SEARCHING

SEARCHING

Practices and Beliefs of the Religious Cults and Human Potential Groups

By

Harriet S. Mosatche, Ph.D.

STRAVON EDUCATIONAL PRESS
New York, N.Y. 10022
ISBN 0-87396-092-0

Library of Congress Cataloging in Publication Data

Mosatche, Harriet S., 1949-
Searching: practices and beliefs of the religious cults and human potential groups.

Bibliography: p.
Includes index.
1. Cults. I. Title
BL85.M73 1983 291 83-4829
ISBN 0-87396-092-0

Composition by Delmas, Ann Arbor, Michigan

Printed in the United States of America

Contents

Author's Dedication and Acknowledgments

As always, I dedicate my work to Ian.

Searching could not have been completed without the contribution of a large number of people, some of whom are acknowledged below.

My deepest appreciation to Ivan Lawner for his extremely instructive editorial comments and wholehearted support of my commitment to this book. I gratefully acknowledge my debt to Dr. Linda Fallo-Mitchell who cheerfully did everything she could—from checking references to cooking to typing—to make my job of writing easier.

I am most grateful to the following for their assistance in various ways: Dr. Tom McGowan, Brother John Muller, Dr. Mary Ann Groves, and Dr. Stephen Kaplan generously shared their time, ideas, and enthusiasm with me. Dr. Paulette LaDoux, Dr. John Miele, Dr. Paul Sharkey, Leslie Hogan, and the librarians at the College of Mt. St. Vincent and Manhattan College found valuable, often-obscure references for me. My unflappable secretary Terry Huvane and my typist Pat Aalders had the difficult task of deciphering my almost illegible scrawl. My students Marie Donnellan, Marilyn Gagion, Edward Thomas, Jim Morrissey, Jeanne Glasser, and Angela Abbati located references, typed, photocopied material, and proofread parts of the manuscript.

I am also indebted to Dr. Marie Thomas, Dr. Jerry Lee, Marty Licht, John D. Mitchell, and Bob Berg who helped me in numerous ways when I needed them most.

I sincerely thank the spokespersons and/or leaders of the groups described in *Searching*, in particular Cynthia Bretheim of the Himalayan International Institute of Yoga Science and Philosophy, Dr. Lawrence Lentchner and Dr. Lawrence Spiegel of the Institute for Psycho-Integrity, Lynn Sparrow of the Association for Research and Enlightenment, Joy Irvine Garratt and Nadine Hack of the Unification Church, Nancy Fouchee of *est*, Dr. Alfred Sunderwirth and Andrew Carlin of Wainwright House, and Tim Skog of Scientology. They gave me information and pertinent material, acted as sources for some interviewees, and often facilitated my activities as an observer and group participant.

Harry Taylor of the Citizens Freedom Foundation and Arnold Markowitz of the Cult Clinical Service of the Jewish Board of Family and Children Services were most helpful by providing me with relevant documents and books, and by contacting or suggesting interviewees especially former group members.

I also acknowledge the work of Elvin Abeles, my very capable and meticulous editor, and the support and freedom given to me by my publishing house, Stravon Educational Press.

Finally, I thank my parents, my sister, my brothers, and my grandmother for encouraging me in all my endeavors.

Additional Acknowledgments

The hymns "Song of the Heavenly Soldiers" and "My Promise" appearing on pages 31 and 32 are reprinted by special permission of the Holy Spirit Association for the Unification of World Christianity (HSA—UWC).

Picture Credits

Pages 28, 187, 279, 346, United Press International. Pages 96, 276, Wide World Photo.

Introduction

MOONIES, Scientology, *est,* deprogramming, Hare Krishna—these words have enormous power. One has only to utter them to elicit strong opinions, pro and con. Almost everyone reacts, though often with very little knowledge or understanding of the complexity of the issues involved. Moreover, I found, as I was conducting an investigation in this controversial area, that people were constantly attempting to persuade or dissuade, and everyone I knew or was to meet in my search for answers had a relevant story to tell me. Religious cults (or new religious movements) and human potential groups have deeply touched the American scene. The purpose of this book is to provide much-needed information and analysis of this psychosocial phenomenon in contemporary society.

As a start, some definitions of terms are provided. The importance of language cannot be overestimated—the use of one word rather than another itself connotes a particular meaning and suggests evaluation of the underlying concept or organization. For example, the term "cult," while certainly value-laden, has meaning to most people and is therefore used in the title of this book. Frank K. Flinn, a theologian, writing in a recent newsletter of the New Ecumenical Research Association (an interdisciplinary, interdenominational organization affiliated with the

Unification Church), pointed out: "The word 'cult' is derived from the Latin verb *colere*. In the ordinary sense the verb meant 'to till the soil.' As the fertility of the soil was believed to be dependent upon the favor of the gods and goddesses of fertility, acts of piety and worship were often associated with the ploughing of the fields. Thus the term *colere* took on the associated meaning 'to worship' and the noun derived from it *(cultus)* came to designate 'acts of ritual piety.'"[1] Later in the same article Flinn noted: "At its best the term 'cult' is a sociological category used to describe certain religious phenomena; at its worst it is a prejudicial term used to put down other people's religious beliefs."[2] In an often cited article, Margaret Thaler Singer stated: "The term 'cult' is always one of individual judgment. It has been variously applied to groups involved in beliefs and practices just off the beat of traditional religions; to groups making exploratory excursions into non-Western philosophical practices; and to groups involving intense relationships between followers and a powerful idea or leader."[3]

Some writers use the term "cult" to describe any group that deviates from traditional orthodox Christianity. For example, for the purposes of his book, theologian James W. Sire defined a cult as "simply any religious movement that is organizationally distinct and has doctrines and/or practices that contradict those of the scriptures as interpreted by traditional Christianity as represented by the major Catholic and Protestant denominations, and as expressed in such statements as the Apostles' Creed." Sire suggested that while the term cult "is heavy with negative connotations... [o]ther terms such as *religion, religious movements, alternative religion* are too general and do not give the sense of exclusivity associated with groups commonly termed cults."[4]

On the other hand, Robert S. Ellwood, Jr., also a theologian, preferred to use the term "emergent religion" rather than "cult." He stated: "An emergent religion, then, is one which appears suddenly and unexpectedly, and which stands out from the sea of established religion like a new volcanic island or a rock revealed by an unusually low tide. Though it may be a result of an understandable process and even something which in a sense was there all along, it gives an appearance of both novelty and striking contrast to the established faiths that surround it."[5] Ellwood contrasted these emergent religions with those he calls "established." He described the latter as "culturally and institutionally pervasive in the society, and which is also assimilated by folk culture and embodied in many of its motifs."[6]

Many of the specific terms that are chosen to describe aspects of the cults or new religions are also subjective, reflecting the bias of the writer. For example, the term "deprogramming" has been employed to describe the process of forcibly retrieving members from a religious cult. The word implies that individuals were programmed or brainwashed in the first place and therefore need to be deprogrammed or deconditioned. Thus it is a term used most often by individuals opposed to particular religions. Unification Church members who, of course, do not believe that individuals join as a result of programming, prefer the term "faith-breaking" for this practice. Clinicians sometimes use the phrase "exit counseling" to refer to therapeutic efforts that are applied when individuals leave organizations either voluntarily or as part of a forcible deprogramming.

"Brainwashing" is another word that is often used by critics of new religious movements. Joost A. Meerloo, in his classic book on brainwashing called *The Rape of the Mind,* noted that the term is derived from the Chinese *hsi nao,* literally meaning "wash brain" or "to cleanse one's thoughts." Meerloo applied the term to the coercive techniques used by the Communists during the Korean War to extract information and confessions from prisoners of war. Those who are antagonistic toward religious cults suggest that these groups use the same or similar measures to recruit members. Members and leaders of the religious organizations, on the other hand, contend that people "convert" to these movements and that the process occurs gradually rather than through a sudden "snapping," as has been suggested in a recent popular book.[7]

In the present book, various terms are employed and readers, of course, may view them and their associated phenomena in a positive, negative, or neutral fashion, depending upon their own perspectives on the subject.

Groups that are part of the "human potential movement" are also addressed in this book. Sociologist and "evangelical Christian" Ronald M. Enroth described this movement in the following way: "The decade of the sixties was the period when large numbers of Americans embarked on a journey of self-discovery and self-improvement through what came to be known as the Human Potential Movement."[8] Jane Howard, who spent a year participating in various human potential groups, wrote: "The human potential groups were striving to reacquaint us with the 'affective domain,' and to help us be less 'cognitive.' They aimed to remind us that we have bodies below our necks, and senses other than sight." She noted that human potential groups represent a continuum. "One extreme, which for reasons more emotional than political might be called the left, is represented by fifty or so 'Growth Centers,' . . . concerned with self-knowledge and with reducing people's inhibitions. They do not primarily care, as people do at the other end of the continuum, about what happens to organizations and institutions and systems. They figure that the way to change systems is to start by changing people. The right-wing end of the continuum has the opposite notion: that if a system is changed the individuals in it automatically will change too."[9]

Marilyn Ferguson, publisher of *Brain/Mind Bulletin*, a widely read newsletter, described in her book *The Aquarian*

Conspiracy the history of the human potential movement and its present manifestation as a powerful network working to create a radical change in consciousness. Some of the early leaders of the movement were the writer Aldous Huxley, who, according to Ferguson, encouraged Michael Murphy and Richard Price to open Esalen, the first "Growth Center," in California's Big Sur area in 1961. Some of the most influential forces of the movement, including humanistic psychologists Carl Rogers, Rollo May, and Abraham Maslow, led seminars at Esalen in its early days. In 1964 and 1965, *Look* magazine senior editor George Leonard traveled throughout the United States for a story he intended to call "The Human Potential." During the course of his investigation he met Murphy and began to work with him not only in "planning residential programs at Esalen but seeking ways the insights of this new human potential movement could be applied to the larger society. They saw its relevance to education, politics, health care, race relations, and city planning."[10] Esalen received a tremendous amount of publicity, much of it evidently unwanted, which consequently led to the establishment of human potential organizations throughout the country, some of which are described in later chapters of the present book.

In a rather scathing look at a large part of the human potential movement, Kenneth Cinnamon and Dave Farson, both psychologists, wrote: "The Human Potential Movement or Emotional Growth Movement is an umbrella concept used to protect and encompass many different kinds of therapeutic techniques and offerings. There are group and individual therapies, mental and physical techniques, and various combinations of each, whose purposes purport to be enhancement of psychological growth within the person and the breakdown of barriers between people."[11]

Questions that arise at this point are: Why do these two movements appear in the same book? How are emergent religious movements related to the human potential movement?

Interestingly, some of the human potential groups that I approached in the course of my research shied away from inclusion in a book that would be dealing with religion in any sense and, perhaps, particularly with religious groups which have strong negative images in the public's eye. However, in questioning the actual participants of those reluctant organizations, rather than public relations spokespersons, I found that religious and spiritual issues and motivations were frequently discussed. On the other hand, some groups that were clearly religious in nature were not especially enthusiastic about being part of a book that would focus on human potential as well as religious movements. They argued that readers would lose sight of the religious dimension of their church and would see all of these groups as part of the same fabric. Some of the organizations were hesitant about being discussed in any type of book that focused on the cult phenomenon. As one high-ranking group member told me: "We don't want to be the one 'good guy' in a room full of 'bad guys.' We'll be guilty by association even if the chapter read alone is generally positive in its analysis."

Regardless of these misgivings by some of the groups studied, I went ahead with the book as planned because I do see some important connections and overlap between these two kinds of organizations. I am not alone in this perception, although my reasons may differ from those cited below. Cinnamon and Farson suggested: "The Human Potential Movement or Emotional Growth Movement, as religion of old, claims to have the answers for the questions of the multitude."[12] These authors also categorize religious cults and growth groups together when the dangers of such groups are described—that is, when the groups are packaged to "represent themselves as *the answer*" for life's problems and when they offer a *"new dependency"* as a substitute for old ones.[13] Moreover, Cinnamon and Farson commented: "Yes, religion and growth psychology are philosophical neighbors. Their rituals differ, yet the pay-offs are similar. Ultimately, in both, the search is the pay-off and the pay-off is in the search."[14]

Similarly, no clear distinction between the two types of groups was made by author Dave Hunt, who took a dim view of "cults" of all kinds. He wrote: "Cults by the hundreds that were unknown a few years ago have sprung up almost overnight, many of them based upon Buddhism and Hinduism: *est* (Erhard Seminars Training), Scientology, TM, psychosynthesis, Silva Mind Control, Arica, biofeedback, Divine Light Mission, International Society for Krishna Consciousness, Nichiren Shoshu, Eckankar, guided fantasy, Ananda Marga, and a host of others. Eastern concepts such as karma, reincarnation, maya, self-realization, and the unity of man with everything in the Universe have gained popular acceptance."[15]

Hunt and others noted that not all groups considered to be cults are religious; there are political, flying saucer, and psychotherapeutically based groups. Clinical psychologist Herbert Freudenberger, addressing the 1981 American Psychological Association Convention in Los Angeles on "Cults and Their Impact on Society," stated that there are 8,000 techniques to expand the mind and three to ten million individuals involved in at least 3,000 groups obeying some kind of leader or guru.

One important reason for considering religious cults and human potential groups in one book is that many of the same issues are pertinent. For example, both types of groups have had similar charges leveled at them, such as brainwashing of participants. Additionally, adherents often have similar reasons for joining the groups, and the organizations frequently appeal to potential members using similar techniques. Some of the group goals are alike and the roots of the movements demonstrate some uniformity as well.

The overlap between religious and human potential groups makes joint consideration appropriate. There are religious and spiritual aspects of the human potential movement and there are consciousness-raising and personal development dimensions of the new religious movements. For example, many of the human potential groups use ideas and practices, such as meditation and yoga, derived from Eastern religious traditions. It is not even always clear how a particular group should be classified. Thus, at a 1979 conference Marilyn Ferguson asked: "And what *is* a new religion? Is est?"[16]

This book will not be divided into two distinct sections, one representing the human potential groups, and the other pertaining to religious cults. Rather, each chapter will be devoted to consideration of a particular organization.

Although the above discussion suggests some of the relationships and similarities between the contemporary religious and human potential movements, I was not initially equally familiar with both areas. My formal educational training in psychology (Ph.D.) and job as a college professor included the study of the human potential movement and some of its major theoreticians, including Carl Rogers and Abraham Maslow. However, I became interested in and involved in the study of the new religions quite by accident. A panel was in the process of being formed to speak at the induction ceremony of the honor society in the Department of Religious Studies at Manhattan College. The ceremony was to take place just a few months after the tragedy at Jonestown, Guyana, where 900 members of the People's Temple lost their lives. That event had certainly increased public awareness of the phenomenon of religious cults and I was a part of that interested public. The honor society decided to present an interdisciplinary panel discussion on that timely subject with the fields of theology, political science, sociology, and psychology represented. I agreed to be the representative of the psychological perspective even though I had never formally studied the topic. However, I had done some reading in the area and had some ideas that I felt could be relevant to an interdisciplinary approach. From that simple panel discussion grew a college course. It was called Cults in America the first time it was offered and New Religions in America on the second occasion. The same multidepartmental team that had given the presentation to the honor society taught the course both times. My interest in this important psychosocial phenomenon grew. As a trained researcher, rather than a clinician, I felt that I could apply my knowledge of psychological concepts and methods in an objective look at what really exists in the world of religious cults and the human potential movement. This book is the outcome of that extensive and intensive investigation.

One of the decisions that had to be made regarding this book was which groups were to be analyzed and how many. Rather than writing briefly about a large number of organizations, as in a guidebook, I decided to select ten or fewer groups (I ended up with nine). In-depth coverage of a limited number of organizations would provide insights and understanding that could potentially be generally applicable to other groups. With that goal in mind, I decided to sample different types of movements: those that are well known as well as those that are lesser known; groups that are controversial and those that are not; large organizations and small ones; old ones and ones that are in their infancy. This approach will enable the reader to gain a sense of the variety of organizations, activities, and individuals involved in this phenomenon. I did not ask the groups for permission to study them. I selected them first on the basis of my own criteria and then I sought their cooperation. Although some expressed initial reluctance, almost all were extremely helpful.

As a first step in the preparation of this book, I read everything I could find in the field. There is already a tremendous published and unpublished literature. However, much of it is heavily biased, and the sparse literature that is psychological is largely clinically oriented rather than research-oriented. The clinical approach tends to see problems and pathology because that is its framework. In addition to the literature review, I conducted more than one hundred structured interviews as well as at least a hundred other less formal interviews. In the structured interviews, I asked a set of particular questions and then probed further so that I could obtain as much detailed information from each respondent as possible. Because I sought to present an objective picture of the religious cult and human potential movements, I was determined to collect information from a variety of sources, some of whom have been underrepresented in the media. Thus, I spoke to individuals who are presently members of the groups under discussion; former members who were forcibly "deprogrammed" out; former members who left groups of their own accord without external pressure; leaders and spokespersons of the groups covered in this book; clinicians who are relatively neutral about the subject and clinicians who are involved in deprogramming or "exit counseling"; individuals who have never been members of religious cults but who are active in anticult organizations; parents who are deeply disturbed by their children's participation in these movements and parents who accept or feel positively about the role of the group in their children's lives; other family members, including children of group participants; and finally many other interested parties who learned that I was writing a book on the subject and offered me their opinions and stories about people they knew who were involved in some way in these movements. In most cases, the names that appear in the following chapters are pseudonyms to protect the privacy of the individuals who were kind enough to share their innermost feelings with me. In some instances, it was necessary to change small facts concerning the respondents' lives for the same reason. The only individuals who are identified by their actual names are those in leadership, public relations, or some other kind of official position within the group or those who have written material for public distribution. If the pseudonyms chosen coincide with the names of actual persons, that occurrence is totally unintentional.

In addition to the interviews, I also participated in many of the activities of the groups, where feasible, in order to gain a better appreciation of the experience of membership. Thus, I chanted Hare Krishna; attended numerous church services, receptions, and lectures; took a personality test; participated in a dream workshop and an aerobic dance class; ate various types of unusual food, drinks, etc. In addition, I conducted naturalistic observations of group activities where I tried to be as unobtrusive as possible while tape recording or taking copious notes. I could not do everything; there were constraints of time, money, and interest, and I always left my investigation of a particular group feeling that there was more to be learned, additional people to talk to, other perspectives to understand.

I titled this book *Searching* because that is the common underlying theme that I encountered. People are searching for all kinds of answers to a great variety of different questions and they find them in various sorts of places. In the remainder of the book, people speak for themselves in describing their own search.

I have organized the book by covering each group in a separate chapter. Each chapter is organized somewhat differently, depending upon the nature of the movement, but I attempted to include the following information in each one: origin or history of the movement, including past and present leaders; basic principles, theology, and activities; recruiting practices; characteristics of members; reasons for joining; reasons for leaving; evaluation of the group; and future outlook. The last chapter is devoted to an examination of such pertinent issues as deprogramming, recruitment, type of members, and reaction of family members. In addition, comparisons of and relationships among the organizations are discussed. Finally, some areas for future investigation are described.

Searching is not a theological book, nor is it a political or sociological treatise, although the book contains material in all of these areas. Rather it is a social psychological analysis of organizations and the people in them. This book will certainly not answer all questions on the subject and the methodology is flawed (the sample of respondents, for example, was not randomly selected), but it provides information and raises questions about a topic that has left deep marks in the American psyche in the past few years.

1: Unification Church

HE has been called everything from "the Messiah" to "another Hitler." He has been compared to Jesus Christ as well as to Jim Jones. The man is Sun Myung Moon, spiritual leader of the controversial new religion, the Unification Church.

Moon was born on January 6, 1920, in a rural town in what is now North Korea. He was named Yong Myung Moon, which translates to Shining Dragon. He changed his name in 1946 to Sun Myung Moon, meaning Shining Sun and Moon. When he was 10 years old his family converted to Presbyterianism and when he was 16 he had a religious experience. He reported that Jesus came to him to tell him that he was chosen to attempt to complete the messianic mission. During the next nine years he spent much time in prayer, meditation, and the study of various religious scriptures. After studying electrical engineering in Japan in 1938, he returned to Korea.

He began his religious mission in 1946, by preaching to the public in Pyongyang, which was under Russian Communist occupation. The agitation caused by his preaching led to his arrest and in 1948 he was sent to a labor camp. According to journalists Carroll Stoner and Jo Anne Parke, Moon was excommunicated by the Presbyterian

Church in 1948 because they "had enough of Moon's 'heresy.'"[1] He was freed in 1950 by United Nations forces and, according to Unification Church sources, fled with two disciples to Pusan. There he preached the "Principle," which he had begun to develop years earlier after his vision. He completed the writing of the scriptures of the Movement, the Divine Principle, in 1952.

Moon's new church, Holy Spirit Association for the Unification of World Christianity, was established in 1954 in Seoul, South Korea, and spread to Japan in 1958. In the following year, the first missionary, Young Oon Kim, came to the United States. In 1965 Moon traveled all over the world, including the United States, on his first large-scale public speaking tour.

Other details of Moon's life, particularly his personal life, are less well known. He married Hak Ja Han in 1960, and they are the parents of 12 children. Moon and his family now live on a luxurious estate in Tarrytown, New York. An earlier marriage had dissolved because of his wife's opposition to the religious role she was forced to play. Stories of other marriages have been hinted at in some accounts, but have not been reliably documented.

Frederick Sontag, a philosopher and theologian, during his investigation of the Church in the mid-1970's, talked to Moon's earliest still-living disciple, a woman named Mrs. Se Hyun Ok. She reminisced: "At that time in North Korea, all the members came to Reverend Moon. He did not seek them out. They came to him. They were seeking revelation from God. I received a revelation about the coming of the messiah. God said that very soon the messiah would come...

"Before Reverend Moon went to prison he had twenty followers. Then he was arrested by the police and went to prison. The followers lost confidence in him and they scattered..."[2]

Sontag conducted extensive interviews in Korea in order to collect information about the early significance of the movement to both members and non-members. A university teacher, who was not a church member, told Sontag: "I was looking for some place to really rely on spiritually. One characteristic is that all the intellectuals are there. They are very rational; . . . I had the impression that they didn't just believe like a machine, out of routine—they believed with some foundation, some basis . . . "[3]

A Protestant Church mission leader in South Korea described the early Unification Church: "It has the Korean method of what we call syncretism. This has been the favorite religious method in Korea, take a little bit of something and something else and make your own thing."[4]

An early follower from Korea revealed his perception of the beginning of the Unification Church and how it changed through the years: "The Christian churches in Korea started to have internal struggles and separation among the different denominations. . . . I almost lost my faith in the Christian churches. . . . I was deeply concerned with the future of Christianity and also about the Second Coming. . . . I received a message from God not to wait for the messiah; not to expect him like a miracle, but to seek him among normal human beings. I was told that I was living in the last day, that God will send one group of people on this earth to lead other groups to fulfill his providence. They will be persecuted very much. Then I felt very strongly that this was the group God was talking about. Since that time I gave up my faith in the Presbyterian denomination and joined the group. . . .

"To call one 'Father' would be the most intimate relationship one could have with someone. It means you are closer to that person. Twenty years ago members didn't use that word as much as they do now. They call him father now because now Reverend Moon does not only give the strict word but he gives more love. . . . Twenty years ago he was very strict. Just teaching. Because of that people used to call him master."[5]

Moon explained in an interview that Korea was chosen by God for a special role because its people are homogeneous and united, deeply religious, and have undergone great suffering.[6] In the same interview, he also expounded on his position in the movement and why he was chosen by God for that role: "I have an unchanging will; I am deeply religious, and I, too, have been tested and strengthened by tribulations and hardships. When God revealed himself and his mission to me, I could readily understand his heart. I couldn't help but weep. I determined then to give my life completely to ease his broken heart. It has been my honor and privilege since then to carry his sorrow on my shoulders. My every action is to liberate God from his sorrow."[7]

The Unification Church presently consists of many organizations (critics of the movement call them "front" organizations), such as the International Cultural Foundation, The World Peace Academy, the New Ecumenical Research Association, and the Collegiate Association for Research of Principles (CARP). Moreover, the Church has its own seminary, the Unification Theological Seminary, which opened in Barrytown, New York, in 1975. Although the school applied for a state charter in April of that year, it has not been granted by the Board of Regents as of this writing.

The Seminary currently offers formal two- and three-year graduate programs in Religious Education and Divinity, but valid Master's degrees cannot be conferred because of the absence of a state charter. After the New York State Court of Appeals ruled in June 1981 that the Board of Regents had properly refused the granting of a provisional charter, the Seminary decided that it would consider an appeal to the United States Supreme Court on constitutional grounds.

At the 1981 graduation ceremony the president of the Unification Theological Seminary, David S.C. Kim, presented Reverend Moon's commencement address. Moon was unable to attend because he was in West Germany at the time as part of "God's dispensational plans for the entire European continent."[8] In that address, Moon noted that his "heavenly mission" to Korea, Japan, and the United States had been completed as of April 30, 1981. That mission, dating from his marriage in 1960, consisted of three 7-year periods or one 21-year course which all Unificationists must go through.[9] In that same address Moon stated that the Unification Church has three critical unfinished tasks in America:

1) Stop the spread of Communism, an atheistic ideology which is the greatest threat to the whole world,
2) bring about a revival of declining Christianity,
3) and, based on its traditional Judeo-Christian ethics, America must prevent the decay of morality, especially of the young people.[10]

These and other important aspects of the Unification belief system and theology will be explored below.

Unification Thought

The basic purpose of the Unification thought is the promotion of Christian unity (the unity of Christian theologies, denominations, and churches) and the achievement of an interfaith movement (thus the Church name—Unification), before the Day of the Lord of the Second Coming, "to build the Kingdom of Heaven on Earth for all mankind to live in peace and order and joy forever." The goal of creation is the fulfillment of three blessings which are simultaneously responsibilities: to be fruitful (the perfection of individuality), to multiply and fill the Earth (creation of the family), and to subdue and have dominion over the creation (entrance into a God-centered relationship). The Unification Church sees God as one who is "beyond space and time, who possesses perfect intellect, emotion and will, whose deepest nature is heart and love, who combines both masculinity and femininity, who is the source of all truth, beauty, and goodness, and who is the creator and sustainer of man and the universe and of all things visible and invisible. Man and the universe reflect His personality, nature, and purpose."[11]

The "scripture" of the movement is the Divine Principle. Moon explained that the teachings that form the basis of the Divine Principle "are not something that he has based simply on what he has studied. He described them as coming from revelations that were given to him by God—revelations which led him to a deeper understanding of God's nature and will and His providence of salvation."[12] Lloyd Eby, a Unification Theological Seminary graduate, further noted: "I think the divine principle is that principle by which God exists, by which God creates, by which God restores mankind."[13]

The Divine Principle claims that Moon is God's messenger. However, the Divine Principle does point out that the second coming of a messiah is expected to occur in the East, most probably in Korea. Many members consider that Moon is the Messiah or the Lord of the Second Advent, while others consider him to be a teacher or spiritual leader. Sontag noted that members are hesitant to inform inquirers that Moon is the second Messiah "[b]ecause the whole doctrine stresses the necessity for preparation, for indemnity to be paid, for study and struggle to precede any affirmation."[14]

In response to the question "Who is Reverend Moon?" posed at a Unification Theological Seminary conference in Barrytown, New York, in 1977, Lloyd Eby responded: "I think the official answer would be, and has been, that he is a prophet, a channel through whom God speaks."[15] Farley Jones, another Seminary graduate, further explicated Moon's role: "We believe that he is coming in the role of the third Adam. . . . Our belief is that Jesus came in that role, but as it says in the Divine Principle, because He was rejected by the people of His age, He was not able to fulfill His role completely. So, we see Rev. Moon as chosen to fulfill that role... He is a prophet, he's the founder of the Unification Church; but more than that, we see him in the role of potential True Parent of mankind, and his wife, the feminine side, as the True Mother of mankind."[16]

Although the Divine Principle is said to be more significant than Moon as an individual, a central figure is necessary for the success of the mission, which is basically the restoration of humankind. This restoration is necessary, according to Unification teaching, because of the "Fall of Man." Unification theology suggests that Satan, the serpent, seduced Eve, leading to the spiritual fall. Then Eve, realizing that Adam, rather than Satan, was her intended partner, seduced Adam to fulfill their intended relationship. However, that union is considered "a sexual Fall and a misuse of God's love,"[17] because Eve tempted Adam into sex prior to the time appointed by God. As a result, all individuals have the potential of being claimed by Satan. It is, thus, "God-ordained sex which will eventually bring about the restoration of creation. Salvation means the ending of Satan's biological hold on humanity and the generation of a new race through the sexual activity of new first parents."[18]

According to Unification theology, Jesus came to Earth, not to die, but rather to raise humankind to perfection, to marry and rear children in a God-centered world. However, Jesus realized that He could not accomplish full salvation for the world because of the lack of faith of His generation of people. Thus He died on the cross for society's spiritual salvation. Physical salvation would have to wait to be fulfilled by another messiah. Moreover, Unification belief suggests that Jesus' resurrection (a central tenet of Orthodox Christianity) was spiritual rather than physical and that Jesus has not entered God's heavenly kingdom.

Another important theological concept of the Unification Church is the "Four Position Foundation." This phrase refers to the interrelationship among four realities: God, man, woman, and child. This concept points to the importance of the family system, implying that "individualism in religious life is self-defeating."[19] Rather, the goal is for a perfected man and perfected woman to get married and form a perfect family centering on God. Because love and the family are God-centered, rather than being based upon human desire, the practice of marriages arranged by Reverend Moon has evolved in the Church. Many of these arranged marriages, in which the couple receives the blessings of Moon and his wife, take place between members

Rev. Sun Myung Moon (right) and his wife (left) officiate at the wedding of 2075 couples on July 1, 1982 in New York.

of different races and backgrounds, supporting the notion of a unified world. The marriage blessing is similar to the more traditional notion of a sacrament. On July 1, 1982, 2,075 young couples brought together by Moon were married in a mass ceremony in Madison Square Garden in New York. These individuals are supposed to be among the 144,000 predicted to be saved first in the Book of Revelation.

There are political and economic aspects to Unification theology, particularly with regard to the division of the world into democratic and Communist nations. The former will allow the creation of the appropriate environment for receiving the Messiah, while the latter countries are seen as being controlled by Satanic forces. Unification thought tends to believe in the inevitability of some kind of struggle between the forces of good and evil in order to bring about lasting peace. It is predicted that World War III will manifest itself either as a physically fought confrontation or as a spiritual one. Unification doctrine sees socialism as the economic system most compatible with democracy.

The Second Coming of the Messiah to complete physical salvation of humankind will be possible only when people fulfill certain conditions through indemnity. A wide range of behaviors are considered to be symbolic indemnity conditions for the removal of humankind's fallen nature: fasting, street cleaning, preparing for a rally, fundraising, or witnessing (in which a Unificationist prepares a potential follower to receive the words of God through proselytizing). One very attractive Unificationist, who had long beautiful hair when we first met, had cut her hair to stylish chin level by the time of our second meeting about a year later. She explained that the act was an indemnity condition, that she had had "too great a concern for my appearance. I was too attached to my hair." Furthermore, Unification belief indicates that individuals have to redeem themselves, to pay indemnity for sin—that God will do 95 percent of the work, but the remaining 5 percent must be supplied by the person.

In addition to the Divine Principle, theological tenets of the Church are also contained in a collection of recorded and transcribed lectures that Moon has made to members of the Church. Excerpts from these talks, entitled "Master Speaks," have been used by both followers as well as antagonists of the Unification Church to respectively support or discredit Moon and his movement. Sontag cited some of these quotations in his book about Moon and the Church.

> Do you think God's Will will be realized by following Western style? It cannot be done. From now, we have to make new customs, new tradition, new culture, new life, a new way of living, new morality, new laws. Are you ready?[20]
>
> We have only a small number of people, but God relies on us.... We must be zealous and enthusiastic in raising money. We must be stingy in using money for ourselves, but generous in using the money for other people... We are the visible incarnation of God; through us, God will be expressed; through us, God will be active.[21]
>
> You must be more strongly drawn to God's love than your spouse's love....[22]
>
> It is immaterial whether or not I can unify the world within my lifetime, for the work will go on and on, and I will continue to lead it, whether I am here on Earth or in the spirit world....[23]

The Divine Principle and "Master Speaks" both contain statements that suggest that Moon anticipated persecution and antagonism from non-Church members because of the Unification belief in a new and human Messiah. Moreover, Thomas McGowan, a professor of religious studies, noted that Unificationists believe that the Messiah "may not be taken seriously by many Christians who have assigned too much exclusivity to Jesus and who await only cataclysmic interventions."[24] Thus, followers of Moon are psychologically prepared for the negative evaluation they and their leader receive from mainstream religions in the United

States. In an interview with Sontag, Moon even suggested: "The greater the persecution, the faster the Satanic world will lose power."[25]

Unification Church Services

To gain a fuller understanding of Unification theology and religious practices, I attended several of their services at the New York church which is located on West 43rd Street near the theater district. The services begin with silent prayer while worshippers file into the church, which was filled to capacity during each of my visits. These churchgoers are a heterogeneous group—old and young (although there are almost no children), well dressed and poorly dressed, black, white, and Oriental, attractive and unattractive. Participants are given a program which includes the Order of Worship, notes on church activities (e.g., parents' conference, street-cleaning campaign, guest seminars, workshops), and the music and lyrics for the hymns to be sung that day. These hymns usually include both a traditional one, such as "Praise to the Lord, the Almighty" or "We've a Story to Tell to the Nations," as well as at least one song composed by Church followers. In the traditional hymns, a word or two might be changed to more accurately reflect the Unification belief system. One Unification hymn, entitled "Song of the Heavenly Soldiers," included the following stanza:

> Beautiful morning sunrise,
> calm above the land of our hope,
> Robed in white chosen people,
> fighting for the land of God.
> Tow'ring high the snow mountain
> stands aloft in majesty,
> Ruling with pow'r over the world,
> shining o'er the universe.

The Chorus is:

Marching on Heavenly soldiers,
  marching on with His love;
Uniting in life eternal with our
  God in Heaven and Earth.

Another hymn called "My Promise" contains the following words:

I'll follow the Way, I'll follow the Way,
I'll follow the path of my Lord,
Though thorny the path, now
  persevere as the brightness is growing,
On to the vict'ry and glorious crown.
Giving my body and soul,
I'll follow the Lord all of the Way;
Giving my body and soul,
I'll follow the Lord all of the Way.

In addition to the communal hymn singing, which appears to be a major part of the service, a solo is also presented. Following the singing of a solo, such as "The Impossible Dream" which fits in with Unification thought, there is a scripture reading and a sermon. Next, red velvet-covered containers, with small openings, are passed around to the participants while offertory songs are beautifully presented by a Unification group, the New Hope Singers International and their accompaniment. Almost every participant appears to donate something, although there is no evident pressure to contribute. A Unification Prayer of Thanksgiving, a closing hymn, silent meditation, and church news are presented in that order, with everyone being invited to a free buffet lunch afterwards. Clearly, a few of the participants are present for that part of the service only—a couple of "shopping-bag ladies" and teenage runaways may be receiving their entire daily nourishment from this meal.

In addition, some parents of Unification Church members use this service as their opportunity to maintain or strengthen ties with their children. I even met one parent (not a Church member) who was attending a service, despite the fact that her son was working for the Church in another state. However, since she had visited this church irregularly for several years, she had become acquainted with numerous people and felt "very much at home."

Moonies

The strong commitment to Reverend Moon and the Unification movement is evident in the behavior of and statements made by the thousands of followers in the United States. These followers are frequently called "Moonies." When I began my investigation of the Unification Church, I had assumed that the term was a derogatory one. However, I soon learned that Church spokespersons and dedicated members use the word as readily as do movement critics. Nadine Hack, the former director of public affairs for the Church (she now holds another official Church position) told me that the figure of 30,000 United States members that is usually quoted represents 5,000 core members who function as "full-time lay missionaries" and an additional 25,000 Church members. The latter accept Unification theology, attend Church services, and raise their children in accordance with Unification principles, but do not make a full-time commitment to the movement. Most have other jobs and/or interests that preclude full participation. Hack also informed me that there is an attrition rate of about 50 percent, contrary to a commonly held public belief that once one has become a Moonie there is no way out of the movement unless one is forcibly deprogrammed. Joy Irvine Garratt, the public relations spokesperson in New York, estimated that there are about 3,000,000 members worldwide. Although the largest number are in Korea, 137 countries have Church members. Accurate data are difficult to obtain, but Garratt remarked that in the United States at present there seem to be more male than female members.

How individuals become members of the Church is an issue of considerable controversy. John Lofland conducted an intensive sociological analysis of the Unification Church which he reported in his book *Doomsday Cult.* When the first edition of this book was published in 1966, the group was quite small and unknown and the actual name of the organization was not used. Instead, Lofland referred to the group as DP and its scriptures as the Divine Precept. By the time the enlarged second edition was published in 1977, the movement had achieved worldwide recognition and it was quite evident that the group under discussion was the Unification Church. However, Lofland continued to use the pseudonym DP because of his "personal and private obligation to the members" and because he is "a sociologist rather than an investigative journalist..., muckraker, or other moralizer."[26]

Initially, the Unification Church attempted to recruit members largely through presentations of its theology in a progressive and logical manner in religious gatherings. Lofland cited many early strategies employed by the group to encourage attendance at lectures where the theology would be explained. For example, a newspaper advertisement in the Special Notices section of the classified section read:[27]

> A NEW MESSAGE
>
> Never told before. Reason and purpose of Creation—What God is going to do in the next 7 years. Lectures Mondays 7:30 p.m., January 9th, 16th, 23rd and 30th. No charges, Bay City Lions Club Hall, 772 Clayton Street.

Another advertisement in the "personal" section read:[28]

A COMPLETE NEW AGE REVELATION
Free Lectures Daily
420 Ash St. WY8-5147

The distribution of handbills and radio announcements promoting lectures were among the other publicity techniques used by the movement. These early appeals, however, were generally unsuccessful. A more successful recruiting phase began in the 1970's.

Lofland described five main phases of the recruitment tactics: First the *picking-up* stage involved a casual contact or "pickup" in a public area such as a college campus or on the road. Potential recruits were invited to a dinner and/or lecture with the religious aspects of the host organization being played down.

The next phase Lofland labeled *hooking,* in which the prospect arrived for a dinner attended by a number of friendly, solicitous members. From the 1960's to the 1970's the strategy changed from a cognitive orientation to a more emotional one. Once the positive emotional foundation was established between a prospect and the group, the organization then began to present its basic principles in a relatively uncontroversial lecture.

The third phase was called *encapsulating* and encompassed the unfolding of the ideology of the movement in a controlled setting in which emotional bonds were simultaneously enhanced. Lofland described five facilitating factors that were at work during this phase, which usually took place during a weekend (or longer) workshop. First, "[a]ll waking moments were preplanned to absorb the participant's attention."[29] Second, collective activities such as communal eating, lectures, games, and prayers filled the hours of the days. Third, workshop participants were strongly discouraged from leaving or from receiving input through the media on subjects other than those selected by the Church. Fourth, the social and physical tempo of activities was quite intense and resulted in fatigue. Fifth, the group used this context to systematically present its theological principles from the most neutral and simple to the most complex.

Loving was considered by Lofland to be the fourth basic state. "Love-bombing," a term used by the Unification Church, describes the approval, concern, and love provided to the prospective Church member.

The final phase is called *committing*. Individuals are invited to make more and more of a commitment to the movement, by staying for longer and longer periods with the group in an encapsulated setting. Lofland suggests: "A part of the process of commitment seemed to involve a felt cognitive dislocation arising from the intense encapsulating and loving. . . . People leaving any highly charged involvement, be it a more ordinary love affair, raft trip, two-week military camp, jail term, or whatever, are likely to experience what social scientists have called the reentry problem."[30]

According to Lofland, the type of individuals who joined the Unification Church changed from the early 1960's to the 1970's. He described the early converts to the movement as "decidedly marginal and rather crippled people, drawn from the less than advantaged and more religiously inclined sectors of the social order."[31] In more recent years, the more privileged alienated youth have converted to Unificationism.

A study by Thomas McGowan was conducted between 1978 and 1980 in order to collect data about some characteristics of Unification Church members. However, it should be noted that most of the respondents were candidates for the Unification Theological Seminary and therefore not a random sample of Church members. Seventy-four individuals responded to a written questionnaire, and eight oral interviews were conducted. Sixty-one percent of the respondents were male; 39 percent were female. Most (74 percent) were American citizens, and 96 percent had at least a Bachelor's degree. With regard to the religious background of the participants, 39 percent came from Protestant families, 38 percent Catholic, 11 percent Buddhist, 9 percent Jewish, and 4 percent agnostic. With regard to their own religious identification prior to membership in the Unification Church, 28 percent considered themselves to be "agnostic or nonpracticing members of a mainline church," 20 percent were practicing Protestants, 18 percent were practicing Catholics, 11 percent were Westerners practicing some form of Eastern religion, 6 percent were Buddhists, 5 percent were theists who had no church affiliation, 4 percent were practicing Jews, and 9 percent gave no codable response.[32]

McGowan also asked respondents how they initially came in contact with the Unification Church and reported the following data: 26 percent met church members in a street encounter; 23 percent through a lecture or workshop; 13 percent through a friend already affiliated with the church; 12 percent through a dinner invitation to a church center; 12 percent through studying the Divine Principle; 7 percent through organizations such as CARP or the Creative Community Project, which were not immediately identified as Unification Church groups; 4 percent through newspaper advertisements; and 4 percent through public lectures by Reverend Moon.

While some made a definite commitment to the Church within three weeks after the first contact, most (79 percent) took between three weeks and seven years before definitely joining. McGowan further reported that the two reasons most often given by respondents for their conversion were "the seeking of answers to questions concerning the meaning of life and the desire to improve the world or at least themselves through this new community."[33] The respondents also indicated why they remained committed to the Church; most gave more than one reason. Almost half noted that the Unification Church had helped them to form a deeper relationship with God, while almost one-third found truth in the Divine Principle. About one-quarter maintained their commitment because of Reverend Moon, while almost the same number wanted to solve problems of the world and build the Kingdom of Heaven on Earth. Smaller numbers referred to personal fulfillment (17 percent) or the friendship and dedication of members (12 percent). Six percent cited the opportunity for personal involvement and action. Three percent mentioned their recent matching for marriage. One member noted self-sacrifice; another stayed to help in the fight against Communism.

A recent study of the Moonies in Great Britain, conducted by sociologist Eileen Barker, is particularly significant because of its use of two control groups of comparison subjects. One group consisted of individuals matched to Unification Church members on the basis of age, class, education, and religious background, but having no connection to the movement. A second control group comprised individuals who had attended Unification Church workshops during 1979, most of whom never went on to join the Church.

The results of Barker's study indicated "no evidence to support the hypothesis that those who actually joined the Unification Church were any more or any less likely to be the victims of poor mental or physical health than anyone else from a similar background in their age group."[34] Another finding from the study was a lack of evidence of a higher-than-average degree of familial deprivation. Moreover, although Unification Church members generally believed that marriages were unlikely to work well in contemporary society, they did not show a significantly greater perception of unhappiness in their parents' marriages as compared to the control groups.

The occupations of parents may be a meaningful

indicator, since Barker found that while few of the fathers of Church members were in jobs primarily concerned with making money (such as the stock exchange), many of the workshop group were. In addition, significantly more Moonie parents were in occupations concerned with caring for people (such as medicine, working with the handicapped) than were workshop participants. Moreover, "caring-for-the-country" parental occupations (e.g., armed services, police force) were better represented in members and workshop participants than in the control group.

Barker further observed that, while many of those who joined in California (recruited through the Creative Community Project, which does not usually mention Moon's or God's name during the initial workshop) were atheists or agnostics, over 80 percent of British members were already strongly convinced of God's existence at the time they came in contact with the Unification Church.

The average age of joining the Church in England was 23 years, and most were in paid employment at the time, often in occupations of relatively high status, such as engineering. Interestingly, individuals "who attended the workshops but did not join were far more likely to have been at some transitory stage or unsettled in their careers."[35] Barker also commented that her research provides "support for the hypothesis that potential Moonies may have enjoyed a protective family environment until a later stage in their development than might be the norm."[36]

Another important conclusion from Barker's study is that, while "the Moonie saw himself or herself as a seeker far more than did the members of the control group, it was also apparent that several of the workshop group who did not join were, in certain respects, more ardent seekers than those who were to join; and in certain other respects, those who were to join and then leave were the most active seekers of all."[37] Furthermore, although the movement is strongly anti-Communist, Barker reported that a Moonie is likely to be "an apolitical animal (as opposed to a social idealist)."[38] Barker's general conclusion from her intensive investigation revealed that "the potential Moonie's experience of life may have left him with an aching desire to do something even though he does not know what or how. He is looking for someone to give him the chance to give, for someone to help him to help."[39]

Joining the Church

In the course of my study of the Unification Church, I talked to a large number of members, some of whom had been with the group for several years, while others were relatively recent converts.

Linda Paten, 29 years old, the second-born of five daughters, was raised in a "liberal" Catholic household in the Midwest, and reported a number of religious experiences as a child. At the age of six, Linda decided she wanted to become a nun. "My parents didn't react with glee to that," she told me. The "searching" theme is evident in Linda's story:

"I went to Germany after college to scare the timidity out of myself. I wanted to do something different. My major had been Spanish literature. I always got good grades. I had a great belief in individualism. I wanted to make sure that I was living it. I wanted to go somewhere where I didn't know the language; it was to be an experiment in living.

"I worked as a waitress and was also a student at the University of Heidelberg. After a year and a half I felt I was stagnating. I wanted to go back to the States to start a new era, to get a doctorate at the University of California at Berkeley. I moved to San Diego where there were Spanish and German and Mexican people.

"I met the people that introduced me to the movement almost immediately. I was staying in a hotel. One day I was waiting for a bus and met a man and a woman. The man, who was 18 years old, spoke to me in Spanish and invited me to the center and for lunch.

"Then I signed up for an apartment. The man and woman visited me again and invited me to a weekend workshop. I had never heard of the Unification Church before. I had a sense that there was something for me, but I didn't want to join a religious group. I had been an agnostic for 6 years. However, I did stay for the rest of the week. Then I left, moved into my apartment, and found a job which was to start in January, but it was only October. I had three months to think. I wrote to my friends about the Church. They sent me clippings of Hitler's propaganda meetings and other newspaper clippings which they thought were related to the Unification Church. One friend from England even came to the United States to talk me out of joining the Church.

"I felt it was definitely a spiritual time of my life. I read the Divine Principle so that I could realize it was sufficiently *not* true enough so that I wouldn't join. But that didn't happen. I felt early on some responsibility to act upon what I had experienced and learned. The Unification Church re-evoked the religiosity of my youth."

In discussing her reasons for remaining with the Church for five years, Linda commented:

"The existence of a personal God is what sustains me, that there is a God, that God suffers and is not an impassive God. Rather He makes an effort to relieve the suffering of the world. Restoration has meaning to me. It is the concept I most often fall back on when I question. When I joined, I was an agnostic, but I had traveled a lot, and I realized that when people from the East and West were together, when they could get away from their governments, they could get along. That vision inspired me. . . . My tolerance level is high because of the concept of restoration. For example, if leaders are misusing money. I don't have the idea that the Church must be perfect.

"I think international marriages are a good idea. I see us

working on many different areas. The basis of my faith is different at different times. . . . This movement is actually good and can offer something, the logical possibility of the perfectibility of this world and that we can work toward it."

Another member, Cindy Walsh, also became aware of the Church in California after being in Europe. She was born in an upper-middle-class suburb of New York City to Protestant parents. She discussed her early religious background:

"My parents sent me to an Episcopal Church Sunday school. Then my parents moved to California. I stopped going to Sunday school there because I became disgusted with the attitudes of the teacher. She would be reading the Bible and kids were throwing paper wads around the room. The teacher couldn't control the kids. It seemed so hypocritical to me. We moved again when I was 14 or 15 to Irvine, California. I became friends with a girl who was a member of Religious Science, a Protestant tradition. The church camp was quite good but the youth adviser died and the regional adviser died suddenly. The wife of the minister took over, but the sense of fellowship and sharing wasn't there any longer. The problem of hypocrisy came up. I stopped going and no one even called me.

"My questions about God had still not been answered by the Religious Science group. I loved Jesus intensely, whatever he was, the Messiah, son of God, prophet, or whatever. I thought I would become a nun. The spiritual life was something I really admired and was attracted to, but I didn't believe in God."

Cindy described the circumstances under which she joined the Unification Church at the age of 21:

"I had been traveling in Europe, spending my Junior college year abroad. I hitchhiked throughout Europe—France, Germany, and other countries. When I returned to the University of California, at Berkeley, I met the Church. It was 20 days after I returned. I had just applied to law school.

I saw this table on campus and there was a sign about a project. I felt really open that day. The sign said Oakland International Reeducation Foundation. I introduced myself and asked for information. They also called themselves the Unified Family. This was before Reverend Moon became well-known. I probably would not have stopped in if the word Church had appeared in the sign. I had been disillusioned with traditional Christianity. I gave them my phone number and my name. They invited me to an evening program, to an open house.

"It was like a spiritual odyssey. To get to the house I had to walk through a long dark alley. There were many obstacles. I had had very little sleep the night before, so I fell asleep during the lecture. I felt bad because I had eaten their food. Then I came back two weeks later to hear the lecture, but I only had one hour of sleep. But this time I stayed awake. There were various concepts introduced which I found interesting.

"My spiritual parent was a male Harvard graduate. He introduced me to the movement. There were all different kinds of people at the Church. I went to a weekend workshop two miles away from my house. I had a lot of questions which were answered. I was stimulated by the ideas. I had been seeking to understand the concept of God for a long time. I went home and had a discussion with my sister and some friends about religion. By the next night I didn't know if I could accept the idea of God, so I prayed. I told God I wanted to put my pride away. I asked God, 'Do you exist?' Spiritually I had put aside my pride. I was wide open now. I took my Bible, which was always a mystical thing. I always felt that God was trying to tell me something, but I couldn't understand. I closed my eyes and opened my Bible and found a quote on the page that the Bible had opened to, that had been used in the lecture. I thought: 'God is telling me that if I just open my eyes I will find God.' I really understood God then as a personal being. The next three nights I had some spiritual experiences. I closed my eyes and opened the Bible and the passages I turned to seemed to be telling me to join the movement.

"I told Mrs. Durst [the wife of the Unification Church President] I wanted to work with the movement, but I had some things to take care of. She understood, but other members were not yet aware of my understanding of the movement, of my wanting to serve Jesus in the person of Reverend Moon. I really felt I was being told something, not in the sense of a surprise, but I had some kind of premonition, some sense of commitment to the community at the time."

Cindy is now attending a prestigious secular graduate school, working toward a Master's degree in Religious Studies. She also works part-time at various secretarial and public relations jobs. She commented on the factors that continue to be responsible for the maintenance of her commitment to the Church:

"As long as the world is suffering, I want to do more. I can't stop if there is suffering and poverty. The idea of the movement is to build a better world. Reverend Moon has tremendous vision and plans which are completely hopeful. I am dedicated to that vision. He understands the suffering of the world because he is from a poor country. All of his work and dedication are to give to people, to get rid of poverty."

Anne Steward has been a member of the Unification Church for seven years, and is currently working toward her doctorate in history. She told me that she had grown up in a New England Catholic family, but had become an atheist during her college years. She explained how this transition took place: "My father died when I was 12. I was the oldest of five children. My father's death threw me into reality suddenly. From then on, my relationship with my mother deteriorated; she was very immature. She couldn't take care of us. I couldn't trust anyone. I had to take care of myself. I started questioning all authority. One of the nuns in the

Catholic Church scared us from going to other churches. We were told: 'If you visit them, they won't let you go.' I realized that she was wrong and if she could be wrong on this, she could be wrong on other things. I stopped trusting teachers. I had to find the truth out for myself. I was ready to start lessons with a rabbi. I went to a priest to tell him about it. But he said, 'Even if you convert, you won't be accepted as one of them.' I wanted to find an identity, to become one of God's people. That was a blow. Then I started giving up on God, I was tired of looking."

Anne was first introduced to the Unification Church when she was in her final year of college. Her narrative of her conversion story follows:

"There was a battle inside me. I wanted to dedicate myself to something, but the only two causes I knew of were Communism and the other was anti-Communism. I had been thinking of joining Young Americans for Freedom . . . I was waiting for graduation. There were Moonies witnessing our campus. I was a little afraid of them, but I wanted to talk to them, anyway. However, I kind of avoided them because I felt uncomfortable. Then I was in the cafeteria at school one day and a French guy came over to me. He was a Moonie also and he asked me to go to dinner. I was shocked, since I didn't know him. He seemed hurt when I said no, so then I said maybe. . . .

"One day I was sitting in my dormitory room—this was a couple of days after I had met the French guy, and I had an urge to sit out in the field. I had been reading some psychology books because I had wanted to figure out something about a friend. I had an urge to go outside. I kept telling myself I should stay in and read, but finally I went out.

"I was sitting in the field when some people came toward me—two guys. My initial reaction was, 'they're coming to get me.' When I was a teenager, I was interested in UFOs. I remembered a story about a UFO that had picked someone up. Sometimes I had thought, 'I wish there were some real UFOs so that I could be saved from the mess the world was in.' So for an instant, I was thinking that these people had come in a UFO and were finally going to take me away. There was a sense of relief.

"They talked to me about God, about making an ideal society, about their international movement. I asked them if they were with the Unification Church. They all had this look. I noticed that they were happy when I told them I had previously met another member, as if they knew they were talking to the right person.

"The Unification Church didn't really mean anything to me at the time. They invited me to go to their center in Boston. I went that night and then went back a second time with a friend. She was more negative and never did join the Church. On the way from the campus, they were singing songs like 'Country Roads.' She sang with them; I didn't. There was a picture of Reverend Moon in the van and I asked who he was. I watched more than I participated.

"When I got to the center, I saw a girl from college who said she had joined a week ago. There was a lecture first, followed by dinner. The lecture was pretty interesting. I asked lots of questions. I asked about the Fall of Man, and they told me that that would be discussed in tomorrow's lecture. I kept pushing her to answer my questions, but she told me that I would have to hear the next lecture. They drove us back to the campus where I was living at the time. I came back the next night but it was the same lecture. I was annoyed, but I enjoyed it still and noticed more things.

"I thought of going to graduate school in biology, but then decided to take a year off. I interviewed for a job as an editor for a science journal, but I didn't get it, probably because I told them that I was going to go to graduate school in a year. Then I got a job as an immigration inspector. I had wanted to be far away, to do something I hadn't done before. I would be working on the border between the U.S. and

Canada. I ordered my uniform and had gotten an apartment. Then my spiritual father called me long distance. The French guy I met became my spiritual father. I was surprised that he bothered and he invited me to a weekend workshop. I declined, saying I was too busy. He called again; his English wasn't too good and I felt sorry for him so I agreed. A guy picked me up. A friend was supposed to go with me, but she chickened out.

"I listened to the lectures and was very critical at first. Then spiritual things started happening. I was all set to refute the lecturer. I was writing down all my criticisms. Then a voice inside my head said: 'While you're doing this, you're not really hearing what he's saying.' Then I realized that there was a lot that he was saying that was appropriate. He provided graphic examples of true love versus false love. Some examples were shocking and brought me to tears.

"There was a lot of prayer during the weekend workshop, like praying before eating. At first, I was just polite. Everyone, at some point, had to say a short prayer. I was scared. When it came to my turn I prayed: 'God, show me how to pray.' I started crying, thinking that God could answer my prayer.

"There was so much talk about God's heart. I didn't know what they were talking about. What does it mean? I was praying about that. In moments of reflection, I asked God: 'What does it mean?' During the first or second night, I had a dream that was an answer to this prayer. An angel came to me and said, 'Come with me and you'll experience God's heart.' I took this person's hand and flew off with him. We came to a place where God was. God said 'You want to experience God. You'll do that.' God warned me that it would be painful but beautiful. Suddenly I was immersed in God's love. I felt that this was a spiritual experience. I felt every cell electric with God's love.

"I also felt God's pain. I also had to experience Satan. I thought I was awake. I looked around the room and saw snakes all over. The girls in the room were screaming, 'You did it, you did it, you did this.' The devil was pointing to me. I was overwhelmed. I said, 'No, I didn't.' Finally, I woke up. I must have been crying in my sleep. A coordinator came over to me. She tried to comfort me and told me it wasn't unusual to have dreams like that during the workshop. It was a very deep experience.

"During the workshop, I questioned constantly. Sometimes I was very sure. Sometimes, I had real doubts. One morning, I was in one of my doubtful moods, feeling depressed. Then something said to me, 'Turn around!' There was a nice window, the sun was shining, it was beautiful. I felt it was God's love.

"I stayed for a week. One day I was mad, so I decided not to have lunch. Another member came over to me and told me he didn't have lunch either (I didn't find out until later that he had already eaten). I felt I had some impact on someone. At the end of the week, people went around with applications to those individuals they felt would join. I had been so argumentative that they didn't give me an application. They were surprised when I decided to join.

"I felt that this was really it. There was nothing more worthwhile I could do with my life. I wanted to devote myself totally to it. I signed the application form. I went back to Maine to get my clothes and to tell my aunt. I was staying with my aunt because I didn't get along with my mother. I was crying when I was with my aunt. She couldn't understand it. But I was overwhelmed. There was so much to explain about the Divine Principle."

David Baum was one of the earliest members of the Unification Church in the United States when he joined in 1969 at the age of 21. He discussed his religious background: "I'm a Unificationist, but that doesn't mean that my Jewish background is wiped out. My religion became clearer to me after conversion to Unificationism. A personal issue for me is that it allowed me to reconcile Judaism and Christianity." The narrative of his joining the Unification Church follows:

"I was a student, a Junior at the University of Rochester at a fairly radical time. People seemed to be searching for an ideal world through drugs or political action. Those approaches didn't solve what was needed in myself. I was a psych and education major. I wasn't interested in spiritual values. I met the Unification Church through a friend. He was in my fraternity and was struggling with his faith. I became involved in discussions with him and was stimulated by his thoughts over the course of three months.

"During Christmas, I visited the Unification Church in Washington, D.C. It was a deep religious experience for me. I had a number of deeply religious and meaningful dreams at the time. I recognized that some of my ideals could be realized through this community, although I fought with the idea of community. I had to learn to love this community, seeing that I wanted to become a part of it. I visited the New York branch first and then went to Washington. I was interested in what caused gaps between people. There must be ways for people to live together without conflict or contradiction.

"My parents were in Pittsburgh. At Christmas, I dropped the bombshell, that I wanted to visit this religious group in Washington, D.C. It was an intense experience for my parents. They thought it was just a fad, but they were pretty concerned. I had been dating someone fairly seriously at the time. My parents really liked her. They were concerned about the relationship. My girlfriend and I heard the Divine Principle at the same time. We stopped dating because of our involvement in the Church. Over the course of many years we took different paths but we both remained in the Church. She's now in Africa as a member of the Church and married to someone else."

At the time of our interview, David was engaged (through

a matching by Reverend Moon) and was eagerly looking forward to married life. In contrast to David's long-term commitment is 24-year-old Gregory Josephson's status. He had not formally made a commitment to the Church, but was planning to do so in the near future. I spoke to him after a Sunday service. As brother to five siblings, all of whom are vocationally successful (his sister, for instance, is a concert pianist), Gregory commented that he has always been different. He further explained:

"My family thinks I'm crazy for joining, but they think that everything I do is crazy. I dropped out of college because I just wasn't interested any longer. I received a pilot's license in Florida. Then I got involved in real estate. I came to New York City to sell real estate.

"I became interested in starting a peace movement after John Lennon's death. I made a plan for world peace and then found out that Reverend Moon also had done much of what I had planned to do. So when I came to New York I was either going to join a movement for world peace or create one. I was searching for the truth about life. What does it really mean? I went to the Unification Church table on the street and asked how I could join. I attended a couple of introductory lectures and had dinner with Church members. I attended a seven-day workshop and started a 21-day workshop in Boston, but was sent back to New York. I was told that I wasn't ready, that I wasn't being spiritual enough. I'm returning to Boston tomorrow to start another 21-day workshop."

Gregory further commented on his changed perspective regarding the Unification Church: "When I first heard of the Moonies years ago, I believed they were crazy, like the media says. Now, I'm ready to die for the movement, for the mission. Your life itself is not important. What is important is your spiritual life. I don't need my material possessions."

The above narratives of Unification Church members suggest generally theological or spiritual reasons for joining. Unification members and non-Unification academician participants, at a conference sponsored by the Unification Church in February of 1981, concurred with this observation. In contrast, ex-members at the conference cited sociological, psychological, and/or ethical reasons for both joining and leaving the movement.[40]

Leaving the Church

I talked to a number of individuals who had left the Church, either on their own or through forcible deprogramming, to find out how their perspectives compared to the viewpoints expressed by current members.

Kevin McVey had been brought up in a Catholic home, attended parochial school as a child, and graduated from a Catholic college. He was a member of the Unification Church for about nine months before leaving. He still maintains some personal and emotional ties to followers of the movement and continues to refer to them as "brothers and sisters." His ambivalence about the Church and his own status is reflected in much of what he says:

"I thought it would be really easy to leave. It has turned out not to be as easy as I thought. Throughout my experience here in New York, I've just constantly been meeting people from the Church again and have been very tempted to go back a lot of times. I'm not quite sure what my feelings are, whether I should go back or whether I shouldn't. I'm trying to work all of that out for myself. Sometimes I feel very confused . . . sometimes I do want to go back to the Church and some days it really doesn't make any sense . . . some days I would like to just head across the country on a bike or backpack across Europe."

Kevin was introduced to the Unification Church soon after dropping out of graduate school. A friend invited him to the Unification Church center for lunch. He described that day:

"It was very strange. There were these Oriental people walking around who couldn't speak English. The Americans who were there had short hair and ties and white shirts. They were just formal. It just seemed really strange to me. They were talking about good and evil at the lecture, using a blackboard. Good and evil, it was really foreign to where I was at the time."

It was five years before Kevin actually joined the movement. He was working in a library at the time and met some Unification people who were witnessing on the street. He had seen the Unification Church table set up on that block "dozens of times" and everything he had heard or read about the Moonies was negative. But on this particular occasion he met a "brother-and-sister team" from England for whom he had positive feelings, particularly the female member, who was to become his spiritual mother. "She was very attractive, very interesting," he recalled. "That male-female attraction was there definitely. I don't know how much it was intended, or how much it was just natural. I mean, she wasn't a ravishing beauty; she wasn't a model." When Kevin later told his spiritual mother, Mary, about his attraction to her, she told him that there was nothing wrong with that, it was only natural, that in time his connection to the movement would be at a deeper level. Kevin again met Mary four days later in another part of town. He described this incident:

"All of a sudden, out of the blue, there I was and there she was. She was with a sister at that point and I talked to Mary. I wanted to know just what her parents thought about it and I stood there for about an hour, asking questions and talking to Mary and the other girl about what they were trying to do. They were trying to build another world, to restore relationships. They invited me to dinner, but I didn't go. So then, two days later, I was out running and I ran into Mary and she was going to pray. It was nice that she was going out to pray. I was attracted to that and she said, 'When are you coming to dinner?' So, I went to dinner and listened to the lecture. The lecture was good, but not anything special, about good, evil, hope, despair.

"And there was the community. There were a lot of people living in the group from all over the world. At the beginning of the evening, everybody stands in a circle in the main dining room and gives their name and the country they're from.... Then they wanted me to go away for a two day workshop. That was the next step but I was working, I couldn't do that. But people came over and wanted me to go. It was important that I go. But I was working; that was my primary responsibility.

"When I left the church that evening, I kissed Mary, I just went to peck her on the cheek, to say thanks. She'd spent the whole night with me and she'd talked to me a lot and I really enjoyed the evening.... It was, 'No, no, no, we don't do that!' I felt terrible, I felt so stupid. It hadn't occurred to me that this was a very religious context....

"Mary proceeded to visit me in the library every day and she started bringing me bouquets of roses and she'd bring flowers to my apartment, tape them to my mailbox when I wasn't there. Love-bombing, that's what it's called, and it worked. It definitely worked. I was very impressed. Mary came and talked to me every day. She wanted me to come to a workshop. She'd bring different people with her, a different brother every day. One of them, a 32-year-old, had been president of an oil company and had just shucked it all. I was impressed with him. They all just seemed to be on a totally different wavelength.

"The workshop was the place to find out about the Unification Church. I went to New Hampshire for two days and it was really wonderful—it was excellent. I really enjoyed it. Lectures were short and interesting, about three hours a day. It was very pivotal—you had to deal with what the lectures were trying to tell you. Above it all, it was really a community. They are people who really cared, people who want to make the world a better place. And the conclusion that came out was that the messiah is here, there is a job to be done. Then the pressure starts and it's intensive pressure....

"Mary came over and everyone came over. They thought it was really important that I come over for a seven-day workshop. And I got this enormous headache; the tension was annoying, it really was. I wanted to go, but I had a job. I couldn't just walk out. It would be completely irresponsible to just walk away. The conversation went on for hours, it was very deep conversation. I decided not to go that night but finally I decided to go.

"I had to set it up. I canceled a trip to California and took some vacation time from the library, ostensibly for seven days. And here I was at a Moonie workshop, but it was very educational, I thought at the time. It was like a whole new world. Five hundred people and they all had a mission. Different people came up for lectures. One man from CARP gave an inspiring speech and I learned a lot. So I stayed seven days and then I agreed to stay further and I finally called up work and told them I wouldn't be coming back. I stayed for the whole 21-day training. Then I went back to Boston, cleared out my apartment and took two bags of clothing. I did go to the library. I didn't want it to be that I called up and didn't go back. I just wanted to let the people know that I was all right. I knew they had all kinds of fears, that I was drugged, being kidnapped, and I just wanted them to know that I was choosing to do this. It was all right."

Kevin became a member of a witnessing team in the South, part of CARP. He stayed in a "beautiful house in an idyllic setting" with nine other Church members. Although he noted that his group was not particularly good at witnessing, they were quite successful at fundraising, which was necessary to support themselves. "So my brothers and sisters could eat, could live in this house, pay off the van, bills and all that. It wasn't for Reverend Moon."

Kevin left the Church, he believes, because he was never

able to fully incorporate the Unification theology, Reverend Moon's role, and many of the practices of the movement. The idea of fundraising at Christmas rather than being with one's own family was difficult to accept. In addition, the practice of arranged marriages was one that was quite foreign to Kevin's philosophy of life. In fact, when he attended his first Unification workshop and found out about the practice, he remembered: "Boy, I almost walked out that day. But then I was told you don't have to deal with it for three years. By that time it'll be all right. Even though my reaction to it was pretty bad, it's a challenging thing, learning to love anyone. I could see the value in it." But he indicated that he could never really agree with the idea. With regard to Moon's role, Kevin explained: "It got to a point where you had to totally believe in the Father and I never got to that point. It's one of those things, and I never reached the point where I could totally trust him." Finally he recalled: "I woke up one morning and said, 'That's it. I'm leaving.' I was getting away, not knowing where, but getting away."

About four months after our first meeting, Kevin and I again had a lengthy conversation. In the meantime, he had taken a clerical job with a Catholic agency in order to pay off a student loan from his college days. He also had been visiting Catholic monasteries with the idea of perhaps finding one that would provide him with the sense of community and dedication that he still sought. The thought of returning to the Unification Church was one that he continued to entertain periodically, particularly whenever he saw or heard from his spiritual mother, Mary—as he did, for example, at a demonstration outside the New York court when Reverend Moon was indicted for income tax evasion in 1981.

Witnessing and Fundraising

Two of the Unification activities mentioned by Kevin, as well as many other Moonies, are witnessing and fundraising.

In addition to being quite visible to the public, these activities arouse great controversy. Those in the movement claim that witnessing and fundraising are integral aspects of Church life, fulfilling vital theological and social missions. James Baughman, a Unification Church member, explained this position at a 1981 conference in San Juan, Puerto Rico, sponsored by the Unification Theological Seminary: "Fundraising and witnessing are fundamental disciplinary practices used to build an individual's character, self-confidence, and parental heart, as well as to develop in the person a broad knowledge and concern about the world's situation."[41] Former members, particularly those who have been forcibly deprogrammed, and critics of religious cults perceive these activities in a highly unfavorable light. They suggest that Church members are being exploited to increase the membership roster and to raise money for Moon's personal use. These dimensions of Unification Church life are explored below.

Mobile Fundraising Teams (MFT's) are composed of Church members who travel together, usually in a van, selling candy, flowers, nuts, etc. to the public. They keep some of the money for their own needs and send the rest to Church headquarters. One eight-year member described her former fundraising experiences (ended three years earlier) in the following way: "I started fundraising and it was fun. It was local fundraising; I was not part of an MFT at that time. We'd go to shopping centers and I did well. We sold candy in tins and flowers. My enthusiasm probably sold them. I would have a hard time fundraising now. I wasn't aware of the negative press at the time." At a later time, this young Moonie became part of an MFT. She described one significant spiritual experience that occurred to her during that period.

"It is important to be connected to your MFT leader. Once, I was feeling very disconnected from everyone. I wasn't talking to anyone on my team. I was aware that I was getting depressed, that I didn't enjoy being in the van. I was withdrawn from everyone. That night I had a dream. I saw Satan pulling something on a rope; then I realized it was me. He was pulling me with the rope around my neck. I hadn't thought about it before in religious terms. I told one of the girls about this dream and asked her to give me a back rub, which she did, and she helped me to relate to the others, to become less withdrawn. I don't have those kinds of dreams now. I guess I don't need them anymore."

Another Unificationist expounded on her view of fundraising as part of setting indemnity conditions for herself: "If it were just for money, I don't think anyone could survive. It gave me confidence that I could offer myself up in that way to God. What lingers for me is the spiritual aspect of it. I don't feel that I was exploited."

A former Church member reflected on his ambivalence about fundraising: "I opened myself up to people and tried to create relationships while fundraising. I enjoyed it sometimes and hated it sometimes." He further described his fundraising activities: "Sometimes I would say I was from the University. I felt it would allow me to raise more money. I handled fundraising differently from other people. For me, it worked to look like I look. I brought decent clothes with me and I dressed up decently. I fundraised in a more 'business' sense whereas others fundraised in a more 'personal-friend' kind of sense. I made just as much as they did. We started selling pictures, oil paintings, ugly little things from somewhere in New York, but people loved them. They loved them and I sold thousands of pictures.

"Early in the day we'd do business sections of the city and afternoons we'd go over to highway strips, popular highway sections. Early in the evening we'd do apartment buildings. Late evening, we'd blitz—do fast-food restaurants on the highways. We would fundraise until 2 in the morning. If they asked me if I was with the Unification Church I would tell them I was. Only twice—no three times, it happened—I didn't tell them, and twice I went back to rectify it."

Moon discussed the purpose of fundraising in a speech in December, 1979: "Fundraising is not easy, but that's why we do it. We do the very things we really don't want to do. You want to be respected by people, but in fundraising you humble yourself to ask people to help with contributions. That is a great experience, because when you receive from someone you learn the feeling of wanting to give. This nurtures you and deepens your character.... When people are negative and nasty and you truly give yourself in return, loving them instead of hating them, you are building your character. You can think that the most spiteful person you meet is a training aid for you."[42]

In a speech, made in January 1979, Moon stated: "When you analyze your own motivation for fundraising from early morning to midnight, do you have shame or dignity in your heart? I recommend that you keep a diary of all the dramatic events in your experience. For instance, record the time someone gives you incredible mistreatment and you just want to throw everything away and knock him down. Write how you were patient instead and thought that your mission will help save not only good people but people like this man, and criminals who are even worse. Think that those people are going to have hope because of you."[43]

Witnessing is considered by Moon's followers to be another means for individuals "to restore true love and humility in relationships with fellow human beings."[44] Moon stated: "Another tough thing is witnessing. People don't want to be bothered by you, say they don't have time for you, but still you try to get their attention to preach the eternal truth. When you forget yourself in concern for the other person's life, it is the most sacrificial heart. If you really care, then you witness. What a noble deed that is."[45]

A former Church member described the difficulties he

encountered with witnessing: "I hated it because I wasn't sure I wanted people to come up for dinner. It was almost as if I didn't want any new members to come in because we had such a nice group. We did not want anyone new to come in for dinner. We would have to watch our conversation, to offer our prayers up to the Lord instead of to Reverend Moon, which is what we did when we were by ourselves."

Fundraising and witnessing are just two of the many ways in which Unificationists manifest a disciplined life style, which they see as necessary for the establishment of the foundations of faith to receive the messiah. Some other conditions of faith include fasting for varying lengths of time, absolute celibacy before marriage, cold showers, and prayer (all-night prayer sessions). Baughman noted that these conditions are "not dictated by legalistic prescriptions or hard-fast rules. For every general practice there is always room for exceptions."[46]

Family Reactions

Another issue of major importance, and one that has received great publicity, concerns the reaction of individuals to having a family member join the Unification movement. McGowan's recent research, described earlier, included the question: "How has your family reacted to your conversion?" Sixty-two percent indicated a currently good relationship with their families, although about two-thirds of these had been initially strained relationships which evolved over time into better relationships. Twenty-eight percent reported "negative" or "very negative" family relationships, some indicating that family members were active in anticult groups. Five of the 82 respondents noted that their parents had attempted to have them deprogrammed. Another four reported that while their families liked the Church, they did not have a positive attitude about Moon. Finally, the parents of four other Church members had either joined the movement or acquired the status of "associate members."[47]

It is ironic that while the Unification Church places the family in a central position in its theology, the criticism that is most often heard concerns the role of the Church in breaking up families. Joseph H. Fichter, a sociologist, who has compared the Unification and Catholic churches, reported: "One of the more inflammatory charges against the Unification community is that the membership is disruptive of family life. The new convert leaves home and family, brothers and sisters, to dedicate himself entirely to the religious calling. Parents sometimes charge that their children have been 'brainwashed.' Similar charges have been made about Catholic religious orders that lured a daughter to a convent or a son to a seminary. God's call must be obeyed even if parents are in opposition."[48]

In each of the interviews that I conducted with present and former Church members, I questioned them about their family relationships. Many of the answers revealed a defensive posture, perhaps reflecting the numerous press reports about the Church breaking up families.

David Baum, whose conversion was discussed previously, commented: "The first four to four-and-a-half years were very painful for my family. When I joined, the thing that was most difficult was knowing that my parents would be hurt. I knew in time things would work out. I constantly asked them to visit. They finally came to see me after four-and-a-half years. They had known a number of Church people before and they felt a lot of love and respect given to them on their visit by Unification Church members. They left with tears in their eyes saying they would never question my involvement again, that it was worthwhile. They began to take an active role with the parents' group in the Church.

"One of their concerns was that they wanted me to continue my education, which I am now doing. . . . My mother had lost another child at birth before I was born.

They had struggled, particularly financially. They are more dependent on me and even closer to me now than before. They are very supportive. They live in Miami now; my mother has a heart condition. Mother knits all kinds of things for babies born in the Church. She answers questions from other Jewish parents. They are deep-thinking, loving people."

In describing the relationship with his older brother, David told me: "My brother and I were very close. My joining was painful for him. He was interested, but he didn't want to change his lifestyle. When he got married, he became influenced by the media and something came between us. But my parents were supportive by that time. My brother died suddenly in 1977, when he was 33 and my religion served to comfort me and my parents. I did have a chance to visit him in the hospital, to talk to him before he died, but it was a great shock to all of us."

David's concluding remark about the relationship between the Church and family was a positive one: "Sometimes, being in the Unification Church allows people to rework ties with families that had previously been severed. The family plays a critical role in the Unification Church. People of all different religious and nonreligious backgrounds have gotten together and can find fulfillment in relation to one another."

Another long-time Church member, who was living with her aunt just prior to joining the movement described her family's reactions: "My aunt didn't express any concern. She said to me 'You're bright, you're old enough to take care of yourself.' My grandmother had been unhappy because I had been an atheist. She was glad that I now prayed. She later began wondering, when there was more negative publicity, but I visited her and was able to reassure her. She died a few years ago.

"In college, I hardly visited my mother. I talk to her now more than before, but it's still hard now. There was lots of sibling rivalry as we were growing up. I visited my sister after I had joined. I wrote my sister letters about God. It had been a radical switch and my sister was concerned. She was relieved when she saw me to know that I was more normal than she expected. My sister, who is a nurse, and my brother-in-law visited Barrytown and they were impressed. But at another visit my brother-in-law was turned off—it was boring. Now the relationship with them is bad, but for personal reasons."

In response to my question about the reaction of her friends to her joining the Church she noted: "I only had a few good friends at the time that I joined the Church. I missed the recent college reunion that was held, but I was told that I was talked about. They were surprised and curious about what I am doing. I have maintained my friendship with my roommate at college, but a high school friend who had become a Charismatic Catholic was very opposed to the Unification Church and wouldn't talk to me."

Cindy Walsh, whose experience in joining the Church was described earlier, also discussed her family situation with me. She had left home at the age of 18, one year after her parents divorced. She recalled: "My family perceived a dissonance between what I had earlier believed and what I now believed," she said. "I had never shared my religious search with my family, so they perceived this dissonance. They were 400 miles away at the time. I wrote to my mother. All the different threads in my life had come together. I wrote a 20-page letter to my mother. She wrote back and said, 'I'm glad you're happy.' The publicity didn't affect them initially. Early on in the movement, we weren't really wise in relating to families. Now things are different....

"I moved into the Church center six weeks after I had signed the membership form. My mother and siblings came to visit. However, I hadn't told anyone at the center that they were going to come, so there was some tension. A place was found for them, but my family felt uncomfortable; they were aware of a certain amount of tension. My younger brother said: 'Everyone around here smiles so much. Why are they all smiling?' I wasn't affected by my family at the time, but my family was affected; there was tension. The first year was rocky. When I graduated from college, my whole family came to the center to pick me up for the ceremony, but one of the other members told them I had already left. She thought I had. My parents and siblings were upset about that. Actually, I was still there. It was not center policy, but rather the way certain members had handled certain situations. There wasn't enough sensitivity toward families.

"After graduation my mother came every week to visit me. I wanted to talk about the ideology of the Church. She was upset about that, but that was what I was most interested in. It wasn't the Church dividing us, but rather my interest in the Church. My mother also joined the Church one year after I did and worked hard within it for almost three years. The Church was not equipped to deal with older people at that time. She's doing counseling now and has left the Church. The Church has gotten better with regard to older people. Her relationship with the Church now is not antagonistic. She and I have problems in our personal relationship, but the problems are unrelated to the Church.

"My father has a positive attitude toward the Church. However, my father sometimes said: 'Maybe you don't love me.' They were affected by the negative publicity. That was a painful period for me and my family. They were influenced by the media. I had to continually reassure them of my love."

Terry Linden, another Church follower, described her family's response to her membership: "They didn't mind when I became an agnostic, but when I became a Unificationist, they became more religious. They are good people, but they never held family prayers. When I first joined, my father wouldn't talk to me for a long time. We still have some problems getting along. But my teachers were always more central to my life than my parents. My parents swallowed all the stuff that was in the press—that

Unificationists were led to believe that their parents were demons. I called them to reassure them. When I joined a fundraising team, that blew their minds. My mother would write letters to me—blasting the Unification Church in every one of them, but also writing nice things to me. My father didn't say anything for a while, and then would erupt. They didn't understand my religious motivation for joining.

"I had had some previous difficulty with them in high school with regard to their racial prejudice. I took it personally. I cared for my parents and still do. I last saw them at Christmas. But it wasn't unusual for me not to go home. I had always been independent. I didn't see them frequently before joining the Church. Because I wouldn't go home the first Christmas after joining they took it as a rejection of them, that the Church wouldn't let me go home. They are beginning to trust that I believe something. My younger sisters didn't come to visit me at my first Christmas home. When I first went home, they felt rejected. It took a few times before they felt less rejected.

"My perspective is not different than it would be if I were not a Unification Church member, but you would have to ask them. I'm sure they would prefer it if I were not a Unification Church member. Also, they have family gatherings now every Thursday night. They all live in the same area and they've expressed to me that someone is missing from their Thursday night gatherings."

Terry's final comment regarding her family was: "They wouldn't 'faith-break' [a term used by this respondent for the practice that is commonly called deprogramming]. I have to respect them for letting me do all kinds of things." As far as her relationships with friends, she said the following: "I have friends both inside and outside of the movement. I alienated my friends from before because of my initial letters. But everyone I was close to I have gone back to."

One fairly recent convert expressed a notion that was

echoed by several other Unificationists: "My relationship with my family is the same as ever. It has never been very good. The media has distorted all that about the strong negative reactions."

A former member who had been fairly active in the *est* organization at one time told me that his mother suggested that he go back to *est* activities after he joined the Unification Church. Now that he has left the Unification Church and is considering a life as a monk, which would mean even greater isolation from his family, his mother has suggested that he "become a Moonie again."

Charles Milton, another ex-Unificationist, expressed his family's response as follows: "They thought I was just totally off the wall. I didn't feel that way. They just didn't understand. I had called my mother and she hit the ceiling. She just went crazy and I tried to explain to her that it was just an experiment and I was going to do it until I couldn't do it anymore, do it until I left. She was going to come up. I didn't think she was sophisticated enough to know about deprogramming but I thought maybe, somehow, she had found out. So I avoided meeting her. I told her I would be gone right away, that I was going somewhere and I didn't know where I was going. I told her I would call her. And I did. I never had any problems about calling her.

"She thought that my spiritual mother was an evil person. I tried to tell her about Jane, but she hadn't met Jane. I did empathize with her, but also I was 29 years old. It wasn't like I was a 16-year-old kid. I'm 29 years old and I can choose to do crazy things if I choose to do them. I don't have to ask my mother's permission to go, you know.

"Church members told me at the time that a lot of people are going to try to stop you from what you are doing, that there is a lot of Satanic influence, a lot of evil. So it seemed appropriate at that time to lie to my parents. Because I didn't want them to come up and stick their foot into it, just create a lot of craziness. They said they just wanted to have lunch, but Jane would say, 'Oh yeah!' She knew stories of people being kidnapped at lunch. And I know that has happened.

"I wouldn't counsel anyone at 16 to just cut off your parents like that, but I was older. I didn't feel guilty about it. I just did it. On our way to North Carolina we drove right past my parents' house. I could look up and see my parents' house. I really didn't feel anything. I just thought it was very curious. I didn't feel guilty that I was going and I never told them that I was that close."

The parents who receive most of the publicity are the ones who are extremely distressed by their children's association with the Unification Church. In fact, almost all parents (except, of course, those who are themselves members) seem to react with concern and dismay initially to the realization that their children have become followers of Sun Myung Moon. However, many, in time, display a changed attitude, either becoming neutral in attitude, demonstrating calm acceptance of their child's new religious affiliation, or even manifesting a favorable attitude toward Church members and their child's association. One father, who expressed great antagonism toward the Church's influence over his daughter, a recent recruit, told me that "parents of long-time Church members have no choice but to show acceptance. They've had a long while to get used to the idea." But he planned "to fight the Church to retrieve" his daughter, Karen, if he could. He further remarked that his daughter had "changed noticeably, particularly when talking about the Church doctrine. My wife and I and my other children are very upset about Karen becoming a Moonie. The other children want me to do something about it. We don't want to lose her—we love her."

Another parent, a mother who had her daughter deprogrammed, described her initial reaction to me: "When I first found out Sally was in the Unification Church, I didn't know what I had to do, but I knew I had to get her out. First, I read everything I could find and learned everything I could. The more I learned, the more desperate I became. The most important thing was to keep the lines of communication open. Every time she spoke to me, I felt that she was not getting something from them. Their influence was that much reduced."

The Unification Church appears to be quite concerned about the negative image it has, particularly with regard to the subject of relationships between Unificationists and their families. In order to combat this unfavorable view and the concern and discomfort experienced by relatives, the Unification Church held a conference on "Family Relations and New Religious Movements" in April 1981, attended by professors in the fields of sociology and religious studies, Unificationists, and siblings and parents of Church members. In addition, the Parents' Association of the Church in Great Britain publishes a magazine whose listed objectives are: "1. To encourage understanding between members of the Unification Church and their families. 2. To provide a means of contact between parents for interchange of ideas and information. 3. To act as a link between parents and the Unification Church and to ensure that the opinions of parents are brought to the attention of the Church. 4. To ensure that the views of parents are fairly represented to the public."[49]

One recent edition of the magazine contained an article entitled "If Your Child Joins The 'Moonies,'" by Laurie Burnett, an excerpt from which follows:

"So many parents have leapt into the first plane, train or boat, in a frenzy of activity which has brought nothing but frustration. Sit down calmly and assess the situation. But, let me warn you that it is extremely unlikely your child will return home again.

"However, what is surely far more important, if you insist on bombarding him/her with emotion, hysterics and reproaches, he may well be lost to you forever."[50]

Two letters to the editor also appeared in the same magazine, one supportive of the organization, while the other was strongly antagonistic. The latter included the following: "He has put his mother into an early grave and I blame him and the Unification Church in America for the harsh treatment handed out to her on her two visits to see Kevin in the New Yorker [a former hotel in New York City, bought for residential use by the Unification Church].... When Kevin's mum was dying would he come home, the answer was *no* he was too busy working and having legal problems over his passport."[51]

The New York headquarters of the Church produces its own parents' newsletter called UP *(Unification Parents)*, which began publication in 1981. The first edition contained a 1980 article reprinted from the *Albuquerque Journal* which described a good relationship between a Moonie daughter and her mother; a Christmas letter from a father to his son; information about the International Conference on the Unity of the Sciences sponsored by the Unification Church; and quotations from Reverend Moon on marriage and the family—for example: "If man is one with God and woman is one with God neither one can say, 'I am higher than you.' There is no higher or lower, but only complete oneness."

Two brochures which reprint positive messages from parents of Unification Church members are also used by the public relations office to contrast the largely negative parental reports found in the media. For example, "A Personal Observation" was written by Judith Harris Carter in 1975; two of her seven children are members of the Church. She wrote:

"In the end, you must decide how you will address the question of your relationship with your son or daughter. If our friends' beliefs differ from yours or mine, we accept them anyway in affection and tolerance. Can we do less for our own flesh and blood?"

The other brochure, entitled "A Mother's Point of View," was written by Peggy Moffit, a registered nurse residing in Texas and the mother of a 26-year-old Unificationist. She wrote the brochure after a 12-day visit to the national Church headquarters in New York. The following passages express some of her feelings:

"... right now, America is turning into a jungle.... I want my son to live a happy life and desire him to become a good parent. I also want him to be strong both physically and emotionally. Before Larry joined Reverend Moon's Crusade he was not fulfilling all of these things.... They [Unification Church members] are not hypocrites, or puppets, and they are not brainwashed. That is a bunch of hogwash. They really feel deeply about what they are doing and are dead serious that their cause is good."

Many parents attend Unification Church services on Sunday because it provides them with the opportunity to visit with their children. One mother, Mrs. Lester, whose husband had died 12 years earlier, five years before her son, Bill, became a member, spoke to me about her feelings toward her son and the Church. Her son was not present during our conversation. In fact, he was many miles away at another Church center. At first Mrs. Lester was hesitant about revealing her thoughts because she did not believe that she was sufficiently articulate and knowledgeable, but after some reassurance she told me:

"I am not a member of the Unification Church and am not interested in becoming one. I usually go to the Lutheran church near where I live. But I come here once in a while. Everyone is so nice. I also have a daughter who is younger than Bill. She is married and lives in Las Vegas and goes to Unification Church services once in a while. Her husband is Catholic, so I suppose she goes to those services also."

Mrs. Lester described the circumstances under which her son became a Moonie: "Bill was taking language courses in preparation for medical school in France. He met

Unification Church members there and joined it. Then he stopped attending school. He has found something to work for; it is important that his life have meaning. He was interested in philosophy and things like that. He now works in Gloucester in the boats and is engaged to a lovely girl. I met her and her family. They were all so nice to me."

When I questioned her about whether her son was coerced into staying with the group, she answered: "There is absolutely no truth to the charges that Unification Church members are prevented from leaving. I would never think of having my son deprogrammed. It's totally against my principles. I may have thought of it once at the beginning. But I would never do it now."

I asked Mrs. Lester whether she had any advice or suggestions for other parents of Moonies. "Parents should visit the centers to be reassured," she said. "The information from the press about brainwashing is untrue. The Church has never prevented me from doing or seeing anything and I've made many friends in the Church."

I also inquired about the reaction of friends and family to Bill's membership in the Unification movement. She answered: "I try not to talk to my friends or family about his Church affiliation. They just don't understand. At the beginning, they kept sending me negative articles or they would tell me about shows they had seen like '60 Minutes.' I told them I have seen the articles and don't need them to be sent to me. Now I just avoid discussing it. It's best that way." Her final remarks were: "I think one of the problems in the past was that college students would drop out of school to join the Church. Now, CARP encourages students who are in college to finish. That's a good thing, because parents were upset that their children left school to join the Church. The Unification Church people are such a lovely group of people. There's just something about them. You can see it in their faces."

Ex-Moonies

Although it has often been said that once an individual has become a Unificationist, that person is a Moonie for life, the attrition rate is actually quite high, at least 50 percent, according to Church spokespeople. I spoke to many individuals who had left the movement, some on their own and others through forcible deprogramming, usually arranged by family members. Their narratives, some of which have already been cited, are instructive and reveal another side of the Unification Church story.

Maria Sanchez, a 23-year-old Puerto Rican woman raised in a Baptist home, stayed in the Church for just five months. She had previously received an Associate's degree, but had dropped out of her four-year college, where she had been studying psychology, because of family problems. Prior to joining the Unification Church, Maria had peripherally been a part of several other movements. She explained: "I knew about Hare Krishna; I had studied with them. A friend had gotten involved with them. I started reading some of their books. I did some meditation and some chanting. I was in college studying psychology. I was curious about them. But I couldn't stand their chanting and I couldn't believe that Krishna was going to pick them up by their ponytails. It didn't make sense to me. I was also involved in other groups like a flying-saucer group. I was curious about all kinds of groups. I used to get involved in anything that was spiritual."

I interviewed Maria about a year after she left the movement. She described her involvement with the Moonies: "I had been in New York for two weeks at the time. I was under a lot of emotional stress. I didn't know anyone here except my aunt. My father had kicked me out of the house in Puerto Rico. My mother was in New York on vacation, but she left to return to Puerto Rico. I was staying with an aunt. My relationship with my parents was never very good. After my mother left, I was looking for a job. I was on 125th Street and Broadway. A tall guy selling candy asked me for a donation to his Church. He seemed like a nice fellow, very warm. I was curious, so I asked about the organization. He said he was fundraising for the purpose of the Church. He kept talking about the wonderful group he had joined. He talked about a workshop, but I really didn't understand that word; my English was not that good at the time. He invited me to hear a lecture. I went to the lecture that night at West 43rd Street. It was a history lecture and it impressed me. I was physically there, but my mind was somewhere else. I needed to cry, to be comforted. I couldn't analyze what was going on. Everyone was love-bombing me. I started crying there. Everyone was really warm and loving.

"The next day they invited me for dinner at CARP on Sunday night. Then I went home. They kept calling me to talk. They invited me to their house. I called my aunt and told her I was going to someone's house. I still didn't know it was part of the Unification Church. I stayed over at the CARP house and I did fundraising without even being a Moonie, to raise some of the fee for the workshop. They took me as part of a fundraising group—selling flowers. They were preparing buckets. I could see that it was important that I was there and they were encouraged. There were some lectures in the house. It sounded like something I really wanted to do. Before noon I was in the van with two leaders. I decided I'd try to fundraise with them. I spent the whole day and made much more than I needed for the workshop. In a half hour I could make ten dollars. The next day, I did the same thing.

"On Friday night I went home and picked up my clothes. I was prepared to stay for the weekend. I knew by then it was a religious group, but I still didn't know it was the Unification Church. I took the workshop, which was really hard for me. I was still under emotional stress. I understood part of the workshop; the other part I didn't understand. I met a lady that weekend who asked if I wanted to stay for a seven-day workshop. It cost 40 dollars, but I didn't have it. CARP said they would pay for it.

"By the time I got back to Queens, I decided I would do the seven-day workshop. That week was a hassle, but a woman from CARP was so nice that I stayed. In the middle of the week, she left. I did a lot of crying, and I couldn't sleep. The CARP woman kept watching me. I couldn't sit through any of the lectures. Then I stayed for another week because they told me I needed it. Then I ran away from the 43rd Street center leader. He kept pushing me, I had to make a commitment to the Heavenly Father. I still didn't know who Moon was. I started getting uptight. I told him to stop pushing me.

"The lady leading the workshop was very supportive. I felt very close to her. She was the one who made me join. She was happy, uplifting, very loving and caring. Now, I think she was just trained to do that. After I joined I saw her a couple of times, but she would block off. After awhile I tried to contact her and I couldn't find her. After that week—it was a Friday night—we had a long talk and I promised her that I would join. She was my spiritual mother.

"The other thing that influenced me was some weird dreams as if I were divided, but I was actually conscious and awake. The first time it happened I was in a lecture room. I couldn't listen anymore. I was feeling very tense. I left the room and went into bed. I lay down and noticed people coming and going. I felt my spirit coming out. I felt a burning in my back and saw two angels. My mind was divided. The angels were saying: 'She will see what has happened to all her ancestors, but she's okay. We are here to help her.' I was struggling to become one with my body. Then finally I stood up and I was frightened, but I kept quiet about it.

"The next night, I'm in bed trying to sleep. Then I have this flash. I see a comet from outer space to Earth. I find myself at the New Yorker. I see Reverend Moon with Jesus. I couldn't see Jesus' face, but I could see Moon. Jesus is saying: 'This is the great prophet that I sent here to give this message.' I look at Moon and think that finally I have seen him. At the end of the workshop, I told them about my dream and they told me: 'You have received a great revelation.' Then the center's leader pushed me to join. I said, 'I can't, I need time to think.' Then I left. I ran out. My spiritual mother ran after me to try to convince me to go back. She kept pushing, but I kept going. I didn't have any money. I asked someone in the street for a dollar. Finally I went back.

"My spiritual mother had started crying when I told her I was going to leave. I started feeling guilty. I thought, 'She hardly knows me. How can she care so much for me?' She said, 'Heavenly Father needs you right now.' I said, 'I don't want to go back to CARP.' She finally agreed. I went to the 43rd Street center, but I didn't tell the CARP person. It was more what I wanted to do. When the CARP person found out, he said it would be harder at 43rd Street. I told him, if I couldn't be at the 43rd Street center, I would just leave.

"I joined the Church without knowing anything. I was totally ignorant. No one was willing to train me. My mission was witnessing, but first I did some handy work at the center. It was more of a job for a man than for a woman. I was also working in the kitchen. Then I fell off a ladder. It hurt, but since I had previously been in an accident, a car accident, my legs always hurt. Somehow I just blocked out the pain. There are indemnities. There was work to be done. After awhile, you just block off everything and keep going. Two weeks later, my back and legs really hurt. Meanwhile, every weekend I went up to a farm for training. I also worked in the kitchen and on the farm.

"My mother was coming to New York because she wanted to be with me. She talked to me by phone and tried to convince me it was the wrong group. Then I went to pick up my mother at the airport. I was allowed to go alone because I was already trusted. I went to my aunt's house, picked up my cousin, and then went to the airport for my mother. We visited for awhile and then I went back to the center.

"I went to a chiropractor for about three weeks for treatment. He was not a Unification Church member, but he agrees with their theology. He sent a note to the Church explaining my condition. He said, 'Either you'll go crazy or all your systems will shut off if you don't start getting more rest.' His diagnosis was that my kidneys and nervous system were in bad shape. Then I went to camp and worked hard anyway. It was my escape in a sense, I didn't have to listen to lectures. I led the kitchen crew and worked with Spanish training groups trying to reach the Spanish community.

"At the 43rd Street center, we got up at 5; 6 was a prayer meeting; 7 was trinity. We got to sleep at 12:30 at night at the earliest. The prayer meeting started at midnight. At camp, at least, I got more rest. I didn't have to get up until 6 or 7 but still I went to bed 12:30 or later.

"In the camp, I met a girl, Betty, who was in for three weeks and I saw her crying desperately. I went over to her, giving her some comfort. I spoke to her. The second time I saw her, we had a good talk. One time when I was gathering everyone for a lecture, she gave me a big hug. She started asking questions about the Bible. She couldn't believe Moon was the Messiah. Then I see that her spiritual parent is really pushing her. She needed someone to talk to about her problems. Everyone ignored her. I started helping her emotionally. We were not allowed to be friends so we would see each other after 12:30 at night. By that time I began to see some racism within the Church. Blacks and Spanish people were treated differently. I became very disappointed with the movement. They really didn't want people who spoke Spanish.

"In the meantime, my group leader told me I was changing and she was proud of me. She felt that I had become part of the movement even though I didn't think

Moon was the Messiah. I spoke to my group leader, who is asked permission to do anything. I asked if I could go to Philadelphia with Betty. My group leader had been told that Betty was in love with me. I said it wasn't true. She let me go to Philadelphia, but she also sent a four-year member, Anne, with us.

"In Philadelphia, Betty contacted her friends; we stayed in a Moonie center, the Home Church that night. We went to bed after 2. We could hardly sleep. A friend of Betty's was trying to get her to leave. Other friends invited us for dinner. They took her into a room and left Anne and me out. Another guy kept us busy while his girlfriend was talking to Betty. After dinner we went outside. Betty grabbed my hand and I realized something was wrong, that she wasn't going back. She asked me not to go back. I told her I had made a commitment and talked with her for two hours trying to convince her not to leave. Betty's friends told me I was brainwashing her. Moonies then showed up, a whole bunch of them from Philadelphia. I was surrounded by Moonies on one side and Betty's friends on the other. They began fighting with each other, yelling. I looked at the show going on and became real confused for an hour. One of Betty's friends said to me: 'The Moonies are not what you think they are. Give yourself a chance. Listen to some ex-Moonies.' I didn't know who to believe. The police came and I was in the middle. The Moonies were calling me to go with them and Betty was calling me. Finally, I go into Betty's friend's house. I told the Moonies I would call them the next day.

"The next day, I read all kinds of newspapers Betty's friends gave me about Moonies. They asked me if I wanted to stay. They contacted an ex-Moonie who talked to me. Betty's boyfriend meanwhile took her away. Then the Moonies came looking for me. Betty's friend said I had left, but actually I stayed for six more days. I felt like I was in the pit of Hell. My mind was off. I felt like I was dying. After a week I left the house and went to the park. That afternoon, Betty's friends took me to a party in a beautiful place.

"Then I went back to New York with Betty's boyfriend to pick up my things from the 43rd Street center. We saw the Moonie who had gone with us to Philadelphia. I started crying, I made believe I had gotten lost, making up stories, saying I was back. They gave me cake. Betty's boyfriend stayed outside, waiting for me. They asked if I had met any deprogrammers. I told them I was okay and was not leaving. They grabbed my arm. Watching me, but not threatening me. They kept questioning me. I asked a Moonie that I trusted: 'What would you do if someone left the movement?' She said: 'I wouldn't talk to them because they have betrayed the Heavenly Father.' I then said: 'I'm going to see my mother and will be back in an hour.' They left me alone because they noticed I was getting angry. I went to my aunt's house and then went back to the center with my cousin. My cousin went to my room and took my things and I walked out. I did leave some of my things but I didn't dare go back. I called the center and told them my mother was sending me to Spain to get married. I just didn't want them to bother me.

"I felt very vulnerable, I would wake up at times and feel like I was still in the movement. I had dreams about going back.

"After that one week in Philadelphia, Betty and I didn't want to hear anything about the Church. We wanted to be left alone. We stayed in an empty house, we wanted to forget. I lost trust and confidence in myself. I was afraid of going back to the outside world. I was afraid that the Moonies would kidnap us. After that experience, I felt I couldn't relate to people.

"I started studying the Bible and the Divine Principle by myself. I started writing. Friends told me there was going to be a conference of ex-cult members. I met some ex-cult members who invited me for dinner and we shared our experiences as Moonies. I was told about a support group for ex-cult members. From then on, I started dealing with my vulnerability and my anger at being used, at my mind and my will being taken away. I am still part of the support group. It has helped me deal with expressing my feelings.

"It took me five-and-a-half months to get a job. I couldn't communicate. I moved from Philadelphia two months ago. I also do deprogramming. Sometimes I get paid $200 a day for a full 24-hour period, sometimes I don't. It's not good to do it alone. It's very intense—you need someone to back you. When someone needs help I do it—even if I don't get paid."

Eddie Pringle spent just six-and-a-half weeks with the Church in 1975. When I spoke with him more than six years later, he recalled some significant aspects of his religious and family background as well as his earlier personal philosophical perceptions and activities:

"My previous experience with religion was somewhat negative. Both of my parents are Jewish, but they were not observant. I was not Bar Mitzvahed. I had three years of Yiddish schooling, mainly focusing on historical, cultural, and language aspects. I was seeing a great deal of hypocrisy—more words than action. The Bar Mitzvah is less a ceremony than a catered affair. It's gift-giving rather than what it should be. It's more of an excuse for a party than anything else. One attains status by how big a party parents can give. My relationship with my family was fair. I was fairly alienated from everything. I was alienated from myself. I was searching for many answers. I was trying to find meaning and purpose in life. I had participated in a few antiwar marches. I was involved in students' rights, I was part of a boycott of classes in high school. I was involved, but not in the forefront. Freedom of the press was my big thing. I wrote for and was editor of a local underground newspaper while I was in high school. I also took part in sensitivity training in high school. I was involved in a lot of different things in college. I worked part-time in the snack bar in college. I wrote the psychology newsletter in the department. I was on the volunteer ambulance corps and volunteered at the counseling center and was a member of the tennis team."

After receiving a B.A. from a branch of the State University of New York and breaking up with a girlfriend, with whom he had been living ("she started going with someone else"), Eddie began to do some traveling. First he went to Florida, then to California where he worked at various odd jobs in the restaurant business. While hitchhiking through Berkeley with a backpack, Eddie was approached by a "clean-cut guy. He asked me to come with him for a free dinner with a group of people who were looking for a better way to live," Eddie remembers. He was not told, until some time later, that this group was connected to the Unification Church.

"When we arrived at the house, I met all these young people who were forever smiling. There was singing, a short meditation, dinner, and more singing. The lecture was given and the concept of God was introduced in a scientific manner. I thought nothing of it as I was so involved with these energetic and seemingly happy people." After the dinner, Eddie agreed to attend a weekend seminar, which was "intense and incessant." At the end of the weekend, Eddie learned of the group's association with the Unification Church. The next step for him was a seven-day workshop at a farm in Northern California, "where the lectures became progressively more emotional." After a group of 50 had climbed a mountain, "it was revealed to us that Reverend Moon was in fact the Messiah and the Second Coming of Christ. His supposed sufferings and miracles he performed were read . . . I found myself getting emotionally involved in the reading and the subsequent deep personal prayer. It was hard not to feel guilty with my small struggle compared with the stories of Reverend Moon and the crying out in prayer all around me.

"My joining was actually not so much a process of joining as not leaving. What intrigued me was a combination of ideals presented. The people were very sincere. They sincerely believe in what they're trying to do." He indicated other reasons for joining: "In the cult, they make it easy; everything is dictated. Sexuality is strictly forbidden, which is good for many people. Getting away from being in a relationship where it was defined in a certain way was attractive. It was an escape from having to deal with sexuality and relationships for awhile."

When I questioned him about the reactions of friends and family members to his joining the Church he told me: "I wrote to my friends when I joined the Church. They thought I was weird, but then they already knew that. I tried to recruit them and my family. I offered them an all-expense-paid trip to come to visit me and to hear the lectures."

He called his family one week after his initial contact with the Church. He explained that after he used the word "family" his mother thought he was with the Manson family. One day, Eddie received a phone message from his father that his mother was ill. His group leader told him that his mother's sickness occurred "because Satan had possessed her." Thus, instead of visiting his mother (who was not actually ill), he became a member of the Church work force in Berkeley and began to witness for the Church, sell flowers, and clean carpets for a Church-owned company. Eddie also indicated to me that he lied whenever it was expedient to do so and that these deceptive practices were clearly condoned by the Church.

Eddie's father flew out from New York to California to see him. Eddie explained the circumstances under which he left the movement: "Because I was still able to see my father's love, concern, and understanding, I could not accept the idea that my father was evil as the Church tried to make me believe—I was able to see how much the Church had made me emotionally dependent on it. I sensed the necessity of leaving the Church if only that I could judge it fairly and objectively despite my emotional attachment and concern for the people in the Church. I sensed that my judgment was impaired and I decided that putting my trust in my father was the right thing to do.

"When I returned it was difficult for my family. They didn't know how to deal with me and I didn't know how to deal with them. I was still under the influence of the Unification Church. I still kept many of the practices. For two months, I felt as if I were still a Unificationist, just not a part of the group."

In the time between his exit from the Church and the present, Eddie has worked as a child-care worker, a camp counselor, a mental health aide, and as an advisor to various YMHA-YWHA programs. He also has been involved in deprogramming efforts and has had several speaking engagements related to his cult involvement. He is presently enrolled in a graduate program in social work and plans to work in the field of gerontology. He has become somewhat involved in his original Jewish faith—attending services occasionally and studying Hebrew. He also feels that he is closer to his parents and sister than ever before.

Criticism

Ex-members of the Unification Church, like Eddie Pringle, are frequently extremely critical of the movement. However, criticisms of the Church have been widely reported from other sources, including present members who do not demonstrate absolute acceptance of all Church doctrines and practices. For instance, one eight-year member suggested: "Zeal may be a weakness. Mistakes can be made. I think that the West Coast people gave the Church a bad name. Weaknesses are from individuals. They are in leadership positions and make mistakes. But," she added, "there is forgiveness in the Church." Another woman, who had been a member for five years, focused on the typical criticism that Moonies are robot-like in appearance, manner, and speech.

She indicated that "a basic problem is the ambiguity that exists with respect to the formulation of individual personal goals." This respondent, like the one just cited, added a positive note to her statement of a perceived weakness: "Our own personal creativity is now being encouraged—to look at ourselves as unique individuals. I just attended a three-week seminar to encourage it. But it has to be repeated to get it into the heads of members."

Another member stated: "There are organizational and structural areas that need to be strengthened." Still another suggested: "There may be some sexism in the Church because the Church does exist in a cultural setting and we have to deal with that."

At a conference on Unification life-style in San Juan, Puerto Rico, in January 1981, Mose Durst, U.S. president of the Church, commented that man is the "initiator," the one who develops a position of responsibility, while woman is the "supporter," the nurturer of man's initiative. Other Church members at that conference disagreed with Durst's perspective and perceived greater equality between the sexes.

One woman, who has been with the Church for about eight years, noted that many of the weaknesses are related to the relative youth of the movement: "I joined at 21 and became responsible for a lot of things very quickly. We've made a lot of mistakes because of our youth and immaturity. Secondly, in Korea members tend to live with their families and have regular jobs. In America the movement has tended to be more mobile."

Criticisms of the Church by various concerned parties fall into several different categories. First, many individuals and businesses are disturbed by the large number of industries in which Moon and his followers are involved. The Church publishes a newspaper called *News World,* owns a carpet cleaning company and a Ginseng tea company, and runs several restaurants and fishing fleets, among many other business endeavors. Critics note that Moonie-run businesses have an unfair advantage, since their labor is supplied freely and they can financially destroy competitors. However, many non-Unificationists avoid doing business with any company that is related to the Church. Ironically, in some instances, rumors that a business is Moonie-affiliated leads to financial hardship for a company that is actually independently owned. In a recent case, a bakery company, part of a large conglomerate, found that its cakes and pastries were being boycotted, resulting in significantly decreased sales, because of rumors that the corporation was owned by the Unification Church.

A second criticism concerns the tendency of Church members to regard Moon as the absolute authority regarding Church-related and other matters. Many former members indicated that while they were part of the movement they would have done anything Moon asked of them, including killing. One present member, a new recruit, told me: "I'm ready to die now for the movement. My physical body is not important." The 120-day training manual, that was formerly used as a teaching guide to explain the Divine Principle and the Unification Church to new recruits, was shown to me by a member of an anti-cult organization. It contained the following passage which is related to the subject of absolute dedication to Moon: "Father, I can give my life. In case of emergency please take my life first. If only You and Mother and Father's family can be saved, I am willing to die."[52]

The totality and inflexibility of Church doctrine is reflected in the following two passages from the 120-day training manual: "So far as you came to Unification Church, you can't go anywhere. You are in prison—you have no other way than to be imprisoned in Unification Church."[53]

"Eventually, if you can catch the mind, then you can catch everything. This is the secret...My feeling, my way of thinking, my imagination, *all* must belong to God. I must deny *my* way of thinking, *my* way of feeling, *my* way of talking, everything. *My* desire, *my* hope, *my* joy, *my* will must be placed on the altar and be given to God."[54]

A third criticism is the deceptive practices sometimes used by the Church. The term "Heavenly deception" was frequently employed to describe instances of deceit in the pursuit of a Unification Church goal. For example, many current and former members indicated that they were initially unaware that the group they had joined was affiliated with the Unification Church. A number of individuals also told me that they lied during fundraising because of the bad name of the Church in the public's mind and the consequent difficulty of soliciting contributions in a direct fashion. Allen Tate Wood, in his book *Moonstruck,* which described his experiences as a Moonie, wrote: "Moon's system was simply one of the many in which the end justifies the means. Lying and stealing were okay as long as you were doing it for the sake of good."[55]

One long-time Church member explained to me why deception or at least omission of information was sometimes necessary: "I applied for a job and was turned down because of my Unification Church membership. On my second application, I didn't say anything about the Church and I got the job. If we tell people about the Church, we don't get the job. If we don't tell people, we're accused of Heavenly deception."

Because of the negative image of the Church, the movement's leaders are very careful about information that is provided to the public. However, this tactic may actually work against the Church by making it appear to be even more controlled and secretive. As an example, the following occurred to me in the course of my investigation: As I interviewed a new recruit named Jim Simmons on the steps of the New York church, a three-year member came over to us and told Jim that someone was waiting for him upstairs in the dining room. She was evidently trying to end the interview. When Jim had left, the woman told me that Jim was a new member and that "he is not a good person to be talking to. Some of what he may say does not accurately reflect the Church's position and ideas."

A fourth major criticism concerns the exploitation and over-working of members, particularly with regard to fundraising activities. Although the soliciting for funds is often related to the fulfillment of indemnity conditions, and thus part of the theology of the movement, the fact still remains that members work extremely hard. For example, one member, describing his fundraising experiences, commented: "We usually get up at 5 or 6 in the morning. Then we have a morning prayer service. Sometimes, we go a hundred days or more without a break.... It's natural to live like that.... I'd sleep about two or three hours a night, but we're inspired by Reverend Moon's word." The importance of money is reiterated in the 120-day training manual:

"Do you like to make green bills happy? When green bills are in the hands of fallen man, can they be happy? Why don't you make them happy? So many green bills are crying. Have you ever heard them crying? Not yet? You must hear. They are all destined to go to Father. This is our responsibility. Eventually, unless everything goes through Father, it cannot be happy."[56]

A fifth criticism is the suggestion of widespread political dimensions and connections of the Unification Church. The training manual states: "The American Constitution is not always...in line with God's word. For instance, the American Constitution allows fornication. In the Messianic country, fornication will not be allowed. The American Constitution says that you can do it under certain circumstances. Therefore the American Constitution must be changed. Therefore, in the Kingdom of God, or Messianic country, fornication and adultery will constitute a felony."[57]

In addition, a number of investigators, including U.S. Congressional committees, have suggested ties between the

Church and the Korean Government, and reports of Church munitions factories have also circulated. The Church has been involved in some clear-cut political activities—most noticeably, perhaps, the demonstration of support for former President Nixon during the Watergate investigation. Moreover, there are significant political implications in the Church's anti-Communist doctrine and the division of countries into "good" and "bad" nations. In an analysis of the political aspects of the movement, Stoner and Parke raised the issue of the origin of the funds used to finance the initial Church crusade in the United States.[58] A related topic that has been the subject of much debate is the tax-exempt status of a great deal of Church-owned property in New York City and nearby Westchester County, and elsewhere in the United States. Because of the many business ventures the Church is involved in, critics have argued that the Church holdings unfairly deplete the tax rolls of the country.

One Church member explained the existence of the political and other criticisms in the following way: "There are always misunderstandings about any new religious movement. There are negative reactions by traditional religions and others because our values are pretty confronting. Some of the concern may be racial. There may be reaction by leftist thinkers who may be threatened by our anti-Communist stance."

Being a relatively new religious organization, the Unification Church has, of course, been the subject of theological critiques. Several interviewees indicated an anti-Semitic aspect of the movement. One told me: "The Unification Church has roots in everything—Eastern religions, Christianity, Judaism. It is an educational, psychological, and philosophical system. However, it is also somewhat anti-Semitic in its claim that Jews had failed, that they were Christ killers. Moon justifies the holocaust by suggesting that six million Jews died because of Christ's death." Others have been critical of the Church's claim to being Christian. For example, a document issued by the Commission on Faith and Order of the National Council of the Churches of Christ in the U.S.A. notes a number of points of conflict between Unification theology and generally recognized Christian doctrines. For instance, the document states: "The fall of man is explained in a way which is incompatible with the Bible and Christian theology. The mythical figure of Lucifer, the fallen angel of light, is presented as the external source of evil and sin, which he transmits by sexual union to Eve, who passes it on to Adam by the same mode. Such unwarranted mythology seeks a facile answer to a most profound and inscrutable mystery, which becomes a basis for questionable teachings and practices of sex and marriage."[59] Another area of disparity posited in this document concerns the doctrine of salvation. It states: "The doctrine of salvation, according to Divine Principle, consists in 'restoration through indemnity.' Because this principle is based, in part, on the failure of Jesus to achieve his mission, it cannot be regarded as Christian." Several other significant theological points are made in the document, which concludes: "The Unification Church is not a Christian Church," and further "The claims of the Unification Church to Christian identity cannot be recognized."[60]

A seventh area of criticism concerns the charge, cited earlier, that when children join the Church, they become alienated from their families. Allen Tate Wood wrote in this regard: "We were generally discouraged from seeing our families, but never forcibly restrained. Force wasn't necessary. If you believed Moon's teachings you believed that the rest of the world was in the hands of Satan. You were told that your family members were your enemies and that you could expect them to try to bring you back to the old evil ways.... When we did visit our families, it was almost always with other Church members, so we would resist collectively and make sure one of our people didn't waver during a period of vulnerability and doubt."[61] However, others (particularly present members) disagree and sometimes even point to improved family relationships after joining the Church.

Another critical issue concerns the Church's goal to unify the world's religions, the ramifications of which are perhaps an unhealthy emphasis on uniformity of belief and an intolerance for differences.

The Future

Turning now to a look at the future of the Unification Church, it is evident that the idea of the Home Church will play a significant role in the movement. One member called Home Church "pioneering and new." Another said: "It is a new and important trend which is based on the idea that God dwells in the family." The idea of a Home Church is to establish the Church in everyone's home, to not be limited to a church building. The individuals in Home Church are responsible for a 360 home district. One Church member stated that Home Church participants "spread the word and act as an example. They are at the disposal of people in their area for shopping, baby sitting, etc." Another Unification follower commented: "The idea is to find a community to serve and build up, to get to know people in an area, to teach Unification theology, to have greater permanence." A former member explained that "while the word recruitment is never used, everything you do as part of Home Church is a recruiting tool." The ultimate goal of Home Church is to have Church members living and working with the individuals in an assigned section. One Church member told me "I see the Church as being dispersed. I've got the sense of God and the Divine Principle within me. I don't have to live in the center." Another long-time member, when questioned about his future, remarked: "I might choose to lead a life that is more private than the one I lead now, but I would not leave the Church." Another commented: "Whatever I do will be beneficial to the Church, whether I work within it or outside of it."

Other followers of Moon, in speaking of the future of the movement, see greater emphasis on world relief programs, missions to other countries, and social activities. Several Unificationists indicated that their lives would be easier or more comfortable if they left the Church, but they felt a commitment to it and wanted to be involved in the programs described above.

Another trend that may change the nature of the Church is its increasing involvement in businesses which may become the primary source of financial support, replacing the massive individual fundraising effort. Whether soliciting contributions by individual members as part of their indemnity conditions continues on a widespread basis, when the practice is no longer the most effective way to raise money, remains to be seen.

An event that may have a significant impact on the movement is Moon's recent conviction for income tax evasion. Unification Church members view the conviction as an instance of discrimination, perhaps demonstrating to them the validity of the prediction of persecution contained in the Divine Principle. Moreover, perceived persecution often serves to strengthen and unify a group. The increased internal cohesion of the Unification Church was demonstrated at the rallies to protest Moon's indictment and conviction. If the appeal of Moon's conviction is unsuccessful, he will serve a term of imprisonment. His absence during that period may have only a negligible adverse effect on the movement since he has played a relatively minor public role in recent years.

The Church may one day become a more accepted part of the American religious scene similar to what occurred to groups like the Mormons or Jehovah's Witnesses. Or it may continue to arouse controversy and strong public indignation and protest as long as it exists.

2:
est

"Outside of my family, it's the most important thing I've ever done."
"For some people it could enforce selfishness, and for others it could enforce selflessness."
"There was a very profound change for me."
"It frightens me."
"It was really wonderful. I really loved it."
"There are parts that are utterly impossible."

THE above are some of the reactions that individuals have had to their participation in *est.* Author and psychotherapist Adelaide Bry described the two meanings of "est": "It is the Latin word for 'it is.' It is also an acronym whose initials stand for Erhard Seminars Training."[1] The letters are written in the lower case and italicized. As of August 1981, 308,000 had participated in this training program at 31 centers, 24 of which are in the United States. There are also centers in Canada, Tel Aviv, London, and Bombay. Some of *est*'s participants are famous—Polly Bergen, Joanne Woodward, Yoko Ono, and Cloris Leachman, the celebrity graduates. John Denver has written a song entitled "Looking for Space," based on his *est* experience. Valerie Harper has applauded *est* and its founder on national television. Four hundred paid staff members and 7,000 volunteers work for the organization, which is now simply called "Centers Network," since "*est*, an educational corporation" was dissolved as of May 31, 1981, with a net worth of $890,000. The organization that sponsors the 60-hour training program is now, according to the organization's financial coordinator, "an unincorporated association which is the simplest financial structure. Moving from *est* to Network allows us to do anything we want. Some can be profit; others can be nonprofit entities. Anything can happen."

The Transformation of est's *Founder*

Werner Erhard, born John Paul Rosenberg on September 5, 1935, in Philadelphia, founded *est* in California in 1971. Erhard's father, Joe Rosenberg, born to Jewish parents, had converted to the Baptist faith and had later become an Episcopalian like Erhard's mother, Dorothy. Thus Erhard attended Episcopal Sunday school and church regularly while growing up and was an altar boy for eight years. His childhood was marked by a series of violent, freak accidents. When he was 3 he fell off a third-story fire escape, incurring serious head trauma that required months of rehabilitation, including learning to walk again. That episode was followed by an accident in which he ran a ruler down his throat; a scalding; and a second fractured skull from an automobile accident. When he was 6 he almost drowned while swimming in a lake.

Erhard first became interested in Eastern religious thought, which was to have a significant impact on the development of *est*. At the age of about 11 or 12 he began the study of hatha yoga. He later developed an interest in hypnosis. Just after he turned 18 he married Pat Fry, whom he had met in high school. She was pregnant at the time of their marriage, but, she explained to historian and philosopher William Warren Bartley, III, who wrote

Erhard's biography, they did not have to get married. Rather, they were in love and wanted to get married.[2] She is presently a member of the Network staff.

After his marriage, Erhard began to work for a meat packing firm. However, according to Erhard, "the inner education, the search, the interior dialogue continued."[3] He perceived a sharp separation between his family and work responsibilities and his private search for meaning in his life. Erhard changed jobs frequently, and for five years he sold cars for several dealers. He also changed his name during that period from Jack Rosenberg to Jack Frost, with the latter name serving as a sales gimmick so that he could be easily remembered. While he was becoming more successful at work and Pat had borne him four children, his marriage was deteriorating and he started an affair with June Bryde, a woman who worked for a real estate agency. During the summer of 1959 he consulted his physician, because he had begun to experience blackouts. Since his symptoms were deemed to be psychological, rather than physically based, he began seeing a psychoanalyst. Erhard described this period of his life: "I was sick of my marriage, sick of my wife and my mother, and sick of myself. My body began to respond, however, to that psychoanalytic therapy."[4]

In 1960, he left his family and went off with June Bryde. While flying from Newark, New Jersey, to Indianapolis, they chose new names to prevent their families from finding them. June became Ellen Virginia, and John Paul Rosenberg became Werner Hans Erhard. He had chosen the name while perusing an article in *Esquire* magazine on West Germany. Werner was taken from Werner Heisenberg, the physicist and philosopher; Hans from Bishop Hanns Lilje; and Erhard from the economics minister (later to become chancellor) Ludwig Erhard.[5] Werner and Ellen took a train from Indianapolis to St. Louis, where Werner began to read books about careers and success.

Erhard discussed the beginning of his own transformation: "Jack Rosenberg had screwed up his life. Werner Erhard was going to do it right."[6] One of the books that influenced him during this period was Napoleon Hill's *Think and Grow Rich,* which contained principles about using ideas to create something out of nothing and the inherent tendency of ideas to be changed into reality. Maxwell Maltz's book *Psycho-Cybernetics,* containing ideas about self-image and cybernetics, was also quite influential at that time.

In 1961 Werner and Ellen left St. Louis, and he became a registrar for a correspondence school which taught the operation of construction equipment. Soon afterwards, they headed for California with two friends, in a car that he had originally borrowed, but because its owner no longer knew Erhard's or the car's location, it became, in effect, stolen. Erhard was reassigned to sell the correspondence program in Spokane. Soon afterwards he became a salesman and then training manager for the *Encyclopaedia Britannica*'s Great Books Program.

In 1963 he went to work for another book operation in Spokane, *Parents' Magazine*'s Cultural Institute. While there he put together a new staff, including Robert Hardgrove, a former journalist, politician, and newspaper editor. Hardgrove discussed the ideas of Abraham Maslow and Carl Jung, important theorists of the human potential movement, with Erhard. The *est* founder explained the significance of the motivational and growth concepts used by these men and others in the movement: ". . . I saw, under the influence of Maslow, Rogers, and others in the field, that people who are healthy and developing as human beings are naturally successful in their jobs. Then *you* don't have to motivate *them;* they motivate themselves."[7]

In the autumn of 1963, soon after the birth of Werner and Ellen's first child, Werner had a mystical or peak experience which apparently caused a shift in his values, similar to that which occurs with religious conversions.[8] His acquaintance with Alan Watts, an English philosopher and advocate of Oriental religions, particularly Zen, also had an impact on the development of *est*. According to Erhard, Watts was instrumental in his understanding of the distinction between Self and Mind.[9]

By the end of 1967, after his study of Zen and while his marriage to Ellen was in crisis (Erhard was apparently involved in numerous affairs), he took the Dale Carnegie course. This was followed in future years by Erhard's investigation of various other disciplines: Gestalt, Encounter, Transactional Analysis, and the martial arts.

Erhard resigned from *Parents' Magazine* in 1969 to become a division manager for the Grolier Society, a subsidiary of the Grolier Corporation. However, Grolier became involved in legal difficulties concerning sales techniques and practices. John Wirtz, then vice-president of the Grolier Society, noted that neither Erhard nor the members of his division were associated with these legal problems.[10]

Scientology and Mind Dynamics also played a role in the creation of *est*. Erhard took the Scientology Communication course which he described as "brilliant."[11] He went through five Scientology levels and received about 70 hours of auditing or counseling. Erhard took the Mind Dynamics course in 1970 and led his first Mind Dynamics training in the San Francisco area in February 1971.

One month later, at the age of 35, Erhard had an extraordinary experience which was widely reported. He was driving Ellen's car on Marin County Highway somewhere between Corte Madera and the Golden Gate Bridge when he was "transformed," finding what he had been searching for. He described the experience: "In the next instant—after I realized that I knew nothing—I realized that I knew everything. All the things that I had ever heard, and read, and all those hours of practice, suddenly fell into place. It was so stupidly, blindingly simple that I could not believe it. I saw that there were no hidden meanings, that everything was just the way that it is, and that I was already all right.

"... I realized that I was not my emotions or thoughts. I was not my ideas, my intellect, my perceptions, my beliefs. I was not what I did or accomplished or achieved....

"I was simply the space, the creator, the source of all that stuff. I experienced Self *as* Self, in a direct and unmeditated way. I didn't just experience Self; I became Self. Suddenly I held all the information, the content, in my life in a new way, from a new mode, a new context. I knew it from my experience and not from having learned it. It was an unmistakable recognition that I was, am, and always will be the source of my experience."[12]

Erhard decided that there were three tasks that he had to fulfill: share his experience with others, take responsibility for his ego, and confront and take responsibility for his actions prior to his transformation. In order to transform his relationship with Ellen, Erhard started a cosmetic, vitamin, and food supplement business which he turned over to her to guarantee her financial independence and to allow her to "experience" her abilities.[13] He believed that their lives together improved at that time, when they stopped trying to figure out what was wrong with their marriage and with each other. Instead of attempting to fix blame, they began to take responsibility both for their marriage and their roles in it.[14]

In 1971, Erhard hired Harry Margolis, a tax attorney, to devise the financial and organizational set-up of *est*. After considering several possible arrangements, it was established as a profit-making educational corporation and its aim was to reach the maximum number of people possible by charging what was considered a relatively low fee ($150 at that time). The first *est* training session took place in October 1971, simultaneously with Erhard's resignation from the Grolier Society and the ending of his association with Mind Dynamics. One thousand people attended the first *est* guest seminar, held at the Jack Tar Hotel in San Francisco. In 1972, about a year after *est* training had begun, Erhard made his first contacts with the family that he had left behind in Philadelphia more than a decade before. First, he reestablished contact with his parents and siblings and soon afterwards with his ex-wife, Pat, and finally his and Pat's four children. Between 1972 and 1975, almost all of Erhard's family participated in the *est* training. In 1974, the one remaining loose family thread was resolved—the reunion of Erhard's ex-wife and present wife, both of whom presently work for the organization and are friends.

Erhard discussed the relationship between his past and present: "My past used to have me. By taking responsibility for it—as those years of disciplines and the particular

Werner Erhard during an appearance in New York on Feb. 4, 1980.

experience that generated *est* enabled me to do—I got to get my past. Now I no longer am my past; now I have my past, and it does not have me. My past is now my past. It isn't sticking into my present and my future."[15]

The Philosophy and the Training

The basic underlying philosophy of *est* concerns the differentiation between Self and Mind. The goal of *est* appears to be the transformation from the state of Mind, an inherently unsatisfying state in which most individuals purportedly live, to the state of Self, an intrinsically satisfying state. "The Self, for Werner, being the context of all contexts, is then the unsubmitting, unresisting, unformed matrix in which all forms, all processes, all metaphors occur. Who is one really?"[16] The state of Mind, on the other hand, is "an automated warehouse of burdened, encumbered memories.... [Its] design function is to ensure the survival of oneself....

"... the Mind scrupulously records those experiences that are necessary for survival.... The most powerful of these records usually relate to one's parents, and originate in the first few years of life.

"Whenever the present environment resembles *in any way* some such painful or stressful memory, whenever one encounters a situation that one *perceives* as threatening to survival—one in which one might lose, be made wrong, be dominated, be invalidated—the past memories are reactivated, called into play in an undiscriminating way, as 'guides' to the avoidance of pain and threat. They exert a total command over behavior in the present, controlling body sensations, facial expression, posture, thinking, emotions, appearance, fantasies, attitudes, states of mind, everything."[17]

Everyone associated with the *est* training explains that it is difficult or impossible to describe what occurs—it must be experienced. Moreover, Bry, author of a book about *est*, explained: "I cannot ethically reveal the training processes, nor would I choose to do so, because I feel that knowing them in advance significantly reduces the experience of them in the training."[18] Nevertheless, an attempt will be made to describe here the basic rudiments of training, the aim of which is "the transformation of the ability to experience living . . ."[19]

The standard training is about 60 hours in duration over two successive weekends. In addition, there are pre-, mid-, and post-training seminars which last about three-and-a-half hours each. The fee was $400 as of January 1, 1982. The weekend session begins at 9 o'clock on Saturday morning and ends after midnight on Sunday. There are bathroom breaks every four hours, down from the seven hours in the early days of *est*. This may be the aspect of training that is most well-known to individuals prior to training. I was assured by an *est* graduate that if someone really had a bladder problem and wasn't just using a bathroom trip to get away from the training, he or she could get special permission to sit in the back of the room and leave whenever it was necessary. Several trainees discussed the bathroom issue with me. One said: "There are bathroom breaks every three to four hours and maybe not. The trainer decides that for the people. That's a whole process in itself. People would come into the training room and right prior to walking in there they would have five cups of coffee. Then, an hour later they would be complaining about it. But they knew the rules. They knew what the set-up was. You could decide either at that point, decide to support yourself or not support yourself. So I didn't have anything from the night before. It was logical. It was interesting that people were in such a rut in their lives that they couldn't change. So there were people who were demanding to go to the bathroom. The trainer would say no. Some people he wouldn't let go and some people he'd say O.K. you can go. It's not whether you go to the bathroom or not. It's not the issue, the issue is your power over yourself, the control you have over yourself. If you supported yourself in coming in here, knowing the ground rules, then you're not going to have any problems."

Pre-training, which occurs in the middle of the week prior to the actual weekend training, presents the rules for the training and prepares the individual for what is to come. The pre-training session is run by a seminar leader, not the trainer. Participants are asked to adhere to the following ground rules: no alcohol, no drugs (except birth-control pills and essential prescription medication); no watches in the training room; going to the bathroom on regularly scheduled breaks only; no eating except during the single meal break (participants generally eat breakfast prior to training); to be punctual; to stay until the trainer decides that the session is over; to stay seated until called on; to stay quiet unless the participant is sharing, when he or she must use a microphone; to wear name tags printed with letters large enough to be read from the stage; not to move one's chair unless instructed; not to sit with anyone known prior to training.

Most of the questions at the pre-training sessions concern eating and using the bathroom. One 30-year-old man, who did the training three years ago, discussed these ground rules with me: "It was very discipline-oriented. Like you can't take anything into the training. One of the first instances of that is watches. You're not allowed to take a watch into training. And you see all the stuff that comes up from people who don't want their watches taken away. They refuse to just let themselves go into this experience. So that we spend about three hours on people who didn't want to give up their damn watches. It was very interesting to watch the trainer because he was centered; he knew where he was coming from. The other people didn't. They were putting up arguments for long periods of time."

About 250 to 300 people take the training together. It

generally takes place in a hotel ballroom. A recent trainee in his early 30's, told me that the size of the group was not a problem: "In a group of 250 people, each person can have a personal experience, you cut through to the core level." Straightback chairs are arranged theater-style facing a platform on which stand a chair, a lectern, and two blackboards. There are four areas which are addressed in the training: belief or mind structures, experience, reality, and self; and three types of activities which allow experiencing of these topics: lectures or presentations by the trainers which provide information and analysis; "processes," guided experiences or exercises, usually conducted with the eyes closed; and sharing, the activity in which participants are encouraged, but not required, to communicate their realizations about themselves, their lives, and their problems, with the trainer and/or the other trainees.

On the first day, the assistant again reads the ground rules to the audience, and then the trainer appears. There are currently 20 *est* trainers, each of whom has undergone three to five years of training. Thirteen are men and seven are women. They represent various former occupations, including medical doctors, psychologists, attorneys, teachers, business people, an actress, a photographer, and a philosopher. In addition, there are 25 trainer candidates. I was informed by an *est* public relations person that professional background doesn't matter too much, but the trainers "must have an incredible commitment to share this experience with the world. . . . People do not work here to get rich." The salary range for trainer candidates was said to be about $18,000 to $25,000 and for trainers about $25,000 to $35,000. Training begins with a barrage of obscenities addressed to the group. Bry reported: "The trainer's response to a woman who questioned the use of these words was, '"Spaghetti" and "fuck" are the same. They're only words. The difference is the significance you add to them.'"[20]

After the trainer describes the training procedure and the

gamut of feelings trainees are likely to experience, he or she explains that they can leave if they want at that point and receive a tuition refund by mail. The first day of training is mainly spent "observing the role of *belief* in defining their experience of living."[21] The trainer makes all kinds of statements "designed to present trainees with an opportunity to examine whether the statement is true for the trainee. Examples are: 'Anything truly experienced will disappear.' 'What you resist will persist.' "[22] Several hours are spent discussing the role of belief, with the trainer shifting from one trainee's point of view to another, without apparently having one of his or her own.

The trainer then prepares participants for the "process" part of training, explaining that there is no right or wrong way to do it. The first process concerns locating a body sensation. "Locate a sensation in your right foot. . . . Fine. Now locate a sensation in your right calf. . . . "[23] Following this short process, trainees are asked to share with the group or the trainer. They may do this by making a comment, asking a question, or sharing an experience, but they may not focus on what others have shared, reinforcing the notion that the training is personal and private. The trainer responds to statements made by the trainee by saying: "Thank you" or "I got that," not to indicate agreement with the speaker, but rather to indicate that he/she "got" what the trainee was saying. Trainees are also taught to respond to the sharing with applause, again reflecting simple acknowledgment of whatever the speaker has shared.

At the end of the first day of training, trainees are asked to "locate in their lives a 'persistent unwanted condition' and to return with a phrase describing it in the morning, when they will observe it during the 'truth process.' "[24] These persistent, unwanted conditions include various somatic complaints such as headaches or chronic insomnia, as well as uncomfortable feelings such as phobias or compulsions.

The second day of training begins with sharing, followed

by the "truth process," in which trainees discuss their persistent, unwanted conditions. For about an hour and a half, trainees observe the sensations, perceptions, thoughts, feelings, evaluations, attitudes, and images that are associated with that condition. Erhard and Victor Gioscia note: "After this process most trainees share that their item has disappeared—and their belief in the condition is the cause of its persistence, without which the 'condition' vanishes. In short, trainees find they have begun to 'observe'—i.e., to transcend belief. The shift from *conceptual* to *experiential* reality has begun."[25] For example one woman, who took the training seven years ago, told me: "I had insomnia, real killer insomnia for three years. I almost didn't do anything anymore. I was always too tired. On the second day of training, there was a technique called 'truth process,' where you look at what's really true of what you say. I said 'I have this fear of insomnia.' The trainer said: 'Is it fear or is it the insomnia?' I had this realization. It could have happened anywhere, on the bus, for example. But it happened during the training. It was so fabulous. On the second day, I went to sleep without a problem. I really got my money's worth."

A long process called the "danger process" takes place during the evening of the second training day. The group is broken up into eight rows; one row at a time goes up to the stage to face the rest of the group. People experience this phase in many different ways. Some are acutely embarrassed, while others become depressed or filled with fear. One trainee's reaction to this process was described by William Greene, himself an *est* graduate: "The screams started coming. By the time the trainer had everyone frightened of the entire universe, the room was alive with screaming. Once again, I could hear people retching all about me."[26] Between the two weekend sessions is a midweek session in which participants "share" and experience another process.

Day three of training is directed to questioning the nature of reality. There are two processes which are designed to enable trainees to discover that they tend to regard things as real and their experience as unreal. Participants also learn a technique for retrieving unconscious traumatic memories. It is on the fourth day of training that participants are expected to "get it." One trainee discussed his experience on that day: ". . . there's a point in the training at the end when you really get it or you don't. I didn't 'get it' initially. To 'get it' is to find out what the training's about."

The fourth training day begins with a discussion and process called "Anatomy of the Mind," which is a core part of the seminar. In fact, the trainer announces that it is on that day that the *real* training will begin. One participant told me: "The training starts when you decide to do it. When you take the leap off the mountain, that's when the training starts. You've decided that maybe life does actually work."

"The Anatomy of the Self" follows the "Mind" process. Erhard and Gioscia described the fourth day of the training experience: "Carefully, thoroughly, completely, with an irrefutable and inescapable logic, trainees create an experience for themselves that propels them first *into* and then irrevocably beyond the way they have contextualized (experienced) all prior experience. At the end of the process, in a part of the training called 'getting it,' trainees experience a transformation—a shift in the *nature* of experiencing—from thinking that things (the *contents* of experience) determine and define what one experiences (mind) to experiencing self as the context, or source, of the *way* they experience."[27] The final group experience is concerned with the problems of communication on subjects such as sex, love, power, and relationships, now approached from the perspective of Self, rather than Mind.

The post-training session takes place in the middle of the week following the second training weekend. Bry described her experience at such a session: "There's a feeling of being among dear friends and of belongingness. It's not unlike a reunion of an encounter group or college class—we had all experienced similar input. The significant difference, however, is the absence of judgments."[28] A great deal of sharing goes on during the post-session.

Although most *est* training occurs in hotel ballrooms, the *est* experience has also been offered in prisons. Prisoners have provided commentaries on *est*. One related: "Cool, man, cool. And I *got* that what happened to me ain't no mistake. I planned it that way."[29] Another said; "I'm here for bank robbery. It doesn't take too much smarts to walk into a bank and tell them to hand over the money. I kick myself in the ass every time I think about it. I know I got more potential and qualifications than to do something like that. But I was impatient. I wanted it *then*. *est* brought me a lot of realizations and I guess you could call it waking up."[30] Another prisoner who had served two years of a five-year sentence commented: "I took it because there wasn't anything else to do.... But I really roll with the punches now. Sure I'll be glad when I get out of here... But right now I'm paying attention to right now."[31] A convicted rapist and bank robber said: "What I got out of *est* is self-control and self-awareness.... Some days my mind just can't stop wishing I were out. So then I say, 'Why wish to be out there when you can't? Just relax and flow with it and take it as it comes.' "[32]

There is also a special *est* training for children, called the Young Persons Training. The use of the phrase "Young Person" rather than children was clearly not a haphazard decision. It fits in with the underlying philosophy of the organization and its training. Hal Isen, a trainer in the Young Persons' program, explained: "Children are people in small bodies. Their problems aren't much different from ours, it's just that the nuances get subtler as you get older." He noted that the children's programs and the standard *est* training make the same three assumptions: "(1) People are perfect and have barriers to the expression and experience of their perfection; (2) change causes persistence; and (3) recreation causes disappearance."[33] The training, offered for children between the ages of 6 and 12, is held for about 50 children at one time. The hours are shorter than in the standard training (9:00 A.M. to 4:00 P.M. on two successive weekends). Bry remarked about this time difference: "... they get it quicker, I'm told...."[34] Another difference is that lunch is brought in for the children. On the second day, parents can participate in training by sharing and asking questions. Moreover, comparisons of the standard and Young Persons Training certainly suggest that the latter are milder and are run on a somewhat less cognitively complex level.

Phyllis Allen, another trainer in the children's program, further explained: "People interact with children for the most part as if children are less than able." When Hal Isen was asked why children would want to take the training, he replied: "They notice what has happened in the lives of their parents or brothers and sisters. They often share that their parents seem more able to handle things, that they experience being loved by their parents regardless of the circumstances."[35] Isen further suggested that children discover during their training that to be responsible for themselves gives them power.[36]

A representative account of the Young Persons Training, in which Phyllis Allen was the trainer, was written by Ann Overton.[37] Children are told at the outset: "There is no punishment, no retribution in the training. There are no good people and bad people in here. All the assistants have a purpose in being here: to support the training."

An interesting exchange takes place between the trainer and a 6-year-old boy who has removed his name tag for the second time that first morning:

"Are you going to find a new problem after this one?"

"No."

"Did I talk to you earlier?"

"Yes."

"How old are you?"

"Six."

"Maybe you can't have a discussion with a 6-year-old. Is that it?"

"No."

"What did I ask you about?"

"I heard you, but I forgot."

"Kelly, tell him."

"I just remembered."

"Did you just remember because you've been playing a game called 'Stupid' with me?"

The trainer then addresses the group: "Start noticing the games you play with people. Pretending you're stupid is a game. You've got to be real smart to pretend you're stupid."

One of the exercises on day two of the training addresses the question: "In life what have you done for which you have not yet been acknowledged?" One particularly moving exchange between a young girl and the trainer occurs as follows:

" 'Two years ago my mother died,' Sharon says, 'and I was real sad. But my little sister was more sad than I was, so I helped her instead of being sad myself.' Sharon is crying now, and Phyllis, who is sitting between the two microphones, asks, 'So you gave up your own feelings to help your little sister?'

" 'Yes,' Sharon sobs, 'and my dad never acknowledged me for that.'

" 'Sharon,' Phyllis says looking at her, 'I want to acknowledge you for supporting your sister when she was sad and for giving up your own sadness to do that.' Then, turning to the group, Phyllis says, 'Rarely in life do we get acknowledged for the space we create for others.'

"Sharon's tears are beginning to subside. 'Sharon,' Phyllis continues, 'now all the people in this room know what you did. Never again are you going to be able to remember what you did without knowing that we know you did that.' "

Prior to the last process of the training, the children shared their final reactions with the group. One said: "I had a really nice time, and I discovered myself. You helped me see what kind of person I am." Another acknowledged: "It was real fun. . . . I got to find out about my life and my brother's life and everyone else's life, too."

Anyone who has completed the standard *est* training may sit in on a training for a nominal fee or may take a special review for graduates, also at a very low rate. In addition, there are specialized graduate seminars. Bry, a psychotherapist, explained her positive evaluation of these seminars: "From my professional viewpoint I feel it's important, and often essential, for any system that jolts the psyche to provide a follow-up for those who experience it. This is both to help the person integrate the experience and to ground him if he's frightened or disoriented by it."[38]

Another participant that I spoke to expressed some reservations about the Graduate Seminars: "I attended a Graduate Seminar called *Be Here Now*. It took place twice a month for ten sessions from 7:15 to 10:30 on Monday nights. It cost $50 and builds on the training sessions. It focuses on upsets in your life so that you can understand why things are upsetting, how you confront upsets. Are they natural? You learn how you can creatively deal with upsets. I completed the course in May and still feel some of what was learned." When he was interviewed two months later, he said: "I may do another graduate course. But the Graduate Seminars can be a very social thing. A lot of people use it as a social vehicle."

There are several other Graduate Seminar programs. One, called *What's So*, is described as follows: "This is about discovering—or uncovering—what it is you really want to accomplish, what your purpose is in life."[39] Another is entitled *About Sex*. "Experiencing yourself as the *cause* of your sexual experience works; being the *effect* doesn't. In the seminar you will have a chance to locate and dissolve any barriers between you and communicating about sex."[40]

I was informed by a public relations spokesperson that the

term graduate, for an individual who has completed the first training, has recently been dropped because of the connotation of exclusivity. Thus, the magazine of the movement, *The Graduate Review*, will have to be renamed.

There are numerous other courses, events, workshops, and projects sponsored by or associated with the *est* organization. For example, a series of courses called Making Relationships Work was held in the late 1970's. The following are some of the ideas Erhard shared with the thousands of participants in Part IV of that course: "This is about the realization of ecstasy, of joy, of pleasure—but not pleasure in the way we ordinarily hold it, in which we find we're a little reluctant and a little bit guilty about the expression of pleasure. We're talking not about pleasure as a measure of gratification but pleasure as an expression of love, pleasure as ecstasy. An incomparable pleasure."[41] In discussing going completely into each individual relationship, he said: "Many people keep a hole card in reserves, just in case something goes wrong, just in case the person we're with isn't 'the one.' "[42]

A Communication Workshop is advertised as "a breakthrough in the technology of communication" and takes place during 40 hours from Thursday to Sunday, charging a tuition of $300. The following are the promised results: "In *relationships,* it produces harmony, resolves problems, and dissolves feelings of separateness. In *families,* it clears up misunderstandings, conflicts, and resentments. In *organizations,* it transforms a group into a team. Work is done with less effort, fatigue, and struggle, and with more accuracy and efficiency."[43]

The *est* Foundation, the Holiday Project, and the widely publicized and controversial Hunger Project are among the many other organizations that function as separate entities from the Centers Network, formerly "*est* an educational corporation." However, these individual entities are clearly related to Centers Network even if they are legally distinct organizations. They are located in the same building in San

Francisco as the Centers Network. The *est* Foundation was established in 1973 and has provided totally over $1,000,000 in grants to more than 100 projects ranging from research on sonic and visual communication between humans and dolphins to a pilot program of "intercultural contemplative training for the priesthood."[44] An unincorporated entity, called Werner Erhard and Associates, also exists. Its purpose is described by Erhard: "To have a place from which to work and from which to relate to the rest of the network.... Unencumbered by formal structure, it will serve as a space from which to produce and contribute contextually."[45]

Established in 1977, the Hunger Project's goal is to educate the public that hunger exists and that it can be eradicated. It does not directly collect or contribute to the malnourished in the world. As an example of how this project functions, about $90,000 was spent purchasing newspaper space urging individuals to make contributions to charities that send food to the starving in Cambodia. About $1,000,000 was donated, apparently in response to these ads. The Hunger Project is not without its critics. John Weldon, writing for Spiritual Counterfeits Project, an anti-cult group, calls the Hunger Project "a notable addition to the world's list of rip-offs ... *est*'s 'responsibility' does not involve a moral obligation to *do* anything. Erhard does not need to feed the hungry—he can move about in plush surroundings and assert his authorship of a positive world food situation."[46] Suzanne Gordon, in an article in *Mother Jones* magazine, concurred, stating that "consciousness is everything; distribution of wealth and power, nothing."[47]

The Holiday Project, formerly the *est* Hospital Holiday Project, attempts to touch the lives of individuals in institutions such as prisons, nursing homes, and hospitals during the Christmas and Hanukkah season through visits, contributions, and gifts. A new program, certainly a sign of the times, is Growing Older: The Continuing Challenge Workshop.

est *Participants*

Who participates in *est?* A survey sent by the *est* organization to a random sample of 5,800 graduates early in 1980 yielded 2,200 responses. The data revealed the following demographic statistics:

The average *est* participant is 36, with 54 percent female and 46 percent male. They had obtained an average of 15.5 years of education; about 23 percent held degrees above the Bachelor's. Less than 13 percent earned salaries below $10,000; almost 30 percent received salaries over $35,000. The greatest proportion, 36 percent, were married; 29 percent had never been married and were not living with anyone; almost 18 percent were divorced; 9 percent were living with someone; 5 percent were separated; and a little more than 1 percent were widowed. The average number of children was relatively small—1.08. While 32 percent did not indicate a religious preference, 25 percent were Protestant, 16 percent were Jewish, 14 percent were Catholic, and 12.5 percent indicated some other religious orientation. The participants were 94.3 percent white.[48]

Individuals participate in *est* for various reasons. One man in his 30's who was enrolled in a doctoral program in counseling psychology told me: "I went to *est* out of curiosity, out of a desire to find alternative ways of working with patients in counseling."

Many psychotherapists have participated in *est* training. One psychologist explained his reason for training: "You're going to find my view clearly atypical because I didn't go through *est* for the normal reasons. I think that people get caught up in looking for something more in their lives and they see *est* as a possibility of giving that. They're looking to attain higher levels of consciousness. Those were not my reasons for going through *est.* I had attained the level of consciousness that I needed to attain some years before that. I went through *est* because I wanted to see what it was out of professional curiosity. I suppose that was it. I really was interested; it was another human growth experience for me too."

A financial officer in his 30's described the circumstances of his life prior to training: "I was living in New York and was in therapy with an enlightened therapist and thought: 'What's the next thing?' She had done the *est* training and she suggested *est* for me. I was searching for the next thing. I had another friend who had done it. I had an outstanding therapist who knew what her client needed. It was clear to her that the training was what I was looking for."

A woman, formerly an educator, who now works in a public relations capacity, told me that she and her husband had been having marital problems. "My friend said, 'Do this thing called *est*.' He [her husband] went to a guest seminar. I was a little apprehensive. I had never participated in anything labeled human potential or religious. There were very few trainers at the time, so there was a long waiting list. I waited several months."

A high-level business executive in his 50's took the training with his wife and subsequently took a couple of graduate seminars. "We got involved in *est* because one of our daughters said we could communicate better with her if we did it, so we did it. And it did help."

Nancy Fouchée, a member of the communications team at Centers Network, explained: "'Word of mouth' is the best advertising. The way it usually works is that someone takes the training and tells her mother and all her friends. It's like seeing a great movie. You tell everyone about it. People bring friends to guest seminars—there is no charge."

A woman in her late 20's, who is now vehemently opposed to the *est* training, described her initial attraction to *est:* "My father is a psychiatrist-psychoanalyst, so I always grew up on household psychology. I was always intrigued about how many people think the way they did and I think that was reflected in my interest in comparative religion.... I was in my second semester in college and that was the semester that I took the *est* training. I belonged to a coed fraternity where two of my fraternity brothers convinced me to take it. And from their descriptions it did not sound like something like the Unification Church. So I thought that it sounded interesting. . . . Looking back on it I feel very certain that I was drawn towards it as, possibly, an optional thing to do—other than what my father was doing. That I'd always very much admired what he was doing and then I saw this as part of the human potential movement. This was a new way of dealing with therapeutic situations and I was really interested in that. . . . I think I did to a certain extent fall into a classical model—that I'd broken up with a boyfriend right before that."

Tom McDermott, an unemployed 30-year-old man, related his moving life story to me including his involvement with *est:* "I was born in New York City and attended Catholic grammar school. My father was an alcoholic, so he slowly deteriorated to the point where my mother and my sisters had left and I stayed around because I didn't want to desert him. They seemed to all just be walking away from him. I thought maybe there was still something I could do. That was when I was in college. I was at home living with him and it didn't help at all. So I eventually left and moved in with this family that I'd known for three years. They lived up in Larchmont too, where my girlfriend lived. My whole life just sort of moved up to Larchmont."

After graduating from college, Tom went to law school in Boston. "At that particular point I didn't really want to go, but I applied and I got accepted and there was a chance to get away, so I went. It became very clear very quickly that I wasn't supposed to be a lawyer. I wasn't on the same level with these people. It was also my first time away, so I tended to go crazy. I just got involved in a lot of different things, like partying, abusive drinking, and drugs and girls. Just partying all the time. It was enjoyable. I won't put myself down for it. I enjoyed it; I had never done it and it produced nothing. But while you are in the process it was fun."

Tom left law school after the first year and took a job in a public library. "So I just proceeded to tread water for the next three years—just working, and I started another relationship with another girl. We were together for a year and then she wanted more independence, so she stayed in the building and I got another apartment. Then her family moved out to California and got involved in something called *est.* Her family was encouraging her to take the training. I had been familiar with *est* because during this period I was studying Eastern religions and taking a lot of drugs—psychodelics, marijuana, a lot, like every day....

"But I couldn't communicate with the people that I was surrounded with, mainly because I found most of them were doing it just to get as unconscious as they could get. That wasn't my purpose; my purpose was to heighten my experience, was to open myself. I was stoned most of the time. The drug always wears off and you always need more. I was spending a lot of money on pot. So I'd give it up for two or three days, then struggle back. Then, after my girlfriend moved away, she had decided to do the *est* training. Then I met her one day and she was aglow. She invited me to a seminar. She just said she'd decided to do it and she got a lot out of it and she thought I might like it.

"So I went to a seminar and I had heard about *est* being involved in all this stuff. I was open to it and I'd visited their center once just to find out about *est.* I'd read some articles about it; they were all negative. I decided that I really didn't know anything about it from newspaper articles. So I went to the seminar and I was very impressed. Then I went through a whole process of pressure to sign up that night. But it wasn't evident pressure, just very loving concern."

After attending a special guest seminar, Tom decided to sign up for the training. "I said 'Well, there's nothing else happening. Why not try this?' It was $300, which was a lot of money, and I hate things to have money associated with it. But maybe there's something here. So I did it and it was really wonderful. I really loved it.

"The agreement in taking the training is that you don't use alcohol or drugs. So the very first night, that first session, I go home and start to smoke pot. I'm there and I'm saying: 'Boy, like where are you? I mean, you've made this agreement. But where have I gotten to where this is such an automatic thing?' So that was it and I haven't gotten high since then, which was two-and-a-half, almost three years ago. So that was a process in itself. As they say, the training is a very small part of it."

Mark Monroe, a 33-year-old who was later employed by Centers Network in a media production capacity and was recently married, had been involved with *est* for about eight years. After graduation from high school he had entered the military service and soon afterwards had started a small advertising firm with some friends. Mark suggested that his early experiences strongly influenced his decision to become deeply involved in the *est* organization:

"I grew up in Richmond, Virginia, in the early 1950's, when it was racially biased. As a child, I was unable to understand our reaction to blacks. I was literally being taught that these people were not human, that they didn't have souls or property. I couldn't understand that. I also noticed that there were sick people, diseased people, that things weren't wonderful for people. I thought I could be useful to people, that I could be an agent in being beneficial to people in some way. As I grew older I still had those dreams and ideals, but it got worse rather than being actualized. I went through the drug culture; there was racial violence, the Vietnam war, the inflationary spiral. My personal life was developing well, but my sense of what I thought I was going to do was unfulfilled. I understand that phrase now, that I wasn't useful to the human species.

"I acted successful, fulfilled; I walked around pretending

to be fulfilled, but I wasn't happy. But I didn't discuss it with people; there was more and more internal anxiety. I had a lot of thoughts that I was secretly keeping from people. My long-range plans and goals didn't fit the dreams and goals I had when I was younger. I heard about the training from a friend who is an accountant. He had heard about the training and was going to do it with his wife. He said: 'We'd like you to do it,' so the three of us did it together. It turned out to be the single most impactful thing in my life, so impactful that I decided to become involved."

Wilma Fey, another *est* training graduate, discussed her perception of *est* and its participants: "People take the training believing that *est* has an answer for you, that there's a formula that Werner has discovered about how life works. My perception about this has changed also as the years have gone on. But essentially their position is that they don't have that. There is no answer there. If you come wanting to know how to lose 50 pounds, you're not going to find it in *est*. They don't have a way to do that. People come in there with all kinds of different reasons for being there. They want to lose weight, they want to stop smoking. Their relationship isn't working or their relationship is working too well. Or they want enlightenment or whatever. They're not freaked-out people. They're very middle-of-the-road, mainstream people—corporation presidents, doctors, lawyers, and young people. They're just sort of searching around. The essence, I guess, of the training is that what you've been searching for, you've always had it. You spend your life looking for the keys to doors that aren't even locked. I remember the trainer saying that."

A phrase often used by individuals who take the *est* training is, "I got it." Trainees also informed me that they are told that if they keep their "soles" (not souls) in the room—that is, they do not leave training—they will "get it." I pursued the meaning behind that phrase "getting it" with many of them. What did they "get"?

Joan, a psychology graduate student told me: "You get what you get. If you have any expectations, basically, you are reacting as you would react to anything else in your life."

Another participant, who was later employed by *est*, related the following: "I got nothing; we use the term because it's as close to representing what we're trying to say as anything. It's a symbol, it represents something. You don't end up with something you didn't have. You don't end up with more than you had. You end up with less unclarity about yourself. You come out knowing more about who you are, what you're about—less unawake and more awakened, particularly about who you are, not about the individual next to you, except for the realization that you share something deeply in common. You don't benefit quantitatively from training. There is nothing concrete, not even information. It may take awhile to realize what it is, to become closer to an experience of yourself."

Sticking to one's agreements and taking responsibility for one's life are themes often repeated by trainees. An executive in his early 50's, who took *est* training with his wife, told me: "I'm looking at life in a different way, taking more responsibility for the way we perceive things. I tend to be pretty rigid. It helped me to be more open, more receptive... *est* taught us that life doesn't work unless you keep your agreements. It's very practical. You have to take responsibility for your decisions, even as a child. It allows you to recognize that you made certain judgments because you were a child. Those judgments may not make sense today. You can change those decisions. You are responsible for living in the past or moving into the present."

An accountant, who believes that he is working at full capacity, reported that prior to training he looked successful and was paid well, but was "operating at three cylinders out of six." A public relations specialist, in her mid-30's, told me how her life changed after experiencing *est:* "I moved from being a player in my life to being an author. There was a shift from content to context. Like, there's been a peacefulness. I went from being shy to being participatory. I had this realization and got in touch with a vision or dream that life could work for everyone. I can see now that I did think that things just happened to me. After training, I realized, 'Here I am.' These things are in there. You have to acknowledge that they are true, but you have the choice of being the victim of them forever. The bottom line of training is, 'What is, is.' I used to wish that it wasn't that way. If you've had a rotten life, that is what it is. What are you going to do about it?"

A man I met at a dinner reception held by another group that I was studying, provided me with a concrete example of how *est* had transformed his life. Art Wilson was the vice-president of an advertising agency and was 32 years old. The participants at the other group's function were largely over 45. He explained his new perspective: "Previously I would go somewhere and say 'Why am I here?' When I arrived at dinner tonight, I noticed the age of the guests and at first wondered why I was here. But I decided I would enjoy myself regardless of who was here. If I stayed alone all evening I would still enjoy myself." I quickly left him alone so that he could test out his theory.

A number of individuals reported significant influences on their relationships as a result of training. A 30-year-old woman told me: "If your relationship isn't working, you can always leave that relationship. You don't have to stay there. You decided to get into it in the first place; you can decide to leave. I learned that relationships can actually work. It was just hope, really. In my life I was surrounded with marriages that did not work. Almost every family I knew had been divorced or should have been. I knew things about them that they did not know. I knew their relationships were horrible."

A man in his early 30's, who had not lived with his family since the age of 19 and had "almost no contact" with them before training, discussed the effect of *est* on that aspect of his life: "I liked my family, but they were not much a part of my life. After training, we didn't have much of a relationship for several years. But over a period of time I began to discover how much I loved them. They haven't done the training, but they recognize that it is useful for me."

Another man compared his family relationships before and after training: "I have an incredible relationship with my parents. We had the potential to be close, but now we are closer than ever. My mother has done the training and loved it. My father has not done it yet. We're an independent family. We don't do things because the others are doing it.... I stopped blaming my family... *est* gave me the opportunity to become very clear about who's responsible. How you appreciate life is independent of what you've experienced."

The effect of *est* on one's religious or spiritual life has also been suggested by several participants. Mark Monroe talked about the various phases of his life from a religious perspective: "As a child up through 13, I was devoutly Christian, a Methodist. I was going to study to be a minister. I started studying the Bible." Because of all the world problems he saw around him, "I came to the conclusion that if there was a God, He must be extremely weird. Then I concluded there was no God. For the next ten years I was a practicing atheist. I believed in the finiteness of human nature, that human beings are a tragic entity, that it is a tragic condition to be human. One or two years before the training, something about that didn't make sense, didn't fit the whole universal thing. Something about what I was seeing was lacking. I was intensely confused in that area. It was, in general, a very confusing period in my life, a period of some awakening. Then I took the training. Now, I see myself as very religious. I have come to love religious traditions. It doesn't matter what type. They are uplifting to me. I do not belong to any church. I am not specifically Christian or Jewish or Buddhist. It's almost mystical. I sense or believe in or experience that there is a self, a God, something that we are."

Tom McDermott's experience was somewhat similar to Mark's: "For me, the training was very spiritual. It was very religious. There was no mention of God in the training, but for me it was very God-centered. Everything's O.K.; the world is O.K. It's us that makes it not O.K."

Evaluation

Although most participants who have been willing to talk about their *est* experience have been generally enthusiastic about it, many criticisms have been addressed to the training, the organization, and its founder. For example, Kevin Garvey, in a series of articles about *est* in a local New York City newspaper, pointed to some financial peculiarities of the *est* organization prior to its dissolution in May 1981: "To increase *est*'s flexibility in the use of tax shelters, [attorney Harry] Margolis set up a system which directs *est*'s revenues into Switzerland. The arrangement is that *est* pays its owner of record, the Werner Erhard Charitable Settlement, located on the tax-free Isle of Jersey, all accrued profits from operations. The U.S. government would take thirty percent of *est*'s profits, but to avoid showing any profits *est* pays for the use of what is known as 'the body of knowledge.' This is their primary asset and consists of the expertise Werner Erhard contributes to their success. The copyright on this 'knowledge' is owned by a Dutch Corporation, Welbehagen, B.V., to whom *est* pays royalties for its use. Seven percent of this is paid out in Dutch taxes. The remaining revenues are placed in the Werner Erhard Foundation located in Berne, Switzerland. *est*'s international operations are also located in Berne. This is the funnel through which *est*'s international activities receive their funding."[49]

Although its adherents state that *est* does not interfere with one's religious beliefs, some individuals have criticized *est* on religious grounds. John Weldon stated: "Although a Christian believer would be told *est* would not interfere with his religious beliefs, this is not true. The *est* belief system is designed to destroy the validity of the Christian world view. *est* is supposedly nonreligious, but since its purpose is to alter one's epistemology and instill a monist and/or pantheistic belief in impersonal divinity, *est* qualifies as religious. In the *est* philosophy, it is Christianity which is detrimental, even harmful, to growth and enlightenment."

Weldon further noted: "*est* and Christianity function on two entirely opposite principles. *est* is a system of 'self-salvation' that appeals to human ego and personal 'divinity.' Christianity recognizes only an agency outside of humanity, Jesus Christ, as its sole instrument of salvation. Erhard teaches self-glorification; Jesus teaches self-sacrifice."[50]

In the same vein, Walter Martin wrote: "The important element to remember about *est* theology is its claim that man is God and God is man." Martin refuted this world view: "The scriptures categorically deny that God is man or that man is God. According to the truths of the Bible, there is an infinite gap between Creator and created. Man is not God and can never become or realize the deity. One cannot be transformed into God."[51]

est offers scholarships for its training to individuals in religious organizations, including non-mainstream ones, making it easier for them to participate. For example, I spoke to several students at the Unification Theological Seminary at Barrytown, who were recipients of $300 scholarships, thereby enabling them to take the *est* training for just $50 each.

Numerous individuals have been critical of the *est* training in terms of the intensity and harshness of some of its procedures. Weldon stated: "The experience transforms people because through intensive, at times brutal and cruel, physical and mental conditioning, the individual undergoes a 'conversion experience' where the 'old' way of viewing reality is supplanted with the *est* way."[52]

In a talk given at Women's American O.R.T., M. Norman (a pseudonym) described some aspects of training that were particularly difficult for her. "From the beginning we had to abide by 'ground rules' dictated to us by the *est* staff. The staff were not obligated to keep the same rules. This put me in a dependent situation from the start. I was not permitted to have a watch in the training room. By confiscating my watch *est* robbed me of all sense of time. I thus became dependent on the staff to dictate my reality, tell me what I was feeling and coerce me to act accordingly. They served little by little to break down my sense of personal autonomy."[53]

Martin cited the following report from a trainee about the "Truth Process": "Soon the room was filled with moans, sobs, whimpers, and cries. Then there was an ear-splitting scream. A man cried out, 'It's on my chest—get it off!' I felt I was the only normal person in the place. I sat up and saw hundreds of people writhing and flailing the air. I was in a snake pit and I wanted out."[54]

A psychotherapist who had taken the standard training and a graduate seminar was critical of some of the processes used in training: "I found the process was very primitive. The technique that *est* uses for process is very primitive. It's not a very sophisticated technique. So I was somewhat disappointed in the process part. I didn't like the dehumanizing stuff. I went through *est* at a time when they were more dehumanizing than now, although there is still dehumanizing now. Werner is a pragmatist. He uses what works, and he doesn't care what it looks like, what it doesn't look like. If it works he uses it. Breaking people down by depriving them of sleep, depriving them of food, depriving them of an opportunity to go to the bathroom, works to break down people's defenses."

A couple who had completed the *est* training expressed ambivalence about it: "We had to strain to get at the content, which was most irritating. But they are dedicated people. The mechanics irritated me quite a bit."

A question that arises regarding *est* is whether or not it acts in a therapeutic manner. Psychologists Donald M. Baer and Stephanie B. Stolz, in a systematic behavioral analysis, noted: "Some of the procedures used in the *est* training resemble those used in a considerable variety of therapies." They suggest that the trainer has considerable power in shaping the behavior of the trainees: "Trainees are instructed from the start to acknowledge with applause all contributions by trainees, regardless of their content. In practice, however, the signal to applaud generally is withheld until the exchange between the trainee and the trainer is completed. Often the trainer shapes a trainee's verbal behavior in the course of their interchange. He does so by withholding his acknowledgment until the trainee tells the group something that seems self-revelatory, self-exploratory, non-'act'-asserting, and relevant to the trainee, rather than to any other trainee or to the trainer. Then, by saying 'Thank you' or 'I got it,' the trainer commands a potentially powerful form of social reinforcement, the applause of 200 to 300 peers, all presumably in the same uncomfortable situation as is the trainee receiving the applause. Thus the applause may be well valued."[55] Joel Kovel, a psychiatrist, commented: "In sum, *est* has discovered how to compress and intensify the basic psychotherapeutic maneuver of breaking down defenses."[56]

Another issue that has been of concern to critics is whether the *est* seminars can be described as brainwashing. In a survey of graduates undertaken in 1980 by the *est* organization, 31 percent responded "*est* is brainwashing" to the question: "Circle the two below which best fit your impression of what bothers other people about *est*."[57] However, when these same respondents were asked the open-ended question: "What, if anything, bothers you about *est*?", very few expressed this concern directly. It is difficult to compare these two questions, since the former question offered brainwashing as a choice while the latter did not. In addition, the survey itself has been criticized because of the relatively low response rate (11 percent) and the resultant implications. Andy Sewell, in a letter to *The Graduate Review,* wrote "...the 11% return is an indictment that graduates' view of the organization is so low that only one out of ten graduates are [*sic*] willing to spend 20 minutes to fill out a survey to make a difference in their organization. This 11% is the 'tip of the iceberg,' and would tend to be those graduates who are active in, and in agreement with the organization.... We need an organization that recognizes its faults, and says: '89% of us won't even play.' This is a sad commentary on how we have alienated our graduates."[58]

Mark Brewer, in an article in *Psychology Today,* stated: "Such efforts, of course, are commonly known as brainwashing, which is precisely what the *est* experience is, and the result is usually a classic conversion."[59] Weldon, writing for the Spiritual Counterfeits Project, agreed, stating: "The question of brainwashing seems to depend on the degree of force/coercion used to effect this change of belief system. The evidence indicates to me that *est* should be labeled a mild form of brainwashing, or at least intensive indoctrination."[60]

One young woman, who thought she had been brainwashed by the *est* regimen, explained her situation to me: "What happened was, I got there and the first thing they said was that there were certain ground rules and you had to keep the ground rules and they make a point of saying that, before I ever took the training. I mean I was in their pre-training seminar and I was sort of, of the mind that I didn't see any point in making a fuss about ground rules. I thought doing something like that would be immature. It was obviously a part of their game and why make a big stink of it. So I didn't do anything. Quite frankly, I didn't think at that point I had enough of a background to know what that was beyond being part of their game plan. It was so much tougher than what I was prepared for. And it didn't take me very long before I was going along, agreeing with what they were saying. I think with all these groups, they have these hooks, emotional hooks. They get you to agree with certain things that feel right or sound right and then they'll throw in something that will throw you off if you're not prepared for it. Then you sort of accept that and then they move on to the next emotional hook and so forth."

It has also been suggested that *est* may be psychologically dangerous for certain individuals, perhaps even precipitating psychotic episodes in some instances. Several studies have been conducted regarding this issue. For example, a study commissioned by *est* and prepared in 1977 by J. Herbert Hamsher of Temple University in Philadelphia, surveyed 242 psychiatrists, psychologists, and social workers, all of whom had taken the standard *est* training and had worked with over 1,700 *est* graduates. Sixty-eight percent of the clinicians reported that they applied *est* processes in their own work. These therapists suggested that individuals with neuroses and character disorders could take the *est* training without serious risk, but that compensated psychotics should not. In addition, the Hamsher study found that of the 163 individuals who had been hospitalized before *est* training, 119 had no record of hospitalization after training, 33 had fewer hospitalizations than previously, 11 had the same number, and none had a greater incidence of hospitalizations than before. This study also investigated 26 psychiatric emergencies following training and found slightly more improvement in functioning after the emergency than before (as rated by their therapists).[61]

A psychiatric study by Glass, Kirsch, and Parris, reported seven cases of serious emotional disturbances following training, but suggested that these cases do not imply a cause-and-effect relationship between *est* and a psychotic episode.[62] In a 1977 interview reported in *The New York*

Times, Glass stated: "We don't know if more people become psychotic after *est* than after riding on the F train."[63]

Some critics have suggested that *est* applies high-pressure techniques and an inordinate amount of time recruiting participants for its programs. Prospective trainees are often introduced to *est* through Guest Seminars which frequently use a hard-sell approach. One participant, who basically found the training valuable, commented: "They spent a disproportionate amount of time urging you to come to other meetings or to bring guests to meetings. I was much more interested in getting at the content."

Another issue that has been raised is the possible exploitation of *est* participants as volunteers. One woman, a social work graduate student in her 20's, was deeply involved in *est* activities as a volunteer for about two years, until she became quite disillusioned. She spoke to me about her experience as a member of a logistics team: "The whole process is done with an extreme amount of precision. If you are on a logistics team, you are expected to have all the chairs perfectly lined up. There is no deviation from that. It's rather compulsive—we spent some time picking up pieces of stuff off the carpet floor with masking tape. I did a lot of assisting. I never got paid for it. My motivation was: first of all, I was interested in it. They believed that if you assisted in training, then you will not only relive the experience of training but you will also have a chance to work out any additional problems. The whole thing was justified, you see. You will be able to move into another space. People used to pat me on the back and tell me I was a great player. People used *est* vocabulary and jargon to justify their behavior or their responses about all kinds of things. An example is, I was working loading and unloading trucks at one point for something. I got my period and I got terrible cramps. I was really beat and in great pain and I said so, and I was told to get off my female act. I find it curious that they've not discovered that this is a physiological problem rather than a psychological problem, which is what people believed for years. I did not take kindly to that at the time, even though I wasn't convinced that it wasn't psychological. If you were not doing what they felt you ought to be doing then you were on your act."

Another volunteer, whose experiences were considerably more positive, commented: "It was also an opportunity. I hated my job. So this was an opportunity to get involved in something else. So it was like an opportunity to expand maybe your social horizons. I liked being in the office. The efficiency really amazed me. People seemed to be actually getting their jobs done and they enjoyed doing it. I'd still be working, I'd still maintain my job but I had to be available 24 hours a day when needed."

Some individuals, including graduates, criticized the imitative behavior of those deeply involved in *est,* in language as well as dress. For example, Tom McDermott told me how people change when they start to do volunteer work for the organization: "Something transforms. I don't know how but they start to look better. They get their hair cut and they all get little Werner sweaters and brown loafers and they look just like Werner. I did it too. I had three or four Werner sweaters. You're not told to do it. Just very subliminally, you pick it up. It's like a uniform. You get the brown loafers, gray pants, blue sweater, white shirt."

A final question to be considered is whether *est* works, both in terms of changes in the psychological and physical health and interpersonal relationships of participants and in terms of *est*'s system of transformation in the ability to experience life. Results of studies, such as one conducted by sociologists Earl Babbie and Donald Stone,[64] indicated that *est*'s graduates are generally quite favorable in their reports of benefits from training and that these positive effects are long lasting. However, whether *est* works in its intended purpose to actually transform the ability to experience life is a question that is yet to be answered.

3: Scientology

"The creation of dianetics is a milestone for Man comparable to his discovery of fire and superior to his inventions of the wheel and the arch."[1]

"Scientology is a do-it-yourself psychology course which grew into a cult and now lays claim to being a religion."[2]

"Scientology is one of the oldest, wealthiest—and most dangerous—of the major 'new religions' or cults operating in America today."[3]

As the three examples above suggest, Scientology and its precursor, Dianetics, have been described both in glowing, enthusiastic terms and in critical, derogatory words. It is such a controversial system that it is difficult to discern facts about Scientology from opinions of the organization and its ideas.

Both Dianetics and Scientology are the creation of L. Ron Hubbard, who is at least as controversial as the systems he has developed. The word "scientology" is formed from the Latin *scio,* "to know," and the Greek *logos,* which means "doctrine." Hubbard defined scientology as the study of knowing or "Knowing about Knowing" or the "Science of Knowledge."[4] George Malko noted that the name Scientology was first used by Dr. A. Nordenholz, a social psychologist, who published a book entitled *Scientologie:*

Science of the Constitution—Usefulness of Knowledge/Knowing, in 1934.[5] Dianetics, from the Greek *dianoetikos,* "intellectual," deals, according to Hubbard, "with a system of mental image pictures in relation to psychic (spiritual) trauma."[6]

The details that have been written about Hubbard's life are contradictory. The following information is based upon many sources—some favorable (including an official biography from the Public Relations Bureau of the Church), others critical of Scientology.

Hubbard was born on March 13, 1911, in Tilden, Nebraska, the son of Commander Harry Ross Hubbard of the United States Navy and Dora May Hubbard (née Waterbury de Wolfe). He lived on his grandfather's ranch in Montana until he was 10. When Hubbard was 14, his father was sent to the Far East for a tour of duty, and young Hubbard thus had the opportunity to travel to China, Japan, and India. His travels in Asia sparked his interest in the mind and its functioning and permitted him to meet Commander Thompson, purportedly one of Sigmund Freud's students, who taught Hubbard about psychoanalysis. In 1930 he enrolled in the Engineering School of George Washington University in Washington, D.C., and left in 1932 without having received the Bachelor of Science degree in civil engineering. Some of the earlier Scientology publications refer to Hubbard by the title of Doctor. His doctorate was awarded by Sequoia University of California, "a degree mill where 'qualifications' could be bought for suitable sums."[7] According to psychologist Christopher Evans, Hubbard repudiated his degree in March 1966, "possibly tiring of suffering on behalf of this valueless embarrassment."[8] Hubbard defended his academic qualifications against the press's criticisms: "'He is not a doctor of philosophy,' they have to assert. They are never quite bold enough to say it [Scientology] is not a philosophy.... In actual fact, the developer of the philosophy was very well grounded in academic subjects and the humanities, probably better grounded in formal philosophy alone than teachers of philosophy in universities. The one-man effort is incredible in terms of study and research hours and is a record never approached in living memory. . . ."[9]

An article by H. Latana Lewis, II, in the July 1934 issue of a magazine called *The Pilot,* described some of Hubbard's activities: "Whenever two or three pilots are gathered together around the Nation's Capital . . . whether it be a Congressional hearing or just the back of some hangar, you'll probably hear the name of L. Ron Hubbard mentioned accompanied by such adjectives as 'crazy,' 'wild,' and 'dizzy.' For the flaming-haired pilot hit the city like a tornado a few years ago and made women scream and strong men weep by his aerial antics."[10]

During the 1930's, Hubbard also began to write, mainly adventure and science fiction stories, sometimes using pen names such as René Lafayette and Kurt von Rachne. In 1932, he is said to have completed the first complete mineralogical survey of Puerto Rico. He was elected to membership in the exclusive Explorer's Club in 1940, the same year in which he carried the club flag on an expedition to Alaska. During World War II, Hubbard served in the U.S. Navy in the Pacific as an officer. In the spring of 1942, he was flown home because of injuries, but recovered sufficiently to return to the Pacific in 1943. His official biography states that in 1944 he was "crippled and blinded," but by using his therapy he fully recovered by 1947.[11] Eugene Methvin questioned some of the official biographical notes. He stated that Hubbard "served in the Navy, but Navy records do not indicate he saw combat or was ever wounded. He was discharged and later given a 40-percent disability pension because of an ulcer, arthritis, and other ailments."[12]

By the end of the war Hubbard was married to Margaret Louise Grubb and had become the father of two children, a son, L. Ron Hubbard, Jr., nicknamed Nibs, and a daughter,

Katherine May. Nibs was once active in the Scientology movement, but years ago severed his association with the organization. Malko reported that "Hubbard himself has said only that his first wife died."[13] Evans reported that in 1947 the couple filed for divorce and that Hubbard then married Sarah Northrup, who sued him for divorce in 1951. Hubbard had a daughter, Alexis, by that marriage.[14] He subsequently married Mary Sue Whipp of Texas, and they had four children.

During the 1940's Hubbard had become acquainted with John W. Campbell, Jr., the editor of *Astounding Science Fiction,* a popular magazine, which published some of Hubbard's science fiction stories. Campbell was interested in the philosophical and psychological theories and methods Hubbard was generating and even experimented with them himself. The editor attributed the cure of his chronic sinusitis to Hubbard's techniques and thus decided to publish Hubbard's article about Dianetics. It received significant prepublication promotion in the form of Campbell's preview announcement in the April 1950 edition of *Astounding Science Fiction* magazine:

"Next month's issue will, I believe, cause one full-scale explosion across the country. We are carrying a sixteen-thousand word article, entitled 'Dianetics . . . An Introduction to a New Science,' by L. Ron Hubbard. It will, I believe, be the first publication of the material. It is . . . one of the most important articles ever published. . . .

"This is no wild theory. It is not mysticism. It is a coldly precise engineering description of how the human mind operates . . . it makes only one overall claim: the methods logically developed from that description *work.* The memory stimulation technique is so powerful that, within thirty minutes of entering therapy, most people will recall in full detail their own birth. I have observed it in action, and used the techniques myself."[15]

These editorials were so persuasive that numerous

individuals sought therapy and training with Hubbard. To meet this need, the Hubbard Dianetic Research Foundation was incorporated in April 1950 in Elizabeth, New Jersey.

Campbell's article suggested that the system of Dianetics was a breakthrough in psychotherapy, that individuals with a few hours of simple treatment ("auditing") could be cured of chronic disorders. Shortly after its publication, Hermitage House published Hubbard's classic book, *Dianetics: The Modern Science of Mental Health,* which remains the cornerstone of Scientology. It became a bestseller almost immediately and Evans reported that "within weeks a Dianetic fad was sweeping the United States."[16] From the outset, well-known personalities were associated with the movement. Movie star Gloria Swanson and jazz pianist Dave Brubeck both received Dianetics training.

Another influential early supporter of Hubbard was Dr. Joseph A. Winter, who described his work with Hubbard: "I observed two of the patients whom Hubbard had under treatment at this time.... After some observation of the reaction of others, I concluded that my learning of this technique would be enhanced by submitting myself to therapy. I took my place on the couch, spending an average of three hours a day trying to follow the directions for recalling 'impediments.' The experience was intriguing; I found that I could remember much more than I had thought I could, and I frequently experienced the discomfort which is known as 'restimulation'.... I was convinced that dianetics as a method could produce effects."[17]

By November 1950, branches of the Hubbard Dianetic Research Foundation had been established in New York, Los Angeles, Washington, Chicago, and Honolulu with Hubbard, his second wife Sarah, John W. Campbell, Dr. Joseph A. Winter, Arthur Ceppos (publisher of the *Dianetics* book), and C. Parker Morgan, a lawyer, making up the Board of Directors.[18] Each branch employed trained auditors and instructors of Dianetics. Simultaneous with the establishment of branch centers was the emergence of small informal groups practicing Dianetics. The movement spread outside the United States, particularly to Great Britain.

By 1951 the Foundation was in a financial crisis and Campbell, Morgan, Winter, and Ceppos resigned from the Board of Directors. Hubbard himself resigned in April 1951 because of his creditors' demands and impending financial disaster, and went to Cuba.[19] Don Purcell, a businessman from Wichita, Kansas, used his funds to assist the Foundation and became its president. When Hubbard returned from Cuba he was made the vice-president and chairman of the Board of Directors. However, the financial problems had not been resolved and in February 1952 Hubbard resigned his posts and sold his stock in exchange for an agreement that allowed him to set up Hubbard College in Wichita. Subsequently, Hubbard established the Hubbard Association of Scientology in Phoenix, Arizona, where his parents lived. According to Roy Wallis, who analyzed the movement from a sociological perspective, "Hubbard sought to move Scientology away from the amateur practitioner basis of Dianetics. . . . While Hubbard sought to exert control over practitioners and other followers in the field, he also tightened control over his central organization, dismissing officers who failed to perform precisely in accordance with his requirements."[20] Wallis further asserted: "While the basis of the theory has changed relatively little since 1952, the techniques employed to secure the ends specified by the theory have changed frequently as one thing after another was tried in an effort to find the set of techniques which would routinely achieve these ends."[21]

The Hubbard Association of Scientologists International was incorporated as a "religious fellowship" in Phoenix in 1952 and the *Journal of Scientology,* reporting on the movement and its beliefs, began publication. In 1953, the Church of Scientology, represented as a nondenominational church, was incorporated and a year later independent churches of Scientology were being franchised in other states. Hubbard and the Scientology movement ultimately became involved in various corporate structures. As it appeared to Wallis, "...complex corporate structure maximizes the difficulty of surveillance, or investigation of the movement's affairs, and also maximizes the number of public images through which the movement can be promoted. These exoteric 'faces' to the movement can then be differentially stressed (at different times) depending on public receptivity at any given time to any given image."[22] For example, Hubbard promoted an organization called the Freudian Foundation of America, which is at present credited with establishing the reliability of the personality test administered to prospective Scientology members.

After the mid-1960's, Hubbard played a less evident leadership role in the Scientology organization. However, after that time, his daughter, Diana, and son, Quentin, from his third marriage, played increasingly more important leadership roles in the group.

Another important aspect of the present organizational structure of Scientology is the Sea Org, a fleet of vessels, "an elite order of Scientologists, with a broad authority to intervene in the affairs of Scientology organizations."[23] Wallis noted that "Sea Org personnel are generally trained on the most advanced procedures...commanding widespread respect within the movement." He further suggested that "the Sea Org, whether formally or informally, has a considerable commitment to Hubbard personally, and provides an executive force mobilizable by Hubbard to maintain his authority and carry out his policy anywhere in the world."[24]

An Applied Religious Philosophy

Scientology calls itself an "applied religious philosophy" and is based upon a rather eclectic set of principles and techniques. Moreover, the concepts of Dianetics continue to figure prominently in the Scientology movement. Dianetics is more technically oriented, while Scientology is broader and more of a philosophical system. In his various writings, Hubbard credited numerous individuals as sources for his ideas, including Sigmund Freud, Aristotle, Descartes, William James, Confucius, Mohammed, Buddha, Thomas Paine, Issac Newton, Socrates, Voltaire, and Jesus of Nazareth.

Some of the important aspects of the theory and practice of Dianetics are described below. Hubbard suggested that an individual functioning at an optimum level is called "clear," a state to which almost all Scientologists seem to aspire. At this level, the individual is supposed to have perfect memory and significantly better mental facility than the average person. He or she would be free of all mental and emotional disorders, such as neuroses, and physical defects, such as imperfect eyesight. Theologian Robert S. Ellwood, Jr., in his book *Religious and Spiritual Groups in Modern America,* quotes an enthusiastic Scientologist who has achieved the state of clear: "There is no name to describe the way I feel. At last I am cause. I am Clear—I can do anything I want to do. I feel like a child with a new life—everything is so wonderful and beautiful."[25]

One of Hubbard's earliest difficulties with promoting Dianetics to the public occurred when he permitted the observation of Sonia Bianca, a college student majoring in physics, whom he considered to have attained the state of clear. Cy Endfield, a film director, was present at the demonstration and asked Bianca some simple formulas, but she was unable to pass even these simple memory tests.[26]

Those who have not risen to a clear state are considered to be pre-clear. This category includes most Scientologists, although 1978 statistics from the organization indicate an increasing number of clears. A state of dianetics "release," while not the optimum state of clear, is, according to Hubbard, "superior to any produced by several years of psychoanalysis," takes less than 20 hours to achieve, will not allow relapse, and frees the individual "from his major anxieties or illnesses."[27]

Dianetics further posits that there are two aspects of the mind, the analytical and the reactive. In most instances, the analytical mind is dominant; it consciously perceives, thinks, remembers events. However, in situations that are painful to the individual, either physically or emotionally, the analytical mind stops working and the reactive mind begins to function. The reactive mind operates on an unconscious level and records "engrams," a "definite and permanent trace left by a stimulus on the protoplasm of a tissue,"[28] or "a recording of the full perceptic content of a moment of pain, unconsciousness, or emotional loss."[29] Hubbard provides the following example of an engram: "A woman is knocked down by a blow. She is rendered 'unconscious.' She is kicked and told she is a faker. A chair is overturned in the process. A faucet is running in the kitchen. A car is passing in the street outside. The engram contains a running record of all these perceptions: sight, sound, tactile, taste, smell, organic sensations, kinetic sense, joint position, thirst record, etc."[30]

Hubbard attributes all kinds of problems, from the common cold to unhappiness, to the existence of engrams. Thus, Dianetics was established as a technique to rid the body of these engrams, thereby eliminating a whole host of difficulties and permitting the person to function in a clear state. According to Hubbard, "The *engram* is the single source of aberrations and psycho-somatic ills."[31] There are three types of engrams: First, there are "contra-survival engrams," which contain physical or emotional pain. "A child knocked out by a rapist and abused receives this type of engram," according to Hubbard. A second type is the "pro-survival engram," which appears to be in favor of survival. Hubbard uses the instance of an abused child being ill and "told, while he is partially or wholly 'unconscious' that he will be taken care of, that he is dearly loved, etc." The final type is the "painful emotion engram," "caused by the shock of sudden loss such as the death of a loved one."[32]

The purpose of Dianetics therapy is the eradication of engrams. In a release, most of the emotional stress is removed from the "reactive engram bank," and in a clear, "the entire content is removed."[33] An "auditor," an individual skilled in the practice of Dianetics therapy, uses "reverie" so that the pre-clear individual can begin to return to earlier times in her or his life and ultimately remove the engrams. Reverie is induced by the auditor in the following way:

"Look at the ceiling. When I count from one to seven your eyes will close. You will remain aware of everything which goes on. You will be able to remember everything that happens here. You can pull yourself out of anything which you get into if you don't like it. All right (slowly, soothingly): One, two, three, four, five, six, seven."[34] The auditor continues to count (or uses letters if numbers make the patient tense) until the patient closes his or her eyes. Then the "canceller" is installed; that is, the auditor tells the patient: "In the future, when I utter the word 'cancelled,' everything which I have said to you while you are in a therapy session will be *cancelled* and will have no force with you."[35]

The reverie procedure is employed to guard against accidental positive hypnotic suggestion, although Hubbard maintains that it is distinct from hypnosis. Once the canceller is installed, the auditor returns the individual to an earlier time in his or her life, perhaps the fifth birthday. The "file clerk" (an internal "monitor" which retrieves material from the individual's memory bank) selects relevant data that are worked on by the auditor and patient until the engram is reduced or erased. That is, the individual re-experiences all aspects of the episode that resulted in the engram, until the auditor feels that the patient has done enough for that session. The patient is then brought to the present time; the auditor says "cancelled," and then restores saying: "When I count from five to one and snap my fingers you will feel alert."[37]

When an engram has been deleted from the reactive bank, a greater portion of the mind is freed for analyzer functioning, thus purportedly increasing one's intelligence. Hubbard suggests that when a pre-clear is in the state of Dianetics reverie, he or she will tend to yawn and become sleepy, indicating that the therapy is going well and that an engram is being brought to the surface. During each therapy session, the auditor tries to help the patient contact the "basic-basic," the very first engram after conception, "the first moment of pain." Once basic-basic has been erased, all other engrams will vanish.

Hubbard offers explicit advice to prospective practitioners of Dianetics therapy. For example: "Do not take on a Junior for your first case if you can avoid it. If father was named George and the patient is called George, beware of trouble.... Mother says, 'I hate George!' 'That means Junior,' says the engram, though mother meant father. 'George is thoughtless.' 'George must not know.' 'Oh, George, I wish you had some sex appeal, but you haven't.' And so go the engrams.

"... Such cases resolve, of course, but if parents knew what they did to children by giving them any name which might appear in the engram bank, such as that of parents or grandparents or friends, it is certain the custom would vanish...."[38]

Hubbard offers a number of other "Dianetics Don'ts," such as: "Don't get a case snarled up and then take it to a psychiatrist who knows no dianetics. Only dianetics can unsnarl dianetics and yesterday's methods won't help your patient one slightest bit when all he needs is another run through the one you snapped him out of too fast. Take a cinch on your nerve and send him back through the incident again. In dianetics today's obvious nervous breakdown is tomorrow's most cheerful being."[39]

"Don't evaluate data or tell a patient what is wrong with

him. . . . Don't crow. If the pre-clear is your wife, or husband, or child, don't rub it in that the favorite argument phrase was out of an engram. Of course it was!"[40]

In Dianetics, four dynamics or motives, are posited by Hubbard. He suggested that the best solution to a problem is one that produces the optimum benefit to the greatest number of dynamics. He further notes: "None of these dynamics is necessarily stronger than any of the others. Each is strong."[41]

Dynamic One is "the urge toward ultimate survival on the part of the individual and for himself."[42] *The Dianetics and Scientology Technical Dictionary* suggests: "Here we have individuality expressed fully. This can be called the self dynamic."[43]

Dynamic Two is "the urge of the individual toward ultimate survival via the sex act, the creation of and the rearing of children."

Dynamic Three is "the urge of the individual toward ultimate survival for the group."

Dynamic Four includes "the urge of the individual toward ultimate survival for all mankind."[44]

In Scientology, these dynamics were increased to eight. The Fifth Dynamic is "the urge toward existence of the animal kingdom. This includes all living things whether vegetable or animal. . . ." The Sixth Dynamic is "the urge toward existence as the physical universe. The physical universe is composed of matter, energy, space, and time. . . ." The Seventh Dynamic is "the urge toward existence as or of spirits. . . . This can be called the spiritual dynamic." The Eighth Dynamic is "the urge toward existence as infinity. This is also identified as the Supreme Being." It is noted that the science of Scientology "does not intrude into the dynamic of the Supreme Being. This is called the Eighth Dynamic because the symbol of infinity ∞ stood upright makes the numeral '8'."[45]

The coverleaf to Hubbard's *Scientology: A New Slant on Life* states: "The way up to a capable human being is the realm of Dianetics—Scientology reaches from a capable human being upward. Dianetics was the ultimate development of the mind of human beings. Scientology is the road from there to Total Freedom."

Thus, as Evans remarked: "Dianetics, which deals largely with the technique of clearing engrams, is a relatively slow and temporary measure. Scientology, its bouncing progeny, takes up where Dianetics leaves off. . . ."[46]

A basic notion of Scientology is that "[b]ehind every reactive and analytic mind, it appeared, lay an entity known as the 'Thetan.' Thetans are the really important part of the human being. . . . They are entirely non-physical and also quite immortal."[47] Thus, Scientology suggests the existence of "past lives" (which is the phrase preferred over "reincarnation" by Scientologists). Hubbard posits that when the Thetan enters a new body, it contains engrams from previous existences. Since becoming clear would then require the erasure of engrams of prior lives, "[m]ost people would have to rest content with the prospect of one day becoming a MEST-Clear (those being the initials for the universe of Matter, Energy, Space, and Time). . . ."[48] The highest form of clear is the "operating Thetan."

Two concepts that are important in the practice of Scientology are taken from Dianetics: "the ARC triangle" and the "tone scale." In the former, the *A* stands for Affinity in the sense of liking, loving, or other feelings about people. The *R* represents Reality, that which people agree is real, and the *C* signifies Communication which consists of a message sent to someone who is prepared to receive it. The tone scale is a classification of human emotions ranging from -8.0, which reflects the state of "hiding," to +40.0, which indicates serenity of beingness. Some of the other points on the emotional continuum are: 0.05, apathy; 1.1, covert hostility; 1.8, pain; 2.5, boredom; and 4.0, enthusiasm. One of the goals of Scientology auditing is to raise an individual on the "tone scale."

A significant technical aspect of Scientology auditing or

processing is the use of a piece of equipment called an "electropsychometer," "electrometer," or more commonly "E-meter." This device is composed of a box with a meter, wires, batteries, and terminals which look like small tin cans. It was developed by Volney Mathison in 1950–1951 to spot engrams or blocks in dianetic therapy, but "it was little employed until the emergence of Scientology in 1952."[49]

The E-meter appears to be basically a rough approximation of a skin galvanometer, which measures the galvanic skin response (GSR), a change in the electrical resistance of the skin. Psychologists who have studied this response for over a century have found that a change in the electrical conductivity of the skin will occur during periods of arousal, excitement, or stress of any kind. The individual holds a terminal in each hand, thereby becoming part of an electrical circuit. Voluntary responses, such as squeezing the terminals, will cause a reduction in the resistance of the circuit. Moreover, sweating, even in small amounts, causes the needle on the meter to be deflected. Finally, in states of arousal, even of a mild sort, there are changes in electrical skin resistance which can be picked up by the meter. When psychologists have worked with the GSR in the laboratory, they have generally implemented procedures which measure the third type of change only, which is done by attaching electrodes, generally coated with petroleum jelly, to the palms. Various studies have found changes in the GSR during states of fear, embarrassment, sexual arousal, etc.

The E-meter, as used by Scientologists, with its hand-held terminals or cans (rather than electrodes), however, is sensitive to intentional squeezing of the terminals, sweating, as well as the more unconscious changes in electrical conductivity of the skin. According to Evans, Scientologists defend their manner of using the E-meter by arguing that trained auditors can detect and thus disregard needle deflections caused by intentional squeezing as well as increases or decreases in sweat production.[50]

Various terms are associated with particular types of needle deflection on the E-meter—for example, theta bop, rock slam, speed rising, each of which is characteristic of a particular emotional or spiritual state. A rock slam, which is reflected in a wild, erratic movement of the indicator gauge, indicates contact with a major trauma. The "pinch test" is used to demonstrate the E-meter to first-time users. Holding the cans, the individual is pinched. Afterwards, the auditor asks the person to recall the moment of pain. The meter registers, demonstrating that people can remember moments of pain.

During processing, which occurs in an invariant sequence of procedures, the pre-clear holds the cans of the E-meter while answering questions or commands posed by the auditor. For example, "What are you willing to tell me about?" or "Recall something real," or "Tell me a problem." When the needle moves in a particular way, that is a signal that a significant insight has been achieved. In addition to being audited by another Scientologist, individuals can also engage in self-auditing, in which they read the E-meter and ask themselves questions or give themselves commands.

Scientology training is arranged in hierarchical levels ("very much like formal education," I was told by one Scientologist). Completion of each level of training is followed by the award of a certificate and/or the applause and congratulations of his or her auditor and classmates. He or she is also asked to write a "success story" indicating the gains achieved by the course.

One former Scientologist whom I interviewed described some of the training for me: "Ten people teamed up by pairs. We would just look at each other. Next, one person would get a command across from the other. Then the other person would do it. I would acknowledge the command by saying 'Thank you,' 'Yes,' 'O.K.,' or 'I got it.' When you're learning to confront, first your eyes are closed, then you do it while your eyes are open.... There are totally weird courses—people yelling obscenities at you and you're trained not to react. They flatten your buttons on using obscenities. Hubbard likes to use computer terminology. Flattening your buttons is behaving in a way that is unemotional and uninvolved....

"At the end of each course, there was an announcement: 'John Smith has finished—that's it John!' Then they said: 'Tell us your wins John' and everyone applauded. I filled out a success story form because I knew that that's what they wanted. You have to be bright in Scientology."

Some of the underlying philosophical ideas of Scientology along with reasons to become part of the movement, are expressed by Hubbard in his book *Scientology: A New Slant on Life.* The Registrar at the New York City church told me that this was the book that best explains Scientology to a novice. The book begins by asking a simple question that is pertinent to everyone's life: "Is it possible to be happy?" The following are some excerpts from the book, which is filled with common-sense, folk-type advice and examples:

"Very often an individual can have a million dollars, he can have everything his heart apparently desires, and is still unhappy."[51]

"The true story of Scientology is simple, concise, and direct. It is quickly told:

1. A philosopher develops a philosophy about life and death;
2. People find it interesting;
3. People find it works;
4. People pass it along to others;
5. It grows."[52]

"Despite the amount of suffering, pain, misery, sorrow and travail which can exist in life, the reason for existence is the same reason as one has to play a game—interest, contest, activity, and possession."[53]

"One could say then that life is a game and that the ability to play a game consists of tolerance for freedom and barriers and an insight into purposes with the power of choice over participation."[54]

"Children are not dogs. They can't be trained as dogs are trained. They are not controllable items. They are, and let's not overlook the point, men and women. A child is not a special species of animal distinct from Man. A child is a man or woman who has not attained full growth."[55]

"The ingredients of successful work are: training and experience in the subject being addressed, good general intelligence and ability, a capability of high affinity, a tolerance of reality, and the ability to communicate and receive ideas."[56]

"The first step of handling anything is gaining an ability to face it."[57]

"Whenever there is an excessive commotion amongst a people against its government, the government is then invited to act as an opponent to the people. If a government is acting toward its people as though it were an opponent of the people and not a member of the team, it becomes obvious that many of these points must exist in the law codes of the country and must violate the customs of the people. Whenever such a point exists, turbulence results."[58]

"A man is as dead as he cannot communicate. He is as alive as he can communicate. With countless tests I have discovered, to a degree which could be called conclusive, that the only remedy for livingness is further communicatingness."[59]

An interesting aspect of both Dianetics and Scientology is its emphasis on the written word. In this regard, Evans observed: "Like many other heads of bureaucratic organizations Hubbard seems to believe that anything that is not written down is not true; the spoken word is ephemeral and has no mass to it, while something written on paper becomes fact. This perhaps accounts for the obsession with paper-work, the countless bulletins, directives, sub-orders, memos, policy letters, etc., which Scientology Orgs circulate and file."[60]

Almost every Dianetics and Scientology book includes the notation: "In studying Dianetics and Scientology be very, very certain you never go past a word you do not fully understand.... The only reason a person gives up a study or becomes confused or unable to learn is that he or she has gone past a word or phrase that was not understood.... If the material becomes confusing or you can't seem to grasp it, there will be a word just earlier that you have not understood. Don't go any further, but go back to BEFORE you got into trouble, find the misunderstood word and get it defined."[61] One former Scientologist who had been a member for several years told me: "You never see a Scientologist without a dictionary."

Scientology claims to be not just a philosophy, but an applied religious philosophy. Whether or not it truly is a religion has been a widely debated issue. Robert S. Ellwood, Jr. suggests that Scientology has much in common metaphysically with Buddhism and other Eastern religions "despite totally different (and, Scientologists would argue, much more effective) terminology and techniques."[62]

The ambiguous religious status of Scientology has been evidenced in numerous instances of litigation. Burkholder reported on two court cases. In one[63] the court ruled that "the Founding Church of Scientology has made out a *prima facie* case that it is a *bona fide* religion," thus allowing as religious doctrine the theory of auditing and the use of E-meters. However, Judge Wright, presiding in this case, also stated: "We do not hold that the Founding Church is for all legal purposes a religion."[64] A second case[65] involved "the Second Circuit Court of Appeals, which granted an application for discharge from the Army Reserve for Aaron Barr, who had become an ordained minister of the Church of Scientology."[66]

John B. Snook, a professor of religious studies, compared certain aspects of Scientology to Christian Science. "In the first place, like other groups devoted to religious healing, these base their appeal on extraordinary personalities—Christian Science on Mary Baker Eddy and Scientology on L. Ron Hubbard. Both have developed theories that depend on the cultivation of ever higher levels of spiritual reality and regard such attainment as the fruit of attention to correct religious principles and disciplines. In practice their organizations depend on networks of trained practitioners who communicate the teachings of the founders to others as the basis for what the groups consider effective therapy for a wide variety of ailments. Both groups have become churches in the sense of creating liturgies for services of worship, thereby placing themselves among the established denominations."[67]

Other dimensions of similarity were noted by Snook: "Like Christian Science, Scientology proclaims itself a gospel appropriate to the modern age—the age of science and technology—for the realization of age-old spiritual benefits,"[68] and "... Scientology was from its beginning a kind of Western yoga, just as Christian Science was."[69]

Many present and former Scientologists discuss its ideas from a religious stance. For example, one interviewee told me: "The basic point of Scientology is that man is a spiritual being. The other point has to do with karma." Another told me: "You don't go through a conversion process. You don't give up your first religion, but if someone asked my religion, I'd say Scientology." Statistics supplied by the Public Relations Department of the Church confirm that most still practice their original faith. In response to a 1977 survey question, "Do you consider yourself still to be a practicing ________?" 70 percent responded "yes."

Snook's overall evaluation of Scientology as a religion was mixed: "It is apparent, on the one hand, that the church makes no very great investment of effort in corporate worship. In fact, the book of 'background and ceremonies' it publishes begins with the distinction between religious philosophies and religious practices, to the detriment of particular practices.... On the other hand, there are in the teaching some recognizably religious ideas—not very original ones, to be sure, but perhaps therefore all the more effective."[70]

Scientology services are rather informal, generally a discussion of principles contained in Hubbard's writings. One of the Sunday services that I attended at the New York City church was run by a female minister wearing a Roman collar. Prior to her addressing the group, another Scientologist, the director of public contact, played the piano for a few minutes and people in the large auditorium engaged in light conversation. There were only 15 people present, including myself and two young children, but the number of participants varies from week to week, from as few as 3 to as many as 40. Moreover, the Sunday service had just recently been re-instituted. Tim Skog, assistant director of public relations of the New York church, later explained to me: "The Sunday Scientology service is unlike the traditional concept of Sunday service, where everyone would get together giving testimony to their faith. In Scientology, the Sunday service is only one day of involvement. It's not even the biggest day. It's the other days when most of the training and counseling takes place."

The minister used the blackboard to illustrate the ARC triangle described earlier. We were asked to participate in two exercises to further demonstrate the relationships among Affinity, Reality, and Communication. First, we were asked to jump up and do something physical with someone. Several people shook my hand, smiled brightly, and asked for my name or how I was that day. Others, who obviously knew each other previously, interacted more intimately, kissing and hugging each other warmly. Secondly, we were asked to communicate with someone. A woman turned to me and told me that I had a very nice complexion and that she liked the color combination of my clothes. The service was adjourned within about twenty minutes.

Some ceremonial practices do exist within the Scientology Church—for instance, for marriages, funerals, and the naming of a child.

The issue of whether Scientology is a religion is far from resolved and as of the date of this writing several key cases on this topic are in litigation. For example, the California commissioner of the Internal Revenue Service has filed suit against the Church in California in an attempt to deny it religious status. However, Tim Skog informed me that most government agencies presently recognize Scientology as a religion.

Relationship to Psychotherapy

Scientology is also often compared to psychotherapy. Many writers, including Snook, have suggested that the process of auditing "resembles deep psychoanalysis, and part of the popularity of the book *Dianetics* seems to have come from the hope that the results of psychoanalysis could be obtained in a shorter time, and at much less expense, by the process of auditing. Not least of all, the work could be done by laymen trained only by undergoing the process themselves."[71]

From its inception, however, Hubbard's teachings have been questioned by practitioners of psychotherapy. Malko reported that in September 1950 the American Psychological Association (APA) asked psychologists not to use Dianetics therapy. APA unanimously adopted a resolution which stated: "While suspending judgment concerning the eventual validity of the claims made by the author of *Dianetics,* the Association calls attention to the fact that these claims are not supported by empirical evidence of the sort required for the establishment of scientific generalizations. In the public interest, the Association, in the absence of such evidence, recommends to its members that the use of the techniques peculiar to Dianetics be limited to scientific investigations designed to test the validity of the claims."[72] Malko further noted: "In January of 1951, the New Jersey Board of Medical Examiners instituted proceedings against the Hubbard Dianetic Research Foundation, Inc., for conducting a school which, it was charged, was teaching medicine, surgery, and a method of treatment, without a license."[73]

The practices and concepts of Dianetics and Scientology have been compared to various psychotherapeutic and psychological systems. For instance, Dianetics reverie is similar to hypnosis, and the concepts of the analytical and reactive minds are analogous to the conscious and unconscious dimensions respectively.

Wallis suggested that "Dianetics was a form of abreaction therapy," and further commented: "The therapeutic role of abreaction had been systematically explored first by Breuer and Freud, whose investigations revealed that the root of many hysterical symptoms lay in the experience of psychological trauma."[74]

In 1929 Otto Rank, in his book *The Trauma of Birth,* developed an important theory of neurosis positing its underpinnings in the birth trauma, years before Hubbard suggested that events during and prior to birth could have a significant impact on the development of the individual in the form of engrams. Moreover, the concept of engrams is closely related to the Pavlovian idea of conditioning, which suggests that traumatic events and associated stimuli continue to have emotional and behavioral effects even if the individual has forgotten the original incident. Hubbard's notion of the chaining of engrams is also similar to the chaining of responses or stimuli, an aspect of standard psychological learning theory, familiar to most students of introductory psychology. Furthermore, Wallis suggested that Richard Semon's work on engrams described in his books *The Mneme* and *Mnemic Psychology* published in the 1920's, is "reminiscent of Hubbard's theory." Semon used the term engram to represent the modification of organic tissue as a result of stimulation. "The stimulus impression could be reactivated or, in Semon's terminology, 'ecphorised,' by the complete or partial occurrence of the 'energetic conditions which ruled at the generation of the engram.'"[75]

Given that much of what Hubbard has written is evidently derived from, related to, or in agreement with psychological theories and practices, it is incongruous that there is so much antagonism toward and misunderstanding of psychology and psychiatry by Scientologists. For example, in a 1975 Dianetics brochure called "Dianetics In Action: Your Chance to Help Others Become Well and Happy," Hubbard wrote: "And psychiatry, since it has no understanding of the workings of the mind, can also offer only increased dependency on drugs and no alleviation of psychosomatic pain." Trevor Meldal-Johnsen and Patrick Lusey noted that, during an annual convention of the American Psychiatric Association in the early 1970's, Scientologists hired a plane to fly a banner that read "Psychiatry Kills!" over the convention hotel beach in Miami. Scientologists claimed that the action was a protest against moral support given to Hitler's programs in Germany, in which thousands of inmates of psychiatric hospitals were murdered.[76] In the 1981 Glossary of Terms for the film *The Problems of Life,* psychology was defined as follows: "This word originally meant 'the study of the soul.' 'Psyche' is Greek for 'Soul' or 'Spirit.' 'Ology' is Greek for 'the study of.' Over the years, aided by the 'theory' that men were animals, first proposed by Wilhelm Wundt in Leipzig, Germany, in 1879, the subject of psychology has degenerated to the point where today it is merely a study of the brain and the nervous system and its reaction patterns." According to the same Glossary, a psychologist is "a person who is a specialist in Psychology."

One young woman who recently left the Scientology movement explained her perception of the advantage of Scientology auditing over psychotherapy: "There is never evaluation in session; the intention is to get the most out of a person. We are taught that psychotherapy is judgmental." She was surprised when I told her that psychotherapy can be nonjudgmental. Another former Scientologist told me that because of the similarity between techniques utilized in Scientology processing and psychotherapy, "Scientologists run into problems when they leave the group and then go into therapy."

Recruitment

Although the movement appears to be moving away from its psychotherapeutic emphasis toward a more religious orientation, one of its recruiting techniques uses a psychological test. A young, attractive Scientologist who works at one of the centers described the circumstances under which she became involved two years earlier, at the age of 18. She was walking down the street and met someone who asked her to take a personality test. A staff member analyzed it for her immediately and, based upon the results, suggested a course. "I figured I could do it for $15," she said. "Then I signed up for other courses and began to work at the center."

The test is a 200-item personality inventory called "The Standard Oxford Capacity Analysis," copyrighted first in 1968 and then in 1980 by Hubbard. The cover of the exam states: "Your First Step to Self-Improvement Is Knowing What to Change! This Personality Chart Gives You That Knowledge." The directions, which are standard test instructions, request that respondents "answer each question as to how you feel RIGHT NOW. The accuracy depends upon the truthfulness of your answers. Each question may be answered 1 of 3 ways: + means yes or mostly yes . . . M means maybe or uncertain . . . and - means no or mostly no. . . . " The following are some of the questions:

2. Is it hard on you when you fail?
5. Do you browse through railway timetables, directories, or dictionaries just for pleasure?
20. Are you considered warm-hearted by your friends?
77. Are you inclined to be jealous?
105. Are you a slow eater?
145. Do you frequently stay up late?
171. Do you find it hard to get started on a task that needs to be done?
183. Do you spend much time on needless worries?

The results are depicted on a chart with ten categories of personality dimensions, each on a continuum from scores denoting a desirable state to those indicating an unacceptable state ("attention urgent"). There is also a middle range, the upper end of which indicates "acceptable under perfect conditions" while the lower end means "attention desirable." The dimensions measured are stable-unstable; happy-depressed; composed-nervous; certainty-uncertainty; active-inactive; aggressive-inhibited; responsible-irresponsible; correct estimation-critical; appreciative-lack of accord; communicative-withdrawn.

The personality profile is scored in a few minutes while the individual is waiting, and subsequently a staff member provides an analysis and generally a recommendation about courses that can be taken to compensate for the deficit reflected in the test. One concern is that people who administer and interpret the test are not appropriately trained and may be giving information that is potentially devastating to the examinee—for example, by scoring in the "below broken line-attention urgent" domain on seven out of ten categories, as happened to one man I interviewed. Moreover, although the test description indicates that the test has a reliability of 96 percent (meaning that the test yields consistent scores upon retesting) and has been thoroughly validated by the Freudian Foundation of America, that organization is an offshoot of Scientology, and not an independent body. I requested further information about the psychometric characteristics (such as standardization, reliability, and validity) of the test, but the staff at the New York City Scientology Center could not find any formal material for me on this matter.

Another recruiting technique used by the Scientology organization is their sponsorship of free events or shows and lectures charging nominal fees. For instance, the Celebrity Centre of the Church of Scientology Mission of East Manhattan invited the public to attend a free introductory presentation entitled: "Is it possible to be happy? or What is Scientology?" on Tuesday evenings from 8:00 to 9:30, and "How to understand your mind—An Introduction to Dianetics" on Friday evenings from 8:00 to 9:30. There are also celebrity shows that star Scientologists who are involved in the performing arts. On August 24, 1981, for the price of a book from the Celebrity Centre bookstore or $3.00, the public was invited to the Friday Night Celebrity Show, which starred Maryann White, who sang ballads, jazz, and blues music. A major all-day celebration with no admission fee, called "The World Peace and Freedom Celebration," took place on August 22, 1981, in the heart of New York City's theater district with "balloons, refreshments, speeches, displays, music and other surprises."

Individuals are also recruited by "word of mouth," as Tim Skog informed me. Scientologists are strongly encouraged to urge others to participate in the movement. Moreover, a recent flyer promoting a two-day seminar entitled "The Dianetics Book One Auditing Seminar," at a charge of $50 in advance and $60 at the door, requested: "Each person doing the training is also asked to bring a family member or friend to the second day of the seminar when students use their newly learned Dianetics skills." Ostensibly, the relative or friend is there to facilitate practice of the newly acquired techniques, but it is also a convenient way to introduce others to Scientology. Scientology's own statistics appear in *What Is Scientology,* a book published by the Scientology organization. According to this book, a survey of 3,028 individuals undertaken in June 1977 revealed the following about how members become interested in Scientology:

Interest	*Percentage*
By own personal research	35.0
Through friends	17.6
Through other relatives	12.3
Through books on Scientology	11.0
Through word of mouth	16.1
Through public lectures	3.1
Through advertisements	1.5
Through personality tests	1.2
Unspecified	3.6

The statistics indicate that more than one answer was given to the question in some cases and that a large number of respondents did not respond to this item at all on the survey.[77]

Scientology Followers

What types of individuals are drawn to Scientology? Evans suggested that Scientology offers a real "alternative to both psychoanalysis and mainstream religion. It answers philosophical questions by combining psychology, computer terminology, and science fiction language. Scientology is not for poorly educated working-class individuals, who have little time for and interest in questions of the mind. Nor is it a system that is attractive to sophisticated, highly-educated professionals. Rather it is for the moderately intelligent, reasonably well-read and self-aware individuals who by reason of lack of opportunity of one kind or another are denied higher education or who are temperamentally unsuited for it, that Scientology makes its strongest pitch. For them the self-assurance of Scientologists, the rapid induction into a private jargon and the acquisition of Certificates, Diplomas, etc., the immediate feedback from others of their kind, and the promise of achieving miraculous goals, provide a glowing beacon of hope. Once within this movement, with the feeling of identity with a cause building up, it would be odd indeed if major personality changes failed to take place. All along the line in Scientology, from the lowest rung to the misty heights of Operating Thetan, the willing individual may get attention at any level—provided that he pays his way—and there is nothing that the unsettled souls of our society require more desperately than the personal, unqualified, unjudging attention of another human being."[78]

Furthermore, Harriet Whitehead pointed out that Scientology is "a comfortable meeting grounds for both the old style Occultist, the ex-'head,' and the dissatisfied or unfulfilled mystic (a category that includes many ex-'heads'). In addition it reaches out to the many Americans who are fascinated with things psychological but either intimidated, disillusioned or repelled by the established psychological sciences. Scientologists acknowledge that whether one gets onto it by drugs, by dabblings in Occultism, by some peculiar experience in one's own life, or simply by a desire to understand humanity on a deeper level than that provided by the material sciences, one is all the same in touch with a sense of things that is essentially Scientological. In regard to those who dabble in other practices, or who have had some contact with Scientology but abandoned it, one man said, 'Oh, they'll get there eventually. Maybe it won't be through Scientology, and maybe not in this lifetime, but they'll get there. Once you're on the road to Truth, you never get off.'"[79]

In his sociological analysis of Dianetics and Scientology, Wallis cited a 1952 survey of the readers of a Dianetics newsletter, *The Dianews*. Of the 198 replies received, the estimated average age was 38, with more than twice as many men as women responding; 126 of 184 were married and 115 had one to four children. Most respondents could be categorized as either agnostic or Protestant, with very small percentages identifying with other religious affiliations. With regard to occupational level, the data revealed a disproportionately large number of engineers, Dianetics auditors, and homemakers; but psychologists, teachers, students, and research scientists were also represented. All levels of schooling were reflected by the respondents' answers, with the greatest number holding one or more degrees.[80]

Wallis' own research, although confined to only nine respondents who had been associated with Dianetics during its early days in England, concurred with the above-cited characteristics. He also noted that these early Dianeticists were very similar to science fiction fans with regard to sex, age, occupation, and education.[81] With regard to the early Dianetics adherents, Wallis posited three basic types, although certainly multidetermined motivation was possible. The first type, the career-oriented, was attracted to the movement because it offered a possible alternative therapeutic technique to clinicians. The second type, the truth-seeker, came to Dianetics out of "a lifelong search for meaning and truth." Included in this category were individuals who had examined popular philosophy, psychology, religion, metaphysics, occultism, and science fiction. The third group, the problem-solvers, were the predominant group, according to Wallis. They sought solutions for their physical, social, or psychological deficits. These are the individuals who were aware of their failure "to attain the standards of achievement normatively approved and culturally reinforced in the society around him."[82]

Dianetics, Wallis asserted, found a place within both the self-improvement and healing movements in the United

States and offered professional competence in their respective practices, something very attractive to many individuals.

With regard to the present members of Scientology, detailed statistics (an important aspect of the movement) from 1978 offer a comprehensive view. In the organization's *What Is Scientology?* the introduction to the chapter, "Statistics of Scientology," states: "Each statistic is backed by an individual story. For society is composed of individuals—and each statistic here represents one person, their win, their success."[83]

The official membership figure as of June 1977, was 5,437,000 worldwide, with about 4,000,000 of those in North America, a substantial increase over the reported estimate of 200,000 members worldwide in 1954. Several writers suggest that membership figures have been overestimated through the years. For example, in the early 1970's Evans commented: "The extravagant claims made for Scientology's worldwide membership are very likely exaggerated, and are probably based more on all who have at some time taken an interest in it, rather than those who remain actively involved."[84] In the United States, there are 38 churches and 118 missions staffed by over 4,000 members. Churches and missions exist all over the world—in Australia, Belgium, Canada, Guam, Puerto Rico, Rhodesia (now Zimbabwe), South Africa, etc.

The detailed, worldwide survey of 3,028 Scientologists previously mentioned, revealed the following demographic information:

Age	*Percentage*
under 20 years	10.7
21-25 years	33.8
26-30 years	27.8
31-35 years	12.9
36-40 years	6.6

41–50 years	4.6
51–65 years	3.1
over 65 years	0.4

Duration of Membership	*Percentage*
less than 1 year	17.6
1–3 years	31.2
3–7 years	28.6
7–11 years	11.5
11–16 years	4.0
over 16 years	4.6
No answer	2.4

Educational Level	*Percentage*
High School	47.0
College	37.4
"Specialist education"	13.9
No education reported	1.7

Social Class	*Percentage*
Middle	78.5
Upper	11.7
Working	8.3
No answer	1.6

Occupation	*Percentage*
Arts	19.8
White collar	15.7
Student (non-Scientology subjects)	14.7
Blue-collar	13.7
Technical (including engineering)	9.3
Teaching	8.4
Armed Forces	5.7
Medical (including nursing and dentistry)	4.8
No occupation	4.0
Sales and marketing	2.6
Law	0.3
Civil Service	0.2
Professional sports	0.1
Other	0.6

Marital Status	*Percentage*
Single	50.2
Married	34.0
Divorced	10.6
Separated	4.1
Widowed	0.6
No answer	0.6

The picture that emerges is of a membership of middle-class young adults involved in the movement for one to seven years, many of whom are college educated. The arts, as an occupational category, yield the greatest percentage followed by an almost equal number of white- and blue-collar workers. Several differences between the early Dianetics followers and present-day Scientologists are evident, probably resulting from the change in focus of the organization. First, there are more single than married participants at the present time. Secondly, the arts, rather than engineering, is the most highly represented occupational group. Third, the predominant age of followers has dropped sharply.

The fact that people in the performing and visual arts make up a significant part of current Scientology is not surprising in view of the emphasis on those areas within the movement, ranging from courses in communication to the existence of Celebrity Centres. Which came first—the outreach to the arts or accommodation to the many Scientologists involved in those fields—is not clear. However, it is evident that these individuals play an important role in the organization. Celebrity Centres exist in both Los Angeles and New York City. I was told that there are two reasons why these centers were established: First, people in those industries, "actors, dancers, etc., have very different schedules. They require specialized hours for training. Also, they would be disturbed by others; people in the theater, movies, arts have social recognition and they need their privacy." Moreover, some celebrities, who can afford it, have their own counselors or auditors who travel on the road with them.

In a 1976 publication of the Information Service of the U.S. Churches of Scientology, called *New Viewpoints,* edited by Michael Baybak, several biographical and autobiographical statements of well-known individuals are included. The individuals describe their motivation for becoming Scientologists and how the theories and practices of the movement have changed their lives.

Bert Salzman, a writer, director, and producer, received an Academy Award in 1976 for his film *Angel and Big Joe.* In 1969, he was working on a screenplay when he experienced classic signs of "writer's block." He remembered having met a few weeks before a Scientologist whose "communication was beautiful, free and safe." He thus decided to visit the Church of Scientology one morning and found himself staying until 10 o'clock that night after taking the communication course. He returned for some auditing sessions and eventually achieved the state of clear. Salzman described how his life has changed as a result of his involvement in Scientology:

"My biggest win in Scientology was finding out who I really am and once that happened I think things really changed in my life.

"Your dreams, your visions, are important because they are yours and no one else can ever have them. . . . I never doubt my own work now. I know I continue because I have a unique point of view of life and that's the real value of my work."[85]

Karen Black, a Scientology clear, is a well-known Hollywood actress and Academy Award nominee who appeared in numerous films, including *Five Easy Pieces, The Great Gatsby, The Day of the Locust,* and *Nashville.* She reflected on some of the changes she has seen in her life as a result of Scientology: "One of the things that Scientology auditing does is expand your attention . . . In acting, you can direct your attention to what you have created.

"Say you've got a role in which you love some guy. So when you create this, you are free to direct your attention to your role and put it on the guy you're in love with. . . ."[86]

Another artist who has achieved the state of clear is 1976 Grammy Award winner, Chick Corea, a jazz musician. He became involved in Scientology in 1971, after years of searching for ways to improve himself and increase his self-awareness. Corea had tried macrobiotic diets and drugs before turning to Eastern philosophy and religion. In 1971 a friend introduced him to Dianetics and the process of auditing, which immediately changed his life. "I resolved problems and misunderstandings and achieved a kind of physical as well as a mental and spiritual well-being that I had been striving for for years and years and years through meditation and study of other philosophies," he explained.[87]

Larry Gluck was already successful as an artist at the time he was introduced to Scientology. However, he remarked that his marriage was in a "precarious" state, he was bored with his work, and his self-esteem was poor. After he and his wife were audited, his life changed for the better in all of these areas. Both have attained the clear state in Scientology. Gluck described the change: "I recognize now that I was asleep. . . . Now, nothing else woke me up. Money didn't wake me up. Success didn't wake me up. Going on trips to Europe didn't wake me up. Talking with my stimulating friends didn't wake me up. Drugs didn't wake me up. The only thing that woke me up was Scientology."[88]

A sportscaster, writer, and former star quarterback for the San Francisco 49'ers, John Brodie became acquainted with Scientology during the 1969–1970 football season. He had been having problems with his arm that were severe enough so that he could no longer throw. The various medications he tried were of no value. His secretary, who was involved in Scientology, suggested that the pain might be psychosomatic and that auditing might be helpful . Four or five hours of processing resulted in alleviation of the pain and Brodie continued the auditing procedures until he attained the level of clear.[89]

Probably the best known Scientologist is television and movie star John Travolta, who is quoted as saying: "My future in terms of Scientology is going to be terrific. . . . I'm in a good position now. I'm getting into a bigger game. My career has always done well, but now I'm getting into a bigger game. And with Scientology, it's going to be a really big game because I'm going to have that much less in my way. Those little things that used to stop me before just don't stop me anymore."[90]

It is important to look not only at the lives of well-known personalities in Scientology, but also to examine more "ordinary" individuals who have been associated with it in recent years. I was fortunate to have had the opportunity to meet a woman who left Scientology about a year ago after a ten-year affiliation with the movement, and who presented a rather well-balanced picture to me. Liz Jordan became involved in Scientology when she was just 16, "a poor Irish Catholic girl from Brooklyn," one of eight children. Her sister had joined Scientology in California about six months before she did, and remains a member. As Liz was describing her life at that time, she interjected: "I was a prime candidate for Scientology." She was using drugs—marijuana, LSD, even heroin once or twice. Two of her friends had recently died from drug overdoses. Liz's health was poor. She was in a cast from her ankle to her thigh with paralysis from a muscle disorder. She was a self-described hypochondriac and "preoccupied with death." It was during that period that she met her mother's first husband, who was a Scientologist. She discussed their conversation about Scientology:

"I was on drugs. He told me I had to dry out in six weeks and he would tell me things that would better my life. . . . He told me about spirits, that I'm an entity, that I can perceive, create, love, make decisions. He told me that I had the ability to handle my problems. He guaranteed it 100 percent and I believed in that. He also said, because you're a spiritual being, how can you die? When it comes time to die, you won't be afraid.

"My parents said I couldn't get into Scientology. I wanted to run away from home. Being as frisky as I was, I left. I didn't see my parents for five years. They thought I was weird, but they didn't do anything. They had too much else to deal with. I was one of eight children. Everyone had run away at one time or another. My dad didn't make enough money; we left because we needed more freedom."

Liz joined her sister in California, who was living in "a big Scientology house." After being in California for a year, she and her sister and 15 other Scientologists rented a "giant mansion with 17 rooms." She continued: "No one was fooling around sexually with anyone else. It was really platonic. I ended up moving out because my sister wasn't as dedicated as I was. She stayed in contact with non-Scientologists. She smoked pot sometimes, which was taboo. Scientology was my parents at the time."

Liz rented her own apartment for a short time and then met her future husband, 14 years her senior, with whom she moved in after two months of acquaintance. She described their relationship: "When I met my husband, I realized he had potential. Scientology costs a lot of money. But I didn't love him; he didn't love me." Even though, Liz confessed, they started fighting as soon as they moved in together, they got married two years later. She continued, "I never understood why he married me. He said he didn't need me." Five years after meeting each other they had a daughter.

Liz's ambivalence about Scientology is evident in her comment "I still say 'we' when talking about Scientology," and in various other remarks about the group, some positive, some negative. For example, she first commented, "I thought it was a religion to evade taxes. But I can see religion in it. I have had religious feelings." Immediately afterwards, she noted: "My upbringing is Catholicism. I guess I don't feel it's [Scientology is] a religion." She also remarked: "At the time I didn't know it was so bad. What I loved were sessions. I had a lot of things going on in my life that I needed to talk about. They give you counseling on drugs.... You go up a spiritual ladder. At the time it was very serious. Now I laugh at it.... You can't be late. There is public ridicule if you're late. I had to paint a whole room when I was late and was pregnant.... You're used to giving your blood. You stay up until six in the morning.... They keep you in mystery. You're not allowed to discuss Scientology. You're not allowed to discuss sessions. There's lots of peer pressure. People at a higher level can't tell other people about it. You become so helpless in their hands. It's weird. You're told, 'That is what you have at this level. But wait 'til you get to the next level.'"

Liz also indicated that her emotional life changed as a result of Scientology: "I lost my compassion in Scientology for many years.... Scientologists think they can do everything. They never curse. They never get angry with each other.... One thing I started to hate—if I wasn't walking around smiling, if I was low tone, I had to force myself to change. It's too black and white, there are no shades of gray. You are trained in body expressions.... I always felt Scientologists were the most honest people I ever met. When I got out I realized people were using Scientology for their own gains."

In spite of some negative feelings, she explained her reasons for staying in Scientology for ten years, part of that time at the Los Angeles Celebrity Centre because of her artistic pursuits: "I stayed with Scientology because it keeps you involved. You get hooked spiritually. You come to believe that this is the only salvation on earth. They make you feel you have supreme intellect and a better religion than anyone else. Scientology is the way. Auditors are revered.... You stay in because it's a group, a purpose. Scientologists are very positive. They keep people out of reality." Liz also noted some positive dimensions to her Scientology experience. Several times she reminded me (or herself): "My time there was not wasted." She told me that her 5-year-old daughter "is being raised completely Scientology so far.... We have three things: spirit, mind, and body. I teach my daughter that she's in control of her mind. It's nice to teach a human being that she has a mind and a spirit, that she has control." She described her surprise visit to her parents on their anniversary after a five-year absence. "I surprised them by visiting them with my 6-month old baby.... I came back home that first time to show them that I had done well. I had a husband, a house, long nails, a baby. It was a fun time for me. My parents listened to me about Scientology for the first time—an Irish girl from Brooklyn that makes good." She also remarked that since leaving the movement, she has become a hypochondriac again, is afraid of death, and is extremely sensitive. "The news on television can make me cry," she noted.

Liz Jordan finally left Scientology ("When you leave, you call it blow") after spending $26,000 to attain the status of clear ("If you have bucks, you get up there quickly," she explained), and suffering a "nervous breakdown" (which she did not explicitly attribute to Scientology). At the same time, she also left her husband (who remained a Scientologist). Her move away from both the movement and spouse occurred gradually. She wavered back and forth between Scientology and the "wog" world (the outside world) for some time. She described that period: "I cried for three months. My heart was crying. I paid for a session, a review session. I was crying and crying. I tried to explain that I was crying for a real reason. They didn't believe me. They said if I paid $5,000, I could have intensive sessions. My husband was treating me like I was nuts. I said to them: 'I paid $26,000. Why can't you help me?' They said: 'If you don't pay for it, you can't have it.'" She recovered from her emotional difficulties with the help of "a compassionate maid" who cared for her.

Scientology had prepared Liz for being a success in the outside world. She told me that she had learned to do many things as a result of Scientology training that she was previously incapable of. For example, she lectured without anxiety in front of 1,500 people. Moreover, they "teach you how to make money," she said. "I was able to sell, I'm personable and I looked nice. Within a year I had gone from $100 a week to over $400 a week. It gave me confidence. I was still a Scientologist then, but people were saying things in the wog world that Scientology said only Scientologists knew.... I lied to the people I worked with because of the reputation of Scientology. Then I decided to leave Scientology. I just made the decision that I was going to do it. I visited New York and people loved me here, my parents, my old friends. They showed me compassion. I was really ready to be loved, to be regular again. If I felt bad, I wanted to show it, not to be smiling all the time. I thought that maybe I was copping out. With Scientology you have to be on your toes. This new life would be more relaxed. Scientologists try to predict your thoughts. You always feel that you have to explain your actions. There's always a reason why. There's a lot of pressure.

"I told the Scientologists I was leaving California to make money, that I was coming back. I told them because I didn't want to be bothered. If they were right that this was to be the salvation on earth, I had better not leave in a bad way in case they are the good guys. My husband has custody of our daughter now because I needed time to get myself back together. But she visits me and we love each other very much.

"People from Scientology contacted me. Four people came to New York, supposedly my friends; now, they hate my guts. My best friend doesn't talk to me anymore. Only one good friend in Scientology still talks to me.

"I still like the idea of spirituality.... I'm re-sorting things out. It's like trying to get your personality back. I'm still 30-percent involved, still thinking of Scientology. But I've applied a lot of the information to my life. But I'm now applying it because I want to," Liz concluded.

Another woman, now in her mid-20's and a recent law school graduate described her brief flirtation with Scientology: "I took a course when I was 16. You had to start at the bottom and work your way up. It cost me $50. I knew quite a few people who had done it. I was dating someone who was too old for me—about 27 or 28; I've always liked older men. He was prominent in the underground blues music movement. Then he became very involved in drugs. He then found Scientology through someone in the street who pulled him in and he went off drugs.... He found in the group a great source of women to go to bed with. One day, he said 'Let's go—I'll take you there....' I took the communication course; my parents signed for me since I was too young. You would read sections of a book every day. There was a drill where you would be sitting across from a person staring; blinking meant a lack of understanding. It was like group hypnosis....The person who ran the communication course was just out of the army and was very regimented. He was very mean and I was in tears. But the person above him was very nice and smoothed my ruffled feathers.

"You build up false loyalty; you pay them very little at first in the promise of getting clear some day. I'm very strong-willed, more than most.... I met someone else who thought Scientology was a bunch of crap and I left them.

"There are a few good points. People in the group who came from horrendous homes did find something better. People who were junkies—it kept them from drugs or killing themselves. But you were considered bad if you didn't bring people in. The course related to me the amazing power of the human mind."

Frank Johnson, now 25, had been a member of

Scientology about three years when he was forcibly deprogrammed by his family. He is openly hostile to the organization and described to me his early life, his time as a Scientologist, and his life subsequent to leaving the group.

Frank was born and raised in a suburb of Boston, one of six boys and one girl. He described his family life when he was growing up: "Typically, there's lots of shouting, but we all get along. My mother was overwhelmed by seven children. She's a really lousy housekeeper. I was really critical of that and of her having too many children. My father is an accountant who traveled frequently. They are super-Catholics, but they don't go to church everyday. However, they certainly go once a week. Mother is always saying Novenas for me. My mother is more easy-going about Catholicism than my father. Mother would like me to go to church, but being loved by her sons was always more important to her and she wouldn't do anything to jeopardize that. My father and I argued often about religion. He took it very seriously.

"In the sophomore year of high school, I decided I was no longer Catholic. I had a lot of arguments with my father about that. My father was really tolerant; he was totally willing to accept anyone else's not being Catholic, but he really thought that I would go to Hell if I didn't practice Catholicism. I take the subject of religion, including the lack of religion, very seriously. I therefore told my father in my sophomore year of high school of my decision. I remember my father clutching his stomach. He told me he couldn't attend my wedding if it wasn't in church. The others in my family told me I just shouldn't say anything to him, but I felt that I had to tell him. We can discuss any other subject except for that issue."

Although he is obviously bright, Frank flunked out of college during the first semester. "I didn't know what I was doing in college," he explained. During the first year in college he tried transcendental meditation. "I saw an ad in a college newspaper that said there was something I could do that was supposed to help you to be at peace with yourself. For four months, I did it, but not regularly. Actually, for two months, I did it twice a day for 20 minutes each time. I was open to that kind of thing. Then I stopped. I felt silly doing it. Then I thought of doing *est,* but it was too expensive. Everyone was doing *est;* it was a way to get over all your problems. I had met a professor who had done *est.* I thought, 'They're professors; they know what they're doing.' "

Frank's father suggested that he write a letter to the college to appeal his dismissal. His father wrote the letter, his sister typed it, and Frank signed it. He continued: "Then I went back to school and did well the second semester, but I left anyway. I wanted to go to California."

He moved out to San Francisco, where some friends were living and got a job as a nursing assistant. "My intention was to live there for a year, then go back to school." A few months later he met a friend of his roommate. "He didn't tell me he was a Scientologist, but I knew he was up to something; I didn't know what it was. I teased him and told him he acted like a psychoanalyst. This friend told me he was into Dianetics. I had never heard the term.

"I was very upset with my roommate and this Scientologist was working on my upsets with my roommate. My roommate borrowed money and didn't return it. He was also an incredible slob. At some point I asked Bob, my roommate's friend, if he was involved in Scientology. He said yes and asked me if I was interested."

Frank further described his life at that time: "I was 19 years old, having the normal adolescent problems. I was living in California and didn't want to admit that I missed my family. I thought being an adult meant not talking to your family.

"I was hanging around doctors and nurses at the hospital, but I really felt too young for them. However, I was too old for college kids, I thought. I had no very pressing problems. I was receiving excellent work ratings. I didn't have complaints about my job, except that I was overqualified. The orderlies that I worked with had made the job a life-long career and I had plans to do other things with my life.

"My social life was not too bad. Sometimes, I worried that I was not dating enough, that I was not partying enough. I asked myself: 'Was I being social enough?' I had girlfriends, but not really as many as my brother Billy had, but now I realize that that is a dream that cannot be realized.

"My Scientologist friend told me about the Scientology communication course. He told me I could learn to communicate better with my college professors, with girls, with friends. He hit all the right buttons. It was virtually guaranteed to be successful. He showed me success stories Scientologists had written. The guy who got me in asked if I would be willing to check it out. The communication course was $25 and the study course was $100. He also told me there was a 100-percent money-back guarantee.... He tried five times to get me to go down to the center. The first time I had to work. The second time, he wasn't around. The third time I was on call at the hospital. The fourth time something else happened. The fifth time we were just sitting around and I suggested that we go down to meet the people that he had wanted me to meet.

"I knew that they had a personality test.... I took the test at a center and noticed a sign which said 'Church of Scientology.' I questioned Bob about that, but he said that Dianetics, which is what you're doing, is not a religion. I knew something was going on. But I didn't question him further. I saw pictures of L. Ron Hubbard, and was told that he was the founder, but has very little to do with the organization.

"I had $25 in my pocket, so I took the test. I was below the gray area in 8 out of 10 areas. In the other two I was in the gray area. A girl who was about 18 evaluated the test. She had no personality herself; she was dumb, used double negatives, the whole bit. I thought that she seemed too dumb to be doing this, but Bob was fluent in several languages; he had graduated with honors from college. Out of politeness to him I stuck with it. She wanted me to put down the $25 that night. I lied; I told her I didn't have the money. I put down $15. She seemed desperate for the money and I was annoyed at the heavy sales pressure. But, there were some good things about the course. . . ."

Frank openly discussed his relationship with his family during his time as a Scientologist: "When I became involved with Scientology, my father's first line of argument was: Why bother getting involved in Scientology if you have a perfectly reasonable religion? My father researched Dianetics and Hubbard, but he never talked about the religious aspects again. He thought that Scientology is one thing, and religion is another. At first, he had assumed I had joined another religion. Scientology had me believing that my father was a homosexual. First, they had me believing that he was an SP, a suppressive person, a person who talks in generalities, only relates badness, not goodness, someone who is controlling you. SP's have committed crimes. They are psychotic, but want to appear normal. SP's control you, but hide it; they commit crimes. I couldn't find those crimes on my father. He didn't talk in generalities, but he did attack Scientology. He doesn't live in the past, as SP's do, but since he did fit in with part of the definition—by attacking Scientology—I just accepted the rest.

"They get you behaving before you're believing. They had me using the term SP before I believed it. SP's have heavy crimes, like cheating on your wife. I came to believe that of my father. I also came to believe that he was a homosexual. I would believe anything about him at the time. My job was to stop my father. The Guardian's office [a department of the Scientology church] wanted me to manufacture evidence that he was a criminal because they had a hard time finding evidence on their own."

Frank described his letter-writing campaign against his

father, first involving his sister-in-law, then his sister, then his closest brother. One of his brothers, John, "realized what was going on, what I was doing, and put a stop to it. He said I was manipulating them, to get everyone to turn against my father. But they encouraged me to keep writing, hoping that I would come home eventually, but I didn't know about John's actions or why they were encouraging me to write.

"Letters were sent by Scientologists to my father's company saying that he was cheating on his expense account. He had the lowest expense account in the company. I had not known about this action prior to its occurrence. I would have told them not to do it. My father realized who was behind this. Then they suggested that pictures be taken of him with prostitutes. I argued against that. I figured that we might get caught on this one like the other. I did not talk against the plan out of moral reasons, but rather, I argued against it because I thought we'd get caught.

"I had a session training me to call my father obscenities. I agreed to use the word asshole. It was very difficult. While I was on the phone, there was another Scientologist in the room who kept telling me, 'Call him asshole now.' Finally, I called him that on the phone and hung up. I felt exhilarated for doing that to a suppressive person....

"I took 10 courses all together and it cost me $6,000. I continued working at the hospital, but then I quit because I began to believe people were sick because they want to be sick. I became a window washer and took other menial jobs for a company that was owned by a Scientologist. I had my doubts about Scientology, but not serious ones. I thought that your weaknesses are your own. I didn't get to clear. I couldn't be clear because I had a suppressive person in my life."

Finally, Frank described his deprogramming to me. His father spent more than $15,000 trying to locate him, and on the deprogramming, itself. "I was in a car accident in San Francisco. My car was totaled and I went home [to his brother's house]. I went home because my insurance was canceled. Meanwhile, my father was getting together a deprogramming. My sister-in-law and brother were trying to talk some sense into me. Then one day I walked in and was introduced to an ex-Scientologist. The sirens went off in my head. I hated his guts.

"Then later, we were supposed to go to the airport and I was seated between my brother and some strange person. My mom pulled up in another car and my brother John said to me, 'Talk to your mom.' I said, 'Your tears don't impress me,' when I saw her crying. My younger brother then said, 'He's obviously brainwashed. Get him in the car and get it over with.' I finally realized what was going on. The group had told me that deprogramming was no food, torturing, being stripped and so on. They drove me to my aunt's house and I slept 12 to 15 hours. I spoke to the deprogrammers for about six hours a day. It took place in my aunt's living room. About half-way through I asked for a beer. One of the deprogrammers ran right out to get it for me. They were doing their best to make it easy.

"The deprogrammers were an ex-Scientologist, his girlfriend, and an ex-Moonie. My family was there throughout the whole thing. I didn't fight the deprogrammers because I am not a fighter. I couldn't picture myself fighting my way out of the deprogramming. I was afraid of the physical torture that I thought was involved in deprogramming. After about four hours, I realized that they were not going to use it."

Frank has partially supported himself since leaving Scientology by deprogramming others and by giving talks, sometimes with his father. According to Frank: "My relationship with my father really improved. No one really forgave anyone for anything. They were really happy that it was over with." He is now planning to return to college and leave behind the world of Scientology and deprogramming.

A very different view of Scientology comes from Steven

Tinson, a current member who has been involved in the group for about five years. He is married to a Scientologist and recently celebrated his first wedding anniversary. He told me: "I was a typical middle-class kid from the Midwest. I liked my family, but had the usual family problems in communication, an inability to understand someone else. I'm the oldest with four sisters and one brother. . . . A lot of people get turned off to groups. I went through that in high school. Early in life I was enthusiastic about participation in some groups, but later found out that they never quite made it. In grade school I was a cub scout. I was active in the Catholic Church as an altar boy."

Steven described the circumstances under which he became a Scientologist: "I found out through a friend. He told me about the philosophy after he went to a lecture in Arizona. I was fascinated. I was looking for something that would provide answers. I never tried anything else before, although I was aware. . . . There were particular things I had questioned: What is the purpose of life? Why do people do what they do? In grade school, I wondered, 'Can you create a safe, sane environment?'

"I was impressed by the Church of Scientology in Arizona. People knew what they were doing, what they were going after. I joined at 24. Before that I was in college, but didn't like it and dropped out. I worked in an upholstery shop. I liked working with my hands. Then I became a printer for a newspaper."

I asked Steven what had happened to him as a result of his being a Scientologist. He responded: "I became aware of increased understanding of my relationships with others. Through the course on communication, I came to a better understanding of myself and my problems with others. I can relate to them in a very real sense. It has definitely improved my family relationships. Our relationships are vastly improved. We have greater affinity. We're more open. Our relationship has gone beyond the barriers of dealing with them as relatives. I see them as spiritual beings, as persons. It's more of a loving, caring relationship. My communication with others in business and social situations has also improved. I can communicate freely and openly about things they're interested in. I can confront situations that are unpleasant. I get to the real problem and resolve it. My overall affinity for others has gone up greatly. I understand and know that each person's a spiritual entity. . . . I used to take drugs; I smoked pot. I don't take drugs any longer. I feel more in control. I'm in the present time."

He talked further about his family's reaction to his membership in Scientology: "My parents, in particular, understand. Both of them had a Protestant upbringing, but they converted to Catholicism. They were looking for some religious semblance of life for raising a family."

Is It Effective?

The issue of the effectiveness of Dianetics and Scientology in transforming people has been answered in contradictory ways. In a doctoral dissertation conducted by Harvey Jay Fischer, three groups of individuals were administered alternate forms of psychological tests before and after a two-month period. Group I received two one-hour sessions of auditing per week; Group II received two two-hour sessions of auditing per week; Group III received no auditing. According to the investigator, the results revealed that Dianetics therapy did not have either a systematic positive or negative effect on intellectual functioning, mathematical ability, or personality conflict.[91] A study to qualify for an M.S. degree by John Colbert, also concerned with the effectiveness of the auditing procedure, found no significant changes in IQ before and after the process.[92] The data concerning personality changes were not clear, but certainly did not point to improved functioning.

However, early studies reported by Hubbard and described

in *Science of Survival* presented a different view. Of 88 individuals who were administered the Wechsler-Bellevue Intelligence Scale, 74 demonstrated an IQ gain, ranging from less than 1 point to as many as 26 points, after about 60 hours of Dianetics processing. Only 14 showed a decrease, ranging from less than 1 point to 7 points, after equivalent auditing. On the California Test of Personality, average increases were exhibited in all 12 categories except the "sense-of-belonging" subscale. Particularly strong gains were shown after processing in occupational relations, sense of personal worth, community relations, family relations, social affinity, and physical and mental composure. The widely used psychiatric instrument, the Minnesota Multiphasic Personality Inventory, was also utilized for 21 men and 7 women. Again, the average scores moved towards the normal range (one exception being manic tendencies for both males and females and masculine-feminine imbalance for females) after 60 hours of Dianetics training. It is interesting to note that the average pretest scores were in the "severe-maladjustment" area in schizoid, obsessive-compulsive, and depressive tendencies, and undue bodily concern for male trainees and for schizoid and depressive tendencies for females.[93]

More recent data supplied by the Scientology organization about their members indicated that 52 percent were not absent from work at all during the previous year due to illness, 29 percent were out for fewer than seven days, and only 9 percent were out seven days or longer.[94] With regard to alcohol consumption, 33 percent reportedly drink rarely (one to six times a year), 19 percent drink monthly, 14 percent drink weekly, 7 percent drink on special occasions only, 1 percent drink daily, and 22 percent are nonusers.[95] Moreover, 71 percent indicate that they drink less now than they did prior to their involvement in Scientology.[96] Prior to Scientology, 62 percent took drugs, while 36 percent did not. Currently, almost all report being drug-free.[97] More than half of the respondents surveyed (56 percent) smoke cigarettes, while 42 percent report that they do not, including about 14 percent who gave up smoking since their participation in the organization.[98] Although these statistics are interesting, no control group data are presented, making their interpretation questionable.

The Controversy

From their very inception, Dianetics and Scientology have been embroiled in controversy. The issue of whether Scientology is really a religion and the antagonism between Scientology and the fields of psychiatry and psychology have already been noted. The group has also been part of massive litigation involving various government agencies such as the Federal Bureau of Investigation, the Food and Drug Administration, the Internal Revenue Service, and the Department of Justice, as well as private citizens. Journalist Omar V. Garrison wrote in 1980: "In the United States, various agencies of the U.S. Government had joined the conspiracy and had initiated what was to be a 25-year programme of spying upon and harassing the Church."[99] Garrison's book details the far-reaching dimensions of government action against Scientology in the United States and elsewhere.

A book published by the Guardian Office of the Church of Scientology includes documents and reprints of newspaper articles related to these court cases. The book notes: "The purpose of the Guardian office was to help enforce and issue policy to safeguard Scientology Churches, Scientologists and Scientology, and to engage in long-term promotion."[100] The book further notes that the Information Bureau of the Guardian Office was established to protect "the sanctity of the Church so that counseling and other Church work with parishioners can continue in privacy and without interruptions. This was found to be necessary over the years as Church officials discovered plants and agents provocateurs who had been sent into Scientology churches by various government agencies."[101]

One major court case began in 1977, when the Federal Bureau of Investigation raided Scientology headquarters in Washington and Los Angeles. As expected, Scientologists (and their supporters) view that incident (and subsequent related events) in one way, and critics of the movement see it in a different light. For instance, Rev. Arthur J. Maren, national spokesman for the Church of Scientology, in an interview reported in the June 1978 issue of *Freedom,* the newspaper of the Scientology Church, stated: "The FBI's raid on the Church of Scientology on July 8, 1977 was simply the Bureau's response to our reform efforts.... They claimed they were concerned about certain 'documents' they said we had. What they carried off, however, were over one hundred thousand pages of documents which included our strategy and correspondence with our attorneys on current legal cases we have pending with four or five different government agencies. The documents included various *Freedom Journal* reports we had done on the government previously and our sources of information."[102]

However, Methvin, a strong anti-Scientologist, reported that on the day of the raid the FBI "seized 23,000 documents, many stolen from the U.S. government, plus burglar tools and electronic surveillance equipment. The scope of the espionage operation was staggering. In a Justice Department agency, a Scientology employee-plant actually worked in a vault containing top-secret CIA and defense documents. Other Scientologists entered on nights and weekends and ransacked offices, including the Deputy Attorney General's, stealing highly secret papers and copying them on government copiers."[103] On October 26, 1979, nine Scientology officials, including Hubbard's wife, Mary Sue Hubbard, were found guilty of theft or conspiracy charges against the government. L. Ron Hubbard and 24 other Scientologists were named as unindicted co-conspirators.

As mentioned previously, numerous private citizens have

also been involved in lawsuits involving Scientology. One of the most widely publicized and longest legal struggles (much of the litigation is still pending) involves Paulette Cooper. Soon after she wrote a book entitled *The Scandal of Scientology,* which was published in 1971, she and her publisher, Tower Publications, Inc., were sued by Scientology. The group charged that the book contained false information. Her publisher withdrew the book and Cooper was required to sign a statement indicating that 52 passages were "erroneous or at the least misleading" in exchange for payment of her legal fees by Scientology. In all, 14 lawsuits were filed against Cooper by Scientology throughout the years.[104] Cooper, in turn, sued the organization, claiming that they put her name on pornographic mailing lists, followed her, harassed her publisher, "succeeded in framing me to the FBI leading to my indictment, arrest, and potential 15-year jail sentence, sent depraved, horrible, obscene, and untrue anonymous smear letters about me, including to the tenants of my building (to get me kicked out), to my parents (to get them to cut me off financially), to governmental agencies, my boyfriend, his boss, etc. (to discredit me)."[105] Cooper partly based her case on documents seized in the 1977 FBI raid of Scientology headquarters. As of this writing, her case has not been resolved.

Scientology has not even been free of controversy in areas such as personal and social reform. The Citizens Commission on Human Rights (CCHR), a Scientology affiliate, "is dedicated to correcting the many abuses and denials of basic human rights in the field of psychiatry that have come to the attention of Scientologists over the years."[106]

For example, an article in the New York *Daily News* on May 7, 1977, by Vincent Cosgrove, reported that Queens (N.Y.) District Attorney John Santucci said that he was investigating charges filed by CCHR in a 180-page document that six unexplained deaths and other patient abuses occurred at Creedmoor Psychiatric Center. In 1975, the Florida Task Force on Mental Retardation, a branch of the Church of Scientology, issued a booklet entitled "Hope for the Mentally Retarded." It summarized problems and "workable solutions aimed at easing the burden on the taxpayer while increasing the ability of our retarded citizens to lead more productive, joyful lives in a setting that assures them their birthright of freedom and dignity," said Suzanne Joecken, Director of the Task Force.[107] Narconon, based on Hubbard's technology, is coordinated by the Social Coordination Bureau of the Guardian's Office, and was founded in 1966 by William Benitez, then an inmate in Arizona State Prison. The term Narconon means "non narcosis or stupor." The organization was established to prevent drug abuse and rehabilitate those who are drug abusers. Tim Skog, assistant public relations director of the New York church, suggested that "there could be more involvement in social reform. We were active in it at one time. . . . I'd like to see more active involvement in that area. We are beginning to get back to it now, more of an outreach to society." A 1981 edition of *The Winner,* a publication of the Guardian Office, included a message from Rev. Kenneth J. Whitman, president of the Church of Scientology of California, announcing: "This coming year will be the Year of Community Action for Scientology."[108] The same issue also described a prison reform program in New Zealand called Crimanon, founded by Scientologists. The group worked for passage of a law that permitted "alternatives to imprisonment for *all* New Zealand criminals, other than those convicted for violent or sex crimes."[109] Regardless of the motives behind these programs, one needs to look at the "results" in evaluating them.

When Evans wrote about Scientology in the early 1970's, he explained that it enjoyed relative popularity, "not because its techniques necessarily work any better than those of any other cults or systems of belief, but because it plays with the themes and terminology of this century in a way that few other systems do. One might even push this argument further and point out that Scientology seems to respond with immense readiness to the winds of fashion, and that this no doubt is another reason for its success.

"In some cases it even seems to be anticipating public trends in a curious way. The involvement of the movement in the increasingly significant drug rehabilitation scheme in the USA—a number of former drug addicts appear to be facing life afresh through their association with Scientology—is one good example. There is also the matter of the current anti-psychiatric backlash which is pulling in a certain amount of media support at the time of writing, Scientologists for one reason or another have tended to make a platform of Hubbard's views on lobotomy and ECT (electro-convulsive therapy), two aesthetically and emotionally disturbing facets of current psychiatric treatment, and while they have been plugging away on these lines for a decade or more, it is only recently that they seem to have caught a prevailing popular mood."[110]

One other theme that can be found in Hubbard's writings which may not have received broad support at the time, but has certainly received increasing attention recently, is the area of psychosomatic disorders. Current research in physical medicine and psychology, although still somewhat out of the mainstream, suggests the important role of psychological factors, such as stress and lifestyle, in contributing to all kinds of physical illnesses ranging from the common cold to cancer. Another example of Hubbard's writings anticipating a future trend is in the area of computer terminology. While computer concepts and language are at present part of popular jargon (for example, feedback, psychological overload, input-output), they were rarely used in the 1950's when Hubbard's works did contain such references.

Scientology's future is unclear. It does not appear to be successful any longer in the anticipation of significant societal trends. However, the organization will probably continue to arouse interest and to be surrounded by controversy, regardless of its particular direction or focus.

4: Association for Research and Enlightenment

THE following are excerpts from psychic discourses given by Edgar Cayce while he was in self-imposed trance states over the course of a 43-year period:

"Walking is the best exercise, but don't take this spasmodically. Have a regular time and do it rain or shine."[1]

"Q-4: What can I do to overcome my husband's lack of generosity to me financially?
"A-4: Be just as generous to your husband as you expect him to be to you and these will be more in accord and will bring greater harmony in the relationships throughout the experience.

"These each have ideals. Make them coordinate with the material, the mental, and the spiritual lives of each. Know that it must begin in the spiritual. Then material results will be brought into the experience as the mind is controlled towards those ideals set by each as to the spirit with which they will control and act in relationships one to another."[2]

"Q: What can I do to prevent the teeth from wearing down?
"A: Use more of an alkaline-reacting diet, as quantities of orange juice with a little lemon in it, as four parts orange

juice to one part of lemon; also grapefruit, raw vegetables, potato peelings. . . . "[3]

"Q: What caused growth on foot and what should be used if it repeats itself?
"A: This was from irritation. Massaging with baking soda which has been dampened with spirits of camphor will be good for anyone having callous places or any attendant growths on feet, for it will remove them entirely!"[4]

The Association for Research and Enlightenment (A.R.E.) is an organization founded by Edgar Cayce in May 1931 for the purpose of studying and testing the material obtained during those trance states. Melissa Vaughn, a reporter for a Virginia newspaper, described A.R.E.: "It is neither a church, nor a laboratory, although spiritual growth and experimentation are practiced. Rather, the Association for Research and Enlightenment is a meeting place for people in search of answers to physical and spiritual problems." She described Cayce "as a cross between a prophet and a pop psychologist."[5]

Edgar Cayce's biography is contained in a number of books, including *There Is a River* by Thomas Sugrue, *Edgar Cayce—The Sleeping Prophet* by Jess Stearn, and *Many Mansions* by Gina Cerminara. In addition, numerous other books have contained material about the life of Edgar Cayce and his readings (transcripts of his psychic discourses). In addition to his ability as a "psychic diagnostician," Cayce's life also showed evidence of telepathy, clairvoyance, precognition, and retrocognition.

He was born on March 18, 1877, near Hopkinsville, Kentucky, where his father was a justice of the peace. Stearn reported that Cayce's grandfather may have been psychic but in every other way his family appears to have been an average traditional one. As a child, Cayce showed interest in the Bible and enjoyed going to the Christian Church. At the age of about 6 or 7 he told his parents he could see and talk to his dead grandfather. He was about 7 or 8 when he reported a psychic experience that was to shape the direction of his life. Stearn described this incident:

"Off by himself, in a secluded outdoor nook, he had been reading in the Bible of the vision of Manoah, for he loved dearly the story of Samson. Suddenly, there was a humming sound, and a bright light filled the glade where he usually hid to read the wonderful stories. As he looked up, he saw a figure in white, bright as the noonday light, and heard a voice: 'Your prayers have been heard. What would you ask of me, that I may give it to you?' The boy was not startled. Even then it seemed natural to see visions. 'Just that I may be helpful to others,' he replied, 'especially to children who are ill, and that I may love my fellow man.' "[6]

The next day, Edgar did poorly on his schoolwork because he was thinking about the vision. That night, unable to focus on his lessons, he heard the same voice he had heard the previous day. It said: "Sleep, and we may help you." Edgar did fall asleep and when he awoke, he knew every word in his spelling book.

Another significant incident that occurred during Cayce's childhood involved his telling his parents to put a poultice at the base of his brain to treat an injury from a baseball accident. The morning after the treatment, his semi-stuporous condition had lifted and he was well; Edgar Cayce's first health reading had been successful.

He left school after the sixth grade, and worked on a farm for a while, then in a dry goods store and later in a bookstore. He fell in love with a neighbor, Gertrude Evans, who "had a knack of putting him at ease, encouraged his Bible work, and his teaching Sunday school." She felt "that he should use his burgeoning powers to help others."[7] Edgar Cayce married Gertrude Evans in 1903.

When Cayce was 21 and was working as a salesman, he developed a case of severe laryngitis, which prevented him from continuing his job as a salesman, so he became a photographer's assistant in Bowling Green, Kentucky. During his work in that trade he met a hypnotist named Hart, who attempted to cure him through the use of hypnosis. During the hypnotic trance, Cayce was able to follow Hart's suggestion and speak in a normal voice. However, after reawakening, his voice again returned to its abnormal state. A posthypnotic suggestion to continue to speak normally was unsuccessful. Hart was unable to continue treating Cayce, but another hypnotist named Layne showed interest in working with Cayce's problem. Layne suggested that Cayce describe the nature of his own disorder while he was in a hypnotic trance. Cayce did this and reported: "In the normal state, this body is unable to speak because of a partial paralysis of the inferior muscles of the vocal cords, produced by nerve strain. This is a psychological condition producing a physical effect. It may be removed by increasing the circulation to the affected parts by suggestion while in the unconscious condition."[8]

Layne followed Cayce's suggestion and the latter was cured. Moreover, Layne had become aware of the important ramifications of Cayce's ability. It occurred to Layne, according to psychologist and Cayce biographer Gina Cerminara, that "if, in the hypnotic state, Cayce could see and diagnose the condition of his own body, he might also be able to see and diagnose that of others."[9] Cayce finally agreed to experiment with his talent, to help people who needed it, but not to take money for doing so. Layne began to record everything that Cayce said during these trances and called these written transcripts "readings."

One of the significant aspects of the Cayce readings is that, while they were sometimes unclear and ungrammatical, they displayed an amazing awareness of medical technology, physical illness, anatomy, and physiology. Cayce continued to work as a photographer to earn a living, while giving readings, first to local people and later, as his gifts became better known, to outsiders. One of his early interesting cases came to Cayce's attention via a long-distance phone call from C.H. Dietrich, the former superintendent of the Hopkinsville public schools. His 5-year-old daughter was showing signs of retardation, apparently stemming from an illness three years earlier. The Dietrichs consulted several specialists who were unable to help the child and one had told them that their daughter had a rare brain disorder which would probably prove to be fatal. As a last resort, they sought the assistance of Edgar Cayce. He accepted the railroad fare to go to Hopkinsville, the first time he accepted financial remuneration of any kind for his services. In a hypnotic trance, while in the presence of Layne, who transcribed his words, Cayce said: "A few days before her illness, the child slipped getting out of a carriage and struck the base of her spine in the carriage step. This injury weakened the area, and led to the mental condition."[10] Cayce went on to suggest specific osteopathic adjustments which were given by Layne to alleviate the abnormal condition, and "within three weeks the child was free from all convulsive attacks and her mind showed definite signs of clearing. She called the name of a doll that had been her favorite plaything before the onset of her illness; then she called her father and mother by name for the first time in years. After three months the grateful parents reported that the girl was normal in all respects, and was rapidly regaining the ground lost in the three clouded years."[11] This episode was a remarkable example of retrocognition, in which Cayce was able to describe a significant event that had occurred years earlier.

The first 20 years of Cayce's psychic career were devoted to readings dealing with the physical body and its many ailments. However, Cayce had always perceived a connection between the mind and the body and recognized the importance of attitude and other psychological factors in the etiology and treatment of physical disorders. Not only would Cayce prescribe particular remedies and medications, but he would also refer the patient to a specific doctor when necessary. In many of these instances, Cayce had had no prior knowledge of the specialist. Cayce's suggested treatments were often rather unorthodox in terms of current medical knowledge and practices. Although most physicians were evidently quite skeptical of Cayce and his psychic gifts, a few were drawn to him. Wesley Ketchum was one such physician. Ketchum employed Cayce as an adjunct in diagnosis, although his patients were generally unaware of Cayce's participation in their care.

When Cayce awoke from a trance state he had no memory of what he had revealed and was often surprised by the information. Throughout his life, he expressed doubts about his special gift and it was his wife Gertrude who helped to resolve these misgivings. According to Peter

Edgar Cayce (*circa* 1944)

Sherrill, a former A.R.E. staff member, Edgar Cayce was able to provide a reading for Gertrude Cayce, who had been diagnosed as suffering from incurable tuberculosis.[12] Cayce prescribed a diet, some simple medication, and the inhalation of apple brandy fumes from a charred oak keg. The treatment, unorthodox as it was, appeared to be successful and Mrs. Cayce emerged from it cured. Edgar Cayce also conducted a reading on his son, Hugh Lynn (who became chairman of the board of A.R.E.), when his eyes were severely injured in an accident. While playing with his father's flashlight kit, some of the powder flared up into his eyes. Although doctors suggested surgery to remove one eye in order to save the child's life, Edgar Cayce had other ideas. In a trance, Cayce spoke: "Keep the boy in a completely darkened room for 15 days, keep dressings soaked in strong tannic acid solutions on his eyes, frequently changing same. Thus will the sight be saved and restored." The physicians were concerned that the solution would damage the tissue of the eye. "'Which eye,' Cayce demanded, 'the eye beyond hope, or the one you want to take out?'"[13] After 12 days of treatment, the dressings were removed and Hugh Lynn's sight had been restored.

Cayce evidently did not want to take money for giving the readings that took place regularly at least twice a day over a period of more than 40 years. However, as his reputation grew, he found himself spending more and more time in a trance state trying to help the thousands of people who came to him for advice or suggested treatments. It thus became necessary to quit his job as a photographer so that he could devote himself to diagnosing and prescribing for those who sought out his services. Those who could not afford to make a donation were treated free.

While his early work was conducted in close proximity to the person who was being studied, Cayce soon realized that if he were given the name and location of the subjects (street address, town or city, and state), the reading could take place at any distance. At first, Layne recorded the information revealed by Cayce during the trance state; later the job was taken over by his secretary, Gladys Davis, who continued to be associated with the Association for Research and Enlightenment.

In 1929 the Cayce Hospital was established at Virginia Beach, Virginia, through the financial help of a beneficiary of one of Cayce's readings, Morton Blumenthal. The hospital opened in 1929 in order to provide a medical center where "readings could be given and the somewhat unusual prescriptions of the readings carried out by a sympathetic staff."[14] The Depression and its subsequent financial losses to the hospital's backer led to its closing in 1931. Ironically, Cayce had predicted these great losses of the Depression, but his warnings had gone unheeded by Blumenthal. A.R.E. was organized three months after the closing of the hospital.

During the 1920's Cayce's readings had taken on a different and quite unusual turn from his previous work. Arthur Lammers, a printer from Dayton, Ohio, had asked for a "horoscope" reading, which Cayce gave. At the very end of the reading Cayce noted: "He was once a monk." Since Lammers had never been a monk, he was excited by the possibilities inherent in that brief sentence. He questioned Cayce further to discover more information about previous lives and reincarnation. Though Cayce was somewhat reluctant to delve into that area, his readings were certainly pointing in that direction. Soon he found himself giving readings that came to be called "life readings," because they dealt with past life incarnations. Cayce would begin life readings by noting "the astrological conditions present at the time of the subject's birth, pointing out the most important signs and planets, and then give a brief description of mental, physical, and spiritual traits inherent in the subject. He would then outline several incarnations."[15]

Readings on himself indicated that Cayce had once been "a high priest in Egypt, many centuries ago, who was possessed of great occult powers; but self-will and sensuality proved his undoing. In a later incarnation in Persia he had been a physician. Once he had been wounded in desert warfare and left to die on the sands; alone, without food, water, or shelter, he spent three days and nights in such physical agony that he made a supreme effort to release his consciousness from his body.... All of his virtues and defects of the present were frankly appraised and attributed to one or another of his many previous experiences."[16]

The life readings presented a real problem to Cayce, a conservative Presbyterian. Sherrill posed the dilemma in the following way: "Should he accept the information given by these readings, or should he hold to the traditional Christian beliefs he had learned as a child?"[17] After carefully examining the concept of reincarnation, Cayce decided that it did not conflict with his own religion or with any other religious belief system.

In giving life readings, Cayce emphasized that only the information that was useful to the person was provided. If the information contained in the readings was followed, the result was supposed to be happier and more productive lives for the subjects. For example, Cerminara cited the case of a young woman telegraph operator in New York City who was told in her life reading that "she was wasting her time as a telegraph operator, and that she should study commercial art, as she had been a competent artist for several past lifetimes and could be one again.... To her surprise she found that she had genuine talent; she soon became a highly successful commercial artist, and incidentally transformed her personality in the process."[18]

The last section of a reading, either of the physical or life type, consisted of questions and answers. This section provided subjects with the opportunity to obtain further information on a subject that had been touched on by Cayce.

In addition to doing readings about specific individuals, Cayce predicted world events, such as World Wars I and II and the stock market crash of 1929. He also gave a great deal of information about geological disturbances such as earthquakes, particularly predicting great upheavals beginning in 1958 and lasting for about 40 years. Cayce also spoke of Atlantis and other lost civilizations.

Over 14,000 psychic readings were left by Cayce at the time of his death. In the years just prior to his death, Cayce worked harder than ever because of the tremendous publicity that he had received because of the publication in 1942 of Sugrue's biography, as well as various newspaper and magazine articles about his life and psychic abilities. As Cerminara noted: "To work in one's sleep might seem to be an easy way of life, but it was a tremendous drain on his nervous energy. The strain of this constant service told on him, and on January 3, 1945, he died, at the age of 67."[19] His wife died three months later.

The A.R.E. Organization and Its Programs

The Edgar Cayce Foundation was chartered by the Commonwealth of Virginia in 1948, and in 1956, the old Cayce Hospital, between 67th and 68th Streets on Atlantic Avenue in Virginia Beach, was repurchased and made the national headquarters of the A.R.E., a nonprofit institution. The institution now houses the completely indexed Cayce readings in its library, which was added in 1975. About two-thirds of the readings deal with physical ailments. Cayce emphasized that the purpose of A.R.E. was "not the revelation of psychic phenomena, but 'better understanding of the purpose of life.'"[20]

A wide range of services are offered to both members and nonmembers of the organization. The organization is divided into the following five divisions: Association Services, Research Services, Enlightenment Services, Sales and Marketing, and Individual Services. In addition, the Edgar Cayce Foundation, "a sister organization," is housed in the Library/Conference Center building and is the owner/custodian of the Cayce readings and all the memorabilia pertaining to his life and work. The foundation works closely with the A.R.E. Clinic in Phoenix, Arizona, where medical research based on the readings and holistic health is being conducted. A descriptive brochure states that the clinic offers "the chance to be treated as a whole human being, in body, mind, and spirit... the highest standards in traditional medical diagnostics and treatment... an invitation to accept and overcome disease as a challenge to personal growth... the opportunity to strengthen the body naturally through exercise, physical therapy, biofeedback and acupuncture... the opportunity to open the mind to its potential through education, counseling, relaxation, meditation, and dream interpretation." One important offering of the clinic is the Temple Beautiful Program, a 17-day residential experience focusing on building health through spiritual, medical, and therapeutic means. The clinic sponsors research in areas such as human prenatal development, Down's syndrome, and rheumatoid arthritis.

Association Services of A.R.E. include in-house functions such as accounting, printing, data processing, and personnel. Research Services include the library, which contains the 14,256 Cayce readings plus 32,000 books on parapsychology, philosophy, world religions, holistic health, interpersonal relationships and personal development. In addition, the Braille Library provides free braille cassette tapes and large-print materials to those with visual impairments. Research interests of this division cover a diverse range of fields and are directed by Herbert Puryear, Ph.D., a clinical psychologist. In an article in the *A.R.E. Journal,* which is published bi-monthly by the organization, Mark Thurston, Ph.D., cited excerpts from Cayce readings which focused on the purpose, nature, and strategies of research: "Throughout the readings there are promises that research undertaken with the proper purposes in mind will bring important results." In this regard, Reading 254-82 states: "Again we would insist that we have asked that it be taken as a study, as a thing or condition in the experience of mankind—that this organization may give much to the world on one particular disturbance that has baffled the wise and the foolish. This study on that called epilepsy—for three years!, and you will be undefeatable!"[22] Cayce also emphasized that research should be done *for* enlightenment.

A.R.E. research projects have been conducted in the areas of psychic ability, the effects of meditation, archeology, dreams, and medical disorders and treatment (generally done at the A.R.E. clinic in Phoenix). Dr. Puryear talked to me about some of the ongoing descriptive and experimental investigations sponsored by A.R.E. "Much of what we've done is a validation of the readings. We've collected reports, newspaper articles, etc. to support the readings. The evidence mounts everyday.... One of the most impressive pieces of evidence is the treatment procedures given in the readings for relatively incurable diseases, for example, psoriasis. Cayce gave a procedure to some people and in a few months they were cured...." Puryear also mentioned an interesting new approach to ESP testing that is being conducted at A.R.E. Rather than the typical five-choice problem, a two-choice situation is used. Puryear explained: "Cayce said, 'Pose your questions so that they can be answered yes or no.' My hypothesis is that the subconscious works better with two choices rather than five. We'll run subjects as their own controls and in addition, we'll have a group given five choices and another group given two choices. Also, they'll receive immediate feedback, an important aspect of ESP."

A.R.E. has also sponsored dream research, some of which has been presented in various outside publications. For example, results of a study conducted by psychologist Henry Reed, who is affiliated with A.R.E., indicated that participant-observers, who were chosen on the basis of their desire to experience improved dream recall and who maintained detailed dream diaries, showed increased ability to retrieve dream memories.[23] Puryear commented to me that research in all areas is a growing concern of A.R.E. and that much significant work will be done in the future. A.R.E. publishes *Perspective on Consciousness and Psi-Research*, a monthly research service which contains relevant material from various publications such as *Science News, Science Digest, Parapsychology Review,* and *East West Journal.* In addition, ongoing research being conducted by facilities independent of A.R.E., but pertinent to the organization's purpose, are also reported in *Perspective*. Articles in the early 1980's described the use of electroacupuncture to relieve sleep apnea (an abnormality of sleep in which air passages constrict, resulting in a shortness of breath); psychokinetic metal bending; criticism of the traditional hypnotizability scale; the use of vitamins and minerals to raise I.Q. scores of mentally retarded children; the use of "static" exercises (e.g., push-ups and sit-ups) to facilitate sleep.

Dr. Puryear has also produced a 24-lesson membership course entitled *Covenant*. Issues deal with such topics as "Karma and Grace," "Holistic Healing," "Spirit, Motivation and Ideals," "Reincarnation—The Continuity of Life," and "Sex and the Spiritual Path." The latter is also the title of a full-length book recently published by Puryear.

The third division of the Association is Enlightenment Services, directed by Mark Thurston. This department sponsors seminars and lectures in major cities throughout the United States and Canada as well as at the A.R.E. headquarters in Virginia Beach. Recent week-long conferences included:

> *Keys to the Spiritual Path,* which provided the opportunity to examine spiritual issues, such as: "What can we know of God?" and

"What does a theory of reincarnation do to our view of the spiritual path?"

Exploring Your Dreams and ESP, which facilitated the learning of techniques and insights into how people can deal with their dreams and psychic abilities.

The Art of Loving, which focused on self-love and interpersonal relationships as well as the implications of changes in sexual attitudes and behaviors.

Handling Your Attitudes and Emotions, which emphasized the understanding of and techniques to handle problem areas such as frustration, guilt, and fear.

In addition to the week-long conferences, special free lectures open to the public take place every afternoon. I attended several lectures; some were given as part of a conference, while others were regularly scheduled for the public. In an interesting lecture on health, Ann Clapp, who has studied the Cayce readings extensively, noted: "The key word is balance.... You take the mental, physical, and spiritual, and balance them. If you are not feeling well, it's hard to be spiritual that day." She mentioned the eclectic nature of Cayce's recommendations. "Sometimes it's surgery, sometimes prescription medicine, sometimes chiropractic adjustment, sometimes osteopathy." Some specific Cayce remedies were described, such as fume baths for sinus problems and castor oil packs (using a piece of wool flannel saturated with castor oil which is covered by plastic and a heating pad) for a variety of ailments, from insomnia and migraine headaches to kidney stones and sprained ankles. The lecturer also warned the audience about following any form of treatment or technique to an extreme degree. "Becoming too health conscious is just as serious as doing little or nothing." Some of the Cayce readings on diet and exercise were also described by Ann Clapp. "Cayce suggested that people drink lots of water and that walking is the best exercise. He also talked about following the movements of a cat in exercising. You should stretch like a cat. . . . Exercise above the waist in the morning and below the waist in the evening. . . . Certain combinations of food are bad for the body. Do not take citrus fruits and cereal at the same meal. Milk and citrus should not be combined. . . . Do not eat fried foods, because they cause a short circuit between the heart and the liver. Do not combine a lot of starches at the same meal. Three almonds a day which are raw, not processed, can prevent cancer or tumors. . . . At A.R.E., we are not vegetarians. Fish, fowl, and lamb are best in that order while beef, veal, and pork are bad, worse and worst. . . . To lose weight use Welch's grape juice one half-hour before each meal and at bedtime. Use it diluted with three parts grape juice and one part water. . . ."

The lecturer's final comment was: "Laughter is probably the best medicine, the most healthy thing you can do." That idea was reiterated at another lecture entitled "The Healing Attitude of Humor," given by Violet Shelley as part of a conference called Handling Your Attitudes and Emotions. Shelley is the author of several books, including *Reincarnation Unnecessary,* and spoke in a very humorous fashion to an audience of approximately 100 people, ranging in age from about 8 to 65. She described Norman Cousins' experience when he used laughter and ascorbic acid to treat a degenerative illness as an example of laughter "as the best medicine." Shelley also noted that several people who came to Cayce for physical readings were told: "Make three people laugh a day. It helps you and helps others." Shelley's additional comment about this advice was: "But it doesn't count if they're in a group."

Two other interesting lectures I attended were both concerned with the topic of reincarnation. Hugh Lynn Cayce, chairman of the board of A.R.E. and Edgar Cayce's son, presented one of these talks as part of a conference. He shared a number of stories which reflected the theme of present fears as a function of past life experiences. For example, he told of two women who were afraid of sexual intercourse; one had been raped in Colonial America by a gang of Indians while the other had taken vows of chastity in her previous life as a nun. Another story concerned a little girl who was afraid of loud noises and would awaken terrified at the slightest sound. Hugh Lynn Cayce suggested that in her previous life, she had been killed in an air raid on the French coast. The suggestion to her parents was to sit by her, to make suggestions to her to close the door to her unconscious memory of that past life. The lecturer commented that this advice worked and this little girl grew up normally, got married, "and hasn't awakened to a loud noise in a long time." Hugh Lynn Cayce noted that our dreams may provide clues to our past lives if we are "on speaking terms with our unconscious."

Another lecturer on the same subject, John Van Auken, the manager of the printing department at A.R.E., noted that Edgar Cayce used the term "continual life" rather than reincarnation. The case of a 7-year-old boy who can compose a symphony equivalent to one composed by a trained 30-year-old man was employed to suggest the possibility of a past life in the music field. Another illustration of the significance of past lives concerned a woman who took care of children professionally. Although she appeared to be physically normal, she couldn't have any children of her own. The life reading by Edgar Cayce revealed that in a previous life she had three children who were killed before her eyes. She swore at that time that she would never allow herself to be as hurt again. Once she worked through that past life experience, she was eventually able to bear a child.

In his lecture, Van Auken also discussed three levels of consciousness: the conscious aspect, which is the physical body; the subconscious, which "hides a lot of our secrets"; and the superconscious, which is a "deeper level than the subconscious and is equivalent to Carl Jung's notion of the collective unconscious—we all meet here. Telepathy, Edgar Cayce's readings and ESP are all part of this."

In addition to lectures and seminars, A.R.E. sponsors Wilderness Retreats, which offer "a unique opportunity for exploring and attuning to the beauty of nature," according to a 1981 brochure. Daily study sessions, and training and practice in meditation are part of the trip. Recent trips included sailing among the tropical Virgin Islands in the Caribbean and snorkeling among coral reefs and caves; rafting the Colorado River through the Grand Canyon in Arizona; backpacking in the Wind River Range in Wyoming; bicycling in the foothills of North Carolina; exploring the Mohave Desert of southern California; and whale watching in the lagoons of Baja California, Mexico. A.R.E. also conducts a travel program which combines lectures and workshops with travel. A 13-day Hawaiian tour included a five-day A.R.E. conference covering topics such as *Cayce's Remedies, Mind in Relationship to Dreams,* and *Your Body: Reincarnation Report Card.*

The Enlightenment division of A.R.E. also offers special intensified weekend programs such as the massage workshops, which include demonstrations and practice of various massage techniques; a movement and meditation workshop, which teaches breathing methods and aids to meditation such as music, chanting, and imagery; and *People to People: The Holistic Approach to Communication,* which offers participants "a chance to gain self-confidence, to gain clarity in decision making, to develop awareness of the many levels of communication....," according to a 1981 Intensified Special Week Programs flyer.

In addition, Enlightenment Services coordinate more than 1,700 small study groups found around the world which work to test the usefulness of the Cayce readings in daily life. The A.R.E. introductory brochure describes these groups: "Here, in what are really spiritual workshops, or informal laboratories for creative living, people of all ages and from all walks of life test the concepts presented in the Edgar Cayce readings. Combining periods of reading, discussion, prayer, and meditation, the Study Groups work with principles Cayce described or spiritual laws and observe the changes in themselves." These groups use the two volumes of *A Search for God* as well as the guidelines provided by the *Handbook for A.R.E. Study Groups* and *Edgar Cayce and Group Dynamics.*

The *Over the Wall* program which works with inmates in almost 150 prisons is sponsored by Enlightenment Services. This program includes the donation of books to prison libraries, the organization of prison study groups, and the coordination of a pen-pal program between A.R.E. members and prison inmates.

The Youth Activities Department, a subdivision of Enlightenment Services, developed a model school based on concepts from the Cayce readings. A.R.E. planned to include one additional grade per year. In addition, a number of other special programs are geared toward children and adolescents. For example, the Learning Disabilities Home-Study Kit involved about 75 families. A Summer Camp in Rural Retreat, Virginia, in the foothills of the Appalachian Mountains bordering a national forest, is run for children between the ages of 9 and 15. The activities of the camp include those normally found in a residential camp, such as nature study, gardening, dance, music, arts and crafts, hiking, and sports. However, the philosophical underpinnings of A.R.E. are also evident in the camp program in the form of discussions and workshops on concepts from the Edgar Cayce readings, dream work, "guided reveries," meditation, and prayer.

A prayer service is another aspect of the Enlightenment division. It "coordinates a worldwide prayer chain for all who request help through prayer."[24]

A fourth division of A.R.E. is concerned with Sales and Marketing. A.R.E. Press publishes numerous books and home-study courses based on material from the Edgar Cayce readings. Publications of A.R.E. include *Perspective,* the monthly research report described earlier; *A.R.E. News,* a monthly publication sent to members of the organization; and the bi-monthly *A.R.E. Journal.* Articles in *A.R.E. News* included information about the Over the Wall prison outreach program and a description of a jet lag remedy recommended by an East Indian physician. Articles in *The A.R.E. Journal* included Mail From Members, with comments by Edgar Cayce's grandson, Charles Thomas Cayce, Ph.D., the president of the A.R.E. and a specialist in child psychology. Here are excerpts from some of these letters:

"I read *Cayce, Karma, and Reincarnation* and *Many Mansions* which led me to read and learn more about reincarnation. I lost my son at the age of 16 (cancer). Without a firm belief in reincarnation and karma, I couldn't have kept my senses. The Lord through Cayce helped me through a very sad loss and I still have not lost my faith."[25]

"Migraines—who would have believed enemas would be the cure—but they are."

"I think the concept hardest for me to accept when I started with A.R.E. and which helps me the most now is that the answer lies within self—that I should not search for it outside of myself."

"I'm working with dream analysis and meditation (all reincarnation oriented) and it has helped me immeasurably in understanding myself, my family, every facet of my life."

Some of the letters contained both positive and negative comments: "I have a diagnosis of multiple sclerosis and I studied the readings and used the Wet Cell Battery (with gold chloride) and massages for 2½ years—the body showed no improvement—in fact outer condition worsened. So I've discontinued that. But I still meditate and feel my *attitude* has been greatly healed!"[26]

Other recent articles in the *A.R.E. Journal* were concerned with earthquake predictions; the early history of study groups; a comparison of news items with Edgar Cayce readings on various subjects such as exercise, treatment for warts, and the use of herbal medicine; and book reviews.

The bookstore is another part of A.R.E. Sales and Marketing and contains at least 1,000 titles, many of which are "hard-to-find" books. The audio-visual center "[d]evelops home study courses on cassette tapes and plans original programming for radio and television."[27]

Individual Services provide various benefits to members, including therapy (massage and hydrotherapy). This division is also responsible for responding to the thousands of annual inquiries received by A.R.E., and providing tours, free lectures, and audio-visual presentations for about 45,000 visitors each year at A.R.E. headquarters. One of the major benefits of A.R.E. membership is its therapy services. Massage and hydrotherapy treatments are available by appointment only to staff and members at A.R.E. headquarters in Virginia Beach. The A.R.E. Therapy Department was established in 1966 by Harold J. Reilly, Ph.T., D.Sc., who continued to direct the department from his home in New Jersey. The staff includes a registered nurse, a masseur, and a masseuse who were trained by Reilly. Hydrotherapy includes steam baths, fume baths (steam baths with some added substance such as eucalyptus oil); colonics (irrigation or cleansing of the colon), whirlpool, sitz, and Epsom salts baths; and mud pack facials.

These treatments were often recommended in the Cayce readings, excerpts from which follow: "... at least one week out of each month should be spent in beautifying, preserving, rectifying the body—if the body would keep young in mind, in body, in purpose.... Choose three days out of some week in each month ... and have the general hydrotherapy treatments, including massage, lights, and all the treatments that are in the nature of beautifying, and keeping the whole of the body-forces young."[28]

In a reading given to a 50-year-old man, Cayce said: "... for hydrotherapy and massage are preventive as well as curative measures. The cleansing of the system allows the body forces themselves to function normally, and thus eliminate poisons, congestions and conditions that would become acute through the body."[29]

A.R.E. Members

Membership, which now numbers about 40,000, is divided into three categories: Associate, which charges $20 dues annually; Sponsoring, with annual dues of $40; and Life, which provides all the rights and privileges of Sponsoring for a one-time fee of $1,000. Differences between Sponsoring and Associate memberships include the number of circulating files that may be borrowed each year. These files contain complete Cayce readings on specific medical conditions, such as arthritis, acne, hypertension, measles, and multiple sclerosis, or nonmedical subjects such as earth changes, human relations, business advice, friendship, homosexuality, and advice to parents. The Individual Reference File, consisting of verbatim excerpts from the Cayce readings, are provided free of charge to Sponsoring members, while Associate members are charged $15. Moreover, Sponsoring members are entitled to a discount on doctors' fees at the Phoenix A.R.E. Clinic. Other membership benefits include three books a year, subscriptions to *A.R.E. News* and the *A.R.E. Journal,* the opportunity to participate in research projects, discounts on conferences, referral to M.D.'s, osteopaths, and chiropractors who are cooperating in A.R.E. research and treatment programs, library borrowing privileges, and the opportunity to participate in summer camp or wilderness trips. The final reason for joining cited in A.R.E. Membership Benefits for You and Your Family, a promotional flyer by the organization, is: "You are part of one of the oldest, most respected organizations of its kind in the country. Through your membership in the A.R.E. you support and nurture the most stimulating work going on today in the field of medical research, psychical research, soul growth, and human potential; thereby helping yourself and others to usher in the New Age."

A.R.E. has shown interest in acquiring information about the characteristics, attitudes, and practices of its members. At least two detailed surveys have been conducted to learn about A.R.E. members and whether the organization is meeting their needs. Actually, A.R.E. is constantly soliciting information from members. For example, in their mail order catalogue for 1981, the following request is made:

"We would appreciate your taking a few minutes to let us know of any concepts from the Edgar Cayce readings you have tried to work with and apply to your life.

"We want to know about your experience. Was it successful or unsuccessful? Was it of help or benefit to you? Did you have any problems, frustrations, etc.? If so, what were they? . . .

"Just mail this completed form to us with your next book order. Your comments and thoughts will help shape the future of A.R.E. Thank you."

One survey was sent to the 16,000 members of A.R.E. in August 1973. Those who indicated interest in participating in future A.R.E.-sponsored research projects were then sent a 17-page Workbook Questionnaire containing about 200 questions regarding meditation, dreams, reincarnation, diet, psychic experiences, involvement in other organizations, and demographic information. Richard L. Kohr, Ph.D., an educational psychologist, reported in the *A.R.E. Journal* on some of the findings, which were coded under the direction of Charles Thomas Cayce and Mark Thurston. Of the 2,000 Workbook Questionnaires sent out, 28 percent or 570 were completed; they may or may not be representative of the entire group. Of the respondents, 68.1 percent were female, 31.4 percent were male, and 0.5 percent did not specify sex. High school graduates with some additional training (e.g., two-year technical programs, RNs, Associate degrees) comprised the largest group—39 percent. About 6 percent had not completed high school, 14 percent were high school graduates, 25 percent were college graduates, 11 percent had received Master's degrees, and 3 percent had Doctoral degrees. Most participants (68 percent) were married and for the most part over 30 years of age. Only 8 percent were 24 or younger; 12 percent were 55 or older. The median age was about 40, with a range from the teens to the 80's. With regard to geographic location, all areas of the United States were well represented.[30]

Another more recent survey, undertaken in January 1980, which had not been completely analyzed by A.R.E. at the time of this writing, suggests some preliminary information about current members. About one-third belonged to A.R.E. for at least ten years, another third had joined within the previous three years, and the final third were between three- and ten-year members. With regard to age, 68 percent of Associate members and 77 percent of Sponsoring members were between 31 and 64. Less than one-third of the members belonged to a Study Group, and those who belonged were more likely to have Sponsoring rather than Associate status.

Members belonged to other "awareness" groups, such as Wellness, Spiritual Frontier Fellowship, Course in Miracles, Silva, and Self-Realization Fellowship, in addition to maintaining ties to their churches or synagogues. As Puryear told me: "Cayce encouraged people to stay in their own religion. He didn't want them to stop being Catholic or Jewish. He said 'Don't let this pull you away from your religion.'" This idea was reiterated by Hugh Lynn Cayce: "We're not trying to take the place of a church. . . . We're not a cult of some kind."[31] The survey results further indicated that members in a two-to-one ratio felt that the dues were primarily an exchange for valuable information rather than donating to a cause. Only 30 percent of Sponsoring and 26 percent of Associate members had used the A.R.E. library during the past year. In fact, most members do not visit A.R.E. even once a year and some have never been to Virginia Beach at all.

The preliminary data suggest that "most people support A.R.E. because it aids their growth, they are believers and because of the information they get—not because of loyalties or to receive monthly mailings. A.R.E. has awakened in them a oneness of life and it is their contribution to what they believe in. From nonmedical files the members gain new insights, finds them inspirational and a help to spiritual growth. Medical files are helpful but hard to interpret—although doctor commentaries are helpful."

Recruitment

Lynn Sparrow, communications manager of A.R.E., told me about the recruitment of members: "Up until 1979 it was pretty much a matter of people coming to us the way I came to them—through books, friends, etc. So I would have to describe us as responsive, totally. And then in '79 we experimented with direct mail. We did very small tests—10,000 letters, which is fairly small. We rented mailing lists of magazine subscribers, *Time, Prevention,* and others, and we got a 2 percent response, which is considered a success for direct mail. There was a decision made then to work with direct mail—we were under pressure to expand. We were called the best kept secret in America. So that test was successful, and since '79 we've had three major direct mail efforts, with a fourth coming in September 1981. In 1980 we doubled our membership, primarily through direct mail."

Sparrow indicated the major reasons for joining A.R.E. First, "the people like myself who found that what goes on here pieces together a lot of loose ends. They join to be part of something. They support the effort going on here. They also like the fact that there are no set doctrines. You line up several members and ask them questions and you would get very different opinions. So, it's not that we all believe the same things about God, the soul, and life, but there is some common thread of understanding that kind of builds a sense of community."

A second major reason for joining, according to Sparrow, is to obtain membership benefits, such as the opportunity to borrow the circulation files, receive A.R.E. books, etc. She further commented that the readings are the major strength of A.R.E.; the diversity of the membership and the staff is a second strength: "Where a cult tends to have a monolithic approach to life, people in our study groups can sit side by side each with their own concept of God and apply those principles individually and never come to blows over it. I think those are the two major strengths. Another would be that A.R.E. continues to pioneer." She also pointed to the emphasis on holistic health and meditation, that has been part of A.R.E. since its inception, as other attracting factors.

A.R.E. Participants

I interviewed numerous participants in A.R.E. activities, most of whom were members or staffed the organization. They shared with me their own reasons for joining and/or participating in A.R.E. functions. A couple in their late 20's, from New Orleans, had both joined just a month prior to their visit to A.R.E. headquarters. The husband, Kenneth Sherman, had been a bartender but was, when interviewed, attending college full-time for a degree in geography. His wife worked as a secretary to support the family, which included a 19-month-old child. They also had plans to open a day-care business, but geography was clearly his "real love." The couple had never been involved in other similar groups, but both had been active in a number of environmental groups. Kenneth described his reasons for joining the organization: "I joined because I'm interested in the subject matter. I saw Hugh Lynn Cayce on a T.V. talk show about three months ago. He talked about a presentation at the Holiday Inn. I went to it and was impressed by the level-headedness of Cayce and Puryear and Thurston. They seemed to be well-grounded on earth and in the spirit."

Kenneth also reflected on his and his wife's religious and spiritual backgrounds in bringing them to A.R.E. "My wife was raised in Brazil and was involved in spiritualism; it was part of her childhood environment. I've had a long interest in parapsychology. My father was interested in astrology and holistic health. My mother never developed an interest in the subject, but I read about Edgar Cayce when I was a child. My father believed in freedom *from* religion. My mother and sister recently plunged head on into Evangelical Protestantism. My own religious feeling is evolving. We're on this earth to manifest love and I'm trying to find out how to do that. I've never been in a church I liked. This was the first group that made me believe that Christianity made some sense."

In discussing the significance of the A.R.E. philosophy and practices, Kenneth told me: "The important parts of A.R.E. are finding out how to serve God, holistic health, and astrology. . . . I have tried meditation, but it's too early to tell if it will work for me."

Alice Cunningham, a 35-year-old woman, had "been interested in Edgar Cayce for many years" before she joined the organization. "I've been searching for a more meaningful existence. I have been interested in parapsychology and holistic health and have taken classes in these areas. I'm also interested in psychic things. I've had a psychic reading done, but not at A.R.E.; they don't do them here, and the results are in the mail. . . . I'm changing my life style and I thought that this seminar on attitudes and emotions would be helpful. I had lived with my family and have just left home to start a new career. I was an art major in college and became a teacher. I've worked in both elementary and high schools as an art teacher. I was frustrated and restless. Now, I want to go into the commercial field, into commercial art." This was Alice's first visit to A.R.E. headquarters in Virginia Beach and her evaluation of the experience was a favorable one: "Everyone here is caring and nice. It's stimulating to be here, very helpful, actually inspiring." Her concluding remark was: "I want help to like myself better so that I can better help people. That's what I'm here for."

Thirty-eight-year-old Lorraine Newberg, a member for ten years, was attending an A.R.E. conference as part of her vacation from her job as an audiologist in Maryland. She reflected on the organization, its members, and her own motivation in joining the group: "I'm not a joiner; I've never joined another group. Every five or six years I move somewhere else. I get a better job and I move on. I'm not married, so I don't have to worry about my family. I decided long ago that my career was most important to me.

"I heard about Cayce long ago. Some people think reincarnation is really kooky. My parents aren't interested in this. But I noticed a change in the past five years or so. Now—and I've tried this—if I'm at a table with eight people, at least one of them is open about reincarnation. A.R.E. is not like other organizations. Most people here are not into organized religions. I'm from a loose Protestant background. But I am interested in spiritual things. A.R.E. is everything from soup to nuts. Some people like soup, some like nuts. People feel free to choose what they like. There's holistic health, ESP, reincarnation, psychic readings, and so on. You don't have to believe all of it. Certainly you meet some kooks here once in awhile, but they are the exception."

John Russell, a 55-year-old married man with three adult daughters, was attending his first A.R.E. conference when I met him. He had been a member for three years and was working as a train dispatcher in Ohio. He related his story of joining to me:

"About five years ago I came into contact with a study

group of A.R.E. and I also read the book, *There Is a River*. A friend of mine had been a member and I seemed to see some real truths in what he was saying. I find that there are answers in Cayce readings that I don't find in organized religions. I had a desire to know more. A.R.E. answers all my questions. The greatest strength of A.R.E. is their truth, going within to the real center to find the truth within. They have a flexibility in their teachings. They do not necessarily have a dogma. Everyone is accepted. The majority I've met are sincere and searching for the truth. The few who are seeking the psychic phenomena are not really interested in learning more about themselves. I used to feel there was a conflict between my old orthodox beliefs and my belief in reincarnation. I used to have questions about deformities and illnesses. How could these be if there is a just God? Gradually, I came to the realization that a belief in reincarnation would make sense of all these loose ends."

John also talked to me about the reaction of his coworkers and family to his participation in A.R.E. activities: "I'm from a family that is deeply Orthodox Protestant Pentecostal. My wife lets me do my thing but she has no interest in this. She'll talk about it with me sometimes. My oldest and youngest daughters are easy to talk to. We discuss the readings and they are very open-minded. A couple of my coworkers know about my involvement in A.R.E. and are in agreement with me in some areas. Most of my family members have confidence in my ideals and my reasoning, so there is no real disagreement concerning A.R.E."

When I asked John if he had used any of the remedies described in the Cayce readings, he replied: "The main remedy that has worked tremendously has been maintaining correct pH balance through changing my way of eating for the last four or five years. I have noticed a sense of well-being, fewer colds. But I've always been rather healthy. I use Aura Glow. I swim a lot and I use it for my dry skin and that's cleared up."

Helen Barker, the mother of two college-aged children, joined A.R.E. 7 years ago, soon after her divorce. She was employed by a New York advertising agency. "I was and still am an account executive during the day," she told me. "I needed to do something for myself at night. I needed to find something that I could enjoy, that would be stimulating. I started reading books about witchcraft and the occult and I realized that wasn't for me. I come from a Protestant background and although I was on a spiritual path I didn't see that as the answer. My sister and I live about four hours from each other, but we're very close. We don't usually talk about spiritual things, but we usually wind up doing the same kind of things at the same time. Now I'm involved in A.R.E. activities and so is she. I began reading about Cayce's life and his readings and it sounded fascinating.

"Then, I began to have problems at work; I couldn't concentrate. My boss told me to take a vacation for a week. I told him I didn't have the money. So he gave me $100 and I scraped up $100 and we came down to Virginia Beach, but there were no vacancies. Then I mentioned to the Chamber of Commerce that I was interested in A.R.E. They told me to go to Marshall's Motel [where most A.R.E. conference participants stay] and I started to get involved in the A.R.E. that way. I asked questions and really enjoyed the atmosphere.

"I'm here for my second week-long conference. I went to another one about three years ago. . . . Sometimes I'm more involved in the activities than at other times. There are some very good speakers and some that are not so good. But the whole group is a very loving group. For example, a lady was walking out of the bathroom saying: 'Oh, my hair looks terrible.' Another young girl was walking in and said: 'Let me fix it for you,' and she did. There are a lot of pleasant experiences here. People are always glad to talk to you."

I also interviewed Larry Scott, a 50-year-old Southern Baptist from North Carolina, who is "sort of religious." He was attending a conference with his two sons, both college students. The only non-A.R.E. member in the family was Larry's wife. He explained: "My wife uses peanut oil for her arthritis and it allows her to function much better than before. She doesn't join because she has all the benefits through my membership. She is highly favorable now partly because of the effective treatment for her arthritis and she has seen a difference in me."

Larry told me why he became an A.R.E. member 15 years before: "I probably had a feeling that there is a lot more to a person than I was being told. I ran into the Cayce biography, *There Is a River,* in 1954 on a military installation. I felt a sense of truthfulness about the readings. I also felt a sense of empathy for the Cayce family. Later in my life, that same need, that there is more to life, came up again. I found more books and called A.R.E. and asked to join. A.R.E. has a large body of information which is personally verifiable, information about the real depths of man and man's relationship to God. Man can get hold of it and do something with it if he wants. In working with information in those readings, it helps to integrate the information with your religion. It is not a matter of killing off what you already have."

Larry further reflected on the influence of the organization on his life: "A.R.E. places a great emphasis on dreams. I've been keeping a dream journal for about 13 years and it has been helpful beyond all question. The greatest help has been in understanding myself and my problems. Another tremendous help has been in working with my sons. It has helped to avoid parent-child relationship problems. I've helped them to examine their dreams. Gradually, over the years, we talked about the readings, about dreams, psychic concepts, etc. It may have left them somewhat isolated from people their own age, but it's a greater view of things. It has made a big difference to us as a family. There is greater contentment now. One of the major benefits for us is that it has eliminated a lot of medical bills. I've used castor oil packs for prostate difficulties. I once used it for bursitis and it really helped."

Larry also described the reaction of his friends and coworkers to his A.R.E. membership: "Not many of my friends or coworkers know about my membership in A.R.E. Those who know are often members themselves. In my area of the country anything different or unusual is considered peculiar. This is considered a weird part of my personality, but since everything else seems to be going O.K. in my life, they just accept it. I'm a professor of computer science. Not many other professors know about A.R.E., but a number of them have tried various remedies that I've given them. They are not, however, open to the concepts and ideas of A.R.E. That's changing rapidly. More and more people are changing their attitudes about the association and its tenets."

I also talked to Larry's two sons, one an anthropology major and the other a psychology major, about the reaction of others to their participation in A.R.E. activities. Both noted that school and neighborhood friends and acquaintances did not understand their interest in A.R.E. They had been questioned about whether A.R.E. was a cult like People's Temple or Hare Krishna. They laughed at the possibility of a comparison and suggested that there was "no guru, nothing to worship," that the ideas of A.R.E. were "interesting and helpful."

Some of the A.R.E. staff members also explained their early interest in the organization and its underlying philosophy. One told me: "In high school, I had an interest in the Bible; I started reading it. My first term paper in college was about psychoanalysis and religion. I thought there ought to be some way these fit—some way to put together parapsychology and religion and psychoanalysis."

Another staff member, Sara Turner, stated that her involvement began in the tenth grade. "I was doing a term paper. It was an English term paper, and we could write about anything we wanted, and I chose prophecy. My grandfather brought over a book and it was Edgar Cayce on prophecy. So that was my first exposure and I was really taken with it and yet it didn't totally grab me. It was six months later, really, that my reading in the area of philosophy and metaphysics led me to begin reading some books primarily about reincarnation—a case in the '50's about a woman who, under hypnosis, apparently remembered past lives. It made quite a splash then, and I kept reading books that kept referring to Edgar Cayce and this biography called *There Is a River.* And the more I read more references to it, the more I had to have the book. I went to some bookstores, but I couldn't find it anywhere. And while I was searching for *There Is a River,* my mother happened to run into a neighbor, one of those neighbors you may not see for five years running, and this neighbor for some reason was always interested in how I was doing. She asked my mother about me and for some reason my mother mentioned that I was reading all of these unusual books and this woman said: 'Oh, I have some things she might like.' And the next day she came over with this grocery bag full of paperbacks and right on top was *There Is a River,* the book I'd been searching for!

"So, I don't think I'd ever read anything like it. As I read it, it just put everything together. It took the loose ends—it just really made sense to me. And that book traces the beginnings of A.R.E. The narrative of that book ends in 1945, the year Edgar Cayce died. I had an old copy that had nothing about the current organization. So I just kind of wrote this blind letter to the Edgar Cayce Foundation, Virginia Beach, that basically said: 'Are you still there? And if so, can I become a part of this?'

"I was 16. I didn't think they would even still be there and I've since found a lot of people shocked—they'd been reading Edgar Cayce's books for years and they had no idea that all this was still here. So I got a whole packet of material on the man and included in the material was information about the study group. It turned out there was one right in northern New Jersey—about 15 minutes from where I lived. I walked into that group of people and—I was not one to meet strangers, very retiring to say the least—and I felt I was at home. That group became the high point of my life. The thing about that group is that the people are really dealing on a day-to-day level with the issues that confront us. A person who didn't want to disclose anything about their personal life was never pressed to. But the person who wants to lay something on the table to get help, was welcome to it and it's a real nice situation. I never expected to get as involved as I am now."

After studying theology, Sara took up psychology and graduated from college with a degree in that major. After working for a short time at a facility for the mentally retarded, Sara came to work at A.R.E.

Sara described her family's reaction to her early and continued interest in the spiritual and religious dimensions of life, including her work at A.R.E.: "My parents never interfered; my father was a 'live-and-let-live' agnostic. My mother was a Christian but was never really involved with the church. So my religion was always my own. When I was 8 years old, I was suddenly overwhelmed with the desire to go to Sunday school. It's my theory that in past lives the church has been a very near and dear part of me, and if you accept the possibility of past life influences, these are like subconscious urges that begin to surface and I like that better than saying: 'God called me.' I can remember lying there on my bed staring at my Raggedy Ann wallpaper, and suddenly getting this overwhelming urge to go to Sunday school. I was very shy. I knew if I went they would make me stand up and introduce myself. It took me two weeks to get enough courage to go. Both my parents were pleased, especially my father.

"I came home one night for supper and he pulled out a

brand new leather-bound Bible. When I became interested in A.R.E., my mother had almost developed a mode of being interested in what I thought about things. I think she felt: 'Who am I to question it? At least she's doing something about it.' But that night when they took me out and dropped me at the group meeting—I didn't know it at the time, but they told me they felt real apprehension. They didn't know if they were doing the right thing. These people were total strangers. To this day my parents keep in touch with my group members. They've become my parents' friends, even though they aren't involved. But I think my parents were kind of unusual. They gave me a lot of freedom all my life. I didn't have the hassles of the kind of parents who think it's a heresy. I have an older brother; by that time he was married, off on his own. I think he always saw that whatever I was doing was working for me. I don't think he condemned it. I think he just took an attitude of not understanding and not really being interested."

Sara also talked about the usefulness of some of the Edgar Cayce remedies: "I found them to be unbelievably helpful. I've been lucky in that I don't have any major illnesses that I've had to deal with. But on little things, just day-to-day problems that might bother you. For example, he [Cayce] recommended that thing called castor oil packs, and they're good for so many things, whether it's for something internal or whether it's a sprain. I slammed a finger in a door and it would just be normal for that finger to get black and blue, and I immediately put castor oil on it and wrapped it up and it never even bruised. My mother turned her ankle and couldn't even walk, and I put a castor oil pack around her ankle and within a couple of hours the swelling had gone and she could walk. My father had been having terrible trouble with what turned out to be gallstones, and I gave him castor oil packs. That was ten years ago, and he hasn't had the problem anymore. A woman, who works here—who was in a car accident—her face was horribly scarred and Edgar

Cayce made up in his readings this formula for scar removal. You massage it in and it will get rid of scars and she has absolutely no marks on her face today."

A large percentage of A.R.E. members do not renew their memberships after some period of participation in the organization. Lynn Sparrow, communications manager, revealed the results of questionnaire data on this subject: "The number one reason for nonrenewal of membership is lack of funds. Secondly, people will say that they don't have time to read all the material they receive in the mail. Thirdly, people sometimes have misconceptions when they join and are disappointed. And the smallest percentage would be those who have a change of heart. They find that A.R.E. is not in line with their religious beliefs anymore. Those people will usually write a letter saying they pray for us and they hope we'll see the error of our ways and that kind of thing."

I spoke to Karl Benson, who had been a member of the organization in the late 1960's for three years, about his motives for joining and then leaving the organization. He said: "I joined because I had read some of the books about Edgar Cayce and was intrigued by the whole story. I had just returned from a Peace Corps tour in South America and was overwhelmed by what I had seen there. I was asking myself—what is the meaning of life? I saw lots of poverty, primitive living, children with malnutrition, tremendous infant-child mortality. After I returned to the states I found out that one of my best students had died; he was in his late teens. I was a secondary school teacher there.

"I had started teaching at a community college. I had a new job in the states. I had some time and was exploring. I had what I would consider to be a right-brain experience. I read Thomas Sugrue's book, *There Is a River,* a biography of Edgar Cayce. It's a well-written book which related events that would seem far-out or bizarre to some people but I accepted them. They seemed natural to me. I was open to that kind of thing. I had an experience like, 'This is the way things are.' I can't take things on faith. There has to be some logic for me to accept it. The story of Edgar Cayce and the readings are a logical system that can't be explained away.

"I was also interested in healing. I was somewhat hypochondriacal and interested in finding out what these remedies were. I thought that because of the success of the remedies, the philosophies might also be validated. People seemed to be getting better. If the cures worked, I reasoned, then the philosophy behind the cures should make sense as well. By the philosophy, I largely mean reincarnation, which is paramount to the readings.

"I was raised in a Jewish family and I was exposed to Christianity for the first time in South America. The Edgar Cayce readings integrated Christianity into a larger doctrine. I was also into Oriental religions at the time and felt that the readings provided a neat synthesis of Western and Eastern philosophy. As a belief system, they educate the public. They help to create an awareness of doctrines that most people from the Judeo-Christain heritage are unaware of, although there are sects in both of these groups that accept the beliefs of reincarnation. The existence of A.R.E. promulgates that doctrine.

"I found the book *There Is a River* by chance or—if you believe that kind of thing—by destiny. The next book I read was *The Sleeping Prophet* by Jess Stearn, which pushed me further. The study and prayer groups play an important role focusing on helping others in learning about basic truths. I did join a meditation group, although not with A.R.E., so I know how helpful such a group can be. Cayce advised meditation and I think it is important for people to meditate to get to their true source.

"I was never an active member. I mostly sent for and read their literature. I never participated in a study group or interacted very much with other members. I did give a talk and slide show on my Peace Corps experience to A.R.E. members in New York. I didn't become very involved because there were too many other things in my life. I'm not the kind of person who easily joins groups. I'm shy; there's a lot of inertia. I met a very good friend at an A.R.E. meeting place. He left A.R.E. and went on to other things along the same lines. I went to the reading room at a New York meeting, but not to meet people. I don't talk to people easily. If they initiate first, I would respond.

"I stopped off at A.R.E. in Virginia Beach once, returning from a trip elsewhere. I was just there a couple of hours. I was impressed; the people were nice. I went to the bookstore and looked the place over. But I never got into it. I wanted to, but my relationship with my wife would not permit it. She had other ideas about how to spend a vacation. She doesn't agree with the philosophy of Edgar Cayce, although I forced her to read a number of books about him and reincarnation. I kept bugging her, but they made no impression on her. Not only did she not have an 'Ah ha' experience, she had a 'Ha Ha' experience. She totally rejected it."

Karl Benson also described his experience with Cayce-prescribed remedies: "Another important part of A.R.E. is that it makes available Edgar Cayce remedies, particularly castor oil packs. I've used some of the remedies and found them to be helpful. My gums bothered me and I used ipsab, an herbal mixture which is very effective. I put it on and my gums aren't sore any longer. I haven't used some of the more exotic remedies because I believe Edgar Cayce prescribed specific things for specific people. However, there are some general remedies. It is also interesting that many of the things Edgar Cayce said were important in the health field have been validated by modern medicine. For example, he discussed a physical technique using some kind of pin structure and it actually came out later. The diet he recommended in the 1920's is the diet that is widely advised today. Also, his focus on psychosomatic medicine was very strong and preceded today's great interest in the subject."

In citing the reasons for his leaving the organization, Karl remarked: "I got out of it what I wanted. I read the literature; I learned about the remedies. I had gone as far as I could with them. I had mastered intellectually what the readings taught. There was no point in continuing membership. There was nothing new coming from A.R.E. It was just more and more people's teachings of Cayce's readings. I could interpret Cayce as well as anyone else.

"I haven't been a member for a long time so I don't know what is going on presently. But it seems to me that A.R.E. kind of ignores an important religious phenomenon that is sweeping the nation, the holy spirit or the spirit of God—manifested mainly through charismatic groups. A.R.E. is not in tune with what is happening now and they seem to be locked into Cayce readings. The religious phenomenon that I'm referring to includes speaking in tongues, miracle healings—mental, emotional, or physical. People are being immersed in something that was never discussed by Cayce. He was never able to heal anyone by the laying on of hands. He prescribed specific treatments for individuals. A.R.E. is ignoring a lot of the phenomena that occur. Any channel—Edgar Cayce was such a channel—is not faultless. They are flawed, not a pure teaching coming through the unconscious. I don't believe everything Edgar Cayce gave is true. It was biased and should be recognized as such. Some people idolize Edgar Cayce and he had faults. He was not a saint and should not be regarded as such."

Karl mentioned that he is presently involved with a group called The Association for the Understanding of Man, organized by psychic Ray Stanford. "The teachings are clearer than Cayce's," according to Karl. "I've been a member for about four years, even though the organization has changed radically, since Stanford no longer gives readings."

Evaluation of A.R.E.

Present members and staff people certainly recognize that A.R.E. is not without its weaknesses or flaws. Some of the problems seem to derive from individual perceptions and expectations, while others reside within the organization itself. One member told me: "A weakness of A.R.E. is that it is not publicly funded. There are limitations because of the lack of funds. It limits the degree to which the information is made available to people."

The financial situation was also perceived as a problem by one of the staff members I interviewed: "I think a potential weakness is not having a grip on money supply. Edgar Cayce was never able to use his gift, you know, to make money. And he was never even able to support his family well. Not only was it that he couldn't make gobs of money through his psychic ability, he just didn't seem to be able to quite handle money and I think A.R.E. is often guilty of poverty. We're always on a very tight budget, and I don't think it has to be that way, just because you're a nonprofit organization. It's almost a weakness that comes with working in this area."

Another weakness of A.R.E. was described by a staff person: "...some of the weaknesses have to do with becoming so involved with what we're doing that we're not enough involved with the outside world. For example, I found that when I came here to work, everyone I worked with and everybody I was friends with—all were involved with this and I had to go out for balance in my life. I think you can just get too involved in this whole thing and it's not good. Part of life is going to K-Mart, just ordinary things... and I think that that is a potential weakness."

Another potential problem of A.R.E. is the tendency of certain people to regard A.R.E. as an organization that has all the answers, Edgar Cayce as a "cult figure," and the readings as a "pile of magic cures." However, all of the staff members that I talked to warned against viewing the organization and the man in this blind way. One other significant notion to keep in mind as one studies and evaluates the usefulness of the readings is that Edgar Cayce prescribed for individuals, rather than for specific conditions. Thus failure to alleviate a particular disorder after using a remedy that Edgar Cayce had indicated in a similar case does not necessarily invalidate the efficacy of that treatment.

The Future

What does the future hold for A.R.E.? The organization has certainly been showing significant growth in recent years due to a number of factors, including both greater outreach to the general public through direct mailings to potential members and growing acceptance of some of the various tenets of the organization such as psychic phenomena and reincarnation. Even traditional professional organizations, such as the American Psychological Association, are beginning to present research on such phenomena as extrasensory perception at their annual meetings.

Another apparent change is the increasing focus on business, that is the application of the Edgar Cayce readings to the world of business and industry. The Annual Business conference reflects this relatively new interest by A.R.E. For example, the 1981 Management Development Conference revolved around "discovering and developing practical tools to help you manage your business for greater profitability." The promotional brochure indicated that the conference experience emphasized the relationship between business concerns and spiritual values.

A.R.E. continues to attract people because it offers a philosophical and spiritual system that is meaningful to many; it is responsive to the needs of its members; and it allows individuals to make as much or as little of a commitment as they desire.

5: Himalayan International Institute

"...dedicated to the belief that one can achieve a more productive life through reducing stress and strain, that human life at any age means growth, that the realization of one's potential can become a lifelong experience leading to increased health and happiness, that people have within themselves the power to develop self-awareness through self-directed change and that this renewal takes place more effectively through self-discipline and a meditative perspective."

THE Himalayan International Institute of Yoga Science and Philosophy, the official name of the Himalayan International Institute, which has its headquarters just north of Honesdale, Pennsylvania, cites the above as its underlying philosophy. That is, "everyone has the opportunity to explore his inner potential."[1]

This nonprofit Institute was founded in 1971 by Sri Swami Rama, who was then about 40 years old. It expanded to 12 centers in cities throughout the United States, including New York, Chicago, Pittsburgh, and Austin. The Institute derives its name from the ancient traditions of the

Himalayas, which are committed to the understanding of the interaction between the mind and the body. According to Dr. John Clarke, a physician on the staff of the Institute, "Swami Rama had the good fortune of being brought up in those traditions." He came to the United States in 1969 to make that information, which had predominantly been transmitted orally, available to the Western culture. The literal translation of the Sanskrit term *swami,* according to Dr. Elmer Green of the Menninger Foundation, is "master." However, Dr. Green further pointed out that Swami Rama believes that "a real swami is one who has achieved self-mastery," rather than being master of someone else.[2] In 1977, Swami Rama received the Martin Buber Award for Service to Humanity for his spiritual and scientific contributions.

Swami Rama's background is impressive. He spent his childhood in the Himalayas raised by a great yoga master. As a young teenager, he was ordained as a monk and went on to study with a number of spiritual leaders, including Mahatma Gandhi. He received a formal education at Oxford University in England and also studied Western psychology and philosophy in both Germany and Holland. While still in India, Swami Rama attained that country's highest spiritual position in the Hindu hierarchy, the office of Shankaracharya. He renounced that position in southern India to come to the United States to "establish a clear scientific basis for the practice of yoga and meditation."[3]

Doug Boyd, the author of *Swami,* spent over two months as Swami Rama's 24-hours-a-day personal assistant while the Swami was undergoing psychophysiological tests at the Menninger Foundation in 1971. He reported some interesting observations of this very unusual individual. Dr. Green was head of the Voluntary Controls Program at the Menninger Foundation's Research Department in Topeka, Kansas, where Swami Rama initially demonstrated the extraordinary ability to control his heart rate in the spring of 1970. He was able to cause his heart rate to jump from 70 to about 300 beats per minute, resulting in atrial flutter, in effect stopping the heart from pumping blood for about 17 seconds. Dr. Marvin Dunne, a cardiologist at the University of Kansas Medical Center, noted that this type of heart change is associated with a drop in blood pressure and fainting and sometimes even death.[4]

Swami Rama returned to the Menninger Foundation in 1971 to become a research subject and to learn more about biofeedback techniques. These techniques allow an individual to receive information about changes in physiological processes, such as heart rate and brain activity, in response to changes in physical or emotional conditions, such as depression or low temperatures.

Boyd noted that Swami Rama is a "beautiful storyteller. He told incredible stories and told them with great skill. . . ."[5] In addition, Boyd wrote that the Swami "appeared to be an expert in all things knowable—from metaphysics to history to horticulture." However, because he was accustomed to being totally waited upon in India, he was "an interesting combination of self-mastery and incompetence."[6] Boyd provided an interesting and amusing anecdote about Swami Rama. One afternoon, soon after meeting Boyd, the Swami had been scheduled for deep meditation while wired to physiological assessment devices. As Swami Rama showered upstairs, Boyd prepared lunch. When Swami had finished showering, he attempted to turn the water off, but unscrewed the knobs instead, causing increased water flow. For about a half-hour, he remained in the shower, trying desperately, but unsuccessfully, to stop the water. When he realized that he would have to call for help, he dressed quickly while the bathroom flooded, "so that at least his appearance would be as dignified as possible."[7]

Swami Rama was given the title of consultant to the Voluntary Controls Project at the Menninger Foundation. His relationship to the researchers was an interesting one. While he certainly intrigued them because of his unusual abilities, he also appeared to be a threat to them because those same remarkable behaviors played havoc with their knowledge of the laws of Western science.[8]

One of the accomplishments described by Boyd involved psychokinesis (moving of an object without the use of any physical force). Green described Swami's first unsuccessful attempt. A pencil, tied to a string which hung from a desk, began to rotate as Swami said his mantra, but Green discounted the movement, since Swami was blowing on it, as he forcefully recited his mantra.[9] About two weeks later, a second attempt took place. This time Swami Rama wore a mask and an elaborate and controlled set-up was employed. According to Boyd, who sat on a couch to the left of Swami, psychokinesis clearly and dramatically occurred during this test session.[10]

Another episode suggesting Swami Rama's special gifts is related by Boyd. A woman came to see Swami with her 3½-year-old son, who had been very ill but was not responding to his physician's treatment. Swami told the child's mother: "The problem is the child's *heart.*" He further suggested that an electrocardiogram be done and also asked the boy to choose a picture of a holy man from a group of pictures. Swami asked the mother to hang the chosen picture, an image of Christ, in the child's room. When the mother told the doctor about consulting a swami, the doctor requested that she find another physician. The cardiologist who ultimately examined the EKG detected a heart abnormality. Swami explained how he knew about the child's physical ailment: "I called the boy, and he came to me in his astral body. I said, 'What's the matter with you?' And he said, 'In this life I have a defective heart.' "[11] The boy's condition improved and the mother attributed it to the change in doctors, the Swami's blessing of and continued meditation for the child, and the picture of Christ still hanging in the child's room.

A story that was told by Swami Rama suggested his

attitude about his life and his work: "There was an aspirant with an unquenchable, burning desire for the *darsan* of a particular wise and powerful saint. In his youth he traveled a great distance to see the saint, but as he was not received, he returned to his village and spent 30 years of his life preparing to try again. For 30 years he worked perpetually and perseveringly to develop his faith and his concentration and he repeated his mantra so many times and developed such powerful concentration that he found he could produce fire from his mouth at will. Ecstatic with joy, he journeyed to find the saint, to implore him to be his spiritual teacher and lead him to knowledge. Because the saint had been in the man's thoughts for 30 years, the saint gave the man audience.

"The moment the man saw the saint, he prostrated

Swami Rama meditates in a special cubicle on the Institute's grounds in Glenview, Illinois on June 17, 1977.

himself at his feet. He could not help but say, 'For thirty years I have dreamed of seeing you. Thirty years I have spent in constant work and devotion!'

"The saint said, 'So?'

"'I have developed intense faith,' the man declared, 'and intense powers of concentration.'

"Again the saint said, 'So?'

"'I can produce fire from my mouth.'

"'Go and begin doing something useful,' the saint said calmly. 'When we are all having matches, why have you wasted your time?' "[12]

On a visit to the Himalayan International Institute, I had the opportunity to meet Swami Rama. Although I had informed the public relations staff that I was including a chapter on him and the Institute in a book I was writing, I do not know whether he knew that when he came into the dining room where I was eating lunch. I was told that, although he frequently interacts with people in the dining room, he takes his meals alone. Swami entered the dining room wearing a maroon velvet robe. He said hello to a man at one of the tables, looked toward the table where I was seated with two associates, and then came over to us. He inquired as to when we had arrived and how long we were staying. He appeared to be a warm, personable man with great physical presence. When one of my associates told him that I was writing about the Institute, he shook his head in acknowledgment, but did not verbally respond. He then said hello to a group of people who were eating in silence and walked over to a table where a woman was trying to quiet her crying infant. The Swami said to the child, who was about one year old: "Oh, you're a big boy. What's all this about?" When the child continued to cry, Swami picked him up, while looking in our direction, and the child immediately stopped crying. He gave the baby back to his mother, waved farewell to us, and left the room.

The Organization and Activities of the Institute

The Institute, located in the Pocono Mountains of northeastern Pennsylvania, consists of a brick main building constructed in 1954, a small guest house, the Eleanor Naylor Dana Research Laboratory, two tennis courts, two outdoor racquetball courts, a basketball court, a farm, and an organic garden surrounded by 420 acres of magnificent field and forest land. There are nature trails, a clear lake, and springs, all adding to the sense of serenity and beauty. The main building contains over 100 rooms for residents, each containing a sink, closet, lamp, and mattress. There are also classrooms, offices, a dining room, kitchen, an auditorium, a library, woodworking and ceramic shops, a photography studio, and a bookstore. The bookstore contains a wide variety of books covering topics ranging from nutrition to photography to homeopathy. In addition, the bookstore sells pottery, greeting cards, incense, tapes, and records (for example, music for zen meditation).

The Institute staff consists of several M.D.'s, Ph.D.'s, nurses, and therapists, all of whom are trained in both Eastern and Western approaches and who continually participate in self-development programs at the Institute. There are numerous programs which focus on attaining a balance among the physical, emotional, mental, and spiritual dimensions of the individual in order to achieve optimal health and growth. The training programs, research, and courses at the Institute utilize material from the fields of philosophy, psychology, and medicine. "Underlying all of its programs, however, is the philosophy and practice of Superconscious meditation, a systematic method for developing every level of one's consciousness."[13] Although all programs have the same general philosophy, each has a specific emphasis.

Admission to the Himalayan International Institute Residential Program is permitted through the approval of

Swami Rama. The initial residential program lasts for three months, but it can be extended for six months or longer if the Swami approves. The fee was $400 per month, which included room, board, and training. According to its brochure, this program is designed to provide the opportunity for the development of "skills for functioning successfully in the external world. In this setting one can reassess oneself, one's goals and purpose in life." The following schedule of activities is strictly adhered to by the participants six out of seven days a week:

5:30 A.M. Rise
6:00 A.M. Group prayers and meditation
7:00 A.M. Individual practice or hatha-yoga class
8:15 A.M. Breakfast
9:00 A.M. Work duties
1:15 P.M. Lunch
2:00 P.M. Rest
2:30 P.M. Work duties
5:30 P.M. Meditation
6:00 P.M. Dinner
7:00 P.M. Classes, study, recreation or work
10:00 P.M. Group prayers and meditation
10:30 P.M. Rest

From 10 in the evening until the next morning at 8 o'clock, silence is observed. Participants are trained in diet, ethical behavior, hatha-yoga (physical exercises), meditation, and community living. The work chores are an integral part of the program. Residents do housekeeping, gardening, cooking, baking, construction, and clerical work. Cynthia Bretheim, a public relations staff member, explained the rationale for these duties: "They learn how to work with people and how to work in general.... People work in different areas regardless of their backgrounds, which gives them additional skills and helps them adjust to change." However, one criticism of this aspect of life at the

Institute is that residents may be exploited. They are paying a fee for the opportunity to work.

There are a number of explicit rules that residents are expected to strictly observe. Drugs are prohibited because they artificially "alter the mind" and therefore counter the purpose of the residential program. The diet is completely vegetarian. Residents live on campus, and are supposed to demonstrate self-control with regard to mind and behavior. If they wish to leave the grounds at any time, they must request special permission, and must sign in and out when leaving the main building for any reason, including going for a walk. Speech and communication are to be carefully monitored by the individual; there are periods of silence each day. All residents are expected to maintain a spiritual diary which is confidential. In addition, the descriptive brochure indicates: "For the duration of the stay the resident shall have no emotional relationship inside or outside the Institute. This is intended for the student to concentrate his energy in the program in order to achieve the maximum benefit and to avoid distractions."

In general, residents are discouraged from engaging in any activities that will distract them from their work and spiritual practices. Thus, outings to town, extensive correspondence, or deep interpersonal relationships inside or outside the Institute are not encouraged while in the program. However, one year-long resident told me: "Getting ice cream is a big thrill. People sneak out for a few sweets once in a while; everyone does it except Swami Rama. I also go to the movies sometimes." Participation in political activities is also not allowed. As one resident remarked: "Most people who come here are apolitical." Residents are expected to wear "clean, modest, orderly dress." They are not permitted to apply for any kind of public financial assistance, including unemployment insurance.

The rules of behavior of the Residential Program are applied to the Self-Transformation Program as well. The program lasts from one to three months and participants were charged $500 per month for room, board, and training. The brochure for this program describes the program's purpose: "... to make students aware of the reality within and, by increasing their awareness, to gradually lead them to deeper levels of spiritual understanding and experience." The schedule which follows differs in certain respects from the one for those in the Residential Program:

5:00 A.M. Rise, bathe
5:30 A.M. Joints and glands exercises or postures
6:00 A.M. Group meditation
7:00 A.M. Hatha-yoga or breathing practice (class when scheduled)
8:15 A.M. Breakfast
9:00 A.M. Light work duties
11:15 A.M. Study of prescribed books
12:30 P.M. Practice of postures, breathing, meditation
1:15 P.M. Lunch
2:30 P.M. Light work duties
4:30 P.M. Study time
5:30 P.M. Meditation
6:00 P.M. Supper
7:00 P.M. Classes, recreation or study
9:30 P.M. Postures, breathing
10:00 P.M. Group meditation
10:30 P.M. Rest

Students are asked to consider the degree of motivation and self-discipline that will be necessary to achieve the maximum benefit from this program and to make their decision to enroll based upon that consideration.

Another Institute program, described in its brochure as "a unique therapeutic and experiential opportunity, developed to provide medical care in a setting conducive to self-observation and self-understanding," is the Combined Therapy Program. A comprehensive medical and psychological examination, including, if necessary, blood chemistry, breathing tests, nutritional analysis, hair analysis, and exercise stress-test, is provided initially to each participant. The underlying philosophy of this holistic health program is that individuals can reestablish healthier patterns of living and increased personal growth through review of one's life goals, attention to diet, exercise, training in relaxation, resolution of emotional problems, and stress reduction techniques. Exercise programs include yoga training to help quiet the body and aerobic exercise to increase the efficiency of the cardio-respiratory system. Biofeedback is used to aid individuals to recognize and control various physical and mental states. Both Western medicine and traditional Eastern medicine, such as homeopathy, are practiced by the staff of M.D.'s.

According to the staff of the Institute, the Combined Therapy Program is particularly effective for those with psychosomatic or stress-related disorders such as asthma, hypertension, colitis, and ulcers. Improvement for problems such as alcoholism, intense anxiety, depression, obesity, and cigarette smoking has also been cited as a result of participation in the program.

The individually tailored program cost $1,400 for a two-week session. For an additional $300, those who completed the Combined Therapy Program could participate in a follow-up program, which provides the opportunity for a weekly scheduled telephone consultation with a staff physician for a three-month-period.

The Holistic Health Training Program is an intensive ten-day program, costing $500 for room, board, and training in nutrition, breathing, aerobic exercise, hatha-yoga, biofeedback, and cleansing and purification techniques. A Self-Development Research Program is also offered by the Institute in collaboration with the Eleanor Naylor Dana Research Laboratory. Medical, stress, nutritional, and personality evaluations are conducted, followed by research testing to determine the individual areas of greatest stress sensitivity and reactions to that stress. The program consists of training in biofeedback, breathing, and self-study for periods of three, five, seven days, or longer if warranted. During that time, physiological responses including heart and respiration rate, skin blood flow, muscle tension, digestion, and brain activity are monitored.

A Diploma Program, offered at the main headquarters and at branch centers, begins with hatha-yoga and the development of flexibility, stamina, and general bodily control, and continues with courses in meditation, concentration of attention, and expansion of awareness.

The Five-Day Stress Management/Physical Fitness Program, with a fee of $750, is based on the assumption that people who feel well are creative and productive. Its brochure announced: "The goal of successful stress management is to maintain, at a high level, efficient, creative performance, sustained over years and decades, integrated with satisfying human relationships, personal well-being, and deepening insight and wisdom." The Institute suggests that it is necessary to increase our knowledge of and sensitivity to the interaction between the physical and psychological states that are relevant to how we respond to stress. Moreover, the program provides practical training in the use of tools and skills to modify inefficient or undesirable patterns of reactions to stress. Following an extensive evaluation of the individual's physical, dietary, respiratory, and relaxation habits and functioning, specific training and recommendations are offered in areas such as aerobic exercises, stretching postures, time management, motivational techniques, and biofeedback. Special one- and two-day workshops in stress management are offered at branch centers and can be provided as well to corporations at their headquarters.

An Intensive Purification and Self-Development Program begins with a weekend educational seminar followed by a review of the participant's health status and offers practice in yoga, cleansing teachniques such as juice fasting, and periods of silence. The program, with a fee of $400, concludes with a weekend seminar.

A Weight-Loss Self-Awareness Program combines the facilities and staff of the Combined Therapy Program with the principles of self-transformation. This program focuses on enabling participants to resolve the emotional and mental problems that lead to obesity. Medical and nutritional evaluations are provided at the outset, followed by training in biofeedback, exercise, juice fasting, and self-development. The program lasts four weeks and cost $1,500. Participants may choose to remain longer.

An interesting program, with a two-day minimum stay, is the Meditation Vacation. Of all the programs at the Himalayan Institute, this one probably offers the least structure and the lowest fee. Participants are given a room in a quiet part of the main building and are free to relax and practice meditation. They can also engage in sports activities such as swimming and tennis, and attend lectures and classes as they desire. The $25 per day for single occupancy and $20 per person for double occupancy included the room and three vegetarian meals, but not the lectures and classes.

Three-, five-, or ten-day silence programs, which cost $125, $200, and $350, respectively, provide an "opportunity to create the proper inner and outer atmosphere for intensive self-study. . . ." Participants are trained "to quell the agitation of troublesome memories and thoughts and how to bring forth the creativeness of the subconscious."[14]

A special Biofeedback Meditation Program was offered at a cost of $75, for five one-hour sessions. Participants are trained to use modern scientific instruments such as the electromyograph, which reports the degree of muscle tension. This program is intended to help individuals to recognize tension buildup so that he or she can learn to relax the area and facilitate healing. Meditation is also enhanced through the use of biofeedback, "since higher consciousness can only be achieved when one has quieted the body and mind and reaches a state of inner awareness."[15]

Various training programs for professionals are also given at the Himalayan Institute. The Training Program for Counselors and Therapists consists of four days of lectures on meditation, breathing, yoga, psychology, and their integration with psychotherapy; instruction in the use of biofeedback equipment and techniques, meditation, and yoga; and discussion of Eastern and Western approaches to psychopathology and mind/body interactions. In some instances the fee of $175 was reduced through partial scholarships based on need. A three- to six-month Training Program in Combined Therapy is offered for those who want to work as staff members in a setting similar to the Combined Therapy Program of the Institute. The cost of $500 per month covered training in the use of biofeedback, videofeedback therapy, cleanses and washes, herbal packs, steam baths, stretching exercises, hatha-yoga, breathing, meditation exercise, nutrition, and supportive counseling.

A Training Program for Diet and Nutrition focuses either on applied nutrition or nutritional research. Trainees do clinical work, receive practical experience in food preparation and conduct a research project in the nutritional field. The fee and length of training were identical to those of the Combined Therapy Training. A six-month training program for physicians focuses on supervised clinical practice in applying the holistic health model of the Institute.

In affiliation with the University of Scranton, the Himalayan International Institute offers a Program in Eastern Studies and Comparative Psychology leading to a Master of Science degree. All students are required to complete 48 credits of course work including a thesis or its equivalent. Those students who are lacking in knowledge of the techniques of self-knowledge, including hatha-yoga and meditation, are required to take these courses on a noncredit basis. There are three areas of concentration: Eastern Studies, a systematic examination of ancient schools of Indian thought and philosophy, including Buddhism, yoga and Vedanta, and their contribution to an understanding of human nature; Comparative Psychology, a study of yoga psychology, Buddhist psychology, and modern psychology combined with training in holistic psychotherapeutic techniques; and Holistic Therapies, training in the design and implementation of health programs with a holistic perspective.

The program includes courses in concepts in consciousness; yoga anatomy and physiology; comparative systems of psychology; Sanskrit; diet and nutrition; yoga, meditation, and Western science; and yoga: research design, methodology, and analysis. The two-year residential program costs about $5,000 per year and provides seminars, laboratory work, lectures, and opportunities for personal practice of acquired skills.

Apart from the specialized Master of Science program in Eastern Studies and Comparative Psychology, the Himalayan Institute and its branch centers offer numerous courses and lectures to the public. For example, recent offerings have been vegetarian cooking, introduction to meditation, creative use of personality, survey of holistic health, the quest for immortality, reincarnation and philosophy of karma, and science of breath.

Systematic scientific research has been a particular focus of the Himalayan Institute since 1979 and in 1980 the Eleanor Naylor Dana Research Laboratory was established. This laboratory is equipped for exercise stress-testing and psychophysiological measurements of brain waves, respiration, heart rate, and muscle tension. The Institute is interested in further developing valid effective measuring techniques to be used to determine the efficacy of the natural forms of healing taught in yoga and Ayurvedic medicine. The Institute's quarterly *Research Bulletin* contains articles describing ongoing concerns and projects of the laboratory, including findings of experimental investigations. For example, a 1981 edition contained the following articles: "Pranayama" (the science of breath), by Swami Rama; "Respiration, Heart Rate and the Autonomic Nervous System: An Introduction," by John Clarke, a Harvard-educated M.D.; "Stress: A New Perspective," by E. Phillip Nuernberger, Ph.D. in counseling psychology from the University of Minnesota; and "Changes in Respiration with a Mental Task: An Experimental Study," by Edwin Funk, M.D., from the University of Chicago.[16] Funk's article reported on his research, which was concerned with changes in breathing while solving mental mathematics problems. This task was chosen because it was thought to be similar to the common types of mental tasks faced every day. Fifteen women and 13 men were first asked to relax and then to subtract seven from 100 in sevens. A comparison of their breathing patterns during these two phases revealed a marked increase in rate of breathing accompanied by more shallow breathing during the attention-focusing problem. Results of the comparison of chest and abdominal breathing during the two experimental phases are less clear-cut and Funk suggested the need for further research in this area. The applications of breathing research to anxiety and therapeutic modification are cited in the article.[17]

Each June, the Himalayan Institute sponsors an International Congress where professionals and lay people can examine and integrate ancient Eastern traditions and current research in the health sciences through lectures, workshops, and practica over a four day period. Applications to child care, self-improvement, and aging are explored from a body/mind/spirit holistic perspective.

The Institute is also involved in publishing. The Himalayan Institute Publishers and Distributors specialize in books in the areas of philosophy, the health sciences, and psychology, and sell to over a thousand bookstores, health food stores, and libraries in the United States. More than 15 percent of Himalayan Institute books are sold through a mail-order business. A newspaper, *Himalayan News*, with a reported circulation of 32,000, is published bimonthly by the Institute, and distributed free of charge. Its July/August 1981 edition contained articles such as "Breath Awareness and Meditation," by Swami Rama; "Polyunsaturates Pro and Con," by Rudolph Ballentine, M.D.; and "Body Language," by Swami Ajaya, Ph.D.

Beliefs and Practices

To provide greater understanding of the nature of the Himalayan International Institute, some of their basic beliefs and practices will be examined in detail below.

The practice of yoga is strongly emphasized at the Institute. Psychologist E. Phillip Nuernberger stated in one of the Institute's publications, *Dawn:* "Yoga has been described in many ways, ranging from being called a religion to being labeled an occult mystical practice. What has yet to be clearly recognized and understood in this country is that yoga is actually a highly developed and a systematized science. Like any other science, yoga is based on empirical data derived from experimental practices. Where it differs radically from 'Western' science is that yoga is an experiential science rather than an 'objective' science. In other words, yoga is the science of consciousness, not the science of the material world."[18]

Swami Rama has also commented about the widespread misunderstanding of yoga: "I think maybe less than one percent of all people understand the true meaning of yoga. The others—either they think nothing at all about yoga, or they think that yoga is standing on the head. All right. Let them stand on their heads—I also do. But let them not say this is yoga. My dear friends, to stand on your own two feet is yoga and nothing more!

"Yoga is the control of the modifications of the mind. Yoga is a system of understanding one's own nature, becoming the master of that nature, and using that mastery for higher purpose. But here, discipline is required. No self-mastery can be accomplished without discipline."[19]

Rudolph Ballentine, a physician on the staff of the Himalayan Institute, writing in *Dawn* magazine, further described the work of the yoga student: "From the very beginning the yoga student learns to turn his attention inward to become aware of processes that most of us ignore. He finds a quiet place to work, he relaxes the muscles, he calms the mind. In effect he does everything possible to eliminate all the noise and static which can obscure his perception of what goes on inside himself.... He can then learn to regulate and control. He can become aware of developing tension in the neck or forehead for instance, and then, before it develops into a tension headache, he can consciously and voluntarily relax it. It becomes an integral part of his total self-awareness."[20]

There are various forms of yoga taught at the Institute. For example, hatha-yoga was described by Ballentine in the *Dawn* article as "a systematic training program for gradually expanding one's self-awareness so that areas of the body that were previously operating outside awareness and with inadequate regulation can be brought into consciousness and harmoniously integrated with the rest of the system."[21] The introductory hatha-yoga class begins with exercises for joints and glands, and teaches progressive relaxation techniques, and proper posture and breathing.

Diet is also an important aspect of yoga. Certain foods are considered to have a *rajasic* effect, that is, they make individuals feel jittery and tense. *Tamasic* foods, a second category, make an individual feel sluggish. The *sattvic* diet, including such foods as wheat, milk, and fruit, on the other hand, makes the individual feel cheerful and alert. Although a vegetarian diet is often stressed in yoga, Ballentine said in another *Dawn* article that "one should not go to any extremes. To force oneself to do things that are radically different from what is customary is more disruptive than helpful. For a lot of people, a vegetarian diet is an extreme thing.... So it is not essential to become a vegetarian. On the other hand, one should become aware of his habits."[22]

The practice of meditation, an important aspect of yoga, is also stressed at the Institute. There are many different levels of meditation. Pandit Usharbudh Arya, Ph.D., a faculty member of the Himalayan Institute, writing about the relationships among yoga, meditation, and Christianity, suggested: "Whatever meditation you do, a spiritual instructor, a *guru,* is absolutely necessary."[23]

Swami Rama described the meaning and aim of meditation: "The word *meditation* is used in various ways, but it always applies to techniques which deal with man's inner nature.... Meditation does not require a belief in dogma or in any authority. It is an inward journey in which one studies one's own self on all levels, finally going to the source of consciousness.... It is not an intellectual pursuit, nor is it emotional rapture.... It is neither suppression (which makes one passive), nor is it a gaining of any experience which is not already within us."[24] He also suggested that meditation can be practiced "first, by having the right spiritual attitude—by performing selfless action in the external world. This is called meditation in action.... Another method of meditation is to sit in a calm and quiet place, on a firm seat, in a relaxed and comfortable posture. Then become aware of the breath, and then make the mind one-pointed by allowing the mind to attend to the flow of breath. When the mind has become concentrated, the word or mantra (a sound or word to make the mind one-pointed) given for meditation should be remembered. Constant remembrance of the mantra leads the student to a higher state of mind, and such a mind is capable of going beyond its limitations."[25]

Nuernberger has reviewed some of the scientific literature concerned with the unique effects of meditation. For example, he cited reports of the lowering of the basal metabolism rates, and decreases in the amount of oxygen used and the frequency of breathing, as results of meditation. In addition to various physiological effects, he suggested psychological effects of meditation, such as reduced anxiety. He also reported that meditation has been used successfully in clinical settings, in the treatment of phobias and as a suicide preventive.[26]

One of the most interesting practices of the Himalayan Institute is homeopathic medicine. The basic principles of this discipline are described in a book entitled *Homeopathic Remedies for Physicians, Laymen and Therapists,* written by three physicians trained at the Institute: David Anderson, Dale Buegel, and Dennis Chernin. The principles of homeopathy go back to ancient India's Ayurvedic medicine and Greece's Hippocrates. Dr. Samuel Hahnemann, a German chemist and physician, worked with this healing system in the late 1700's and named it homeopathy. The three fundamental laws of homeopathy are the Law of Similars, the Law of Proving, and the Law of Potentization.

The Law of Similars states that the same medicine that cures the symptoms of an individual will produce those symptoms in a healthy person who ingests it. The Law of Proving "involves the systematic verification of the first law"[27] by daily administration of a homeopathic substance to a healthy person. When signs and symptoms arise that are similar to those consistently recorded in a sick person, the remedy that had given rise to those symptoms in the healthy person is prescribed. The Law of Potentization states that the remedy's power lies in its qualitative aspects, rather than in the amount or quantitative aspects. "Potentization is effected mechanically by first diluting the remedy and then by forcefully shaking (succussion) or mixing (triturition). This process can be repeated from one to over one million times. The result of this process is a medicinal substance whose properties are extremely potent, yet nontoxic, as there is very little physical substance to cause toxicity. For example, if enough crude arsenic is taken, death ensues; but if arsenic is first potentized, an effective and safe remedy results."

Another significant concept of homeopathic healing is the Vital Force, which "is the energy which animates and drives the human being and which integrates the mind, body, and soul of man."[28] Anderson, Buegel, and Chernin suggest that while most medicines act only to temporarily improve the condition, homeopathic remedies "act to direct and realign the Vital Force itself, thus fine-tuning the essential balance within the individual."

Homeopathic medicine fits in with the holistic health emphasis of the Himalayan Institute. "Proper selection of the remedy must be based on the whole person. . . . All mental and emotional sensations and physical signs must be integrated into a complete picture."[29] The following are examples of the kind of homeopathic remedies that would be prescribed for particular respiratory infection symptoms:

> "*Aconite:* to be given at the first sign of respiratory infection, especially if it comes on after exposure to a dry, cold draft. Frequent sneezing, fever, thirst, and restlessness at night. Cough is dry, with a hard ringing sound. Generally only useful during the onset of the infection."[30]
>
> "*Nux Vomica:* Infection starts from exposure to dry coldness or after overindulgence of food or sex, and is associated with much sneezing with the nose alternately blocked or running. Generally stopped up at night and streaming in a warm room and during the daytime. Feels extremely chilly and can't get warm. Will shudder after drinking fluids or from the least movement. Alternate chills and fever; excessively irritable. Cough is short, dry, and fatiguing, accompanied by headache and soreness in abdominal area."[31]

Another Eastern idea that is an important part of the Himalayan International Institute is karma. I attended a lecture on that subject at the New York City Himalayan center, given by Justin O'Brien, an Institute faculty member. Tape recording was not permitted at the lecture. About thirty people were in attendance, two thirds of them women. At the reception desk was a box for donations, but no one was asked to contribute. Early in his talk, O'Brien cautioned the audience: "We have to be careful, when we use the term karma, that we don't become fatalistic and think that's fate." He suggested that "an understanding of karma is an understanding of our own lives." He tried to dispel certain myths about the concept. "Karma is not magical; it is not fatalistic. It is not some sort of spooky pessimistic phenomenon. Rather it is a recognition of the basic order in our lives, a cosmic law that affects every aspect of creation, of the Universe." He further explained that the word "karma" is Sanskrit, from a root meaning "action." Basically the nature of karma is reflected in the phrase, "As you sow, so shall you reap." There are two factors working in karma, the inherited aspect ("You come into life carrying karma with you") and the acquired portion ("As you go through life you add new karma . . . you are constantly involved in karma"). He remarked that *samskaras* (impressions from the past), desires, and insight twist together to make karma.

While animals have instincts, they do not possess karma, according to O'Brien. His basic perspective was rather optimistic. "Karma can free you. Karma can liberate you. Enlightenment can occur in and through the world. Live with the reality that you have created. Ignorance is our number one enemy. . . . The law of karma is an expression of your free will."

The notion of karma is certainly intimately associated with the idea of reincarnation. O'Brien noted that more people believe in reincarnation than do not. (He cited the large number of believers in India and Japan.) He continued: "There is something in each one of us that is eternal, that doesn't die. Our being has no beginning; it has no end. Reincarnation is determined by your own free volition. You reincarnate because you want to. You decided you wanted to come back. There is nothing to fear in reincarnation. It is another opportunity to experience life." One of the final ideas expressed in the lecture is that reincarnation doesn't have to hurt anyone's religion.

In general, the Institute is very careful about separating an individual's religious beliefs and practices from the philosophy and work of the Institute. When I first contacted the Institute and indicated that I was thinking of including them in a book about new religious movements and human potential groups, they explicitly stated that they were not to be considered a religious group. I was reminded of that position by several other people that I met at the Institute. However, one woman who was describing what the Institute offered her told me: "It's like religion in some ways. Religion has taught me certain things. They don't really teach religion here, but what I'm learning here is like a religion." An Institute program brochure stated: "All of the programs at the Institute are totally spiritually oriented.... There is no conversion of religion. Students may follow their own religion...." In discussing the relationship between religion and meditation, Swami Rama stated: "The practice of meditation in a systematic way, within a definite and accepted metaphysical framework, is congenial to all religious schools of the world, for their goal is the same—to bring the aspirants to the highest state of consciousness."[32]

Himalayan Institute Participants

Who participates in the programs at the Himalayan International Institute? While there are over 4,500 members, many of those who participate in programs are not formal members. The age of participants ranges from about 17 to 70, the greatest proportion of whom are in their 20's and 30's. There are approximately an equal number of men and women, and the participants and staff are overwhelmingly white. Of more than 150 people I saw at the Honesdale Institute and at the New York City Himalayan center, only two were black; there were a few Indian residents and staff members.

With regard to the type of individuals who participate in programs at the Himalayan Institute, one interviewee told me: "You can't categorize the people who work or live here. They are intelligent and hard-working." My impression is that generally they have a serious attitude about the work of self-improvement or transformation and their behavior is rather subdued. As we walked through the halls of the main building, people did not smile or say hello unless they were addressed first. Those instances in which individuals behaved in a more ebullient manner stood out because of the incongruity with the overall atmosphere of the Institute. For example, three young men talking rather loudly about baseball during lunch were quite noticeable. It was almost as if they were there by mistake.

Michael Meyers, in his late 20's, had been in the Residential Program for a couple of months when we talked about his involvement with the Institute. He had a Master's degree in English literature and had previously been in the book promotion department of a large university publishing house, which he left to live at the Himalayan Institute. His wife is also in the residential program. He explained his motivation: "Yoga has been the focus of our lives for years. Here there are no obstacles to our personal growth. Honesdale is the place to be. I do believe in the work of the Institute. It is helping me to become a better person. This was the next step to take, to actually live here." He described his work duties at the Institute, an integral part of the Residential and Self-Transformation Programs. "There is a mutual trade-off. The arrangement is mutually beneficial."

Another participant, a rather obese man, had been in the Weight-Loss Self-Awareness Program for just three weeks and had already lost 20 pounds. He had been moving up in his business, but decided to give it all up to lose weight at the Institute. He planned to stay for three more months. "I have another hundred pounds to go," he explained.

One of the residents who is also a staff member told me: "The Institute begins to help people live more satisfying lives. Many people come to take a look at their lifestyle to see how it's affecting them. They may not have any real complaints."

Robin Madison, a 17-year-old girl, was taking a course while on summer vacation before her senior year of high school; she was staying with her cousin who lives in a nearby town. I met her as she walked off the tennis court after a game with a friend who was visiting the Institute for the day. Robin described her reasons for being at the Himalayan International Institute: "I have a craving to learn. I'm interested in philosophy, in ideas, in certain things that the Institute has to offer. I've heard about meditation and hatha-yoga. The atmosphere here is more intense. One can learn more quickly.... At first, it seemed rather restrictive. I wasn't sure what I was getting into. But now, I really like it. When I graduate, I'd like to come here for the three-month residence program.... I'm here to find out who I am, my purpose in life. We've been fed a lot of things about life and death.... I got so high being here. They've told me things that I had been thinking of all along. There must be something to it if so many people are involved in it."

I asked Robin about the reaction of her friends and family to her involvement with the Institute. "My parents are very supportive of my doing this. They live in Pittsburgh. My mother would do it if she could. I taught my mother some yoga and she taught me some. Some of my friends have done hatha-yoga and are really supportive. Some of my friends from school tease me, but that comes from not understanding. Most of my classmates are not interested." She laughed as she added, "They're interested in beer, make-up, drugs, and rock 'n' roll."

I spoke to Marie Saunders, a soft-spoken and articulate

high school graduate in her late 20's, who has been a resident for nine months. Before coming to the Institute she had worked in a bank, in a Midwest city, for eight years and had recently completed a training program for a higher position. She had been meditating since she took a transcendental meditation course in 1977. "I decided there was something more for me to do and I gave my notice and I decided to go to the East Coast." She found a notice on a bulletin board requesting a driver to drive a car to the Institute. The car belonged to a staff physician and Marie found herself staying at the Institute for a week. "I loved the place so much that when I left I nearly cried. . . . I felt that I would be back sometime." When she returned to her hometown, she opened up a couple of part-time businesses ("fantasy careers"), but decided she should either commit herself to one of them full-time or go to work for a large company. However, before she had the time to make that decision, she met Swami Rama at an Open House. She recalled, "He said: 'When are you coming out?' And that was it. That's what I had been looking for. It hadn't really occurred to me, but within three weeks, I had finished off all my business ties, packed up my things and moved out here." She spoke about Swami Rama with great affection. "He's a big papa. He knows everybody."

She described her family's reaction. "My mother goes from fear to elation—from wondering what I'm doing here and 'Who is this Swami character? Are you involved in a cult? What is it you are doing out there? When are you coming back? When are you going to be working in a real business situation?' Then she goes through periods of: 'Are you really happy? Are you healthy?' I'm going to visit her in August [the interview took place in July]. . . . I'm her only daughter so she's pretty concerned about me still." Marie repeated a recent telephone conversation in which her mother told her: "You get flak from me, you get flak from Grandma, because we don't understand what you're doing or why you're there, but I want to tell you now that one of the reasons we get so upset is that you're doing what we should be doing. We're not finding the happiness that you're getting. So I don't care what you're getting there, what you're doing, as long as you're happy."

She also described her father's reaction: "He would like me to be home. He misses me very, very much. At the same time he knows I'm doing what I need to do. He wouldn't say, 'Please come home,' but he tells me what is happening in the business world."

Richard Crane, a friendly 20-year-old who had just completed a year of residence at the Institute, described the circumstances under which he became involved: "I was in a very confused state. I had gone from being a straight A college student to failure. I had a really bad experience with a girl. I liked her a lot and she didn't like me. I also had a lot of spiritual questions. It was a lot at the same time—triple play. I had been interested in yoga and Eastern philosophy. My mom is a yoga teacher.... I was also very heavy. I lost 70 pounds since I've been here and have kept it off for about three to four months now. My health was really bad because of my weight. I had always had some kind of weight problem and this is the longest that I've kept the weight off." I had a hard time imagining Richard as a sickly, obese person. When I met him he was a healthy, good-looking young man with no weight problem.

He described his family's reaction: "My mother was for it, but my grandfather and old friends were adamantly against my being here. My father left when I was very young." He also discussed his religious background: "I've had lots of exposure to various religions. My stepfather is Jewish and my mother is Presbyterian, but neither is religious. I liked Bible stories and went to the synagogue when I was younger. During high school I went to a Presbyterian church when I became interested in spiritual matters. But I soon became disenchanted.... I was a physics major in college and started recognizing parallels to Eastern thought. Part of my religious belief now is to be healthy and to take care of my body."

Finally, Richard described how he had changed (aside from his weight loss) in the year he had been in residence at the Institute. "I've found a method to learn about myself. I will be leaving in a month to pursue a career in medicine. My interest in medicine came from here. The kind of practice I develop will be in the direction of what goes on here. I will have to adjust to four years of traditional medical school.... I have become more tolerant of others. We are trying to explore relationships here. We talk honestly with each other. Some people I'm very close to; some I don't like; some I feel neutral about, just like anywhere else.... Even though the brochure says 'no emotional involvement,' I learned the most here about close relationships. I learned a lot here. I thought the focus would be on yoga and meditation. I did learn that, but it was the other things that led me to growth, how to relate to others.

"We are very busy here, but we work together; we're encouraged to work together, to work out problems. But we are discouraged from having close interpersonal relationships with the opposite sex. People are very discreet. People could be asked to leave if they act in bad taste. Sexual pressures are taken off so I can really get to know a girl. Swami Rama does say that ultimate celibacy is actually for very few. Some people are dating, but they do not hold hands or kiss openly.... I've also learned self-discipline. This is a model situation of how people can and should be—working hard for themselves, for others."

Evaluation and Future Outlook

The Himalayan International Institute of Yoga Science and Philosophy may be a model situation for some participants, but it does have its drawbacks. There is a certain rigidity to the structure of the programs. Although an increase in self-discipline is a major goal of the Institute, only certain kinds of individuals have the personal qualities that would allow them to initially follow the rules. In fact, a number of residents do not explicitly follow the rules of the Institute. For example, a public telephone was located in the bathroom off the lounge in the main building. Throughout the day, women could be found engaged in long, serious telephone conversations about family matters. In addition, work roles are more strictly defined along traditional lines than is usually found in modern American organizations. I was told that Swami Rama's Indian background and its rather strict division of labor between males and females has an effect on the activity at the Institute. One of the male interviewees told me: "Women are given serious responsibilities here. I am answerable to many women. But men do the heavy work and sometimes the not-so-heavy work that could be done by women. I sometimes resent that. The regular kitchen work is done by women, while the construction work is done by men. Women generally do the office work."

A second issue that sometimes arises concerns the difficulty some residents have in re-entering "the world." The atmosphere of the Institute is so idyllic and set off from everyday problems—no political activities, no emotional involvements, no work pressures—that there may be a significant period of readjustment, particularly when the individual has been a resident for a relatively long period of time. Another related idea is that there is an almost exclusive focus on self-improvement, thus ignoring world problems.

Fourth, although the goals of the Eleanor Naylor Dana Research Laboratory (attempting to scientifically assess the efficacy of Eastern practices—meditation, homeopathy, and yoga breathing) are admirable, the reports of the research do not appear to meet the criteria for publication in outside professional journals. For example, the article by Funk, cited earlier, failed to report standard tests of statistical significance. If the Institute really wants to affect the consciousness of the Western culture, wider readership of its research findings is necessary, perhaps through publication of research studies in outside journals of health science. Further refinement of research techniques and questions seems to be an important avenue for further development of the Institute.

Another future direction of the Institute will probably concern the interface with industry. For example, an increasing number of corporations are seeking nontraditional ways to deal with traditional problems, such as work stress. The Institute already offers one- and two-day programs to reduce tension and increase productivity in employees.

Finally, as more and more individuals in the United States become interested in such activities and beliefs as yoga, meditation, biofeedback, and holistic health, the Institute will be able to grow and further exert its influence.

6: Institute for Psycho-Integrity

"If your problems make you unhappy, your problems are not your problem . . . your unhappiness is."

THAT phrase can be found on a great deal of the promotional literature disseminated by the Institute for Psycho-Integrity (IPI). The Institute, located in Ironia, New Jersey, has been in existence only since 1977. It is chartered by the State of New Jersey and is described as a "non-profit educational, clinical, and research agency." The founders of IPI, Dr. Lawrence H. Lentchner and Dr. Lawrence D. Spiegel, are New Jersey–licensed clinical psychologists and professors of psychology at a New Jersey community college.

Dr. Lentchner explained to me how and why the Institute was established: "We were quite satisfied with the education we were providing to our college students, and we were quite satisfied with the therapeutic experiences we were providing to our patients, but it was clear that something was missing. In our original attempt we were not thinking of an Institute per se. Our object was to put together an intensive program for transformation and enlightenment."

The philosophy of the Institute is suggested by the following from its 1981 spring/summer calendar: "Human beings need the opportunity to be able to continue to grow . . . to deepen and broaden their awareness and experience... to find the necessary support and assistance for self enrichment... to actualize and discover their greatest potential." Dr. Lentchner noted that, while there are other programs that attempt to do the same thing, "We felt that what was being accomplished could be accomplished in a more direct way." Dr. Spiegel observed: "We are part of a network, a very small part of a very large network of the human potential movement. We have a very specialized focus that no one else has used. We come from an academic, scientific tradition, rather than the Eastern, esoteric route, but it has led to the same path."

The specialized focus of IPI is the application of bilateral brain research to raise people's consciousness. In the 1960's Roger Sperry, a pioneer in the field of split-brain research (who was to win a Nobel Prize in physiology and medicine in 1981), discovered that when the corpus callosum (the connection between the right and left cerebral hemispheres) was cut in an attempt to control severe epileptic seizures, the patients began to show certain peculiarities. Although the patients maintained intellectual functions and lost little of the physical coordination needed for everyday activities (e.g., swimming), they could not verbalize the name of an object seen only by the left eye or touched only by the left hand. Through studying such patients, Sperry and others, including Dr. Robert Ornstein of the Langley Porter Neuropsychiatric Institute of California and the author of *Psychology of Consciousness,* began to recognize the specific functions of each cerebral hemisphere. The left cerebral hemisphere or left brain controls not only movement of the right side of the body, but also is the logical, analytical, verbal part. The right brain, on the other hand, controls movement of the left side of the body, and also is the artistic, emotional, intuitive, creative part. In the Institute's 1981 fall calendar, the founders and directors of IPI suggested: "Inasmuch as neither hemisphere can produce consciousness as we know it without the other, it is the integration of the two which gives our human mental capabilities their greatest potential."

An underlying assumption of the Institute is that most people in the United States are deficient in the use of the right cerebral hemisphere and rely too heavily on the left cerebral hemisphere. Ornstein is credited with inspiring much of the Integrity Experience, the major program of IPI. He noted that our current educational system teaches only half the brain, the analytical part. Thus, students are unable to understand the complex relationships between things, and the perception of whole systems. Spiegel further stated that, as a result of the repression of our right brain, there is "rampant lack of satisfaction and fulfillment, the voices fighting within our minds."

In a newspaper interview, Spiegel suggested that learning only in left-brained ways creates a "whole culture of people who are detached and distant from their feelings."[1] In an IPI brochure, the current state of brain imbalance was compared to a malfunctioning stereo: "What would you do if you came home one day, flipped on your stereo and found that 90 percent of the sound was coming out of the left speaker and only 10 percent of the sound from the right, regardless of what you did to the balance knob? Sooner or later you would have to face the fact that something is not working properly, and off to the repair shop you would go. Well . . . that's exactly what's going on inside most of our heads. Most of our 'brains' work more like the stereo system above—with one hemisphere dominating the other about 90 percent of the time."[2] All IPI programs are based upon the principles of "unifying and harmonizing the two separate hemispheres of the brain so as to produce a new sense of self and clarity of direction," according to the 1981 IPI spring/summer calendar.

The Institute for Psycho-Integrity was designed to serve the community in three areas: "educational programs and seminars for preventive mental health, low cost clinical/consulting services available to the general public and corporations, as well as research programs in bilateral brain theory."[3]

Dr. Spiegel is the director of Educational Services of the Institute. He received his Ed.D. from Rutgers University and is the chairperson of the Department of Psychology at the County College of Morris and faculty consultant to Thomas A. Edison State College. Dr. Lentchner is the director of the Clinical and Consulting Services at IPI. He received his Ph.D. from New York University and is an associate professor of psychology at County College of Morris and an adjunct faculty member of the New York University Graduate School.

The organization also has a developing research program, which is presently engaged in "theoretical, descriptive research... designed to relate directly to improving the quality of mental health services and to provide direct information to be used in helping individuals improve the quality of their lives."[4] According to the directors, the IPI Board of Trustees, composed of several business people, academicians, an attorney, and a physician, is an active, functioning body with a clear commitment to the organization.

At the IPI headquarters in Ironia, there are a number of signs like the following:

When I want what I do,
I do what I want.
When I do what I want,
I want what I do.

When you think you know,
what you know is you don't.

If I am I because you are you
then I am not I and you are not you.

To hold on, let go
To let go, hold on.

If you don't see what you get,
and you don't get what you see,
then you see what you don't get.

If, in order to make yourself right,
you have to make someone else wrong,
then right is wrong, and wrong is right.

It is interesting that, in an organization which attempts to emphasize right-brain, nonverbal functioning, one is surrounded by complex phrases that require left-brain analysis.

The Integrity Experience

The major thrust of IPI is the Integrity Experience, an intense 65- to 70-hour Human Growth Seminar held for four full days, usually for two consecutive weekends. In addition there is a pre-session on Wednesday prior to the first weekend, a mid-session between the two weekends, and a post-session on Wednesday evening following the second weekend of the Experience. It is held at a local university campus or hotel and the current fee is $340, although there is a discount for full-time students. Prior to participation, all applicants are interviewed to determine the appropriateness of the Experience for them. I expressed some concern to Spiegel about the effect of rejection on the individuals. He explained that either he or Lentchner will discuss the rejection with the applicant. Spiegel further noted: "It comes down to the fact that they're not being admitted to the Experience at this time. We will then sit down . . . and either recommend therapy of some kind . . . or other activities and we will tell them very clearly why they are not being admitted. There is only one criterion for not admitting a person for the Experience and that is, we don't feel it's going to give them maximum benefit at that point in time. There is no other criterion. That's what they're told. They're told that 'because of these reasons, we don't feel that this experience is worth the $340 that you're going to have to pay for it; we don't feel that it would be beneficial for you at this time.'"

Spiegel provided examples of the types of individuals who would be screened out—those who are "too intensely involved in their own psychopathology, that is, that they've got too many therapeutic issues going on and we don't think they're going to clear up, or... someone who is acutely psychotic." However, psychotics per se are not necessarily prevented from participating in the Experience. Spiegel explained: "We have had psychotics in the Experience, but our experience with that is that it will normally send them one way or the other way in an extreme sense. Either they go through the psychosis and come out on the other side or they get more psychotic than ever.... We are very clear to any psychotic individual. We will have a consultation with them and their family.... If we feel that there is an adequate support system for that person, in other words, the family member said: 'Yes, we know that this can happen; we are willing to take this person home afterward, not put them in a hospital,' then, one of us will continue to work with that person and we will eventually bring him through it."

About 50 to 75 individuals participate in each Integrity Experience. Lentchner further explained: "It may go up to 75, but no more. We stop at 75 because the experience has to be individualized. The individual has to work through any experiences that come up." The Experience is led by both Lentchner and Spiegel, although others are presently being trained to lead the groups. Also present are an M.D., a nurse, and floor coordinators (who are generally graduate psychology students) and assistant floor coordinators. A floor coordinator and an assistant will be responsible for a particular section of the room and will work with the same 10 to 15 people throughout the Experience.

During the pre-session, individuals are given information about the remainder of the Experience, so that they will not be surprised or shocked by what is in store for them. However, as a descriptive brochure pointed out, "the Integrity Experience cannot truly be spoken about. It can only be experienced." The actual Experience basically consists of three parts: Content, Processes, and Interacting.

The Content, according to Spiegel, "is primarily an understanding of how the left, logical hemisphere does what it does and what kind of an experience of the universe it gives you." Lentchner further explained: "In the Content portions of the Experience, people learn the nature of emotion and thinking, the different contributions of the two hemispheres." Thus, this part of the Experience is similar to a traditional learning situation.

The Process portion, in Spiegel's terms, is, "the antithesis of Content . . . learning the language of the right brain, which is essentially bodily sensations and feelings. There's nothing mystical about it. We teach what is essentially a combination of meditating and focusing. We're teaching people to generate an Alpha state for themselves, which is a meditative state. It's also a state of heightening." Self-hypnosis is also a part of the Process. Spiegel continued: "Everybody has an inherent capacity to go into these levels of consciousness, and they're very restful and very enjoyable levels. Once they're in that level of consciousness, then we are teaching them to listen to what their body is saying. And that's just a simple process of learning your body's language." Spiegel suggested that during the hypnotic and meditative states, issues that have been suppressed for 20 to 30 years will come up. People "will re-experience those kinds of things which they may have thought were dead issues."

A third component of the Experience, the smallest portion, is the Interactive aspect, in which individuals are free to share with each other in particular exercises, but that aspect is optional. While some participants do a tremendous amount of sharing, a minority of participants "stay with themselves," according to Lentchner. He pointed out that it is important that individuals have that option. "The looser ones get more respect from the group. The structure is such that people who need to, end up feeling very safe. Others learn from the ones who open up."

Lentchner suggested that the first day of the first weekend session "is heavily primal in terms of Process. There is a high level of nonverbal release, not an analytical release." In general, the first weekend appears to be devoted to unlearning and therapeutic issues, while the second is devoted to learning, transformation, or real consciousness-raising. It is the first day of the second weekend that is considered the real enlightenment day. According to Lentchner, the "transformation or enlightenment experience is a process of learning and unlearning. Thus the door of some level of consciousness or unconsciousness is opened to [participants]." This occurs on the third day because the participants need "one full day to get away from the door and into the consciousness itself."

During the first part of the post-session, held on Wednesday evening following the second weekend, there is a sharing session. Participants, or "graduates," as they are called at this stage, invite their friends and relatives who are interested in finding out more about the Experience and in understanding the changes that have occurred to the graduates. This is also one of the techniques used to recruit prospective participants for the next Experience. During the second part of the evening, after a brief coffee break, the graduates are separated from the guests. The graduates receive some final training in self-hypnosis and perhaps undergo other processes, while the guests are given information about the Experience (via the Content approach).

I was present during one of the post-sessions and noticed a pertinent sign on the stage:

> If I've lost it, I haven't shared it
> If I've shared it, I haven't lost it.

There is a great deal of kissing and hugging prior to the post-session and during the break. Some participants are young, wearing jeans, while others are older, wearing business suits. Most of the graduates appear to be in their late 20's to mid-30's.

Betty, a friendly, vivacious staff member, begins the post-session by asking: "Did you miss us?" She reminds the group that the Institute is nonprofit, that most of the staff volunteer their time and are not paid, including Lentchner and Spiegel (who are not yet present). While they are consistently referred to by everyone as "the doctors," everyone else is addressed by their first names and most of the graduates wear name tags with their first names on them. Forms are distributed to the participants requesting information about areas of expertise and possible committees individuals could serve on, such as fundraising, or public relations. Future courses are described, as is an experiential two-day Fall conference, The Consciousness of Everyday Life or the Zen of Pots and Pans. In addition, Betty describes a forthcoming couples' weekend Experience, focusing on interpersonal relationships; Saturday afternoon activities for children; and an adolescent Experience, still in the planning stages.

Betty asks the group to "[p]lease find some way to stay in touch. It's important to us and I'm sure to you. . . . It's your responsibility to hang onto it. You may ask: 'Will it stay with me?' It's stayed with me and the rest of the staff because we stayed in touch. The only way the growth can continue is by staying in touch." This theme is reiterated by other staff members. For example, Rick says: "We're all working voluntarily. The reason is we continue to share and stay in touch." Christie, another staff member, tells the audience: "The office is run by volunteers. We need more help. We'd love to have you share some time with us." She distributes cards requesting information about times people had available for volunteering. A separate form is distributed to guests asking for the individuals' name, address, age, sex, occupation, and phone number, as well as how we had heard about the Integrity Experience, and why we were attending tonight's session. A song, which included the words, "sharing all that we can give," is played, reflecting the theme of the session, and signaling the end of one aspect of the evening and the beginning of another.

Lentchner and Spiegel come up to the front of the auditorium. The latter begins the sharing session by saying: "Good evening." The group responds in unison to his greeting. After Spiegel simply states; "We're open to sharing," one graduate nervously laughs and no one else responds for several moments. Finally, Eleanor Longford, a rather outgoing British woman of about 30, addresses the group: "Shall I hang onto it or shall I share it? I never miss an opportunity for a pee break. Maybe I'll give it up or maybe I'll carry it with me. I don't have street directories: I have toilet directories. I was locked in a Parisian toilet, thinking 'Oh, my God.' [There is a great deal of laughter at this time.] A little voice says to me: 'You will not die in a Parisian toilet.' I remembered: there are no problems, only solutions. I started knocking on the door and Fred finally let me out and then ran in the opposite direction. . . . " Spiegel responds to this anecdote by asking: "Was it O.K. with you to be locked in a Parisian toilet?" Before the next contribution Spiegel notes: "That is not what we would call a typical sharing story."

A male graduate first apologizes for not being able to live up to the previous story: "I don't know if I can follow that." He continues: "I've been teaching a class and there is a person assisting me. We started talking about what was going on here. She said: 'It must be terrific; you haven't apologized yet, unlike the last time you taught it.' The class has been going so much better than the last class. It's working much better and it's fun." The leader's response is a simple, "Thank you."

Another male graduate reflects, "One thing I've found

from this Experience is to pay attention to my feelings. I'm gradually learning to express my feelings. Even though I'm Italian, I've never learned it. I always thought things." Spiegel responds: "Ain't that a trip?"

Another man points to Lentchner, who is sitting on the stage, and shares: "This man was doing a Process the first weekend and it was an experience that moved me more than anything that's ever happened to me. There was an enormous amount of power and love. I thought about it later. This man is putting out so much love that there's some for me. It's nice to be so tuned into your job. I also thank everyone who participated."

Allen goes to the front of the room and faces the group: "I'm frightened that I'm going to lose it. I was on a roller-coaster. People say I'm calmer now. Today I was calmer. Someone backed into my goddamn car. No matter what I did I was responsible. . . ." In reflecting on the Experience, Allen tells the audience: "I've paid my money and got a lot out of it."

Spiegel thanks Allen and another male graduate tells the group: "I confronted a monster in my dream. It happened to be someone from my childhood that I had never been able to confront before."

Eleanor Longford takes the floor again and asks: "Is it greedy to share or is it greedy not to share?" Spiegel asks her: "What is the answer?" She quickly retorts: "The hell with it." Spiegel tells her: "The answer is yes to both." Eleanor holds up a picture of her blind nephew. "I take responsibility for his blindness. When his mother was pregnant, my sister-in-law's child had German measles. I talked to a couple of people who told me not to raise a fuss... I've never gotten over the feeling that had I done more... I feel very responsible." "Take responsibility for your own," is Spiegel's reply. "Don't take responsibility for everything. I don't want to see you go back to what you were."

At this point, Carla Winters, a young woman who had walked into the post-session with the assistance of others, speaks in a slow, halting, strained voice. (I had thought when I first saw her entering the room that she was blind.) "I just experienced really being down. My father threw me out of the house. . . . I began to drink again. I was in the hospital Friday night with an overdose of pills. I was in intensive care and they didn't think I was going to make it. I was afraid to call my parents. . . . I had to really struggle to be here tonight. My dad doesn't want me; he's disgusted with me. I begged the doctors to let me go tonight. I needed all of you. It hurts like hell. I'm hurting a lot physically too." "Are you allowing yourself the hurt?" asks Spiegel. Carla replies: "I'm hurt." His quick response is: "No, you're anesthetic. Are you hurting now?" She answers: "Yes, but I don't know how to deal with it." Spiegel reiterates: "Are you hurting now?" Carla's reply is now a simple one: "Yeah." He responds: "Good. Thank you."

There are a couple of other sharing stories and the group breaks up for coffee and socializing. When we reconvene, we do so separately. Lentchner runs the session for the graduates, while Spiegel runs the guest session, which I attended. I observe that many more women guests are present than men. In addition, a number of staff members (wearing blue name tags) stand around the room during the guest session as they did during the sharing portion of the evening's program. We are told at first: "If you have not gone through the Experience, it's difficult to understand the Experience and what went on. . . . If you're using half the equipment, you're getting half the Experience."

Spiegel explains to us why people take the Experience and what it does for them. "People pursue success and when they achieve it—the house they want, the car they want, the job they want, and they land in my office or some other shrink's office, they tell us: 'I have everything and I'm not happy.' Being ready for the Experience means making the admission that you can have a better life. It's about how to deal with anxiety and fears. That's what we mainly deal with here. We emphasize in the Experience: There are no such things as problems—only solutions.

"The logical mind has a capacity to create within you a sense of yourself that is not real. . . . We've been taught not to look at ourselves . . . we receive little encouragement to fully explore who we are. A lot of people go through their lives, and when they're near death, they realize that they never really had the opportunity to do what they wanted.

". . . one of the important things about the Integrity Experience is you find out how your mind creates the reality. You can't understand the Integrity Experience; you can only experience it. What I consider to be most important is the moment they achieve that level of consciousness where they stop worrying about things. People have greater energy, are more open in relationships, are less worried. . . . The Experience consists of a lot of unlearning. A lot of energy goes into worrying. It is wasted energy. You have to be willing to be lost in order to be found. It's learning new rules of a game. This Experience gives you the rules to help you get a full sense of self. Once you've experienced that level of consciousness, you can't forget it. However, you don't achieve that level of consciousness and stay there forever. . . .

"One guarantee: You will not be experiencing things in the same way. What we're going to change is the way you see yourself. You get the ability to enjoy what you are, to change the experience of you. . . . People say they can't figure out if they're in love with someone. . . . It's based upon feelings, not thoughts. . . . If you are in touch with what you are, you'll find that feelings are not confusing. When you get a clear feeling, it's clear. Getting in touch with them will clear up 90 percent of your problems. If you're angry, it comes out. We are raised to be afraid to live and scared to die. Our lives are based on fear. People stay with relationships that are no longer fulfilling. They stay with jobs that were washed out long ago because they're afraid to do something new. . . .

When I ask someone: 'How do you feel about something?' nine out of ten answer, 'I think.' I say: 'No, What do you feel?' and they say: 'I'm doing.' 'No, what are you *feeling?*' They say: 'I don't know.' "

At this point Spiegel quotes one of the phrases that are of the type that are often used at IPI: "When you think you know, all you know is what you think." Finally, we are promised: "The Experience is designed to give you you, but a full you, an ability to reach your potential."

Other Activities at IPI

Although the Integrity Experience is the major activity of IPI, a number of other activities are sponsored by the center. The Institute sponsors an annual conference on topics related to consciousness. For example, a two day conference in 1979 entitled, Educating Both Our Brains, was attended by professionals in the mental health field and lay people. Guest speakers at the conference were Dr. Julian Jaynes, professor of psychology at Princeton University and author of *The Origin of Consciousness in the Breakdown of the Bicameral Mind,* and Dr. George Sheehan, author of *Running and Being.* Both explored techniques that develop right-brain functioning. A second conference was concerned with Consciousness and Culture in the 80's and featured Dr. Thomas Szasz, author of *The Myth of Mental Illness,* and Dr. Arnold Lazarus of the Rutgers University Professional School of Psychology. Experiential workshops in hypnosis, meditation, biofeedback, yoga, and stress reduction were also offered during that weekend conference.

The Institute also offers an individual consultation and referral service at no cost on a one-time basis only. This consultation can serve either as the screening for the Integrity Experience or "to provide support and guidance for anyone experiencing emotional conflicts, stress-related problems, or just a need for direction in their life."[4]

The Educational Services division headed by Spiegel

offers seminars and workshops "designed to promote human growth, potential, and awareness. . . . It is our goal to provide the public with information on important current topics in mental health. . . . We do this without the mysticism often associated with these subjects."[5] Recent course offerings included The Art of Being Yourself, described in the 1981 fall calendar in the following way: "Have you ever wondered what people mean when they say, 'Be yourself!'? This course is designed to help you remove the obstacles that get in the way and to help you perceive and share yourself as you really are. The course is designed to cover hemisphere functioning, parenting, relationships and expressions of love. . . ." Interior Spaces, a one-session course asks: "Are your rooms an extension of you or are you an extension of your rooms?" The course explores the topic "from the perspective of bilateral brain functioning," according to the 1981 spring/summer calendar. A course in which class members are trained to give a stand-up comedy routine based on their lives is entitled The Psycho-Integrity of Humor. Running for five sessions, this seminar was described in the 1981 fall calendar as exploring "the experience of laughter and humorous perspective on the aspects of our lives which usually give us pain." Other courses include hatha-yoga, self-hypnosis, and karate. A Saturday program for 9- to 12-year-olds provides An Experience in Creative Play through the use of drama games, relaxation exercises, and role playing. "This workshop is designed to be great fun for kids and improve self-image," according to the fall calendar.

Clinical and Consulting Services are directed by Lentchner. Individual, group, and family psychotherapy as well as marriage counseling are offered on a graduated fee basis dependent on ability to pay. In addition, the Institute interfaces with corporations in two ways: first, by providing training and consultation to increase "efficiency of productivity, creativity and most importantly, to reduce stress factors within the work environment," and second, by offering, "mental health treatment and prevention programs."[6]

The Integrity Experience Participants

Although no systematic investigation of the individuals who have participated in the Experience has been undertaken, Lentchner shared his perceptions with me. The participants, more than 600 in number, range in age from 18 to 68; most are in their mid-30's. They are generally middle- to upper-middle class. In the most recent Experience the participants, with a mean age of 34, included a physician, a dentist, engineers, a firefighter, a plumber, artists, college students, homemakers, and a bus mechanic. Although there are more white-collar types, there appears to be a trend of increasing blue-collar involvement.

Initially, female participants outnumbered male participants two to one, largely because of a preponderance of women among both the students at the County College of Morris and the patients in therapy with IPI's founders. But subsequently, about equal numbers of men and women were involved as the students and patients who continued to make up a substantial portion of participants were joined by individuals who were referred by previous participants or by physicians. Some individuals do the training after attending a social event or open house at IPI, where they have the opportunity to talk to staff members or graduates of the program. Lentchner further characterized the clients of the Integrity Experience: "Their lives are going fine. They have accomplished most of their goals. They are doing well professionally. Their family life is O.K. or not O.K., but if it's not O.K., they don't know why it's not O.K. They recognize that all of the things that are supposed to give gratification are not enough. They want more out of life. I would speculate that people either have been searching for what was wrong with the culture or have retreated from the culture in an unsatisfying narcissism.... It's for people who are constantly not satisfied, and they keep making one external search after another." As reporter Sheila Lacouture wrote in a local New Jersey newspaper: "The Integrity Experience is not designed to cure those with serious neurotic or psychotic disorders. Its purpose is to remove that vague feeling of dissatisfaction that many know. It helps get rid of the 'Is that all there is?' outlook."[7]

I talked to Bob Hughes, a 20-year-old college student majoring in history and economics, who recently completed the Integrity Experience. Bob said: "I always considered myself a very logical person. I believed there was something else in the world. I had some belief in God. I had my doubts about this experience, but I had Spiegel as a professor and I decided to try it. It was really out of character for me to spend money on something I didn't know anything about. I had been in therapy for about two months. I know how important this is."

Because of his young age, I questioned Bob about his family's reaction to his participation in the Experience. He replied: "My family is very Roman Catholic. At first I was very secretive about this with my family. On Sunday, when we completed the first weekend, my sisters thought that I was going to join the Moonies. Then they thought I was going to be a priest, because I started talking about God.

"I live with my grandmother because her house is closer to my school.... My father was brought up at a time when everything was carefully laid out. He is very conservative, but not a reactionary. I brought him here tonight to the post-session because I want him to do it. Also, because I love him, although I've never told him that. Maybe I will tell him some day. My mother's given up on me," Bob told me with a grin. "She thinks this kind of stuff is cult-oriented. She'd flip out here. If I took her dreams away, she may not be able to handle it. I don't want to change anyone else, just myself."

I further questioned Bob about whether he had changed as a result of the Integrity Experience. "My primary goal is to be rich," he said. (I couldn't tell if he was joking at this point.) "But actually, I want to be a history or political science teacher. I am very pleased now with who I am. Before, I was concerned with trying to be other people. Like I was lifting weights. I was letting other people influence my life, and what I was doing. Now, I am very satisfied with who I am."

Bob's father, who appeared to have a somewhat negative or at least skeptical attitude about the Experience, told me: "One night Bob told me he had to discuss something with me. All kinds of things came to my mind—schooling, an accident, trouble with a young lady. I was tired and didn't want to go out that night, but he really needed to talk so we went. He said he saw Jesus Christ. I still didn't know what was going on—was he drinking, or what? The more he spoke, the more I got a feeling for what was going on. My son had seen the Lord. I asked what did he look like? He said he had long hair and wore a white robe. I came to the conclusion that he wasn't on anything; there were no drugs. But I still don't know what this means.

"He didn't tell me that much, but he said that the food wasn't the greatest, that there was hypnosis, but I don't really know what went on. He told me about his spirit leaving his body. He lives with my mother and sister and they're into that. He got into this when he went to college with these two professors, that and my mother and sister—that's why he's here. To tell Bobby what to do was difficult. He was full of love, kissing his mother, and everything."

When I spoke to Bob's father after the post-session, he indicated that he had "absolutely no intention of doing the Experience," and still couldn't understand what his son found in it.

Prior to the post-session, I went over to William Corbin, about 25 years old, one of the few graduates standing alone.

When I asked; "Why did you do the Experience?" he quickly replied: "Because I couldn't feel anything before; I had no feelings." Since he didn't elaborate, I probed a bit about what was going on in his life presently. Although he then responded, "Now, they're all there; it's great," he seemed almost lacking in affect, emotionless. My final question was: "How did you hear about the Integrity Experience?" His abrupt response was: "I heard about it from my therapist." I observed William later in the evening with two other graduates. He was physically part of the triad, but certainly not a real participant.

Sal Russo is a shop foreman, and the father of two teenage children. He and his wife, both about 40, were very open and friendly, quite a contrast to William Corbin. Sal took the Integrity Experience because he "needed help in several areas. I needed self-improvement that would affect the people I deal with. I had some lack of confidence. I wanted to learn how to express myself more freely. I was under the care of the doctors and they thought it would benefit me. I deal with people every day, but there was a lot of room for improvement. . . . I came with an open mind and attitude. Whatever I could get I took." At first, he told only his wife, children, and boss about his involvement with IPI. "I didn't tell anyone at first at work except my boss, because I didn't know what it would do for me." Sal described various aspects of the Experience for me: "Music is used to get your thoughts back on the right track. Some sessions end with music; some have words. I've heard some songs 50 times, but when I heard one as part of the Experience, it meant something.

"One of the things we did was use hypnosis. It was very scary sometimes. Once I thought it was all over, that I was going to die, that I was going off into another world, going beyond. But it turned out fine. Everyone is here for a reason. They have one problem or another. There's lots of sharing. Seventy-five percent of the people have personal problems. Once people start to share, it gets easier for everyone."

Sal further commented that there are a number of positive

differences in the way he approaches life now. "We were taught one thing: Let it be. To me, it means I'm not going to change anyone.... I seem to express myself more freely. We found out how to improve certain areas of self-centeredness. We're just a speck in the universe.... I want to love everyone now. It has benefited several people in my life besides myself."

Some concerns about long-term transformation were mentioned by Sal. "When you're leaving here so high, you know you have to lose some of it. It's hard leaving. Everyone has a healthy attitude now. Everyone is always smiling. The real test, however, is a crisis. How long does it hold up? I'm not a doubting Thomas, but in an atmosphere like this where there are no problems, it's easy to sit and smile. What happens in other situations?"

Sal's wife, Pat, spoke to me privately and she provided me with additional insights about the meaning of the Integrity Experience for her husband. "Sal was an alcoholic. Since he started the Experience he hasn't had a drop to drink. That has made such a difference in our lives. He would never admit that he had a drinking problem before. Now, he takes responsibility for his actions. It's terrific." Pat spoke further about the changes she noticed in her husband: "Sal is more open with me. He expresses himself better. His attitudes have changed a lot. He has a warmer personality.... The impact really began the last night. Everyone was crying and hugging one another."

Pat expressed some initial reservations about the Experience: "The thing that worried me was that Sal was going to have different views of me and his home life. I was concerned that he would leave me. But things got better at home. My daughter thinks it's fantastic what's happened to her father." Her final thoughts about the Integrity Experience were: "I think the work they do here is fantastic. I'm thinking seriously of doing one in October."

While we were waiting for the graduates' post-session to end, I spoke to Ann Green's daughter. Ann is one of the older graduates, about 55 years old. Her daughter, who lives on her own, told me: "I'm proud of my mother, that she did this. It took a lot of courage. She really got a lot out of it."

Ann Green openly discussed the Experience with me: "I did the Experience because my doctor suggested it. It didn't have to be the Institute for Psycho-Integrity. He actually suggested a number of different groups that might be helpful, but he said I had to do something. I was under a great deal of stress at the time because of my husband's illness. He was seriously ill and it really put a strain on me. He was in the hospital for awhile, came home, and then had to be rehospitalized. He's home now. We've had trouble communicating. I've had to be very careful relating to him because of his illness.

"I was skeptical at first, but I got a great deal from this. I'm more open now. I would have liked to have said something at the sharing session, but I couldn't. I can't talk in front of large groups. I got the most from sharing with my partner when we worked together as a dyad. We became very close.

"I tried to share the things I learned with my husband, but he's not interested. That's a problem. After the first weekend I went home and tried to talk to him honestly. We did for awhile, but he didn't really respond. I was ready to really love him and communicate with him and share with him, but he had not done the Experience and couldn't really appreciate and deal with the changes in me. But I'll keep trying. I thought that the fact that my husband was not going to do the Experience might be a problem. But the doctors said I could do it by myself. Maybe it will work out, I'll see. Some people benefit much more from the Experience than do others. One man kept saying that the Experience wasn't doing anything for him. He completed it, although he didn't show up tonight. But it was clear that it was not very meaningful to him. It was very worthwhile for me."

Evaluation

The founders and directors of IPI were quite satisfied with the effect of the Integrity Experience on its participants. Lentchner told me: "We are superpleased with what that looks like in a number of respects. First, the graduates are pleased. We haven't done any systematic feedback, but we haven't received any negative feedback. We remain fairly close to about 200 and they provide us with constant stroking.... Secondly, it's not simply a marathon high. I'm very sensitive to that.... I spent a lot of time in various confrontational marathons. It's simple to break down defenses. It's maintaining the gains that is difficult. The learning extends beyond the period of learning. We can give them tools where they are not dependent on us. They can continue by themselves to have this new level of consciousness. We need to offer educational and social activities for people to maintain the gains." He further commented about the transformation: "Practically speaking, anyone who left would be leaving with an intensive experience of working through problems rather than working around them, which then serves as a model. They leave here with a clear and tested ability in self-hypnosis. They would be leaving with a clear and tested ability at focusing and defusing. If I had a headache or generalized anxiety, focusing would allow me to identify the physical sensation to allow it to become dominant, to expand. Then it becomes refocused, worked through without analytical or sequential thought processes or logical base."

Although the Integrity Experience appears to have therapeutic effects, it is not psychotherapy. A descriptive brochure of IPI stated that the Experience is not designed to treat neuroses or psychoses. Rather, it is "for all those who wish to improve the quality of their lives."[8] Lentchner discussed the relationship between psychotherapy and the Integrity Experience: "There is an interface between therapy and the Integrity Experience. The Experience is helpful therapeutically, either as an initial introduction to therapy or as a termination device, putting everything together. In the former, the Experience saves six months of therapy as long as it is clear that this is not therapy. You're going to feel better, but the work will not be done. The Experience in the middle of therapy may be the worst thing for a person, or it may not be." The free screening/consultation process that IPI offers attempts to determine whether an individual should be in therapy or participating in the Integrity Experience. As Lentchner explained: "We attempt to make the best guess. Is this an individual looking for therapy? For consciousness-raising? What are they really looking for? What do they want? Perhaps they want education, not the Experience." The directors claimed that for individuals who are currently in psychotherapy, "the Experience should help to accelerate and facilitate their therapeutic goals. In some cases, the Experience has even precluded the need for further therapy."[9] Consultation with one's clinician regarding participation in the Experience is advised by the Institute staff.

A clinical psychologist, who is not affiliated with IPI, but is familiar with its work, suggested that the Integrity Experience is certainly not appropriate for everyone. For example, she explained: "Some people feel too much. They need to learn to be more logical, to do more thinking, the opposite of the intended goal of IPI."

In addition to the Integrity Experience, the Institute offers a form of psychotherapy based upon the principles of "full integration of both Eastern and Western, esoteric and traditional, philosophies and psychologies."[10] Integrity therapy arises out of a body of knowledge called "Psycho-integrity," which includes both theories and techniques that focus on integration of the right and left cerebral hemispheres.

Another interesting issue concerns the relationship

between the Integrity Experience and religion. Religious experiences are right-brain experiences, while our religious beliefs, our ideas of God, are derived from left-brain functioning. Spiegel noted that the Integrity Experience "enriches whatever you already believe." Lentchner pointed out that, although religious practices such as chanting, prayer, and dance encourage right-brain functioning, they are not part of the Integrity Experience. Thus, those religious practices are another route. However, Lentchner did acknowledge that "there is a spiritual flavor or aspect to higher levels of consciousness." Several participants indicated to me that they felt closer to God or had some kind of religious experience as part of the Integrity Experience. In addition, one of the courses offered by IPI is entitled A Course in Miracles, which was described in the 1981 spring/summer calendar as follows: "The Course's aim is revelation—the experience of self which is the level of consciousness called God or knowledge of the true source of the Universe. . . ."

Future Outlook

What does the future hold for the Institute of Psycho-Integrity? The Directory of Services indicated that the scope of the research programs would be broadened in the near future to include experimental investigations of bilateral brain theory with clinical applications. Secondly, there is an increasing outreach to industry, because of the many stresses at work that can potentially be reduced through the application of Psycho-Integrity theory. A third focus was cited by Lentchner: "Our goals have changed over the last four years. Four years ago, we had no thoughts of affecting the consciousness of the culture. Now, we want to have an effect on the culture, although we do not need to become some sort of popularism. Hopefully, the effect would be as indirect as possible." Lentchner indicated that a fourth area of emphasis will be the reduction of structural and administrative problems. However, Spiegel commented: "I don't see things as problems. I see things as situations that need to be dealt with." Fifth, many of the staff members, including the two directors, are not at present receiving money for their services. Both Lentchner and Spiegel believed that the financial picture was beginning to brighten, and this would allow salaries to be given. Spiegel told me that he and Lentchner are not running the Experience for money. "We do it because we love it. Some people paint paintings, or climb mountains; we do this. There is some altruism in raising levels of consciousness. The Integrity Experience can enrich people's lives. Sometimes it drastically changes people's lives. It adds a dimension to most people's lives." When I asked Spiegel about his expectations for IPI in five years' time, he enthusiastically responded: "We are already where we want to be."

7: Divine Light Mission

"When you feel it, you know it; you're not in this body."

"It was hooking up with another type of experience, beyond insight, beyond a peak experience. It is real and beautiful."

"It's really like being on drugs—you're psychologically dependent. You're supposed to accept everything. It makes you more insecure."

"It is the most priceless gift there is."

"It was a heavy session. You are hypnotized into believing you are experiencing God."

THESE are various reactions to "receiving Knowledge," which is the ultimate experience for followers of Guru Maharaj Ji. The Divine Light Mission (DLM) is an international organization which is dedicated to passing along Guru Maharaj Ji's Knowledge.

Guru Maharaj Ji was born Prem Pal Singh Rawat in Harduar, India, on December 10, 1957, the youngest of four sons of Sri Hans Ji. Maharaj Ji's father had come from a wealthy family, but spent his life preaching and ministering to the poor. Sri Hans Ji founded the Divine Light Mission in 1960. He died six years later when Guru Maharaj Ji was just 8 years old. The young guru was named by his mother as the successor to the movement.

Journalists Carroll Stoner and Jo Anne Parke described the beginning of the movement in the United States in 1971: "Divine Light came to the United States after a drug dealer, in India to close a deal, stumbled upon the ministry and persuaded the teenage guru to visit him in the United States. The discoverer of Guru Maharaj Ji (Great King) put a strong arm on his cohorts back in Boulder, Colorado, to finance the trip and they obliged."[1]

Although Maharaj Ji didn't receive a great deal of attention during his first visit, he had built up a relatively large following by the time of his second visit in 1972, when he attended a festival in his honor. In the following year an elaborate three-day millennium festival was held in the Houston Astrodome, although it didn't measure up to the expectations of the group and left DLM in great financial debt. Moreover, Maharaj Ji had begun to live a life of some luxury, with fancy cars and a large house. At the age of 16, Maharaj Ji decided to get married to his secretary, Marilyn Lois Johnson, then 24 years old, a former United Airlines flight attendant. Although his mother was against the marriage, the Colorado court that he petitioned noted that he was sufficiently mature and had enough income to marry. The wedding took place in 1974. Meanwhile, Maharaj Ji's mother had grown increasingly disenchanted with the lifestyle of her guru son and named an older son, Bal Bhagwan Ji, to take over control of DLM. Subsequently, the two brothers became enmeshed in a series of court battles in India over leadership of the Mission. Eventually, both dropped their charges and countercharges. The organization was divided: Maharaj Ji was established as the head of DLM in the United States, while his brother acquired leadership of the Mission in India.

Guru Maharaj Ji has lived in a house in Denver and in a mansion in Malibu, California, with a swimming pool and tennis courts. Both residences were mortgaged by DLM funds. At present he resides with his wife and their two children in Miami, Florida, but spends much of his time traveling. Maharaj Ji refers to himself and is referred to by his followers as Satguru or "Perfect Master." In Sanskrit, *sat* means truth, *gu* means darkness, and *ru* means light. Thus, he explained in a published 1979 interview, it is "One who can take us from the darkness and bring us to Light." In the same interview he explained the use of the term "Perfect Master": "Separate 'perfect' and 'master.' A math teacher may be referred to as a math master. In the same way, one who teaches Perfection may be referred to as Perfect Master... the Knowledge that a Perfect Master reveals is perfect and therefore he is known as 'Perfect Master.'"

Maharaj Ji and his bride, the former Marilyn Lois Johnson, hold hands following their wedding on May 20, 1974 at Lookout Mountain, Colorado.

Premies: Their Beliefs and Practices

I asked several Maharaj Ji followers what would happen to their movement when he dies. None of them was concerned, because they uniformly acknowledged that he is one in a long line of Perfect Masters, including Buddha, Jesus Christ, and Krishna. When Maharaj Ji dies, "another Perfect Master will assert himself; there will always be one around," one respondent told me.

Individuals who are followers of Maharaj Ji are called "premies." One young woman whom I interviewed explained that "the word means 'love' and basically to me what it means is lover of knowledge, lover of that true experience of life." Most premies do not engage in full-time service to DLM, but rather have jobs or go to school, although many work for businesses that are owned by or associated in some way with the movement. There appear to be a large number of businesses affiliated with the Mission—such as food stores, gasoline stations, furniture stores, and import-export firms. A very small percentage of Maharaj Ji followers (according to premie Jeanne Messer, no more than 2 percent)[2] live in ashrams, which are households of devotees. In recent years several ashrams have closed as the organization has run into financial difficulty. Those who reside in ashrams devote all their time and their possessions to the service of Maharaj Ji. They are expected to be celibate, to be vegetarian, and to abstain from alcohol, drugs, and cigarettes. In addition, they follow a rigorous schedule of practices and rituals. However, most hold full-time jobs outside of the ashrams, donating their salaries to the ashram. One person in each ashram has supervisory responsibilities, similar to those held by a house mother or college dormitory head resident. Some premies live in communal households with other believers, but they do not abide by the rules and practices of an ashram. Rather, they are in an alternate residential situation that allows individuals with common interests, problems, and goals to share a lifestyle. Others live independently in their own homes or apartments with their families, who may or may not be premies. Regardless of their living situations, premies are encouraged to visit the ashram as frequently as possible for reinforcement of their beliefs. Stoner and Parke quoted Mission spokesman Joe Anctil, who explained that "the ashram is a state of mind, not a place to live."[3] As Messer pointed out, Maharaj Ji generally does not give specific instructions regarding such matters as diet or occupation. Rather, the focus is on Knowledge.[4]

Knowledge is revealed either by Maharaj Ji himself or through one of his disciples, previously called mahatmas, but now known as initiators. At one time, initiators were all from India, but now many of them are from the West and travel from place to place conducting Knowledge sessions. In the 1979 interview, the Guru described the importance of receiving Knowledge: "Knowledge is the true realization of one's self.... The Knowledge doesn't bring any physical change but just the inner contentment, the Peace within oneself.... " He explained his role after Knowledge has been received by a premie: "Guru Maharaj Ji is there to help in one's life. Without the help of a true teacher, it is very hard to learn, and without learning, the experience of this true Knowledge cannot manifest in a person's life."

Those individuals who are at present followers of Guru Maharaj Ji were rather vague in their attempts to explain to me the experience of Knowledge. For example, one devotee said, "Knowledge is going within. It helps you to find your life force." Another said, "The person feels a certain experience of love. It is a very internal experience, a feeling that you're real, that you trust, that you want this experience." An initiator whom I met at an ashram that I visited said the following about Knowledge: "It's even simpler than learning how to eat with a fork, simpler than clearing your throat, simpler than learning to cough. Once I found that out everything was clearer.... This is the light that lies within you, the divine harmony within you. It's the spirit, the soul that keeps us alive, an energy that keeps us alive. Without the help of the Perfect Master, you can't receive it. I had it when I was born, but without Guru Maharaj Ji, I wouldn't have had the chance of a snowball in hell of receiving it."

One woman who was living in an ashram explained the secrecy surrounding Knowledge: "When you receive Knowledge you take a vow that you will not reveal your Knowledge, the techniques, to anybody, because it could be confusing. Simply, because if a person is not ready, you won't understand the gift you are receiving and they won't practice it."

Those interviewees who were no longer followers of Maharaj Ji and his Divine Light Mission were noticeably less reticent about revealing the particulars of the Knowledge experience. One 31-year-old man, who had been a member of the Divine Light Mission for five years and had been out for just one year, explained simply: "You receive techniques of heavy meditation. It's built up over a long time. You are hypnotized for hours in the Knowledge session. Devotion is the whole key. Eventually you experience Knowledge."

A 25-year-old woman who had been deprogrammed in 1977, after being a devoted follower of Maharaj Ji for two years, told me: "One night, I received a phone call and was told that I was going to receive Knowledge that weekend. I went to Phoenix and received Knowledge, which involved certain techniques—seeing the Light, hearing the Music, tasting the Nectar, and practicing the Holy Name. For example, tasting the Nectar means you roll your tongue into the mucous gland, the nectar of life. Holy Name means you follow your breath up and down all the time."

A social worker's description of the session in which he received Knowledge is cited by Ronald Enroth. In order to allow the aspirants to see the Light, the initiator asked them to concentrate and place their index fingers on the groove in their eyebrow ridge above the nose. They were requested not to turn their eyes upward. Then the initiator turned off the light in the room and began to walk in the dark. The social worker described the rest of the session: "Suddenly I felt him swishing by, and I could feel his finger on my forehead. Then all of a sudden, I felt his fingers on my eyes. Instantly I was zapped with light and was seeing a figure eight of pure white light. It was brilliant dazzling. Then the mahatma took my right hand and put my index finger against my forehead, my thumb and my middle finger against my eyes. My left hand supported my right elbow and in that position he left me."

After the initiator told the initiates to meditate for one hour, he left the room. Upon his return, they went through an exercise that was to permit them to hear Divine Music: "We were to concentrate on whatever we heard on the right side of our head. What we heard on the left side was evil, the left side was of the body—mortal; the right side was immortal. All I could hear was a ringing sound." An hour later, the initiator returned to teach the aspirants the Word or Holy Name of God in which they learned "to pronounce the name through a series of deep breathing exercises." Learning about the Nectar occurred on the Mahatma's final return to the room. "We were told to turn our tongues back and that our tongues would naturally find the passageway to where the Nectar drips down. I didn't taste anything. Nobody tasted anything except one guy over in the corner who exclaimed how everything smelled like roses and how sweet everything was."[5]

Messer wrote a vivid description of the Knowledge session, which is comprised of four events. First, devotees "are shown an intense light" on which they learn to meditate. After the Knowledge session, premies report that the frequency and intensity of the light increases. In its most intense state, it is perceived as either a "brilliant white light" or a "many-hued light show." On occasion, devotees see images or pictures in the light. Second, devotees are shown how to listen to the "music of the spheres" or the "sounds of sounds" while meditating. Messer also noted a wide variety of sounds that have been described by devotees, ranging from "water sounds—similar to, but richer and more varied than, those heard in a seashell or conch—to crickets in the grass on a summer night to stringed instruments and choirs." Third, devotees are made aware of "a Nectar flowing in the body which they can taste, described as tasting like a combination of butter and honey." Finally, devotees become cognizant of an internal vibration which they are expected to meditate on constantly. This vibration is considered to be the "Word or Name of God."[6] Messer noted that while the light seems to be seen with the eyes and the sound appears to be heard with the ears, the blind can see the light and the deaf can hear the sound.[7]

Premies reported a number of significant changes in their lives, their behaviors, and their attitudes after receiving Knowledge. A counseling psychologist in a small community college where most of her coworkers and students are unaware of her premie status, told me: "I found my experience to be a very beautiful experience. It allowed me to see beyond the conditions of society, to give me a security, experiencing a different type of consciousness. When I look in the mirror, I see myself as 31 years old. But there is someone inside me that doesn't change with age. I'm in psychology and I've been in therapy, but Maharaj Ji offered me something that I've never had before."

A former devotee, who was working as a salesman, explained the change in his attitude: "Before I experienced Knowledge, I had been fighting the premies for two months and then I had this realization that the Guru Maharaj Ji was the Lord; his Knowledge was God and I was pretty lucky."

Donald Stone suggested that after receiving Knowledge devotees find themselves in a euphoric state that may last for weeks.[8] Messer, too, commented on the numerous changes in the life of the premies, including heightened positive feelings toward oneself and the world, enhanced relations with one's family and friends, and improved financial circumstances.[9]

Satsang (which premies told me means "in the company of truth") is another important dimension of the Divine Light Mission. Premies are urged to "give satsang" (to talk to others about their experiences) and to "listen to satsang" as frequently as possible. The practice of satsang occurs every evening at ashrams. Those who reside there as well as others in the community, premies and nondevotees alike, are free to participate in it. Maharaj Ji commented on its importance: "Satsang is something which is very, very direct *from* Guru Maharaj Ji, *from* the doctor, to you. It's a direct cure: not just prescribing your medicine, a more direct thing. Premies come, sit down, and Guru Maharaj Ji comes and gives satsang, maybe they are just the nurses, or the assistant, but they can help you too. . . . That is why satsang is so important—to keep our mind where it *should* be, so that it's not affecting us the way it usually does."[10]

I attended satsang at an ashram (an old, beautifully decorated house) in a large Northeastern city. This ashram had recently become coed because of the closing of a male ashram nearby. One room was set aside for satsang and every one of about 30 chairs was taken, with a few additional individuals seated on the floor. Pictures of the Guru adorned that room as well as every other that I entered, including the bathroom.

After a videotape presentation of a speech by Maharaj Ji, which appeared to fascinate everyone present, an initiator who was present that evening sat up front and began to talk. Excerpts from his rambling, rather vague discourse, which lasted about half an hour, follow:

"There's a whole experience beyond this world. There's so

much we get bound into in this world.... Always these masters, these saints would say: God is within us. They always spoke of an experience we can have now. We don't have to wait until we die. What is that thing? What is that experience? It's there. The true master can really show us. What is love? There is an endless power, an endless beauty, an endless love. We're the ones who make the rules. Human beings make the religion.

"Guru Maharaj Ji reveals the direct experience of the Creator. Any person can experience it. This is the beauty of Guru Maharaj Ji. All of the Perfect Masters know. They know the highest perfection, the highest beauty. It's there within us, within all of us. It's within prisoners. Once, I went to a prison where there was a man who killed two people. He had been given Knowledge also. I met a retarded woman with the intellect of a 7-year-old. She had the Knowledge.

"There's a simplicity to what he's offering. It is so completely simple. I used to try to do meditation before. Some are really difficult; it takes years of practice. But Knowledge is simple. It's so simple that if you're really complex, you'll miss it. It's beyond the intellect....

"In the past I had experienced all the pleasures that did quit, that did go down the tubes. But this experience never quits. I could see what was real and what wasn't from my heart, from seeing, from recognizing, a natural discrimination that lies within each person....

"I know one premie who's now an initiator who went from one guru to another. He went to 20 gurus and he would say: 'Reveal the truth to me, the ultimate truth.' Every Swami that came near his village in India. But then when he came to Maharaj Ji—the oceans of love that Guru Maharaj Ji can reveal—he knew he had found it. It's personal.

"And I feel that everyone in this room really needs to know. It cuts across so much craziness. So many religions believe in God and then turn around and kill one another.

Once you know the source of love within yourself with Guru Maharaj Ji's help, if you want, if you choose, you can get on that elevator and go right to the top."

The initiator concluded his talk by saying: "If you are interested in receiving this Knowledge or know someone who is interested, I'll be staying here indefinitely and you can bring them to talk to me." At the end of satsang, as everyone was leaving, a woman I had previously interviwed came over to me to express her amazement that I was able to continue to take notes throughout the talk: "Usually, people begin to write, but they are soon so fascinated that they stop." Others in the room seemed to be equally enthusiastic about the initiator's discourse. One exception was a young woman who confided that she engaged in her own meditation throughout satsang because she didn't particularly like this initiator. "Others are much better," she told me.

Satsang usually occurs without the presence of an initiator or even a formal leader. Rather, it is generally an informal meeting of premies who discuss their experiences. Messer remarked that giving and receiving satsang "become irresistibly delightful, a way to 'get high,' in contemporary parlance."[11]

A third activity that plays an important role in the life of a premie is service. This can include any activity, physical or mental, devoted to Guru Maharaj Ji or the organization and its affiliates, which does not involve financial remuneration. The exact nature of the service is not explicitly specified, but it can include a form of witnessing or giving satsang—letting friends, relatives, and strangers know that Knowledge can be revealed to them through the Guru Maharaj Ji. Service can take the form of preparation for a visit to a particular city by Maharaj Ji or one of his initiators, or working in Maharaj Ji's house or at a festival in his honor. Messer suggested: "Acts of service become extraordinarily rewarding, but the reward is not to the ego or a sense of right action; it is simply the reward of happiness."[12]

Meditation is the activity that probably takes up the greatest amount of a premie's time and accounts for the transformations of consciousness, attitude, emotion, and behavior. Devotees claim various positive effects from meditation, including increased energy, decreased vulnerability, and greater openness to personal change.[13]

Others who have been part of the movement discuss the effects of long periods of meditation in less glowing terms. One young man told me: "I think meditation can have a debilitating effect. You can end up being programmed very easily."

Stoner and Parke pointed to both the positive as well as the negative aspects of the meditation that is practiced by devotees of Maharaj Ji. "It is a medically accepted means of alleviating the ravages of stress. But when practiced to excess, meditation can 'bliss out' a person to the point of inactivity and inertia, stifling creativity much the same way overindulgence with alcohol or marijuana can."[14]

Jim, a young social worker, interviewed by Enroth, concurred with Stoner and Parke's assessment of the damage wrought by excessive meditation. "People around me were saying things like 'Wow, how can you still read?' They said if they meditate, they couldn't read. I myself lost the ability to add and subtract. I could not balance a checkbook. I was always spaced out. At this point, I would accept almost anything my leaders told me, since I was not capable of questioning anything."[15]

Although my impression of the premies I met was generally positive—they were largely articulate, friendly, and alert—one obvious exception was a young woman whom I briefly interacted with on a visit to an ashram. I had used a bathroom but couldn't find the light switch so I stopped a passing individual in the hallway. I asked her if she lived there. When she replied affirmatively, I asked her where the light switch was. She looked at me with a vacant stare and mumbled: "I don't know." Whether her strange reaction can be attributed to the excesses of meditation or not is unknown.

Premies can and do meditate at any time and any place. For instance, while I was interviewing a devotee who was married to another premie—both had full-time jobs independent of the movement—she told me: "When I feel that I need love, I meditate. I'm doing it now as I talk to you because I want to be clear. You can be in that consciousness 24 hours a day."

Experiencing darshan, a state of blessedness resulting from being in the presence of a religious leader, is another dimension of life as a premie. Followers are encouraged to be as physically close to their spiritual leader as possible, as often as possible. Enroth commented: "Devotees who look at Maharaj Ji report seeing nothing but intense light. Some experience a complete stopping of time. Others find in his every motion, gestures, and word the answers to their most troubling questions and doubt."[16]

One woman whom I interviewed described the intensity of her attachment to the Guru: "Sometimes my relationship with Maharaj Ji is more intimate than my relationship with my husband." She further noted: "Being with him, you can feel his power, his love. I felt protected, loved, at peace—even when I'm alone in my apartment. . . . I can also experience it at a large festival with everyone around." Messer quoted another devotee, a Ph.D candidate in sociology: "I once thought I could never prostrate myself before any man, that it was obscene. Now I find it difficult to pass his picture without falling on my face with gratitude."[17]

A possible manifestation of darshan is the propensity of premies to hang or display photographs of Maharaj Ji in every conceivable place—office desks, car dashboards, the bathroom wall, an altar in a college dormitory bedroom, etc. Many have said to me: "He's so-ooo beautiful." They truly seem to feel great joy talking about him, looking at his picture, or even talking about a particular photograph.

A significant phenomenon discussed by premies after receiving Knowledge is the occurrence of events that are remarkably coincidental. Premies suggested that these incidents occur because of "grace": a devotee who was "directed" to pick up hitchhikers, who turned out to be premies; the explosion of a car window without evident cause and no injuries; the payment for DLM building alterations by its owner who had no relation to the organization; the unexpected finding of money in a kitchen drawer. All are cited by Messer as examples of the operation of grace.[18]

One of my respondents described a typical example of grace: "I had a job as an aide at a psychiatric hospital. I met Melissa, who was a psychiatric social worker there and who was also a member of the Divine Light Mission; she still is. I thought it was the grace of Guru Maharaj Ji that we were working together."

DLM Followers

The type of individuals who have been drawn to the Divine Light Mission has changed from the early days of the movement in the United States to the present time. Stoner and Parke reported that Divine Light recruited among drug users and dropouts, "promising a constant high without drugs." But at present, recruits are more likely to be well-educated individuals who are or will be upstanding members of the community.[19] A woman who had joined the movement in the early 1970's and was still a follower of Guru Maharaj Ji, commented on the changing picture of recruits: "When I came, most of the people were dropouts of the hippie generation, on drugs, idealistic people. There were very few old people, poor people, blacks. They were mainly people who had time and energy—middle-class, white, young people. Now, there is a changing picture. There are many older people—in their 50's and 60's—all classes, which is good. Some people are coming from a lack. They couldn't make it in society. They're stupid or ugly or lazy and Maharaj Ji takes care of them. But there are also people who have money and education—people who could make it. That's more inspiring to me. I want to be identified with them. It's more difficult if you're a complex person to acquire a spiritual kind of understanding."

It is difficult to obtain an accurate estimate of the numbers of individuals who are followers of Maharaj Ji, particularly since the organizational structure of the Mission is quite loose. Theologian Harvey Cox, in his book *Turning East,* which is concerned with the attraction of Eastern religions in recent years, commented: "The followers of the Maharaj Ji have sometimes claimed hundreds of thousands for his Divine Light Mission.... Although the spectacular failure of its well-publicized 1973 rally in the Houston Astrodome to attract as many people as expected casts some doubt on the figures supplied by the movement leaders themselves, and the public tiffs between the guru and his family have probably cost members as well as caused severe embarrassment, still the movement has enlisted large numbers of devotees."[20] The explosion of interest in altered states of consciousness, as documented in Marilyn Ferguson's *The Aquarian Conspiracy,* could partly account for the large following of Maharaj Ji's Knowledge techniques. Moreover, Stoner and Parke suggested that premies are "compelling witnesses for their faith. True premies say they are happier than before." They further note that the recruiting techniques used by the Divine Light Mission consist of a "soft-sell approach, and it seems to work." They cited an example of a young female premie, working as a secretary at a Catholic college, who "says she feels confident that some of her associates at work will become interested in Divine Light once they are impressed with her gentle ways and peaceful demeanor, qualities she is sure are fruits of her Divine Light practice."[21]

I spoke to a number of present and former premies about their reasons for becoming followers of the Guru as well as the circumstances under which they joined the Divine Light Mission. A particularly vivacious 25-year-old woman named Marcia Donovan, who has been living in an ashram for about a year, told her story to me:

"I moved out of my parents' house when I was 19 and they weren't going to support me. I had been a Home Ec major at college because my sister was a Home Ec major and was making $18,000 starting teaching salary and my parents thought it was good. I took courses and found out about refrigerators and this and that. I thought, 'I can't take this course for one more week. I've got to get out of here; this isn't it.' Then I got into psychology, philosophy, anthropology. I was a major in everything; every week I had a different major. Then I stuck with psychology. I took this course called Education for Success. It was positive thinking—getting to know yourself, having a positive attitude about yourself. I liked the course and was doing very well. I was a leader. Everyone said this girl was fabulous.

"Meanwhile, my self-image was lousy, but everybody thought I was great so I loved it. I moved out of my parents' place. I finally quit college and got my own place. I started waitressing for a couple of years. Then I decided to go back to school. Then I finally decided to do what I had wanted to do since the time I was 7 years old. I always had the best flowers in kindergarten and all the way through I thought I would be an artist. I'm going to do what I wanted to do—to be happy in my life and I was happy but it wasn't anything like I thought it would be. I mean, I had my apartment, my cats, my dog, my boyfriend, my car and my little drawing and painting, and that was going quite well for me. Still there was something missing in me. . . . My mother would say, 'You're healthy, you're young. What's the matter with you?

You have a boyfriend, a dog, cats, a big career, a car. You're healthy, your IQ's not bad.' The people in China are starving. But what does that have to do with me? There's something in me. I couldn't really communicate with them. I'd be happy one week, then unhappy the next week. No one took me seriously. I didn't take myself seriously.

"It was starting to take a toll on me, sort of wearing me down. I wasn't going up hills as fast; I was just getting tired. I always wondered why my life was so speedy. I was so tired, but I guess my life started early. When I was 14 years old, I was out at discotheques. I was smoking pot already. When I was 7 years old I had boyfriends. I mean, you know, my life started early, but I had two older sisters, one was eight years older than me, so I just followed in their footsteps. I was more wild than any one of them.... My mom's 58 years old and just as tired as I am or I was. Yet, she can't admit it because she hasn't had enough yet. But, I was 20 and I'd had enough.

"Then I noticed this guy, Norman, and he had something I didn't have. He had Knowledge for a few years already and he was studying at this art center. He was in a couple of classes. I didn't know his name but I observed him. I noted that there was a quality about this guy, on a very subconscious level, that I didn't have. We never spoke, and then he said: 'Where are you going?' ... I remember one time, it was summer and everyone was asking, 'Where are you going? Where are you going?' It doesn't really matter where I go, I figure. I go wherever I go. If I'm not happy, wherever I am, it doesn't matter where I go.

"Then the summer recess came and then we went back to school. Now, here's the setting: across the street there is this Spanish deli that Norman happened to be in getting lunch and I happened to be in getting lunch. Norman was ordering a cheese sandwich. So we said, 'Are you a vegetarian?' 'Are you a vegetarian?' 'Yeah.' 'Yeah.' So we decided to have lunch together, so we just sat outside against the wall. The sun was shining; the train was passing overhead. Norman asked me: 'Why are you fasting? Why are you drinking all that juice, for God's sake?' I told him: 'Because I feel closer to nature.' It just makes me feel high, which not eating for 14 days will do to you. I definitely did feel more relaxed. Then I did feel more in harmony with my body which made me relax.... It was my experience with Norman that whenever he spoke it was truth.... He was the only person that spoke the truth. I just felt the steadiness in him that I didn't feel in my life and I didn't experience in anybody else's life. And I had run across quite a number of people.

"Then I went home and my boyfriend Pete had left a trail of his clothes from the front door all the way to the bedroom. And he was zonked out on the bed. I had just gotten home. I had gone from 9 in the morning to 9:30 at night every Wednesday and Thursday at school and the dog wasn't fed, the cats weren't fed, the dog wasn't walked, and he had dinner and left the dishes all over the place and I had had it up to my head and over. I just started freaking out. Then I thought, Norman Wilko wouldn't get this way. Norman Wilko wouldn't act this way. I was this crazy woman; I was this frustrated crazy woman, you know. *Somebody*, give me a break! I needed a break and my boyfriend wasn't giving me a break. I had wanted him to. Even though I had driven it into his head for months, he still didn't give me a break. It's the natural situation that everyone goes through. I'm sure it's familiar to you.... It wasn't that Norman wouldn't or would react that way. I knew that there was something in me that was missing, that was making me so on edge all the time....

"He's a beautiful person, Norman. That day, it happened to be the next day, we accidentally met for lunch. And I told him what happened to me yesterday and he said: 'I've got a pretty bad temper myself.' I said: 'Oh, you do?' And so anyway, for the next eight months he proceeded to tell me about Maharaj Ji and about this Knowledge.... Literally, at times I wanted to run, and he'd get me behind my easel and

I'd say, 'Enough already, I don't want to hear about this.' But there was something in there that kept me interested, something else in me that was drinking it up. I would insult Maharaj Ji. I would say, 'Excuse me, I don't mean to be rude or anything, but I think he's so and so.' And Norman would just sit there and say: 'Really?' Gee, he's not even offended. I can't imagine what would offend this guy—nothing moved him. He knew something and he was trying to communicate it with me, you know. Because I felt something . . . I admired and respected him, too. So, maybe Maharaj Ji had something to do about this.

"Then I started going to satsang. . . . It's a place where you can go and you can hear what is true. Not *just* what is true, like 'Yes, this is true—I ate such and such,' but rather, 'What is the purpose of life?' . . . That when it actually penetrates you, it quenches your thirst, not of your tongue, but of your soul and that's what happened to me. And this Norman talked on for nine months and believe me he asked me to satsang for a million times.

"When I met Norman's wife, Virginia, I realized, he's a normal guy, he has a family. I wasn't trusting him at this point. I mean when I first talked with him, I thought he's some weirdo, hippie-freak guy. That's why it took nine months. I go and find out he was basically like me—basic, level-headed. He had a family, he had roots—my mother always told me about roots. He had good roots, and I started to trust him more. To me, it was a very foreign thing and these days all the cults and everything, you say, 'Oh, God.' But when you get to know this person and he has this Knowledge and he does meditation and he's still normal, someone you can relate to, and talk to, and in fact enjoy talking to, you say, 'Wow.' It's a refreshing experience. . . . I had been depressed. Finally my depression got to a point when it became real.

"Then, I started going to satsang. . . . I'd feel relaxed, so much better and happy and I'd feel hope again. So it was something beautiful because basically I was losing hope and when you lose hope you literally are lost because if you don't have hope you don't actually have anything to live for.

"Then I'd go home and feel good and get along with my boyfriend. He was experiencing a lot of jealousy about Norman because I'd say Norman said this and we did this, oh, Norman, Norman, Norman. But Norman's intention was clear. He saw I was in pain, no dying pain, but saw I was wanting for more and he knew what the more was. At first my boyfriend was very angry because he felt this was something that was taking me away from him.... He, himself, knew there was something else about this. He wanted to do something more about his life. We both knew there's more in this world than meets the eye. But I was starting to understand. My boyfriend would go to satsang, but he'd say: 'I'll go with you because if I don't you'll just be a bitch.' So that's why he'd go.

"Finally, one day, we were sitting in the kitchen eating dinner or something and I said, 'I'm leaving. Satsang starts in five minutes and if you want to come, you're invited.' And he let me have it really. He said, 'I'm sick and tired of going to all these programs,' and he'd be in the back snoring. And everybody would know I walked in with him. I'm just with him; he was definitely not into it. And meanwhile there was something in me that was being awakened and I was, maybe, I was considering the possibility that Maharaj Ji was what he said he was and this Knowledge was what he said it was....

"When I told Pete I was going to satsang, he really let me have it. He was bored and the only reason he'd go was so I wouldn't be cranky, you know. He was bored and wasn't going to spend another Friday night.... And he was yelling at me and I said, 'Look, I'm just looking for God and I'm sorry you're mad.' At that moment he completely got quiet and five minutes later we were in the car going to satsang, going to hear Maharaj Ji. And he told me that the night before he was laying in bed thinking, going through the whole thing, and what came to his head was: 'She's just looking for God. Give her a break.' . . . It's something we search for in our life because we need it. God, creator, energy—whatever you want to use—that supreme power. . . . When Pete heard what I wanted to do, what I was trying to do, he realized he was too. He gave me a break. Then we went to satsang one or two times a week.

". . . when you receive Knowledge, I'll never forget it. It was a spring day and I was standing by my kitchen window stirring up a pot of spaghetti sauce and I was just like involved in my thoughts. And for some reason, I thought, realized, that if I didn't go to satsang, if I didn't have that experience of truth in my life, I was going to go crazy. And the thing that was going to drive me crazy was my very own thoughts. Unless there was something in my life that was going to put a break on my thoughts, give me a break. That my own thoughts had the power to drive me crazy and unless there was something in my life that would stop my thoughts, you know, that everyday voice, that little Howard Cosell that rents a room inside your head . . . 'What's up here? What's going on here?' The thing that's going on inside your head, that's always talking to you constantly. . . .

"These thoughts, for the first time in my life, stirring my spaghetti sauce, I realized, these things could take me right off a cliff, you know. . . . I thought, 'Norman and Virginia are coming back today, I've got to call them and tell them I want to do the program.' At that moment it all clicked, that there was this Maharaj Ji, that this Knowledge was a chance to achieve peace—in my life, not world peace. . . . So I was standing with that pot of tomato sauce hoping that Norman would call me right away. . . . Lo and behold, at 11:30 that night, the phone rang. It was Norman Wilko. He had just gotten into the house, just put his luggage down and said he had to call me. It was the first time I let Norman talk for two hours without interrupting. I was drinking it up. And he said, 'So, whenever you want to come to satsang, just give me a call.' I said, 'Tomorrow.' He said, 'What? You want to go tomorrow?' I said, 'Yes.' So he said 'O.K., I'll pick you up tomorrow.' And from that day on, I went to satsang every night. I realized, man, I was hungry, I was thirsty, and there was food, something inside me.... It was a different kind of food—not the macaroni I just had—but food for the soul. And when a human being eats that, it's something deeper. I mean, you've been through a famine and you just want to feast. And I loved it at that point, but it took quite a while to come to that point. Well, it took a couple of months of seeking."

Both Marcia and Pete are now living in ashrams, Marcia in a center in the Northeast, while Pete resides in the South. Both are following a strict, celibate life and see each other periodically—as friends—usually at festivals for Guru Maharaj Ji.

Other followers of the Guru lead their lives less dedicated to service and renunciation. For example, I spoke to Gloria Taccio, a 29-year-old vocational counselor at a small community college, who is married to a premie. She discussed her and her husband's initial involvement in the movement, before they were married: "Someone came on campus when we were attending college. We were both searching. We were attracted because it didn't cost any money; this is free. Along the way, we fell in love with Maharaj Ji. A teacher, or initiator—who is someone who really wants to dedicate his life—came on campus to explain to people, to reveal techniques of Knowledge."

Gloria commented on her previous involvement with spiritual groups or movements: "I went to a meditation group—Rajireesh, a Buddhist center where there were some meditation rituals. I did some Krishna chanting, but was never part of the group. I went to some *est* meetings and other positive thinking groups.... I was also reading a lot of scriptures; we were practicing our own meditation. But you need a living Master to help you, to guide you toward God."

She turned the conversation back again to Guru Maharaj Ji: "At first, I wasn't turned on. I didn't see a need for a Master. But it was free. There was no trip, no signing up. You could remain anonymous. I didn't have to commit myself. As I meditated I got into it more and more. But we didn't want to get influenced by others. We had the experience and went home and didn't go back for weeks. We meditated by ourselves and had beautiful experiences. It was the last semester of our senior year in college. [She was a psychology major at a small Catholic college.] After a month or so we realized it was something good. We tentatively got more involved; we wanted to be cautious. I really believe Guru Maharaj Ji is the living Master. Maharaj Ji gives a main focus to my life.

"The people are from all different religions. We have festivals. People are from different places—South Africa, Arabs—they all get along. It goes beyond cultural conditioning; it's an experiencing of your life force. . . . I've seen Maharaj Ji individually and I feel that he knows me. Maharaj Ji looked and he saw something inside of me that I didn't even know was real: it was so buried. . . . I've seen a lot of people die. I was terrified of death before, of leaving people. It gives me a foundation. You're on a journey."

In response to my query regarding the reaction of her friends, family, and coworkers to her participation in the Divine Light Mission, Gloria told me: "We both come from Catholic families. I now accept the fact that Jesus was the Master; I accept that now more than before. Before I was not a practicing Catholic at all.

"I talked a lot to my family and they came to accept it. Their initial reaction was, 'Oh boy, she's crazy! Who's this weirdo boyfriend who's taking our daughter away from us.' But my mother and sister came to satsang meetings and eventually came around. Dick's [her husband] mother is now very involved. She's been involved for about seven years and has changed a lot. It took her through very difficult times.

For one, her husband died and it [the Mission] really helped. It's often been very helpful for older people. I have other things pulling me: sex, drinking—I still do them. But she had very little pulling her."

Gloria keeps a photograph of Maharaj Ji on her desk and students have asked her whether it's a picture of her husband. She usually replies simply that it's not. Being a staff member of a conservative school, while following Guru Maharaj Ji, "is not an easy path. You have to deal with people's prejudices, your own resistances. . . . I was hesitant before coming here." In discussing her coworkers, she said that they "usually don't ask questions. One of them talked to me one time about it, but she didn't try to persuade me or attack me or anything like that. Other people tell me I'm sick. At other points, I've tried to talk to people. He *is* the answer to the problems of the world. But I'm not into proselytizing. I don't want people to see me as weird, as a cultist, particularly since Guyana."

Since Gloria made a "part-time" commitment to the movement, I asked her how much time she devoted to its practice. "Previously I went almost every night to satsang, about two hours each time. But lately I found myself getting hooked to the externals, the group experience. It was getting to be too much of a religion, too many rituals. I was getting off the track. I just want to be by myself, not go to meetings, to get to the original purpose, the original point that Maharaj Ji offers. . . . Even though I haven't been as involved, I love to see Maharaj Ji. Sometimes, I feel guilty that I don't do enough. I think I'm going to love him all my life."

Former Members

A very different viewpoint was expressed by those individuals who were one-time members of the Divine Light Mission and have subsequently been deprogrammed out of it. Harry Berman, a follower of Maharaj Ji for five years, was deprogrammed by several people hired by his parents. A year later he was being trained as a salesman, but he also did deprogramming occasionally because he believed he was "helping people." Harry further explained that deprogramming "reinforced the reasons for getting out" and he needed the money he earned from the activity. He planned to return to school soon, to do graduate work either in social work or psychology. He described what his life was like at the time he first became involved in the Divine Light Mission:

"I had graduated from college in 1973 as an anthropology major and I wasn't doing anything with my life. I didn't have direction. I was searching in all areas. I didn't know what to do careerwise. I was searching also for spiritual experiences. I worked at lots of jobs after college—I even sold dope. I went to Columbia as a premed student for a while. I was thinking of becoming a veterinarian.

"When I was 25, I was traveling in Paris. While I was there, I suffered a depression. I had split up with my girlfriend—actually, on the way to Paris I split up with her. I felt very alienated, different from people, like I didn't have the same values as most people in society."

Before continuing with his description of events in Paris, Harry discussed previous relevant events: "I kept meeting premies even in the United States before going to Paris. At a professor's house, I met someone who gave me satsang. I was open; I listened. They can take advantage of anyone searching. My impression is that she couldn't understand why I liked her. I thought she had really been crazy before. Now, she looked better. It was really a positive change. She had been depressed; now she was smiling. Next, in Boston I met a little girl who was a beam of light. The DLM was different then. She was babbling about light, music, and the Holy Name. Lots of people get into groups because they are attracted to members of the opposite sex and they use it.

Then I met Keith Matthews, who is the older brother of a friend from high school, at a party. Everyone left the room, but I stayed and listened to him give satsang. I didn't make a decision then, but I felt good about it. I was doing TM [transcendental meditation] so I already had my guru and I didn't want to change. But I felt I would have to check it out."

Returning to the recounting of his Paris trip, Harry continued: "Then, when I was in a vegetarian restaurant in Paris, I met some premies. They didn't tell me they were premies. I left the restaurant and a mousey-type girl ran after me. She told me she had a job for me in a restaurant. I didn't have money so I went to work in the restaurant. I had a 'snapping' experience. I was working and went to the basement and saw this picture of Guru Maharaj Ji and felt that he had been trying to come into my life. I hadn't gone to satsang. This was my last chance to find out if it was real. Premies were always talking about this fantastic experience. This sounded good. I decided to check it out and began to go to satsang every night. I received Knowledge after four months."

Harry talked about some of the changes he experienced subsequent to his Knowledge session: "I became a vegetarian and became more spiritual. I wanted to move into an ashram, but the one near me had closed. That was in 1976. In 1978, I moved in and followed everything. If you really follow the group, there are really profound changes. I meditated a minimum of one hour in the morning and one hour in the evening. When I was in Boston, I meditated for two-and-a-half to three hours every morning and two hours every night. I meditated a lot. I didn't think very much. In DLM, you're not supposed to think. There are several commandments in DLM: Never put off until tomorrow what you can do today; constantly meditate and remember the Holy Name; always have faith in God; never leave room for doubt in your mind; and never delay in attending satsang. Meanwhile I got a job working for Divine Sales, a DLM used-furniture business. I received a minimal salary, which I turned over to the ashram supervisor.

"When I lived in New York City, I had various jobs like selling pottery for the Big Apple Importers, which are connected to DLM, and turned over all my money to the ashram. I had other jobs in New York—canvassing for a home improvement company, dishwasher, waiter, assistant cook, bicycle messenger."

Harry and I also discussed his relationships with family members and how they were affected by his following Maharaj Ji. "My family is Jewish, but they're not religious at all.... My family thought I was a robot. They tried to get me out. They didn't know what to do. Finally, they had me deprogrammed. When a friend was deprogrammed, they contacted him.

"I still loved my parents while I was in DLM, but I used them for money. I wanted to draw them into the group. But I didn't talk to them much because the Guru Maharaj Ji says, 'No chitchat.' I have two younger sisters. Our relationship has always been pretty close although we did have some communication problems. I would go over to their house but I had to be back by eight for satsang. The other premies and initiators were told that their parents were devils, that their ties with their families are cut when the umbilical cord is cut."

Harry described his deprogramming experience for me: "I was visiting my parents in New York. They paid for my ticket. I was combining my visit with a business trip. I went to my aunt's house and they closed the door. There were five or six guys. I was in a room for one week. When I realized I was going to be deprogrammed, I didn't get really mad. I was going to meditate and pray and get out of it. They were talking and I meditated. DLM doesn't look at the world as reality. During the deprogramming, they gave me information about the Guru's life. They try to hit a point you're not prepared to answer. Finally, I snapped; I was utterly devastated. You find that what you've based your life on is not real. It's your whole life. On the fifth day of deprogramming, I was asked: 'How do you know the Holy Name is God?' At that point, I knew I was never going back. I would probably never have left on my own. I would never have gone in if I had known. They lie, they put on a show."

After his deprogramming, Harry was involuntarily committed by his parents to a rehabilitation center, where he remained for two months. He told me what he was like at the beginning of that period: "I had no feelings. I was a zombie. I couldn't eat at a table with people eating meat. I couldn't ride in a bus with people talking. I couldn't talk to people. I was sexually messed up. I had been celibate for two years. I had learned that sex is for having kids. One is not allowed to have worldly pleasures. The Guru Maharaj Ji is above everyone. I couldn't read or concentrate. When I read Lifton's book,[22] I realized my mind didn't work any longer. I felt like something had happened to me, that the pathways in my head were being rearranged. I couldn't process information. I suffered intellectual, emotional, and physical impairment while in DLM. I have not fully recovered them. . . . You become addicted to meditation. When I got out, I didn't sleep for six weeks. Then I would only sleep for one hour a night for six months. I couldn't stop meditating for a long time."

Harry did make one comment about the positive effect of life with the Divine Light Mission. "In DLM, you work together, serve together with people, and you learn to live with people in a particular environment."

He continued to describe his experiences upon leaving DLM: "After I left the rehabilitation center, I moved in with my parents. We had a communication problem. They didn't believe I was really out. Then I traveled and made friends with ex-cult members. But it's important to have friends who were never cult members. One of the greatest things about getting out of a cult is having real relationships with people who have real feelings and live without any ulterior motives."

Finally, Harry talked about his life at the present time: "I believe in God now. There are still problems I have related to my cult experience. I doubt my ability to know my own feelings. Am I really in love? I question my own feelings. The cult experience is a buffer against reality.... My self-concept now is that I think I'm basically a good person. I'm very sensitive, maybe overly sensitive. I'm more rational than before. I'm not an extremist person; I'm more moderate now. I still have a long way to go, particularly in my career and in my education. Emotionally, and careerwise, I'm five years behind everyone else."

Just as Harry Berman attributed all of his problems and adverse experiences during his five years with DLM to the group and Maharaj Ji, so did Phyllis Bernard. She began her involvement with the movement in 1973 at the age of 18, and continued to follow Maharaj Ji for almost eight years. She discussed with me her life during that period. "Guru Maharaj Ji offered me a solution to all the problems of humanity. The meditation makes you one with God.... I was living in Colorado with high school friends. One had a picture of Guru Maharaj Ji and she started telling me about him. She gave me free satsang. Actually, there are four techniques which they use which are hypnotic.

"I'm originally from New Jersey and I had planned to take a year off between high school and college to figure out what I wanted to do. My parents were not too pleased with that, but they accepted it. In 1973 I went to the millennium festival in the Houston Astrodome. It was real convincing. They used quotes from the Bible and you do get high from meditation. It elevates you, but it's no different from being a positive person. When you're young and searching, this was a solution.

"There were times when I was more heavily involved than

at other times. The last two years I was more heavily involved than ever.... Before I joined I was an atheist. My parents never preached anything about God. My parents believe in God; they're Protestant. I attended a Presbyterian Sunday school. They were seriously upset when I joined DLM. I wouldn't talk to them. But when they tried to talk to me, I would just talk about the Guru....

"During the last two years in DLM, I lived with the man who became the father of my baby; he's still a member. We had some kind of physical attraction. Once in a while we smoked pot or took a little LSD. At one time, I was meditating so much I let everything else go. The effect of meditation alone is damaging enough. You're told to trust, that the Lord will take care of you. I would steal, shoplift. I lived off food stamps. I was on welfare. It didn't matter. They scared you from having regular jobs. They always want you preaching and meditating.... The guy I lived with started beating me. There is an underlying theme of violence in the Divine Light Mission because your true feelings are always suppressed. You're supposed to keep your mouth shut. Eventually there is so much anger that you have to let go. The guy I lived with broke windows and sometimes would beat me. I would be real calm and then I would start screaming.

"Finally I asked the man I lived with to leave. He was 27 years old and all he could do was meditate. He got money from his mother and we lived on food stamps. He was very manipulative and I'm very scared of him. He meditates a lot and then he uses the same ploys. He constantly tries to inflict guilt, to make me feel inferior to him. I would do anything he wanted me to do.

"I'm also afraid of Guru Maharaj Ji. They use a lot of fear. They tell you if you leave, you'll never make it. They tell you it's like dropping a glass. You'll drop into a thousand pieces. And you'll never get back together. It's like your head is wired. You just listen to that experience and nothing else and just digest that. It's totally unrealistic. . . . I had some really rough times while I was in DLM. I lived on the streets for a long time. I was raped while I was hitchhiking once. I was threatened frequently."

At my request, Phyllis discussed the circumstances under which she left the Divine Light Mission: "Four months ago, my parents called me. They wanted me to come home to visit. I was alone with my baby. I was home for nine days. I was feeling well, giving a little satsang to them. My mother told me she didn't understand it. On the ninth day, my parents told me we were going to go roller skating. But then they said we were going to another town to roller skate. Then my father said: 'We'll stop at a friend's house.' I thought that would be fun. They wanted to see my baby and I was very happy about that. We walked into this house and there were six or seven guys there. Immediately, I got scared. I started crying, screaming. I thought they wouldn't understand. I was hysterical. Eventually, after about two hours, I calmed down. Coming out was a gradual snapping process for me. I was asking questions by the second night. I wanted to meditate but they told me not to meditate.

"Then I went to a rehabilitation center. I told the guy I lived with where I was. I wanted to deprogram him. I was still attracted to him, but it was an unhealthy attachment. Then I floated. I was very confused. I didn't know what reality was. I thought of going back to DLM. The rehab center I went to was run by ex-cult kids who were doing their best, but I was still confused. Then I went back to Florida to live with DLM again. But I had no money and I called my parents. They asked me to come back home."

The final part of the interview concerned Phyllis' present life. "My relationship with my family is better than ever. Anything wrong with the relationship is corrected. I'm totally in love with my parents. I really had no contact with them while I was away. I was really high all the time. I had no direction. I saw my parents as crazy, the opposite of what I was involved in. I felt that they were full of hate. Actually, I was the one who was full of hate. . . . Now the only thing I do related to religion is read the Bible once in awhile. . . . I feel like a young kid again. I'm really happy about my baby. I feel very free."

Jennifer Dixon was a loyal follower of Maharaj Ji from 1975 to 1977. She described how she first became involved and about her life during those two years. "I left home at 18 because I had to get away from my mother. I am one of seven kids. I am the middle one, the youngest girl. I always felt my mother was against me; she was overprotective. My parents split when I was about 5. They were always fighting when I was growing up. I moved in with a family, an all-American type, when I was 18. They were the parents of a good friend. I started staying with them and working in a seafood restaurant as a cook and waitress. I was also taking ballet lessons, studying with a company, hoping to join it. I had been studying ballet since I was 10 or 11 years old. My goal was to be a ballet dancer. I was living with Andy, a guy who was in his late 20's, from September to June in a rental on Long Island. While Andy and I lived together, I saw the son in the family that I had previously lived with. Greg had always been a hippie. Now he was sunburned, had short hair. He looked stoned; his eyes were glassy. He said: 'The Perfect Master's here.' I saw such a difference in him. He showed me a tape of Guru Maharaj Ji. My boyfriend walked out of the room. He knew it was fake. Greg invited me to a satsang meeting. I met a man named Dennis there, and was very attracted to him. But I found out he was in the ashram. I told my boyfriend about satsang. He told me to be careful, that Guru Maharaj Ji was a phony.

"In June, our lease was up. We couldn't find an apartment, so we moved into the apartment in Andy's parents' garage. Andy was going through a divorce and his parents thought I was so good to him. I started working for my mother in her restaurant and she accepted my living with Andy.

"I continued to go to satsang. My mother began to be concerned when I was slicing some food one day while looking at a picture of Guru Maharaj Ji. I would always want to bring anyone close to me to the satsang meetings. I wanted Knowledge. Being an "aspirant," aspiring to Knowledge was actually more enjoyable than being a premie, one who has received Knowledge.

"I told Andy I was going to a festival for the weekend. He was mad, but I went anyway. Over the weekend I turned into a vegetarian. I started going to satsang every night. Andy said: 'Go if it's good for you.' Then I left Andy and went home to my mother's house. She was glad I was home. I still had pictures of Guru Maharaj Ji. I had set up an altar. She would break my pictures of Guru Maharaj Ji or throw them out. My mother is Catholic; my aunt's a nun. My father is Protestant.

"Then I left. I felt I needed to get away. I went to see a girlfriend in Tucson whose brother was a member of the Divine Light Mission. The DLM center was a half-hour away from her house and I went to satsang every night.

"One day, I was told that I was going to receive Knowledge that weekend, so I went to Phoenix and received Knowledge. I moved into a pre-ashram. It was for girls who wanted to live in an ashram lifestyle. The housemother was very strict. She had two kids. The father of the two children was in a mental institution. We had to get up at 6:30. I started doing meditation twice a day, an hour and a half in the morning and one hour at night. Plus, I also did two other techniques all the time—Holy Name and Nectar. They kept saying: 'Don't think, don't listen to your mind, just meditate.' All the premies said that. Everything is satsang, service, and meditation.

"I started cleaning houses. I called my family to check in. They were concerned, but they didn't ask too many questions. I decided to move to Miami to be near Guru Maharaj Ji. I wanted to do service. I was with a friend. We had no money, but we charged our trip by car. I called home and my mother started crying, asking me to come home to my sister's bridal shower. I said: 'I can't, I have this festival.' Then the girl I was staying with left me. I stayed at another premie's house, which was really crazy. There was a father and his daughter. He had taken her away from the mother. They would tell people they were a couple. The daughter was 16 years old and was sleeping with two guys. There were other strange people living in the house. One person's arm went through a glass window. They weren't meditating, but they were premies, followers of Guru Maharaj Ji."

Jennifer then described how she finally left the Divine Light Mission: "I called my sister. My sister had gone to a satsang meeting once. She just sat there with a smile. She didn't want to tell me it was a fake. I had been apart from her for two years. We had always been very close. I called her and said I have no money. Then I called my mother who told me that there would be a ticket at the airport for me to fly home. I started living with my sister and brother. I went to see Andy to see if I still loved him. My sister and brother bought me clothes and I didn't go to satsang all week. Then, I called Dennis and he told me to go to satsang.

"I told my sister I didn't know if I wanted to go to the Guru Maharaj Ji festival or to her wedding. She ripped my necklace, which had a picture of the Guru in it, off and we started fighting for three hours. She told me I'd changed, that I had given up everything, that she'd rather see me dead. She said: 'You can't meditate any longer, it's over.' She was holding me down. I was planning ways to hit her with a metal stand. I spit at her. I called her a devil and I kept meditating. I said: 'Guru Maharaj Ji, I'm with you.'

"Finally, something started to sink in. She said: 'Guru Maharaj Ji drinks, sits in his vomit.' I thought: 'If I listen, she'll get off of me.' My brother came home while my sister was still holding me down. She told him she was trying to knock some sense into me. She said: 'I want you back as my sister.' Then the three of us went out and got drunk. Then I started freaking out. My sister got my mother. I was drunk; it was three in the morning. My mother started screaming: 'You little bitch.' She dragged me up the stairs. I was on the bed and started trembling in her arms in a fetal position. I heard my mother say: 'They said this was going to happen.' I felt completely dependent on them. I wanted help. Mother said: 'Do you see this was wrong?'

"In a way, I liked all the attention. It was like I was very sick for a long time and I was finally getting some real care. It was finally my turn for someone to take care of me. I went to lay down. Then Benjamin came; he had been deprogrammed. I said: 'Wow, a real deprogrammer!' In a way I was excited, but I also thought: 'He's not gonna get me.' I started being real nasty. He said: 'If you're going to be nasty, I'll leave.' My mother kept screaming if I gave an answer she didn't like. He started reading all these facts about Guru Maharaj Ji. He said: 'If you saw a baby drowning, and Guru Maharaj Ji said, "Let it drown," what would you do?' I had to think; it took a long time. I said: 'I think I'd save it,' but then I said: 'Well if he were right there I would listen.' That had a great impact, because I realized I would kill for Guru Maharaj Ji. Then Benjamin read Lifton's chapter 22 to me.[23]

"I ate a melted cheese and mushroom sandwich and watched him eat a hamburger. I wanted a bite but wouldn't dare. Benjamin then said: 'Jennifer, you have a choice. Are you going back?' I looked back at him and I knew I was completely back. I saw everything differently; I was happy and smiling. Then we went for a walk. I was so happy. We had dinner and wine with the whole family, my aunt and her children, too. It was very low key.

"The next day a premie came knocking on my door. I was scared and started hiding. My mother told me: 'Don't worry.' Then, my mother said to the premie: 'Call up your parents. Get some help.' She just stared at my mother."

For six months, Jennifer dated Dennis, the man she met at

a satsang meeting. When he left the movement about a year ago, he called her. Initially, she didn't even want to talk to him because she thought he was still a premie, but now that they have both left Maharaj Ji's following, they can share certain problems of readjustment. Currently Jennifer is working as a waitress; she is taking dance lessons again, and attempting to enter the world of modeling.

Divergent Viewpoints

The completely divergent viewpoints expressed by premies and former premies suggest the complexity of the movement and its powerful impact on its followers and their families. The techniques offered by Guru Maharaj Ji can be perceived to be enormously helpful during times of crisis. For example, one premie gave me a moving account of her use of meditation and other techniques associated with following the Guru, during the ordeal of dealing with her mother's gradual and painful death from cancer. When her father-in-law suffered a stroke and eventually died, she and her husband felt that these techniques and their belief in the Guru as the Perfect Master again brought them and the dying man great comfort.

However, others have pointed to the devastating impact of the belief in Guru Maharaj Ji on their lives. Some may be confusing the effect of DLM and other relatively unrelated life events. For example, Phyllis Bernard's account of her life while she was part of the movement included various traumatic situations: she was beaten by her husband and she was raped. In describing those events, she commented: "I can now attribute all that bad stuff to the cult."

Other former devotees noted that DLM contains many or all of the ingredients Lifton cited as aspects of ideological totalism in his book *Thought Reform and the Psychology of Totalism.* One ex-premie named Joe Nelson spent five hours with me one day going through Lifton's chapter 22, entitled

"Ideological Totalism,"[24] for that purpose. For example, he indicated that satsang and the ashram community are instances of "milieu control"; that the grace of Maharaj Ji and the festivals are manifestations of "mystical manipulation"; that the "demand for purity" leads followers to try to be "perfect premies"; that DLM "maintains an aura of sacredness around its basic dogma," which is Knowledge; and that the language is "loaded" with terms like Knowledge, Perfect Master, and satsang. Joe also commented that his criticisms of the group extend to those who maintain a part-time commitment to Maharaj Ji. "I think that even though they maintain normal lives, being dentists, psychiatric social workers, or whatever, they contribute money to the Guru and bring other people in who may not be able to maintain the normalcy of their lives. Also, after many years, they may get deeper and deeper into the practices of the group. Premies don't have very much time to spend with other people. They're meditating, going to satsang for two hours every night." Several former premies also suggested that they were trained to ignore, shut out, or distrust their minds. Harry Berman, for instance, told me: "If you realize that you are thinking, you are supposed to stop mid-thought and begin to meditate."

It is apparent that Guru Maharaj Ji and his teachings are perceived differently by different people. Messer commented about these differing reactions: "I doubt that the entire world population will be caught up in this movement, but the intensity of feeling many seem to have about it—whether for or against—suggests that it poses some issues important to this culture."[25]

8: Wainwright House

SHIATZU: An Oriental Experience, Basic Training in Psychosynthesis, Aerobic Dance, Working with Your Dreams, Born to Win, Putting Your Song Together—these are the titles of just a few of the workshops and programs offered by an organization called Wainwright House, the Center for Development of Human Resources,[1] which recently celebrated its 40th anniversary. Wainwright House describes its aim on its membership card: "To provide an atmosphere where people can find their own best path to spiritual growth. It helps members to develop inner resources for living their deepest convictions, to be enriched for meaningful contribution in the worlds around, and to find encouragement in their quest for love of God."

This nonprofit organization, chartered by the state of New York, dedicated its home in Rye, New York, a suburb in Westchester County, in 1951. The real beginning of Wainwright House occurred ten years earlier, when several business and professional men met "to create and preserve in laymen both the belief that Christianity will work and the determination that it shall be tried."[2] James M. Speer was elected chairman and Weyman Huckabee secretary of the Laymen's Movement, as the group came to be called. They started with meetings and weekend retreats in the homes and offices of members.

From 1941 to 1951 the Laymen's Movement grew rapidly and became more and more influential in the United States and elsewhere. It "was instrumental in shaping the life of the United Nations, founded at San Francisco in 1945 and holding its first meeting in London in January 1946."[3] By 1947, 8,000 churches were participating in the observance of Laymen's Sunday. A meditation room at the United Nations was established in 1949 and each session of the General Assembly was opened and closed with a moment of meditation and silent prayer, due to the efforts of the Movement. During that period its membership roster, which was rather heterogeneous, included prominent and/or wealthy figures such as Dwight D. Eisenhower, J.C. Penney, and Conrad Hilton; as well as labor leaders, insurance executives, and publishers. But garage mechanics, clerks, carpenters, and salesmen were also members. The Wainwright House edifice and most of its furniture were given to the Laymen's Movement in March 1951 by Fenrose Wainwright Condict, who believed that the house she had inherited from her parents was destined to be donated to a worthy cause. The actual house, which was built in 1929, is situated on five impressively landscaped acres with beautiful trees and shrubbery overlooking the Long Island Sound. After the elegantly furnished house was dedicated on May 20, 1951, with the words: "To the Greater Understanding of God," many new programs were implemented. For example, the Receptive Listening program was begun by several individuals who were interested in developing their ability to listen. Robert and Esther Greenleaf, Mary Todd, and others started the program, combining the ideas of the humanistic psychologist Carl Rogers and the depth psychology of Carl Jung. They proposed to provide a supportive environment where individuals could develop greater understanding of themselves and others through listening. The Receptive Listening Program, which has incorporated various philosophies through the years, is now directed by Gene Patton and is obviously a core part of the present Wainwright House.

In the 1950's, the Laymen's Movement also implemented business seminars and a number of participants in those seminars contributed to the movement's study book, *Living My Religion on My Job*. Another developing focus of Wainwright House during that period was spiritual healing. Dr. Rebecca Beard, author of *Everyman's Search,* lectured on the subject of spiritual healing one autumn weekend in 1953. After she conducted a healing service at Wainwright House for a critically ill man, he immediately began to recover from his illness. That experience led to the creation of the Commission for the Study of Healing, which evolved into the present day Center for Wholistic Health. Numerous experiments concerned with spiritual healing and extrasensory perception were conducted under the direction of the commission.

Starting in 1956, the Laymen's Movement conducted seminars and published its reports on the subject of Science and the Nature of Man. The list of speakers at the first seminar was impressive: Ruth Anshed, editor; Rene Dubos, biologist; Loren Eisley, anthropologist; Fred Hoyle, astrophysicist; Kirtley Mather, geologist; Henry Morgenau, physicist; Jaroslav Pelikan, editor; and Gertrude Schmeidler, psychologist.

The decade of the 1960's also brought important changes and growth to Wainwright House. Executives from large companies such as IBM, Polaroid, General Electric, and Gray Advertising Agency met in 1961 to discuss the relationship between religion and work. During the same year, the Laymen's Movement donated $15,000 to be used for the redecoration of the UN Meditation Room. When Secretary General Dag Hammarskjold replaced the "altar" (a four-foot tree trunk section from a 300-year-old agma tree from French Equatorial Africa), the Swedish birchwood chairs, and the curtains of the Meditation Room, they were all donated to Wainwright House. These can still be found on the second floor of the simply decorated Meditation Rome of Wainwright House.

Wainwright House was certainly affected by the world events of the 1960's. An important development was the broadening of the membership base. In 1964, the organization's bylaws were changed to include a special associate membership category for women and members of the clergy. In 1969, full voting privileges were extended, so that thereafter all people could fully participate in the activities and functions of Wainwright House. In addition, numerous programs dealing with such timely social and political issues as international conflicts, race relations, and the generation gap were offered. Other programs focused on business. For example, a sensitivity training course, Therapeutic Values in Group Relations, was held for businessmen in 1966, while the Innovative Management Program to facilitate the development of greater maturity and creativity in managers took place in 1968.

The 25th anniversary of the Laymen's Movement was celebrated in 1967 at the Waldorf Astoria in New York City with Walter Cronkite, the newscaster, as the master of ceremonies and U.S. Senator Charles Percy as the keynote speaker.

By 1970 Wainwright House found itself in a financial crisis with a bank balance of only $1,000. Through the financial support of the members of the board of directors, the establishment of new programs, the addition of summer programs, the finding of new sources of support, and other innovative approaches, the organization was able to survive and continue to grow. At the 30th anniversary of the Laymen's Movement in 1971, a portrait of the honored guest, Fenrose Wainwright Condict, painted by Molly Guion, was presented. This portrait now hangs in the library of the house.

The Rev. Dr. Alfred Sunderwirth became the director of

Wainwright House in 1972, a position he still holds. He received a Ph.D. from Columbia University in Religious and Biblical Studies. He was on the staff of the Rye Presbyterian Church when he was asked to come to Wainwright House as an administrator one day a week. He related the following story to me about his arrival there in the early 1970's: "Mrs. Condict said: 'I'm glad you're here. When I first saw you, a voice said to me that man has to be here at Wainwright House to carry out its purpose and mission.' She said that she had a prophetic sense that I had to be here." Gradually, his work for the center took up more time, so that he had less time for the church. But, as he explains: "My church approves of my working here. Others have asked me: 'Why would you leave the church? I felt like it was the right thing to do at that time in my life. Wainwright House makes a significant contribution to the lives of people. It is in harmony with my vocation.... It is an institution on the move. It's on the leading edge of the human potential movement."

The SCOPE program, "a center for learning, personal growth, and service designed for men and women seeking new life after retirement or semi-retirement,"[4] was begun in the 1970's. It has offered programs in such varied areas as painting, photography, history, literature, and languages. The decade of the 1970's also marked an increased outreach to other organizations, thus further broadening the offerings of Wainwright House. For example, the affiliation with the C. G. Jung Foundation in New York led to the establishment of the Center for Jungian studies at Wainwright House while the association with the Teilhard Association resulted in numerous programs "on the work of the great scientist/philosopher/priest."[5]

There are at present nine individual learning centers within Wainwright House, including the Receptive Listening and SCOPE programs previously described. The main purpose of the Center for Cross-Cultural Programs "is to provide friendship, assistance in cultural adaptation, and improvement in the use of the English language for neighbors from other lands for whom English is a second language."[6] *Tsudoi,* an important component of the Cross-Cultural Center, is a support and discussion group, particularly for Japanese women in Westchester County. A second center offers various courses concerned with Exploring New Dimensions of Consciousness. The aim of the Radix: Education in Feeling program, one of the offerings of this center, "is to grow in the capacity to experience and express deep feelings, to connect up with oneself, and to contact others. As deeply held emotions of pain, anger, and fear are experienced and expressed, chronic unconscious patterns of tension soften and the individual can allow deeper contact with his own aliveness and with others."[7] Other recent Consciousness workshops were Working With Dreams, Mind/Brain/Body, and New Dimensions in Music. The Center for Psychological Studies (which had been the Center for Jungian Studies) explores the depth psychology of Carl Jung and other expressions of psychology and psychiatry. Psychotherapy and the Body and Born to Win: Transactional Analysis were courses recently offered at this center. The Center for Religious and Philosophical Studies provides the opportunity for representatives from different religions to share their personal experience of faith in courses ranging from Clowning: Faith and Fantasy (co-sponsored by the Temple of Understanding) to An Evening on Sufism.

The Guild for Spiritual Guidance, developed in 1977 by a group of 20 individuals called together by Dr. Sunderwirth, is a formal two-year training program. "Its objective is to cultivate in the trainees new depth of inner journeying and comprehension which equips them for a vocation of guiding others along this same inward path of fulfillment and service."[8] The program attempts to bridge the "Judeo-

Christian heritage of spiritual direction" with the depth psychology of Carl Jung "within the context of the Teilhardian myth of cosmogenesis to make it relevant and specific for contemporary men and women."[9]

The Women's Studies and Creative Expression Center offers seminars and support groups for women throughout the life cycle. Aerobic Dance: The Effective Alternative to Jogging; Mother, Wife, Person; Group Leadership Skills; Fighting for Intimacy; and Seeing and Drawing as Meditation are some of the recent catalogue listings of this Center.

A number of programs focusing on "self-responsibility for wellness and care of the body, mind, and spirit through traditional and alternative medicine"[10] are offered by the Center for Wholistic Health and Healing. Recent workshops have included Dealing with Anxiety and Stress Wholistically, Releasing Tensions Through Touch, The Crystal Clear Self-Intensive: A Fasting Program, and How to Heal Your Own Back.

Wainwright House Participants

Although Wainwright House is large in terms of the variety of its activities and the number of program participants, it is relatively small with regard to its staff and membership roster. There are 11 paid full-time and about 13 to 15 paid part-time staff members. In addition, there are two full-time staff members who are not paid because they "have their own financial resources," according to Sunderwirth. Six of the staff members live at the House itself. There are also about 120 volunteers, 90 of whom do some work every week. There are eight categories of membership based on yearly gifts. A regular member pays $40, while a sustaining member who contributes $135 or more receives a discount on tuition and books, plus full tuition for Receptive Listening. Two-together membership is $200, supporting membership is $500, sponsoring $1,000, patron $2,500, benefactor $5,000, and life membership is granted to those who have donated "a one-time gift of $10,000 or more within a one year period."[11] Evidently there are few members in the latter categories, as the present endowment/reserve fund is only $20,000. There are presently about 45 life, patron, sponsoring, and supporting members, and about 300 sustaining and annual members and contributors. Some individuals have retained membership status for years, while others periodically renew their membership. Still others join for one year and never return to the organization.

Sunderwirth explained the drawing power of Wainwright House: "People have a need for personal development. They need a different space. They want to grow, to learn more about themselves, to acquire skills. They are looking for happiness or more happiness. Wainwright House has been around for a long time. People respect and appreciate that fact. In fact, we preceded the human potential movement. People are interested in spiritual growth, transcendent values, depth experiences; they're on a spiritual quest. Here, they can find what they're looking for; they can find their souls. They come here for soul nourishment. They're trying to find their way to a religious experience but they aren't looking for theology or philosophy. . . . Some have been turned off by the church, but want some kind of association with the spiritual, religious qualities of life. Some come to Wainwright House and then go back to the church that they've left. It reinforces what they've already experienced. They can go back to the church with a new strength. . . . Wainwright House is the primary place for many which allows spiritual growth. It provides an atmosphere that is life transforming, the transformation in some instances from a living hell to happiness. There is nothing specific that Wainwright House does, but rather it is what happens while people are here that is important."

A young woman who participated in programs, but was not a member, explained the difference between Wainwright House and other organizations. "I've seen and been to places that have a specialized focus. But just about everything is offered here. For example, church or youth groups are just religious. Other places just do massage or just yoga. This is such a comprehensive facility, an all-purpose facility with respect to personal growth."

Many individuals participate in programs at Wainwright House because of their friendship with a member. A man about 45 years old, who was attending a Dream Workshop, remarked, "I'm here because of her [pointing to the woman seated to the left of him on a couch]. I've never done anything like this before."

Other people come to Wainwright House to take part in particular programs, and have no real interest in the organization per se. For example, at the aerobic dance class one woman said: "They keep the costs down here. The class is of a high caliber." Another said: "Felice is a very good instructor. She's very obliging." Another woman bluntly stated: "I'm a middle-aged female who is interested in keeping my muscle tone. This is nonboring exercise to music. It does work and it's invigorating."

Some individuals may be attracted to Wainwright House, not because of the programs that are offered, but because of the physical beauty and peacefulness of the surroundings. One clear summer evening, a friend who was in a rather bad mood, annoyed with a number of friends and family members, accompanied me to Wainwright House. While I was busy conducting interviews and participating in a workshop, he was watching sailboats on Long Island Sound and the sun setting on the water, and listening to the songs of the birds. By the time I rejoined him at the end of the evening, it was evident that his mood was considerably lighter, and he acknowledged that the physical setting had allowed him to unwind and view his life and his problems in a better perspective.

Although Sunderwirth explained that most who come to Wainwright House are not members, he cited a number of reasons for becoming a member: "First, some have had an experience which is very important and they love the place and want to support it. Second, they see the importance and significance for others and want to make available to others what they have. Third, they want to be involved monetarily and with their bodies, minds, and souls. They make special, nonmonetary contributions, but because of their involvement, they also make a financial contribution. Fourth, membership provides discounts for programs. Often it is that way in the beginning. Depending on what happens to them here, they may or may not be continuous members."

John Hewitt, who has been associated with Wainwright House for 26 years and became its house manager, explains that people join "because they have a hunger for new inner life.... It is a center for growth and change. Our basic purpose is to create an environment for people to become more loving. That is clearly a spiritual motivation. You don't need to believe in a doctrine of God, but you need a reverence for life, a belief in growth and change. This is not a center of authoritarian doctrine."

A physician and long-time member said: "I came here because I had heard of the Laymen's Movement. I was looking for a religious, nondenominational movement and I found it."

Another man who joined about 20 years ago said: "My friends had been here, but I wasn't having any of that kind of nonsense at that time.... My friends had talked of their experience for two years and it rubbed off. I had to find out what it was.... I signed up. It has been a fantastic experience. It's exciting and gratifying to watch people turn on to the Receptive Listening experience."

Several individuals indicated that they had joined

Wainwright House because their spouses were involved. One woman who became a member about ten years ago explained, "In marrying Bill, I married Wainwright House. It was a school for me.... It provided support when I needed it." Others join because their friends have participated in a program that has had a positive impact on their lives. A 49-year-old man who had been a member for about five or six years explained: "Originally I joined because a friend of mine had taken Receptive Listening and liked it and while he was taking it he said that he thought I would like it, that it's kind of useful. I took the Receptive Listening course that May. Being in that building I feel differently about myself, the world, other people and the whole thing." Another member, about 50 years old, also joined Wainwright House because of a friend. "I had been interested in learning how to meditate. This friend told me to go to Wainwright House. I took a course called Centering which is basically meditative techniques, followed by courses on biofeedback and other areas. That was about eight or nine years ago. I was an executive on Wall Street. I perceived myself to be under a lot of pressure. I wanted to see what avenues were open to me. I had done some reading on meditation and I had talked to friends about the human potential movement. My personal life was also in turmoil at the time."

The idea of joining an organization like Wainwright House at a time when one's life is in crisis or transition was echoed by a number of respondents. For example, a man in his 40's who had taken the Receptive Listening course as his first experience with Wainwright House noted: "It's probably the first time of my life that for long periods I was with myself. It was a time in my life when I was just coming out of my divorce. It was a very appropriate time for me to do this." A woman, who had been living a traditional life as an upper-middle-class suburban housewife with three children reflected that when she joined she "tore up that lifescript.... Wainwright House was a lighthouse to me."

She also noted that there were "very strong women models."

Many people joined after they had positive experiences with particular programs. A woman, about 45 years old, the manager of a personnel agency, who had been a member on and off for six years said: "I was a student at Barnard studying psychology. I was very interested in Carl Jung. Wainwright House had a workshop on him and I signed up for that immediately. I've taken a number of other courses and workshops here through the years."

The members of Wainwright House range in age from 20 to the 80's. They come from all socioeconomic levels, but are primarily middle and upper-middle class; there are very few upper- or working-class members. Numerous vocations are represented: physicians, educators, business people, homemakers, scientists, politicians, artists, therapists, lawyers, and artisans.

Wainwright House Activities

I participated in several activities at Wainwright House including their elaborate and well-organized 40th anniversary celebration on June 14, 1981. The event began with a wine-and-cheese hour on the lawn which provided the opportunity to greet old friends. The individuals who attended were older than the average age of participants at Wainwright House activities. There were several elderly women who were present without male companions, and who obviously felt quite comfortable at Wainwright House and seemed to enjoy the evening's activities. The sedate nature of the event and the fact that a contribution of $40 or $50 was required for attendance may have precluded the attendance of a young crowd. However, a note on the invitation stated: "If the donation is a deterrent to your joining the celebration, please get in touch with Dr. Sunderwirth, arrange to give what you can and plan to be present." There was considerably more physical contact—

lots of kissing, hugging, and touching—than would generally occur in other cocktail-type situations not associated with the human potential movement.

After the wine-and-cheese reception, a representation of the history of Wainwright House was enacted by the Rye Presbyterian Clown Troupe, followed by a short musical program. There were a few minutes of Centering (silent meditation) before the dinner, which was informal, buffet-style, but provided tasty, well-prepared food. The dinner conversation consisted of topics that one would expect at a place like Wainwright House. There was a discussion of new techniques for learning more effectively, particularly using the right cerebral hemisphere. There was some disagreement about whether creativity is an inborn talent or due to high levels of motivation. I asked a woman who was a doctoral candidate in a humanistic psychology program, and who was accompanied by her husband, what her dissertation topic was. She replied that she couldn't divulge that information because it would deplete her energy.

After dinner there were several brief but eloquent speeches—actually testimonials—by long-time members, people who played a significant role in shaping present-day Wainwright House. For instance, Jean Houston declared that Wainwright House allows her to "take my scientific research, take my spiritual sense, and be as expressive and implosive as I choose in a totally supportive environment.... Wainwright House allows for healing and wholing, centering and deepening.... It allows sacred time and sacred space to converge." The keynote speaker of the evening, Donald Keys, president of Planetary Citizens and author of *The United Nations and Planetary Consciousness,* spoke on the subject "To Heal the Nations."

Another Wainwright House activity in which I was a participant was a workshop, conducted by Dr. Montague Ullman, entitled Working With Dreams. Ullman, a psychiatrist, has also written a book by that title. He gave up his private practice as a psychoanalyst to start the Dream Laboratory at Maimonides Medical Center in New York. He resigned as director of that Dream Laboratory in 1974 to conduct dream research and develop group approaches to working with dreams. His workshop at Wainwright House was the first he had conducted there, although he has given numerous workshops on the subject in a variety of settings, including the Association for Research and Enlightenment, and for different populations, including psychiatrists ("one of the most difficult groups to work with," commented Ullman). A publicity flyer about this workshop describes it in the following way: "The dreamer and the group will interact in working through the personal meaning of the dream. They will develop a familiarity with the language of the dream through a series of exercises designed to illustrate how the dreamer uses imagery to express feelings, how to identify events in waking life that trigger the dream, and how past memories are integrated into present concerns. In the course of this the participants will acquire an appreciation of the artistry of the images they create, the accuracy with which these images can light up long-hidden aspects of their own past and the way in which these processes come together to shed light on their waking experiences. Dreams are exquisitely sensitive instruments for helping us recognize and respond to novelty in our lives."

People attended the workshop for various reasons. For example, one professional woman in her late 30's explained her motivation in the following way: "I don't have good recall of my dreams and my dreams are like my everyday life, about mundane matters, about the office. It's like working at night. I thought that by taking this workshop, my dreams would be more vivid to me and become more interesting."

There were three men and eight women participants, in addition to Ullman, who considered himself a participant as well. "I am the leader only in the sense that someone has to take responsibility for ensuring the integrity of the process, but I'm actually a member of the group. I share my dreams with the group." The session began with a woman asking Ullman: "Is a swimming pool a symbol?" He replied: "It could be. If you gave it to the group, there would be a dozen interpretations." When the group had settled down, Ullman asked: "Who has had a recent dream you'd like to share with the group?" When a man and a woman both responded affirmatively, Ullman asked them: "How urgently would you like to do it? We may only have time for one dream." The man responded with some urgency saying, "I'd like to do it," while the woman said: "My dream is interesting and I'm curious about it, but it's not urgent."

Thus, the group went on to discuss George's dream, which was rich in symbolism and action. Prior to the session, Ullman had requested that I not report on the actual dream content in order to protect the privacy of the dreamer and the group. After George had vividly described his dream, Ullman instructed us: "The dream is now ours. George, you sit back and don't actively participate." He asked for our feelings. People responded as if it truly were their dream. For example, one participant commented, "I feel fear in my dream," while another noted, "I am anxious. . . ."

The group was then instructed to respond to the imagery. Ullman contributed to the group discussion, which was free-flowing and insightful, although a couple of the members said nothing. When Ullman made a suggestion, it was done in a completely nonauthoritarian way: "I have an idea that I want to try out. It may not be relevant, but here it is." Ullman pushed the participants to dig deeper: "Look at each detail. Look at them in the sequence in which they occur. There are many deeper levels. The dream starts in the present and moves into the past."

The second part of the workshop session entailed the dreamer's response to the group's discussion, and the third part allowed a dialogue between the group and the dreamer. Ullman periodically made comments guiding the group: "I can provide you with hints about what is productive in a dialogue. We want to help the dreamer answer the question: Why did the dream occur last night? The dream is our guide."

When a group member asked George a question that was psychologically loaded, Ullman immediately interceded, stating: "That's the kind of question that a therapist would ask. This is not therapy." He used this opportunity to further explain the group's function. "We want to lower defensiveness enough so that the dreamer can better understand his dreams. We can't ask loaded questions. There are limits to our questions; they must be obviously related to the dream or related to what George has shared."

He concludes the session at the end of an hour and a half by instructing George and the dream group: "You have to use your dream; go beyond the dream group. You lose something if you just go with the global. . . . The dream gives you an opportunity to learn something new about yourself, but you have to keep asking: Why this? What is that? Answers can only come from your life experience. The group can help, but only up to a point." Finally Ullman addressed George: "You've shared the dream. You've shared yourself. You have responded as much as you can, but you have further to go."

An important distinction is made in the group between dream work and group therapy. The Working With Dreams workshop led by Ullman is clearly the former. He discusses a number of differences between the two processes in a chapter in Benjamin Wolman's *Handbook of Dreams: Research, Theories and Applications.* For example, in the experiential dream group, "The focus of the group is on the impact of the dream on the dreamer. The focus is on an intrapersonal field." In contrast, in group psychotherapy, "The focus of the group is on the impact of the behavior on an interpersonal field." Another difference is related to the presence or absence of a theoretical orientation. In the dream group, "The dreamer and the group work along intuitive and shared experiential levels with no specific theoretical orientation." In group psychotherapy, on the other hand, "The leader works from a theoretical base involving personal and group dynamics." A number of distinctions can also be made between individual psychotherapy and an experiential dream group. "There is an unhurried, leisurely approach when a group sets out to work on a dream. It is the only item on the agenda, and it may occupy the group for the entire time they spend together. Dream work has its own tempo, which is more apt to unfold naturally when other constraints on time are absent." In individual psychotherapy, there is usually insufficient time to deal with a particular dream at great length. Other problems or issues are too pressing.[12]

The distinction between therapy and workshops or courses at Wainwright House is made repeatedly. Although the Receptive Listening course, perhaps the most significant activity of Wainwright House, may appear to be therapy, its participants indicate that it is certainly not therapy. One member, who had participated both as a regular member of the group and as a leader (or "experienced participant," the term he preferred), described Receptive Listening as "essentially a composite of a lot of things and it's what you make it." Another individual told me: "The watchword of Wainwright House is listening." According to a program brochure, the leaders of Receptive Listening have themselves completed the course and "function as facilitative members of the group rather than teachers. The program is clearly educational and developmental, rather than therapeutic, in its objectives and structure." The application form requests a statement from an individual's therapist expressing agreement with participation in the program. Moreover, the concluding line of the application blank above the signature explicitly states: "I understand that Receptive Listening is an educational program, not therapy."

The general format is one weekend a month of the Receptive Listening Experience over a six-month period. The basic principle of the course "is that each of us has, within, a spiritual or higher Self which is a source of wisdom, love and energy. To become aware of this Self, or center, is to bring its energy and creative power into our lives."

Several different disciplines and approaches are utilized in the Receptive Listening course. The Rogerian concepts of empathic understanding and unconditional positive reward are combined with the depth psychology of Carl Jung, the experiential practices of psychosynthesis as developed by Roberto Assagioli, awareness techniques of the human potential movement (including spontaneous art and movement), journal keeping, and the spiritual traditions of meditation, prayer, centering, and silence.

Although the program is largely experiential, rather than cognitively informative, some basic readings such as *Experiment in Depth* by P.W. Martin are provided to the participants. "The experiences and sharing take place in a caring community where the space is safe enough for us to really hear ourselves and each other. Attention is given to the characteristics of this safe space in small groups or on a one-to-one situation. Encounter confrontation is discouraged," the brochure states. One participant further explained: "Because it doesn't have professional leadership, it will not encourage or even allow people to go really deeply into trauma.... The program isn't geared for that to happen ... I have a tendency to want things to be done for people and part of the value for me of the whole receptive listening thing at Wainwright House ... is that it is more a place which encourages you to do for yourself and doesn't so much presume to tell you what you ought to do."

Others described in the brochure their Receptive Listening Experience in equally positive ways. One said: "We've been discovering our treasures and sharing the excitements. We've been learning to enjoy a variety of activities as we celebrate our humanness." Another reported: "Don't come to the Receptive Listening course unless you're ready—to learn about yourself, to get rid of hang-ups, and to feel the joy of human beings relating on a safe, caring and equal basis." Still another participant reflected: "I feel the leaders and other group members have enabled me to see the more subtle shadows of my personality. As I learn to respect my own intricacies, I find I'm naturally respecting the various personalities of others." A particularly enthusiastic participant exclaimed: "It is exhilarating to discover new dimensions to yourself and at the same time, to relate in a more meaningful way to others. It is one of the nicest things I've ever done for myself."

An innovative variation of the Receptive Listening program, using a one-day workshop format, was implemented for the first time during 1980. It was successfully given to various organizations, including IBM and church and synagogue groups.

Another Wainwright House activity that is scheduled throughout the year is a support group for women, entitled Making Your Life Work, led by Miriam Lubow, coordinator of the Center for Women's Studies and Creative Expression. It begins with a four-hour session which is followed by four two-hour evening sessions. The brochure for this workshop suggested that, as increasing numbers of women question their needs and roles and face various life options and challenges, they will be "searching for an open space" which will "be supportive to the choices they make in directing their lives. To meet these concerns, Making Your Life Work, a Support Group for Women, provides a unique setting of acceptance and encouragement. Through a thoughtful exchange of dialogue and networking of information and resources, it's possible to clarify opinions and choose priorities; to decide on concrete steps, and to implement specific actions toward making life work."

Women of all ages were said by the support group brochure to have found the "nurturing, information, and resources" they sought. An 18-year-old participant explained: "Women bonded together with the courage to explore in an atmosphere which lends peace to a challenging process by providing incomparable support and leaves us with new understanding and the crying desire for more." At the other end of the adult spectrum, a 73-year-old woman reported: "I came to the support group looking for ways to get a new project started. The suggestions led to a successful plan and the project has been implemented."

It is rather difficult to distinguish by attitude and behavior the members of Wainwright House from the staff. Those who work at Wainwright House give the impression that their work is more than a job, that they would be there even if they were not paid. In addition, there is a large group of volunteers, who are at least as dedicated as the staff to the mission of the organization. One young temporary part-time staff member said: "Everyone hangs together. There's a crisis every other minute, but that's part of the fun." John Hewitt, the house manager, commented: "To be able to work here is a privilege." Sunderwirth, the executive director, also noted: "I would still be a part of Wainwright House without a salary. I attend and have attended many programs." Members of the Executive Committee who do not receive a salary are equally committed to Wainwright House. Andrew Carlin, president of the Executive Committee, called it "a loving, caring community. Even in the 'nuts-and-bolts' business segments of it, I like it. I like the programs. I like what they are doing. I guess that part of me feels that I ought to help to see that it's available for other people."

There are many volunteers who are not in leadership positions, but play an important role in the efficient functioning of Wainwright House. One woman, who retired from a paid receptionist position, has been a volunteer at

Wainwright House for eight years. She spends one full day a week at Wainwright House and it is evidently a mutually beneficial relationship. "I'm devoted," she said. "This is what I enjoy doing. I have done volunteer work at a hospital; I'm giving that up, but I would never give this up. I've grown along with it. I've seen all kinds of things happen here and I've been part of it. The people you associate with, work with—everyone is like family. We work together nicely. . . . It is also one of the most beautiful places I have ever been in."

The volunteers, paid staff, and members work together at Wainwright House within a formal organizational structure. The Board of Directors and Board of Trustees "exercise authentic leadership."[13] A formal Annual Report, including Center reports and a financial review, is issued at the end of the fiscal year. The annual meeting is a "formal, legal event" in the words of John Ballard, the chairman of the Board. The June 1981 meeting which was held prior to the 40th anniversary celebration was open to all members. Thirty-six (equally divided by sex) attended. They were largely conservatively dressed, middle-aged, and apparently middle and upper-middle class, as is the general membership. Even in conducting the meeting, the principles that are part of Wainwright House were applied. It started with centering, a couple of minutes of silent meditation with everyone's eyes closed. One could hear the sounds of birds outside. A break was given after about 40 minutes, with the explanation that research had demonstrated that breaks every 40 to 50 minutes are necessary to maintain the alertness and interest of participants.

The Future

Members were so uniformly enthusiastic about Wainwright House that it was difficult to elicit discussion of perceived weaknesses in the organization. One member commented: "I think the major strength is the diversity and the freedom to be different things. I think that is also one of the major weaknesses and the weakness is a good price to pay. If we can, I'd like to see us make it less of a weakness. Some of the weaknesses relate to lack of money in sections. A lot of energy gets devoted to raising money that could be used, perhaps, more productively, in community things. Conversely, the lack of money is one of the big advantages. It tends to make people be committed to what they're doing, because they've got to do it." Although this respondent was close to 50, he indicated that another problem was the older age of most members. He explained: "The other problem is that I think a lot of the things that bring people to a place like Wainwright House occur in mid-life changes. So it has an older population. I don't like that."

Others preferred to talk, not of real weaknesses, but rather of pursuing new directions or the strengthening of already existing concerns or activities. Sunderwirth, for instance, suggested several areas for additional work:

"First, we are already beginning—we need to continue—bridge building with the corporate world. Our involvement with the leaders of the business community would be in the interest of their expressing higher values and would lead to the enhancement of the business community. Second, we should continue our interest in developing programs that lead to a center for peacemaking and environmental living issues. Third, we might get more involved in the area of human justice, develop programs contributing to greater awareness of political realities—where freedom and justice are denied to dissidents, where adequate food is denied to large portions of the world. A fourth area I would like to see enriched and developed is more personal and financial energy available. The funding of important projects and the meeting of needs have to wait for lack of personal and financial energy. I would like to see a more rapid buildup of our endowment. However, these are relatively minor . . . I would like us to have the resources to do everything with excellence—programs, buildings and grounds, office procedures."

Almost everyone I spoke to discussed a new program called the Learning Methods Group or LMG, a London-based international organization reported in its brochures as "committed to bridging the gap between research into human potential, and the application of that research to human affairs including education, business and government." LMG is expected to have a great impact on the future of Wainwright House. John Church, a former executive with an M.B.A. degree, is the full-time coordinator of LMG-USA at Wainwright House, and is working on selling the program to corporations, while his wife, Fran Church, a social worker by training, is the liaison to schools and government agencies. John Ballard, the chairman of the Board of Directors, became familiar with the program when he was in South Africa and suggested that it might play a significant role at Wainwright House. Tony Buzan, an educational consultant, lecturer, author, psychologist, and the founder and managing director of LMG, explained his approach as follows:

"We deal with all the basic skills required for recording, retaining, and recalling information—the three R's! More specifically, a two- or three-day course would identify personal and group areas for improvement in the handling of information." The course includes such areas as creativity, speed or "range reading," memory, and stress management. Buzan suggested that there are important differences between the usual training in memory and reading and LMG. For instance, the brain is not a compartmentalized machine, but an organically integrated totality. It's therefore somewhat futile to break information handling skills down into isolated components. . . . To teach any particular skill properly we are obliged to cover related areas. Conversely, by exploring the links between, say, memory and note-taking, memory and creativity, creativity and note-taking, and so on, we can get these skills to interact synergistically. And that increases the effectiveness of what we teach—and gives something of a mind-expanding peak experience to the student!"[14]

Buzan's approach is exemplified in the use of "mind maps." Instead of taking notes in a linear fashion which, he said, is not the way the brain functions, he suggested that we begin with an image in the middle of the page. Various aspects of the subject can then be represented by key or trigger terms and/or images which extend from the center, thus providing simplified but comprehensive coverage of the topic. John Church called LMG "an exciting but pragmatic approach to learning and teaching." According to LMG advocates, improvements in areas such as concentration, memory, problem solving, and creativity are available to individuals of all ages.

John Hewitt, who has been associated with Wainwright House for almost three decades, summed up its essence: "Wainwright House is made up of people who are sincere, good-willed, and are working together to bring about a new world where people can live together in mutual appreciation. It requires work. Cultural patterns are very stubborn. It's like taking permanent ink out of a piece of cloth; it doesn't come out that easily."

9:
Hare Krishna

Hare Krishna Hare Krishna,
Krishna Krishna Hare Hare,
Hare Rama Hare Rama,
Rama Rama Hare Hare.

THE above chant can be heard whenever devotees of the Hare Krishna (also spelled Krsna) movement, or the International Society for Krishna Consciousness (ISKCON), as they are officially called, are found—on street corners, in their temples, at airports. Anthropologist Francine Jeanne Daner, who conducted an intensive investigation of ISKCON, translates this mahamatra or great chanting: "Hare means the supreme pleasure potency of the Lord. Krsna is the original name of the Lord, and it means all-attractive, Rama is another name of the Lord meaning the enjoyer, because Krsna is the supreme enjoyer; the function of living is thought to be for the enjoyment of Krsna."[1]

The movement in the United States dates from 1965, when His Divine Grace A.C. Bhaktivedanta Swami Prabhupada, the group's leader, brought his spiritual teachings to New York. Bhaktivedanta was born Abhay Charan De on September 1, 1896, in Calcutta, India. After majoring in philosophy, English, and economics at the University of Calcutta, he managed a large chemical company. During the 1920's he met his own spiritual master, Srila Bhaktisiddhanta Sarasvati, who was a follower of Lord Chaitanya (or Caitanya), a Bengalese Brahman born in 1496. The latter became a preacher of Vaishnavism (a religious sect in India) and introduced Sankirtana (dancing and chanting the praises of Krishna, the highest personality of Godhead). The Vaishnavas include several sects, "all of whom worship the deity Vishnu or one of his forms as the Supreme Personality of Godhead"[2] (Krishna is considered to be the most significant avatar or earthly incarnation of Vishnu). They also follow the knowledge contained in the *Bhagavad-Gita* (The Song of God), a Hindu text, written "somewhere between the fifth and second centuries B.C." This scripture can be called "the gospel of India because of its profound influence on the spiritual, cultural, intellectual, and political life of that country today and throughout centuries past."[3]

Hare Krishna devotees accept literally the stories of the appearances and stories of Krishna that are contained in the *Bhagavad-Gita,* while others might regard them as allegorical or mythical.[4] According to a devotee, Chaitanya taught that God is a Person Who has "Form, Qualities, Names, and Pastimes—but Who is nevertheless Absolute and Transcendental and beyond anything we have experienced in this material world."[5] The followers of Chaitanya believed that he was an avatar or Krishna's manifestation in the flesh. "The reason given for Krishna's reappearance as Chaitanya is that he was to teach fallen souls again the way to Krishna, and to reestablish the fact that there is only One Supreme Personality of Godhead predominating over all living entities."[6]

Bhaktivedanta claimed that in 1936 he was "specifically ordered by his guru to spread Krsna Consciousness to the English-speaking people of the West." Thus Bhaktivedanta purportedly followed an unbroken line of gurus starting with Chaitanya. He is often affectionately called Prabhupada, meaning "One at whose feet many masters sit."[7]

In 1944, the *Back to Godhead* magazine began publication

with Bhaktivedanta as the editor-in-chief. (It is still published in the United States by ISKCON.) In 1950, he adopted the *vanaprastha* (retired) life, breaking his relationship with his wife and children, who were adults. He accepted the *sannyasa* life (the renounced order) in 1959 and by 1962 he had started publishing scriptural texts. Finally he heeded his spiritual master's order, and in 1965, at the age of 69, he arrived in New York City to spread Krishna Consciousness.

Prabhupada distinguished Krishna Consciousness from Hinduism: "... Krsna Consciousness is in no way a faith or religion that seeks to defeat other faiths or religions. Rather, it is an essential cultural movement for the entire human society and does not consider any particular sectarian faith. This cultural movement is especially meant to educate people in how they can love God.

"Sometimes Indians both inside and outside of India think that we are preaching the Hindu religion, but actually we are not. One will not find the word 'Hindu' in the *Bhagavad-Gita*."[8]

Wearing saffron robes, Prabhupada began to chant the Hare Krishna mantra to the sound of small Indian cymbals called *kartals* in Tompkins Park in the East Village section of New York City. A group of individuals whom he met there became his early disciples, including the poet Allen Ginsberg. With the help of these followers, Bhaktivedanta set up a storefront temple and his movement began to attract more devotees, who were trained by their spiritual leader "to preach, to beg, to cook, to chant on the streets, and to carry on the work he started."[9]

Gregory Johnson noted that in 1967 Bhaktivedanta and about half of his New York followers moved to San Francisco for two significant reasons: "to continue as a city organization rather than retreat to the country in order to become contemplative and nature-oriented, like many similar groups; and to make a conscious effort to recruit young persons, whom the swami was convinced were open to the particular message of Krishna."[10] Many of those who became devotees in San Francisco's Haight-Ashbury section were important forces in bringing about the expansion of the movement.

In July 1966 the International Society for Krishna Consciousness was formally incorporated, and during the 1970's ISKCON temples were established in Berkeley, California; Buffalo, New York; Columbus, Ohio; Seattle, Washington; and other heavily populated areas in the United States. Centers were also opened in Canada, Western Europe, and India. In 1968 Bhaktivedanta created New Vrindaban, an experimental farm community in West Virginia. Its success led to the establishment of other Vedic communities in and outside of the United States. Until his death on November 14, 1977, Bhaktivedanta was worshipped "as a pure devotee of the Lord, the latest in the long line of disciplic succession extending back to Krsna's appearance on earth five thousand years ago." However, Daner noted that he "does not ever make a direct claim to be God, only to being His representative on earth."[11] Prabhupada explained the connection between God and himself: "Because the spiritual master is executing God's order, he should be respected as much as God, just as a government officer should be respected as much as the government because he executes the government's order."[12]

Bhaktivedanta's lifestyle changed noticeably as the movement grew. Daner described the changes that were apparent in the early 1970's: ". . . he is always accompanied by a retinue of personal servants who cater to his every whim. It is the duty of his servants to serve the guru his food and drink, to shave him, to massage him, to care for his clothing, to chauffeur him, and to handle all his money matters. He stays in plush quarters. . . . In New York he is driven around in a luxurious Cadillac car. Still, Bhaktivedanta's life seems less flamboyant and simpler than other popular gurus."[13]

Journalists Stoner and Parke cited John McCabe's perception of Prabhupada. While John was a devotee, he lived with the guru and was his secretary. He indicated that the swami was a "fine, dedicated, and totally spiritual man" who "eats meagerly, sleeps but four hours a night and spends hours each day translating the Vedic scriptures into English."[14]

Today, there is no one particular leader of the Hare Krishna movement. Rather, there are 11 ruling spiritual masters all over the world chosen by Bhaktivedanta before his death to carry on his work. In addition, a 23-member Governing Board Commission has authority over material and policy aspects of ISKCON.

ISKCON Beliefs and Practices

The devotees of Krishna perceive that the present time is an age of decline and turmoil. Moreover, they believe that the world is "near the end of the materialistic age of Kali-Yuga, the last cycle of a four-cycle millennium." People are too involved in *máyá,* the materialistic and pleasure-seeking aspects of life. Followers of the Hare Krishna movement believe that if there were a transformation of consciousness (that is, Krishna Consciousness), "a new age of peace, love, and unity would be discovered."[15] They posit that Krishna Consciousness is a spiritual science higher than any other science, higher than Bible teachings. Prabhupada suggested: "Scientists should accept God and His mystic power. If they don't, they should be considered foolish. On the basis of transcendental knowledge, we are directly challenging many big scientists and philosophers."[16]

In another book Prabhupada also noted: "Actually material science is foolish. The scientists are in darkness about so many things. What good is your science? There are so many things they do not know. . . . We don't bother with the scientists. We simply take instruction from Krsna."[17]

Many of the early devotees saw Krishna Consciousness as an alternative to drugs and as a way to establish inner peace in the turbulent political world of the 1960's. I was frequently reminded by devotees that Krishna Consciousness is something to be experienced. It is above and beyond logic or thought or study and thus cannot be understood or dealt with in those domains. Prabhupada, in an interview with reporter Sandy Nixon in 1975, explained his conceptualization of Krishna Consciousness: "When we become interested in knowing, 'What is my connection with God? What is the aim of life?' then we are called Krsna conscious . . . Krsna consciousness is already there in the core of everyone's heart. But because of our materially conditioned life, we have forgotten it."[18] On a morning walk in 1973 with Dr. Thoudam Singh, an organic chemist, Prabhupada commented: "Actually, except for those who are Krsna conscious, no one can have any real knowledge, nor can anyone enjoy it. One simply suffers, but he thinks the suffering is enjoyment. This is called *máyá* or illusion."[19]

Krishna Consciousness, according to Daner, "claims to be the revival of the original consciousness of the living being—the conscious awareness that one is eternally related to God. . . ."[20] Thus, they believe that the soul of the individual never dies, but rather assumes different material or bodily forms. Daner further noted that Hare Krishna devotees do not even use the word "die," but rather prefer the term "disappear." Swami Jayádvaita explained the Vedic viewpoint: " . . . a person is an external traveler who wanders from one body to the next. He appears in different guises—sometimes as a genius, sometimes a fool, sometimes a wealthy man, sometimes a pauper. . . . It is not desire alone that determines our next body; we get not exactly what we desire but what we deserve."[21] As one takes on and identifies with a new body, his/her past life is forgotten. The goal of Krishna Consciousness is to overcome what devotees believe to be "false identification with the temporary body,"[22] and become instead the servant of Krishna.

Bhakti, the constant absolute loving service to Krishna, will allow people to realize their true relationship with God. Bhakti is said to be a state of active love and worship of Krishna. Devotees contend that they receive love and pleasure many times over in return for their devotional service. Moreover, they believe that everything—themselves, their possessions, and their comforts—is the gift of Krishna. Thus, they should use all of their senses, abilities, and resources to serve and be aware of Krishna, with no thought of receiving some kind of reciprocal reward. To heighten their awareness of Krishna, devotees are asked to read and listen to the *Bhagavad-Gita* and the writings of Bhaktivedanta, to count off with their fingers their *japa* (prayer beads) every day, to eat *prasadam* (food offered first to the deity), to smell the incense in the temple or the flower offerings, to think constantly of the name and form of Krishna, to drink the water used to wash Krishna, to learn Vedic knowledge from a spiritual master or guru, and most importantly, to do *sankirtana,* singing the names and praises of the Lord (i.e., chanting the Hare Krishna mantra). Prabhupada explained the meaning of the chant as follows: "... when we chant Hare Krishna we are saying 'O Lord Krsna, O energy of Krsna, kindly engage me in Your service.'"[23] The above description clearly indicates the all-encompassing experience involved in Bhakti. All of the basic senses and faculties are active: touch, taste, smell, hearing, vision, language, thoughts, memories, images. Moreover, a guru is a necessary element in the acquisition of increased awareness. Bhaktivedanta noted: "If you hear about God from authoritative sources, you will become perfect. Simply by hearing. Therefore, the first principle—hearing—is essential."[24]

Krishna Consciousness cannot be achieved quickly, but rather is a matter of gradual growth. Judah outlined the five stages of development, each containing the characteristics of those preceding it. He pointed out that it is difficult to determine which stage a devotee has reached, since humility is an important attribute of advanced Consciousness. Thus, "to brag of one's attainment in Krishna consciousness is regarded as a sign of his lack of advancement."[25]

Bhakti can be followed in two ways. First, one is expected to follow particular rules of conduct about which there can be no questioning or refusal. Failure to obey these rules of conduct or speaking against the spiritual master Krishna, or the scriptures, may result in expulsion from the temple and ISKCON.

The regulative principles include the following:

(1) No gambling, no frivolous sports or games, and no conversation that is not associated with the teachings of Krishna consciousness.
(2) No intoxicants, including all narcotics, alcoholic beverages, tobacco, tea and coffee.
(3) No illicit sex; a sexual relationship is only permitted between married individuals and then only for the purpose of procreation. Dating and courtship are not permitted. Marriages are arranged in order to better serve and worship Krishna.
(4) No eating of meat, fish, or eggs. Food must be prepared under strict dietary regulations, and first offered to Krishna.[26]

The second aspect of Bhakti is manifested as a spontaneous showing of love and attachment to Krishna. In this stage, service to the deity occurs as a function of the "passionate desire for mystic union with the loved one."[27] This second phase can be achieved through following the standard rules of conduct described previously and by chanting the Hare Krishna mantra.

Hare Krishna Lifestyle

Full membership in the group is not attained at one time. Rather, the individual is gradually socialized into the practices of temple life and the beliefs of the movement. When a devotee first enters a temple, one or more devotees are assigned to guide the former in the appropriate behavior of this new life. A new follower is taught "how to behave in the temple during ceremonies, how to prostrate himself before the deities, how to say various prayers and hymns in Sanskrit, how to eat with his fingers Indian-style, how to maintain temple standards of cleanliness and hygiene, how to do a job if he does not already have a skill, how to chant, how to follow temple routine. . . ."[28]

On a visit to the New York temple where I was interviewing devotees, I met a woman of about 65 years of age wearing an Indian sari. I informed her that I was

Hare Krishna members chant and dance in Minneapolis, Minnesota on April 19, 1977.

interviewing Hare Krishna members for my book and asked her if I could talk to her for a short while. She quickly corrected my impression, telling me that she was not a member yet, that she was studying to become an initiate, and that it would take months of work before she was ready for the initiation.

After an initial period of socialization into temple life of about six months or more, devotees are formally initiated with a *harer-nama* ceremony, the holy name initiation whereby the devotee is provided with a new name in Sanskrit. A second initiation ceremony, the fire ceremony, occurs some time later, providing the follower with the new status of brahman. Men only, at this time, receive a sacred thread, which is to be worn over the left shoulder and across the chest. Male and female devotees are given the *gayatri* mantra. For men, there are four orders within the movement equivalent to the stages of spiritual life in the Vedic system: *brahmacari* (celibate student); *grhastha* (householder, married man); *vanaprastha* (retired); *sannyasa* or *swami* (renounced, celibate life). Women are not divided into separate categories, but are expected to marry at some point in their lives.

The devotees in the ISKCON movement follow a rigidly prescribed daily program, similar to the one that had been observed in India by Prabhupada. Although members are not absolutely required to participate in all practices, they are strongly urged to do so. Wake-up bell sounds before dawn at 3:30 A.M. and temple residents begin their day at 3:45 with a shower or bath. The early morning hours are particularly important for spiritual advancement, so the Hare Krishnas take advantage of that time for spiritual practices. Immediately after bathing, devotees put on the *tilak,* white clay marks which represent service to Krishna. They are required to do at least 16 daily rounds of the Hare Krishna chant privately and they do this while holding their prayer beads. The required *aratrika* service, representing the greeting of the Lord, begins about 5:00 A.M. and involves singing praises to Krishna. *Prasadam* (meaning mercy), the food that has been prepared earlier, as well as flowers and incense, are offered to the deity incarnations in the temple at this time. The deities are not idols, but rather are considered incarnations of Krishna appearing in a material form. Classes for the study of *Nectar of Devotion,* written by Srila Rupa Goswani, a follower of Chaitanya, or *Srimad Bhagavatam,* written by Bhaktivedanta Swami, are held next. The breakfast *prasadam* is served about 9:00 A.M., followed by various chores, such as cleaning the temple. Some devotees use the remainder of the morning to continue their work at the temple—sewing, painting, making incense, bookkeeping, cooking, or caring for the deities. Others go out on the streets to chant the mahamatra or sell their products, such as *Back to Godhead* magazine or other publications and ask for donations. At noon, the devotees, who are not far from their home base, return to prepare lunch *prasadam,* which is eaten at about 1:45 P.M. Those who are chanting, selling, or soliciting funds at too great a distance to return for lunch bring their food with them and do not return to the temple until late afternoon. After their lunch *prasadam,* devotees go out to do *sankirtana,* to sell magazines, or to complete their daily duties in the temple. Showers are taken upon their return to the temple. Later they may take sweetened milk *prasadam* (not a full meal, since generally only two regular meals a day are eaten) and attend a class on scriptures. At about 7 P.M., devotees attend another *aratrika* ceremony followed by a *Bhagavad-Gita* lecture and discussion period. There is further chanting and reading of material on Krishna. Some free time before "taking rest" provides devotees with the opportunity to prepare for the next day or attend to personal chores like laundry. At 9:15 P.M. another *aratrika* ceremony is held. Retiring for the night generally occurs at about 10:00 P.M.

The actual schedule for any particular devotee will

certainly depend upon her/his work. For example, the temple treasurer, who has a relatively practical job to do, rises at 3:30 in the morning, and between 4:15 and 7:00 engages in various religious rituals. At three different times daily, he works on treasury business. Spiritual duties are interspersed with practical matters throughout the day. Sleep is scheduled for 9:30 in the evening.[29] On the other hand, the *pujari*'s (a caretaker of the deities) schedule reflects the greater involvement in transcendental worship by the individual who holds this position. The *pujari* also wakes up at 3:30, but spends her day engaged in activities such as *aratrika,* chanting, bathing and dressing the deities as well as sewing their clothes and preparing the *prasadam* for them.[30]

Devotees usually follow the same schedule every day, including Sunday. However, on Sunday there are additional duties concerned with the preparation of the temple and the feast for the guests who participate in worship services and the taking of *prasadam* late in the afternoon. On certain days of the year there are special services and rituals. For instance, *ekadasi* days are fast days which occur twice a month. Although Vedic regulations require that devotees chant all day and night while totally abstaining from food, Daner commented: "In the temples visited, the devotees chant more than the usual rounds of *japa* beads, sleep less, take less care of themselves, and observe a partial fast."[31] Different days are celebrated by the various temples, and the temple presidents decide which occasions warrant observance.

The description of the daily lifestyle of devotees certainly indicates the emphasis placed on cleanliness by followers of the Hare Krishna movement. Besides often cleaning the temple and its contents, devotees also engage in frequent cleansing of their own bodies. Stoner and Parke suggest that another reason for the constant showers is "to discourage lust."[32] As mentioned earlier, one important tenet of the movement is the prohibition against illicit sex. Only married couples may have sex, and for them only once a month for the express purpose of having children. Prior to engaging in sexual relations on the one day in the woman's menstrual cycle most likely to result in conception, the couple must do 50 rounds of Hare Krishna chanting. Sex, like all else in the movement, is for the pleasure of Krishna.

Marriages take place through the matching of a couple, formerly arranged by the spiritual master, and at present by the president of the temple. Most of these who are married continue to live in separate men's and women's quarters at the temple. Segregation by sex is an important aspect of temple life. Faye Levine noted that men and women eat in separate rooms. She further commented: "In the sub-basement is also the laundry, where males and females can wash their clothes according to a posted schedule that insures members of different sexes will not intersect."[33]

A few couples live in rented apartments near the temple, particularly in New York. Many of the male devotees choose the *brahmacari* life, the life of a celibate student, which is fortunate for the movement, since only about one third of the members are women. All women are encouraged, actually expected, to get married, and in fact, devotees contend that marriage is a natural state of affairs for women. One young Krishna woman who was still single told me: "I will get married. It is a woman's natural tendency to want a family life, to be married."

Children born to ISKCON parents are given spiritual names at birth and are generally cared for by their mothers or other female caretakers. Daner cited one devotee mother's description of the movement's permissive attitude toward child-rearing: "Prabhupada has told the devotees that children should do as they please until age five. They should not be stopped from doing anything."[34]

At the age of 5, children are separated from their parents and often sent away to boarding school. The attitude of devotees toward most educational institutions in the United States is rather negative. Many followers commented to me that the emphasis in education should be on the "truth, on spiritual matters, on studying the Vedic scriptures. All else is of little consequence." The movement's major educational facility is located in Vrndávana, India. Prabhupada commented in 1974 on the difference between what he considered to be real education and modern university education: "... one who has not heard the message of Krsna, the Supreme Personality of Godhead—even for a moment—he's an animal. The general mass of people, unless they are trained systematically for a higher standard of life in spiritual values, are no better than animals. They are on the level of dogs, hogs, camels, and asses. Modern university education practically prepares one to acquire a doggish mentality for accepting the service of a greater master. Like the dogs, after finishing their so-called education the so-called educated persons move from door to door with applications for some service."[35]

One high-ranking Krishna devotee told me about educational plans for his 1½-year-old son: "He has to learn practical things to exist in this world. Education is a total experience. I cannot force my son to be Krishna Conscious, but I would be disappointed in myself if he didn't choose to follow Krishna."

In addition to extreme sexual restrictions, devotees adhere strictly to other regulations. The diet is totally vegetarian. In the foreword to the *Hare Krsna Cookbook,* Kirtánanda Swami Bhaktipada described the underlying philosophy of the diet and the cookbook: "This transcendental cookbook is designed to help you transform one of the most important daily chores into a spiritual reservoir of bliss." He explained that the Yoga diet satisfies both physical and spiritual needs "without pandering to the whims of our changing senses. The principle of regulation is strictly adhered to, and the daily fare is almost unchanging. This is very important for a *brahmacari,* or celibate student, for if the tongue is agitated for sense enjoyment, all other senses follow." He described the role of *prasadam* in Krishna Consciousness: "*Prasadam* means food for the body, food for the soul, and food for God. . . . We cook for every conceivable nonsensical purpose. Why not cook instead for the Lord? Why shouldn't this most important and central activity of life be dedicated to the Supreme? Why not cook transcendentally?"[36] Some of the dishes which may be found in the cookbook are chick peas and peanuts, basic split-pea dahl (dahl is made from different types of dried beans); potatoes and cauliflower in yoghurt; fig and date chutney; "celestial bananas"; watermelon sherbet; and banana nectar.

Another aspect of life in the International Society for Krishna Consciousness that is foreign to American society is the appearance of the devotees. Most of the men shave their heads except for some remaining strands of hair called the *sikha*. Daner explained that the *sikha,* which has been worn by devotees for thousands of years as a sign of surrender to the spiritual master will "enable Krsna to pull them out of *maya,* should they happen to fall into her clutches. It is also a haircut which avoids any preening that might foster a false ego."[37] Some devotees wear the *sikha* braided, while others wear it loose.

With regard to clothing, men wear *dhotis,* long draped garments that are worn yellow by married devotees and saffron-colored by celibate followers. On the top of the *dhoti* is worn an Indian shirt, and sometimes a cape tied at the right shoulder is added as well. Leather is not used, so devotees wear shoes of either plastic or canvas. While in the temple, no shoes are worn and preferably no socks either. Guests are always requested to remove their shoes when visiting the temple. Women wear the traditional Indian sari, under which they wear some kind of sweater of blouse for modesty's sake. Jewelry is worn, particularly earrings, bracelets, and necklaces. Some women wear a jewel stud in the nostril or a ring through the middle of the nostrils. Their hair is center-parted and generally braided. Devotees of both sexes often carry a bag around their necks containing *japa* (prayer beads), which they use to chant the Hare Krishna mantra. Beads made of tulasi, a sacred plant, are worn around the neck.

ISKCON Followers

An official statement from ISKCON indicated that there are at present 5,000 to 8,000 followers of the movement in the United States, about two thirds of them men. Many live in the temples found in cities throughout the country, while others participate in many of the practices and follow the belief system of Krishna Consciousness, but they have jobs and residences outside of ISKCON. However, it is extremely difficult to maintain the lifestyle mandated by ISKCON outside of temple life because of the nature of many of the required practices, such as continual chanting and worship services. When individuals become devotees, they are expected to surrender all of their personal possessions, including money and clothing, to the temple. The property then becomes communally owned. The physical appearance and social identity of members are changed in radical ways. Daner commented: "So deep are the changes that most devotees do not wish to discuss their former lives at all, and the average devotee has to be pressed to reveal any facts of his former life."[38]

Moreover, Stoner and Parke noted that individuals must clearly and consciously decide to become devotees, "for the differences between Krishna and the rest of society are too well-defined for a convert to miss."[39]

Individuals join ISKCON for a variety of reasons that have been delineated by a number of people, both within and outside of the movement. In an interview with Ray Ruppert, Srila Hamsadúta Swami, one of the spiritual masters that Prabhupada selected to initiate new disciples, explained the attraction of ISKCON to young Americans: "The attraction is that it is practical. Everything people do begins with someone else giving them a practical example . . . in every country there is some religious community. . . . But almost everywhere the leaders have become deviated. They don't follow their own principles, their own disciplines. So naturally the young people reject them. They are seeking some alternative. . . . Young people by nature will search out higher ideals. That is always the nature of young people, especially in America, where there is so much freedom—they get education and religious freedom. . . . This movement is a genuine spiritual movement. But one must examine it very carefully, rather than lump it together with everything else that has disappointed people." He further noted: "And the reason it attracts people all over (of course, especially in the West) is that its principles are universal spiritual principles that do not depend on any particular place, time, or circumstance."[40]

J. Stillson Judah, in his study of the movement, cited seven values that were particularly relevant for membership. First, he noted that Krishna Consciousness provided devotees with "more happiness than they had known before, and a greater pleasure than drugs had ever been able to supply."[41] Second, the movement focuses on the spiritual rather than the material. The case of a young man (cited by Enroth), who had been involved in occult and astrological practices prior to joining the Hare Krishna movement, is an example of this type of motivation: "At this time in my life I wanted to devote myself to the pursuit of truth. I was seeking God with all my heart. Quite by accident, I met a young man who was a devout member of the Hare Krishna sect. . . . He cared for nothing, obviously, but his relationship to God. . . . Here I was honestly and earnestly seeking God, and this man had found the way."[42] Third, the followers can identify with the "ever loving, eternally young Krishna." Fourth, the practice of chanting and dancing before Krishna permits the emptying "of their emotions" which "becomes a way of ridding themselves of normal aggressions and allows them to sublimate their physical sexual drives." Fifth, the group's emphasis on the importance of devotion over knowledge appeals to an anti-intellectual attitude. Sixth, the philosophy of nonviolence was considered to be "an important antidote to the question of the war in Vietnam. Moreover, its lack of demonstrable concern about political, social, and worldly matters must be indeed a respite from the frustration many youth had formerly felt." Finally, Judah noted that Bhaktivedanta offered an "absolute authority" to youth "who have been confused about what they should believe about so many questions."[43] Even with Bhaktivedanta's death, the Hare Krishna movement continues to offer absolute answers to the problems of the individual and society. One devotee told me: "I joined ISKCON because their philosophy is complete; it is very satisfying. My questions were all answered."

In his analysis of the movement in San Francisco, Gregory Johnson suggested: "Logical discourse was not nearly so important to the devotee as the surges of joy and ecstasy generated by the mantra."[44] He also noted: "For many devotees, the hypnotic quality of the mantra seemed to be an experience equivalent to hallucinogenic drug use. Not only did the mantra generate feelings of ecstasy or transcendence, it also involved a community—something lacking in the drug experience." Johnson further suggested that the fact that the roots of Hare Krishna extended far into the past was of importance. "The practices, symbols, and doctrines of the movement were centuries old, conveying an impression of timeless wisdom."[45]

Stoner and Parke commented about the significance of a certain type of freedom that the devotees experience as a force that attracts them to the movement: "Yet with all its rules and repression of the individual's personality, Krishna does offer freedom from the rigors, challenges and laws of contemporary society, a society in which these young people could not or did not want to find a place."[46]

Although many of the devotees informed me that there is no active recruiting of members, a number of techniques are employed by the group to gain followers. Stoner and Parke contended that "[a]lthough their primary goal in streets, airports and malls is to sell literature, the Krishnas rarely miss a chance to convert a potential member."[47] Faye Levine concurred, writing that their "elaborate theology" and ceremonies prepare them for the real work, which is "winning converts."[48] While I was a graduate student, I was frequently stopped on my way out of school by ISKCON members. First, they would discuss the tragic plight of the world—hunger, poverty, and disease—and then they would invite me to chant with them. Devotees have often done their fundraising and recruiting in and around college campuses. The temples also offer free banquets with music and dance, an attraction to many lonely and/or poor young people.

Many present and past devotees of Krishna explained to me their attraction to the movement. One young man who had just recently joined said: "I was in an airport in Denver. I had never had any religious inclination. I was given the movement's magazine, *Back to Godhead,* which I found very attractive. It described things in an understandable way, how one can become enriched. There is progressive advancement and great philosophical depth."

A 21-year-old woman who had been in the movement for almost three years described the circumstances under which she became an ISKCON member: "I was in St. Patrick's Cathedral. I was sincerely praying to God: 'What should I do with my life?' I had just graduated from high school at the time. I walked out of the church and immediately met some devotees. I knew that was the thing to do; here was the answer to my prayer." I asked this young woman about her family's response to her involvement in the movement. "My mother," she replied, "is happy that I'm happy. My father died when I was young. My sisters and brothers are curious and interested in Krishna because I am, but they're not involved in the movement. I seem much happier so my mother is happy for me."

Jack Adams, a 28-year-old man, who was formerly an insurance investigator and had received a college degree with majors in both communication and psychology, told me about his involvement in ISKCON. Although I found that many ISKCON members, particularly the men, are arrogant and sarcastic, Jack was warm, friendly, and open in discussing his life with me. He is the younger of two children of an interreligious marriage; his mother is Jewish, his father Protestant. His parents were divorced many years before he became a devotee. He talked to me about his adolescent years: "I smoked pot, took cocaine before I joined. I was always a thinker, a philosopher. I was active in sports and always went with a number of girlfriends, but felt no responsibility toward a particular one." He also talked about his investigation of other religious movements: "I investigated other movements, like Christianity. I spoke with priests when I was in high school and college. I investigated the Jehovah's Witnesses, but they did not have a solid basis. They couldn't answer my questions about God. 'Why does this person have to die? Why does this person have to suffer?' The priests gave vague answers."

In 1971, when Jack was 18, his older brother joined ISKCON. (His brother is still a member and works in the theater at the West Virginia center.) Jack described his reaction to his brother's participation in the Hare Krishna movement: "I was in Florida in 1971. I came home and my mother embraced me with tears in her eyes. I thought someone had died. Then she said David—that's my brother's name—has shaved off his hair. I burst out laughing; I was so relieved. Then I went to see him. My mother was really disturbed, so was my father, but my mother was more disturbed, but she continued to see David. . . . I thought it was all right for him, but not for me. I wasn't willing at first to give up my sense of gratification—my sex, my drugs, my material things. My brother was always preaching and I was always arguing about the existence of God. . . . " Finally, he "gave in," he explained, after having made a part-time commitment for several years. "I had examined many other religions. Nothing else answered the questions. God is a person, but a supreme person. I had read more and examined more and this held the answer for me." He took on the status of *brahmacari.*

I asked Jack about his family's reaction to his joining. He commented that, while his mother was initially upset, "now, she is very favorable toward Krishna. She comes to the temple to visit every two weeks." He hasn't seen his father in years. "Our relationship was never close," he explained. However, he noted that "Krishna promises its devotees that 21 generations before and 21 generations after the generation of the devotee will be liberated. That is true even for parents who are totally alienated. That is the highest gift I can give to my father."

Jack talked to me about the significance of his devotion to Krishna. "At the time of death, everything is lost. But this religion offers me something after death which is very attractive. Those who don't follow Krishna Consciousness have to pay at the time of death. No one knows what will happen to them. Everyone wants to live forever, to be happy. We found a way to be happy. Why limit yourself to just 100 years of living? . . . The longer you are here, the greater the realization that this is a jewel; it is very special. It is a science. . . . One must recognize that the body gets old, that you cannot do certain things any longer. For example, an old man walks across the street, sees a pretty girl and is sad because he cannot carry out the thoughts that he has about her. There is no enjoyment for him any longer. That doesn't happen in Krishna Consciousness. . . . The philosophy is sound. We'll always be protected by Krishna. We lead a very simple life with high thinking."

Jack and I also discussed recruitment of others. "If people are open," he explained, "I can guarantee that they'll come to realize Krishna Consciousness because it's the science of Krishna Consciousness, because it's the truth beyond other truths. One who does it sincerely will come to a realization. It's a change of consciousness, rather than a change of life. We won't force it on anyone."

When I asked Jack about weaknesses in the movement, he quickly responded: "There are no weaknesses in the ISKCON movement because it stems down from Krishna in an unbroken chain. If we follow it strictly, there can be no wrong... weaknesses are in ourselves. But these can be overcome."

Finally, I asked Jack about the devotees who have left the movement. He commented: "The only reason people leave is that they feel that they're missing things, that there are things to enjoy out there. Some who leave eventually return. That's very common." He talked to me about one particular friend who left ISKCON. "I don't associate with him because he's engaged in sinful activities. I try to get him to come back because he's suffering. He's committing spiritual suicide. You can't force him. He's doing the same activities that he hated before, so we try to rekindle the spark to help him return."

One of the original members of ISKCON, who has achieved the rank of full-fledged *sannyasa* (a renounced life) or swami, talked to me at length about his experiences. Currently, he is writing a book about his participation in the movement. Swami is the only child of divorced parents, both of whom are Jewish ("but in a nominal way"), and is a high school graduate. He joined the movement, he told me, for reasons that are "completely theological and philosophical, a result of primordial searching." He continued: "I finally came to the belief that God and self are the same. I had tried meditation and LSD when I was between 16 and 18 years of age. I was not an LSD tripper. When I used it, I ordered all of my girlfriends out of the house; it was not an orgy.

"I met Prabhupada in 1966 and I began to follow him. He was not a flatterer; he was very hard and disciplined. He quoted scriptures; he didn't take drugs. He was on Second Avenue at that time in 1966 with no support and no future. He chanted with us and gave us classes Monday, Wednesday, and Friday. Chanting replaced any form of intoxication for me and the others. We chanted for 30 to 40 minutes, then had classes for about an hour and a half. Then there was more chanting. Many people came. All were educated: there were lawyers, historians, and so on. We learned that God is a person, but an all-pervasive person. God is transcendental. A scholastic attitude is not enough. Books do not understand the truth of Krishna. God is a supreme person. We worship Krishna. It is not like mundane sex.... All of the beautiful ideas find their epitome in the *Bhagavad-Gita,* which is more scientific than science."

Swami went to India in 1967 and remained there for 12 years. He described those times and how he returned to the United States: "I toured India as a lecturer and found myself famous. I talked to many crowds. I went to India because of the draft. I tried to go to Canada, but that didn't work out so I went to India instead and learned the language there.... When amnesty came, I had developed a friendship with the American consulate and they were able to arrange for my return here."

In response to my query about his parents' response to his participation in the Hare Krishna movement, Swami indicated that initially his mother, who was studying psychology, thought that Krishna Consciousness was good therapy. Now his mother (at present a clinical psychologist) "would be happier if I got married, divorced, etc., led what she thinks is a normal life. Now, I'm a threat to her philosophy, a threat to her entire materialistic world." He sees her occasionally but "she doesn't try to persuade me to leave the church."

His father lives quite a distance from the temple. According to Swami, his father is "very proud of my status, of my rank.... He introduced me to yoga and has a great interest in the Buddhist tradition."

We also discussed the financial status and fundraising practices of ISKCON. Swami informed me: "We receive street donations. We also run a restaurant. Some people sell books or magazines or have fruit carts. The Indian community has adopted this as their place of worship and they've made lots of donations. In order to survive, some people have outside jobs, regular jobs, but we try to think of ways to include them here. For example, we'll create a restaurant or a business. It's difficult to maintain the four regulatory principles if one is not closely related to the temple."

Swami's response to my question about weaknesses within Hare Krishna was similar to the one given by Jack Adams. The former said: "I would like to see the world have Krishna Consciousness. All the weaknesses are within myself. There are no weaknesses in Krishna Consciousness."

Criticisms of the Movement

However, numerous criticisms have been addressed to the Hare Krishna movement, many of them coming from former followers. For example, I interviewed Lou Paris, who had been a devotee for over five years before becoming a "blooper" (a term used in the movement to denote dropping out of ISKCON) two-and-a-half years ago. Lou is one of five children, with an older sister and three younger brothers. He remarked that his sister was "always doing other things, so we were never very close, but my brothers and I were pretty close." Although his parents had problems while he was growing up, they did not get divorced until he had joined

ISKCON. His mother was "nominally" a Quaker who later became Episcopalian like his father. Lou was a chemistry major at college and then switched to liberal arts, but was "kicked out" because of poor grades. However, as a high school student, his grades had been good, particularly in math and science. Lou joined Hare Krishna at 26 years of age under the following conditions:

"I guess I was searching for some values. I worked for a while doing odd jobs and didn't really like that. I took a trip to Canada and cut off contact totally with my family. That was two years before moving into the temple. I met some people who were into vegetarianism, yoga, Eastern thought, mystical kinds of things. I was taking drugs for about two or three years—pot, hash, LSD, magic mushrooms. I had previously met the Krishnas in New York City. They were chanting in Washington Square Park. I observed their chanting. They appeared to have a very blissful existence. Their high was equal to or greater than anything I had experienced on LSD. I started chanting and stopped taking drugs. I could see from what they were saying and doing that they were renouncing the material world. I had done enough reading that I thought that the separation from the physical world was attractive. Also they had feasts; the Indian cooking was good; it was free food. Also, I made friends there—not that I didn't have friends before, but I was able to give them up easily. I moved into the temple gradually, from January to November. I stayed at the temple two hours a day chanting, the minimum you're allowed.... Each time, I went to the temple, I felt more and more of an affinity for the group."

While Lou was a member of ISKCON he traveled throughout the United States and Canada and lived in several different temples. Since he had avoided contact with his family, they were initially unaware of his joining the movement. However, he reflected that even when his friends and family became aware of his activity in the group, they were unable to do anything. "No one was strong enough to keep me from doing what I wanted to do. There was a certain defiance. The Krishnas are totally against Western thought, education, and psychiatry." His mother kept trying to contact him and managed to visit him once a year while he was a follower. Lou contends that he was brainwashed by the Hare Krishna devotees and that belief was strengthened by his reading of Lifton's book *Thought Reform and the Psychology of Totalism* and Meerloo's book *The Rape of the Mind.*

Lou Paris described his leaving the movement as an evolutionary process, although the ultimate "bloop" occurred through a deprogramming arranged by his mother. He had been fundraising for a few years and "burned out. . . . I had lost about 20 pounds, going from about 135 pounds to 115 or 120 pounds. I went to India and became ill with a number of different diseases—I don't know their names. I went down to 110 pounds. I couldn't do fundraising any longer, so I was given cooking and light duties to do. My health deteriorated. It was a combination of diet and stress; I was going downhill. Then I was in a car accident and suffered some torn ligaments and I couldn't walk. I was useless as far as they were concerned. They agreed to send me home to a hospital, but they changed their minds. I had been seeing a chiropractor. They thought that was O.K. as long as my mother was paying for it. Chiropractors are closer to their way of thinking than are physicians.

"I was walking outside the chiropractor's office. I happened to be alone that day. Two guys grabbed me and put me in a car, in the back seat. My mother was in the car and we drove to another county. It was very traumatic for me. Anything that takes you away from God is of the devil. My first reaction was I wanted to kill my mother because she was the devil. The Krishna doctrine justifies killing demons.

"For the first day, I just chanted; my mind was totally against what was going on. During the second day, it happened in a flash. As soon as I started to think, everything changed. It was very difficult at first to adjust."

I asked Lou whether he had ever entertained the idea of leaving the group on his own. He responded: "The thought never occurred to me to leave on my own. Those who left were seen as having a weakness of the heart. Whatever the doctrine said, we believed. The doctrine said, 'the shorter your life, the better.' I was ready and willing to die in the temple. I knew I only had about one year to live at the time I was deprogrammed."

In answer to my query about perceived strengths of the ISKCON movement, Lou said simply: "The most beneficial thing was that I got out. The benefits of that are priceless. Now, I know what to avoid in life. I also learned a certain amount of discipline, to be punctual. Religiously, I got nothing out of the group."

On the other hand, he had much to say regarding problems and weaknesses of the group. For example, he noted that "the Krishnas are very pro-violence. I was more violent than most in the group. I tried to kill people outside of the group. I felt indignation and reacted to it. I never really harmed anyone, just got involved in some scuffles. I thought violence was justified. They teach that anyone against them is an animal, is a flapping dead body, is a ghost. If a devotee kills someone, they are relieved from torture, so it's not bad. They feel the same way about money. All money belongs to God. So regardless of how they get it, they'll take it. They often use deception, saying they're collecting for some group, when actually it's for themselves."

At the end of the interview, Lou described his present life for me: "I'm finished with organized religion for the time being. I read quotations from other people; I read philosophy. I have a few ideas, but I have such a bad taste for religion. I was a real soldier." In addition, he is involved in deprogramming. "I do that occasionally. . . . I'm also writing. I started taking notes when I left. I intuitively felt it was necessary to try to understand about mind control. I read Lifton's book and other first-person books. I do a lot of reading. Most of my money is from deprogramming. Every once in a while I get a part-time job. For example, last year I was a bus boy for a month. Also my parents have helped me. Occasionally, I live at home. Now, I'm living with my girlfriend." When I asked about his current family relationships he said: "The present relationship with my father is not good. I hardly ever see him, but the relationship with my mother is excellent, better than ever. We've both changed a lot."

Not all parents are opposed to their children's participation in ISKCON. For instance, an article in *The Idaho Statesman*[49] described a mother who became a devotee soon after her son had joined ISKCON. She had been brought up in a strict Catholic home and had tried other Christian denominations, but it was her decision to become a Hare Krishna follower that "ended a process of fifteen years of intense searching." She conceded that she did not initially understand her son's decision to join the movement, but she respected it. She began to read the movement's literature and also visited her son's temple. When she herself joined the group, important changes in her own life occurred, including following the movement's regulatory principles and prohibitions. Although her husband and other sons are not members of the movement, she is trying to pass on the principles of Krishna consciousness to them.

In contrast to the above story, Sheila Dean, a 27-year-old woman from a "moderately religious Catholic family" in the Midwest, who had been a devotee for 14 months, was recently deprogrammed upon her mother's request. Sheila described her reasons for becoming a Krishna follower: "I was attending a state college majoring in psychology and nutrition. My husband was studying for his Ph.D. at the time. I signed up for a yoga course that was being given at the school and found that the Krishnas were teaching it. I was open to it; I wanted to hear what they had to say. I hadn't previously heard of the Krishna movement. But I had read about Zen Buddhists and this was just another slant. I was looking for transcendental consciousness, something above and beyond....

"I had a good relationship with my parents at that time but with my husband, it was different—we had difficulty communicating before I joined. I had lost respect for him. It was easy to transfer my trust to someone else. I felt belittled by him. I wasn't intelligent enough, I didn't have enough degrees. My self-esteem was pretty low. They gave me self acceptance immediately and I needed that."

While Sheila Dean was a Hare Krishna follower, she worked as a typist on an ISKCON book about Prabhupada for several months, and then moved to a temple in another state where she did fundraising, mainly selling candles. In the six months of fundraising activity. Sheila claims to have made between $18,000 and $20,000 for the movement. She said that she often used "transcendental trickery" to raise money. She described her strategy: "I told people that I was a college student working my way through college selling candles. I never mentioned Hare Krishna."

Sheila's husband visited her at the temple, trying to convince her to leave, but as she explained: "I wouldn't listen to him. I was taught that he'll lead you back to animal life. He divorced me because he thought that's what I wanted.... Women can't marry if they've already been married. I was working toward being a widow, being renounced, since I had already been married once."

Sheila continued to maintain contact with her parents while she was a Krishna follower. "I couldn't accept the fact that they were demons," she reflected. "The Krishnas felt that contact was good public relations if my parents supported me and would spread good things about the movement."

I questioned Sheila about the circumstances under which

she left the movement. "I was fundraising, walking down the street when two guys grabbed me and put me in a car. My mom and a driver were in the car. I was definitely scared. . . . The deprogramming was paid for by my parents. I was talked to by ex-cult members for seven days. They just talked; they didn't touch me except to get me into the car. I was the one who was violent. I tried to grab the wheel. After seven days, I came to the realization that I had been lied to, that if the Krishna system was correct it would have stood up to the questioning, but it didn't."

Sheila Dean summed up her feelings about the Hare Krishnas: "The thing that makes me angriest is that people go in with values and ideals; they want to do something positive and that is exploited, particularly by the Krishnas. They're sincere in what they're doing, but they're sincerely deceived. Now, I'm on hold. I've had enough of organizations. I believe in God, but you don't have to belong to an organization to practice religion."

I asked Sheila why she had not left the group on her own since her feelings about it were so negative. She responded: "I wouldn't have left on my own—I know that. My fear was too great, the fear that the outside world was so bad. It was a mental fear that I wasn't living up to a higher purpose. I believed everyone else was blind to the truth."

Various criticisms of the Hare Krishna movement have been enumerated. For instance, the exploitation of women and their treatment as second-class citizens were noted by many of my interviewees and by other writers. One former male member told me: "The treatment of women is pretty bad, but it didn't strike me as wrong at the time. Women are considered to be less than men, but they do most of the fundraising because they collect more money than men. But they are considered to be less capable than men. The women in Krishna cannot look men in the eyes. Those who are brought up in the movement are married when they are 14 because they are only allowed to have one man in their lives.

Their husband is treated as a master. It's like a slave/master relationship."

Faye Levine noted: "In the Hare Krishna oral traditions the male body is considered better suited to 'spiritual science' than the female. They postulate that to be born into a female body is a punishment for mistakes or sins in previous lives." She also stated: "The women's eating place is dirtier, dingier, and colder than the men's, comparing with it as a basement warehouse compares to a finished rumpus room."[50]

An ex-devotee remarked to me: "Women are definitely considered less than men. A woman is considered to have been a man in her previous life who was too attached to his wife. As a punishment, he comes back as a woman. Women are perceived as being less intelligent; it's a lesser birth."

A male member of the New York temple explained his perception of the different roles for men and women in the movement: "Women are not suited for a complete celibate life. Women want to be married, have protection, a husband. There is nothing like an order of nuns in the Catholic Church. We do not ask women to take harsh vows because they are not strong enough."

A devotee, who expressed satisfaction with her treatment as a woman in the group, noted: "Materially, there are differences, but spiritually, there is no difference and I accept the material differences. When there is no division of labor, there is chaos, there is friction, bad feelings. It is very harmonious this way."

Another concern expressed by critics is the potential for violence within the group. Allegations of criminal activity within the Krishna temples have been reported. For example, Paul Avery, Joe Quintana, and Peter Knutson in the first of a four-part newspaper series on ISKCON, reported:

"Law enforcement officials on at least four continents have arrested Krishna devotees for crimes ranging from drug trafficking and burglary to kidnapping and illegal weapons possession. Other devotees . . . are fugitives, commonly traveling with assumed names and false identification. Authorities in several states and countries say that guns and ammunition have been stockpiled in Hare Krishna temples."[51] However, spokespersons for the movement deny any connection with devotees arrested for various crimes. In the third article of the series, a high-ranking Krishna is quoted as saying: ". . . I never hear Catholic robbery, Catholic fugitive, Jewish fugitive. All I hear is Krishna fugitive and that's unfair."[52]

The movement has been criticized for its isolation from the mainstream of society. Furthermore, critics charge that ISKCON is particularly likely to attract young people to this all-pervasive spiritual community before they have had the opportunity to explore and experience other lifestyles. That is not the case in India, according to Stoner and Parke, who wrote: "In India, the segments of a man's corporal and spiritual life are clearly delineated. A man is first a student, then a husband and father and a member of the community. Later, after his worldly duties have been discharged, a man can, as the Swami has done, discard his worldly life for spiritual pursuits."[53]

The Future of ISKCON

Many individuals had predicted the disappearance of ISKCON in the United States upon the death of Bhaktivedanta Prabhupada. However, as of this writing, the movement is still very much alive, although certainly not very large. Its followers are less evident on the streets of this country than previously, since devotees have adopted the habit of wearing Western dress during fundraising activities and while they go about their everyday business in the "outside" world. They also appear to be more attuned to public relations concerns and are becoming increasingly sophisticated in their dealings with the media. This blending into the mainstream may actually prove to be a disadvantage for the movement, since their distinctiveness in the past may have been part of the appeal to potential members and may have facilitated a sense of group cohesiveness.

Finally, it remains to be seen whether the 23-member Governing Board Commission of ISKCON can replace Bhaktivedanta Prabhupada in maintaining the devotion of followers to Krishna. The lack of charismatic leadership can certainly erode a group's attractiveness and sense of purpose, although devotees claim that the movement will survive because it presents the truth.

Conclusions

As I was writing this book, numerous people asked me questions such as the following: What do you think of the Hare Krishna movement? Are the Moonies really brainwashed? Why do people participate in *est* where they are cursed at? Should parents have their children deprogrammed? Are the people who participate in human potential groups lacking in something? Is Guru Maharaj Ji a fraud or does he really believe he is the Perfect Master?

I was obviously expected to give simple, clear-cut answers. While I was working on *Searching,* I was able to give the excuse that my investigation was ongoing. But I still do not have the answers to these very complex inquiries. And I am planning to continue my own search for more information and further insights.

However, I would like to offer some general impressions on a number of significant issues that have been raised in previous chapters.

Sources of Controversy

First, why is there so much controversy surrounding the new religions and the human potential movement? One likely reason is that these movements contain many ideas that are foreign to the average person.

The unusual practices, philosophies, and beliefs that have been described in these pages may be threatening because of a general apprehension of the unknown. Moreover, the media have generally been preoccupied with the more sensational and bizarre aspects of the cult and human potential movements, often taking a certain aspect out of its appropriate context. The tragedy at Jonestown also called negative attention to the new religions.

The Alliance for the Preservation of Religious Liberty (APRL) views the Guyana affair as being atypical. Thomas Hopkins, a regional chairman of APRL and a professor of religion at Franklin and Marshall College, stated: "Jim Jones's enterprise had very little in common with other new religious movements in the United States, especially in its bizarre conclusions. Both the media and the opponents of new religions continue to exploit the tragedy. But the more we know of the events in Guyana the less they tell about other religious movements. It is time to stop drawing false parallels and try to understand the new religions in their own terms."[1] However, members of groups generally considered part of the human potential movement, such as the Himalayan International Institute and the Association for Research and Enlightenment, were not untouched by those tragic events. Several members mentioned to me that, since the tragedy in Guyana, their participation had been called into question, and looked upon with some disfavor by family, friends, and/or coworkers.

Another reason for the strong negative reaction to new religions is that some groups may truly pose a threat to their members and to society in general. There have been reports of arms build-ups and the willingness of members to fight to the death for their cause. In the same vein, there is evidence to support some of the allegations of exploitation of young, naive followers who are made to feel guilty about any thoughts of leaving their groups.

Dick Anthony, a research associate in the Program for the

Study of New Religious Movements in America at the Graduate Theological Union, discussed another aspect of the controversy at the Rockefeller Foundation-sponsored conference described earlier. He commented that some critics have argued that the new religious movements and human potential groups such as *est* are "essentially rationalization for narcissistic self-concern" and "social inequity."[2] Edwin Schur is one of those critics who has suggested that these movements, which comprise what he calls the "ideology of awareness," may be pushing society in an undesirable direction in which self-absorption is encouraged and social and political outreach is ignored.[3] An *est* official, however, attempted to refute this criticism, telling me: "*est* is beyond getting better. It's not part of the 'me' generation philosophy. It's a tool and if you use it, it's very powerful. It's very individual."

Another dimension of many of the new religious movements and perhaps of human potential groups as well, which may add fuel to the fire, concerns the all-encompassing nature of the members' involvement in their groups. Erving Goffman, in his book *Asylums,* described the "total institution" experience in which one's identity, clothing, behavior, etc. are determined.[4] Many of these characteristics can be observed in the groups under consideration.

A further source of controversy concerns the fear of unfair business competition from various new religions. If member labor is provided at subsistence cost, other businesses will be driven out and then monopolies will be created. As noted in Chapter One, some of the hostility toward the Unification Church may be of this type. The hostility manifests itself as religious in nature, but it is actually economically based. Furthermore, with a sufficiently large number of church members in a small community, the cohesive group may have political influence as well.

Why Do These New Movements Arise?

A second major issue centers on the question: Why and under what societal conditions do the groups under consideration arise? The literature is rife with theoretical explanations. For example, anthropologist Weston La Barre suggested that new cults tend to arise in societies under stress as a response to culture shock.[5] Allan W. Eister noted: "Religion and religious movments, regardless of what else may properly be said about economic or political status-deprivation and other 'factors' in their formation, development, and structure, have always been tied to a very fundamental need in human beings, individually and in groups, for shared 'reliable' *meanings* in their life experiences."[6] Joel Colton, director for humanities of the Rockefeller Foundation, noted that anxieties associated with the Vietnam War, the threat of atomic destruction, the competitive work world, and the civil rights movement have contributed to the emergence of new religious movements.[7] David Hanna concurred, stating: "In times of great insecurity, people are apt to turn to mystical, nonrational explanations. The current passion for superstitious cults results from a pervasive feeling of helplessness. People want desperately to believe in something. Many feel that the world of reason has failed, so they rebel and seek to gain control over their lives by turning back to the nonrational."[8] Later in his book Hanna continued: "Of all the reasons intended to explain the proliferation of cults during the 1970's, the cause most easily understood is that 'isms' are products of stress. They sprout in difficult times and are nursed by people's insecurities, their fears and loss of faith in old values."[9]

It should be added that a survey of the vast literature on fringe groups in American society clearly indicates that their presence is not a new phenomenon—they have always been in existence. Indeed, a number of today's mainstream religions, such as the Church of Jesus Christ of Latter Day

Saints (Mormons), started out in the 19th century as cults engaging in what were generally considered to be alien practices and were led by charismatic leaders purportedly imbued with divine guidance. It is not surprising that, in a nation founded by religious and political dissenters of their day and which has often prided itself on its religious and political diversity, new religious movements come onto the scene in times of social, cultural, and political stress, such as the era of the drug society, the sexual revolution, the Vietnam War, the civil rights movement, and Watergate. Some of the groups expand on the new forces in today's society and others arise as a counterreaction to them.

Contemporary societal conditions may be particularly ripe for the establishment of human potential groups. According to the late humanistic psychologist Abraham Maslow, in his book *Toward a Psychology of Being,* it is only after satisfaction of our more basic needs for such things as food, water, and safety, that we can concern ourselves with the actualization of our potential in other areas. Large sectors of American society have sufficiently satisfied their primary needs so that they can move on to focus on self-development and raising of the consciousness of society, two dimensions of the human potential movement. Consequently, a significant portion of the membership of that movement is made up of members of the middle- and upper-middle class of American society, who have satisfied their primary needs of existence.

Relationship to Mainstream Groups

Another issue concerns the relationship between and comparison of mainstream organizations and fringe groups. Martin E. Marty wrote: "To a complete outsider the traditional faiths may look as arcane and idiosyncratic as the 'marginal' ones do."[10] Certainly such practices as "speaking in tongues" and "laying on of hands," which are standard in certain well-established religious groups, are no more "unorthodox" than such practices as the Hare Krishna chant. It is evident that ideas and practices that are perceived as radical when they are first introduced are often eventually accepted or at least well tolerated by a large proportion of American society. Ellwood noted: "Indeed, we may expect to see our 'non-normative' groups appear more and more normal, and even prestigious, at least from a sociological standpoint."[11]

In terms of actual practices, meditation, which is an important activity of many human potential and new religious groups, is also engaged in or has been tried by many nonmembers. Most who have had no personal experience with the practice consider it at worst to be harmless and are tolerant of its practice by others. Yet I did speak to members of anticult organizations who saw as much danger in simple meditation as they perceived in full-fledged membership in a countercultural religious cult.

Another example of the growing acceptance of ideas that were at one time quite alien to the general public is the current fascination with right-hemispheric brain functioning, such as that emphasized by the Institute for Psycho-Integrity. The awarding of a Nobel Prize in 1981 to Roger Sperry, who spearheaded the research in this area, will probably lead to still greater tolerance of this innovative approach to human functioning. In addition, the control of areas of functioning, such as brain waves, which were at one time believed to be totally out of direct human control, has been demonstrated (sometimes dramatically, as in the case of Swami Rama of the Himalayan International Institute) to be capable of being manipulated, as in the practice of biofeedback. This technique is now widely used in medical facilities throughout the world.

Ellwood presented an interesting point regarding the acceptance of many practices from Eastern religions: "Innumerable non-Hindu Americans meditate in the Maharishi's manner or do yoga—but very few non-Roman

Catholics say the Rosary, and very few synagogues have a regular plurality of non-Jewish visitors."[12]

Comparisons of the Nine Groups

A fourth issue that naturally follows from consideration of the relationship between new religious/human potential movements and mainstream religion is the comparison across the various groups that have been described in this book. Common roots are evident in several cases. For instance, Eastern religions and philosophies are obviously significant in the development of all the groups, although their manifestations are more apparent in some cases than in others.

Moreover, many of the groups engage in similar activities, such as meditation. In fact, an investigation of new religious movements conducted by Egon Meyer and Laura Kitch found that about 80 percent practice some form of meditation, although the activity may take several different forms and serve different purposes.[13] Some groups practice individual meditation, while others, such as the International Society for Krishna Consciousness and the Divine Light Mission, stress group meditation. Frederick Bird explained the existence of this variety in the following way: "Often, when the higher reality to which one seeks to attune one's mind is felt to transcend individual persons..., then greater emphasis is placed upon group meditation. Whereas in movements in which this higher reality is believed primarily to be within one,... then individual meditation is felt to be of greater importance."

Bird further noted: "Some groups have meditation rites... which foster a still quiet state of mind as an end in itself.... Others... have developed meditation techniques for realizing a more trancelike state of mind as an end in itself. Finally, there are movements... in which meditation is not an end in itself, but a means to achieve other ends."

A further source of similarity is the initiation rituals

practiced by the groups. Bird pointed out that groups such as Scientology "have established a series of initiation rites to mark the spiritual progress of adherents." In the Unification Church, the complete theology is revealed to followers of Sun Myung Moon in a piecemeal fashion, much in the spirit of initiation rites. Other organizations provide one clear initiation point. In the case of the Divine Light Mission that point occurs during the Knowledge session.

Another aspect of similarity is the relationship between adherents and some kind of guru, teacher, or leader. Bird noted that the initiation rites serve to "enact a shift in personal status such that adherents become devotees, disciples, or apprentices of some honored lord, teacher, or discipline."[14] Except for Wainwright House and perhaps the Institute for Psycho-Integrity—although Lentchner and Spiegel may, at some future time, attain a status equivalent to *est*'s Erhard—all the groups under discussion have such a figure at the center.

Witnessing or testimonial-giving is an activity engaged in by members of all of the groups described in this book, although, again, form differs significantly from one organization to another. Bird explained the dual purpose of this activity: to gain converts and also "to express one's faith and devotion." Maharaj Ji premies give satsang, ISKCON devotees chant Hare Krishna, Moonies proclaim the truth of the Divine Principle, Scientologists describe their "wins."

Many of the groups subscribe to a belief in reincarnation or past lives. That tenet is particularly prominent in the Association for Research and Enlightenment, Scientology, and the Hare Krishna movements.

The nine organizations may also be compared in the degree to which they foster a sense of community or group cohesiveness. All of the groups show this attribute to some extent, although it is reflected in different forms of community. For instance, most members of ISKCON live communally in a temple, while only a small percentage of

Maharaj Ji followers choose the ashram life. But most Divine Light Mission adherents attend communal satsang at an ashram as frequently as possible. The Unification Church is changing its focus in this area from the large church center, where most followers live, to the Home Church, where the members are dispersed throughout the larger public community. Other groups, such as Wainwright House and the Institute for Psycho-Integrity, provide a sense of belonging when they meet, but membership does not include, for the most part, a communal life. The Himalayan International Institute stresses the development of a group lifestyle in some of its programs where members live on the grounds of the facility (for example, the Residential Program), but the communal life is generally considered to be of limited duration and eventually members go back to their homes and families, presumably with an altered perspective.

Some groups share certain structural and philosophical aspects. Similarities can readily be observed between *est* and the Institute for Psycho-Integrity, Wainwright House, and Scientology. However, members of the last three organizations are quick to point out that there are potent differences between their groups and *est*. Lentchner of IPI conceded that his institute is often compared to *est* "perhaps because of the weekend structure." In addition, there are similar components of the training (such as process, content, and sharing) in these two organizations. However, Lentchner pointed out, as a major area of difference, the presence of a trained licensed clinician at all IPI experiences to allow participants to completely work through a process. Moreover, while *est* usually allows 250 to 300 participants, IPI experiences limit enrollment per session to about 75 individuals. An *est* spokesperson indicated that her organization was aware of the many attempts to imitate it in some way, but was not disturbed by that trend. A Wainwright House member who had also "done" *est* compared the two in the following way: "*est* is a mass-produced experience, while Wainwright House is a much less pressureful experience. A Wainwright House activity may involve 20 people, while *est* deals with 200 to 300 people at a time. Both have sharing so that other people may benefit. At *est,* you share with hundreds while at Wainwright House, you share with one or two people. We think we're on a path. The *est* experience is a more jolting, accelerated, fast experience and it may be tougher to accommodate to it. The Wainwright House approach is not to deal with people in a threatening way. We are a support group helping each other to grow. *est* is also a support group, but to get movement quickly, they use a number of techniques that may be questionable."

In comparing *est* and Scientology, it should be noted that Werner Erhard participated in the latter prior to the development of his Seminars Training, and *est* was evidently influenced by it. A former Scientologist told me that in her group "*est* was considered bad. I went to an *est* meeting after leaving Scientology. I was not interested in it. It just mimics Scientology. They're all robots; meetings were just like Scientology meetings. I realized that they're all the same."

The narrowness or diversity of interests and activities of the groups is another important aspect of comparison. Some, like ISKCON, have basically a unidimensional focus. Hare Krishna followers display a single-minded devotion to Krishna; all of their rituals and beliefs converge in their worship of this deity. Other groups, such as Wainwright House, are considerably more multidimensional, almost a conglomeration of different subgroups. Still other organizations are beginning to diversify, although they may have one evident primary emphasis. Falling into this category are *est* and the Association for Research and Enlightenment. In the latter group, the major focus remains on testing the validity and using the readings of psychic Edgar Cayce. However, the Association also has programs dealing with holistic health and meditation, among other subjects.

Another area of comparison concerns the similarity of each group to traditional cultural values and behaviors. Members of the International Society for Krishna Consciousness, chanting Hare Krishna on street corners and at shopping centers while wearing Indian dress, are clearly countercultural in American society. In sharp contrast, many of the members of Wainwright House are the "pillars of society"—business people, physicians, lawyers, members of the "establishment."

Who Is Attracted to New Religions and the Human Potential Movement?

A fifth basic concern revolves around the complex questions: Who joins these groups? Do the members of the various groups share common motives and values, randomly falling into a particular organization, or are specific people attracted to particular movements? Many of the respondents interviewed for this book reported that, although they had investigated other groups in their search for meaning in their lives, they did not find the answers they sought until they joined one particular organization. For example, one former Unification Church member told me: "I had been approached by the Hare Krishnas in college. I thought they were absurd with their chanting and weird dress."

A present Divine Light Mission member remarked: "I went to a meditation group—Rajireesh, a Buddhist center where there were meditation rituals. I did some Hare Krishna chanting, but was not part of the group. I went to some *est* meetings, some positive thinking groups. I had very bad vibes about groups, like *est.* They are very rigid, perverted. You couldn't go to the bathroom when you wanted to. They were arrogant, into their own ego trips, very weird."

Psychiatrists and psychologists such as John Clark and Margaret Singer suggest that individuals join groups when they are in a particular state of consciousness, resulting partly from the individual's life circumstances and partly from situational manipulations practiced by the group. According to them, the particular group may be far less important than the individual's receptivity to what a cult—any cult—has to offer. Singer noted that individuals are likely to join religious cults "during periods of depression and confusion, when they had a sense that life was meaningless."[15] Psychologist Dr. Joyce Brothers is quoted in Hanna's book *Cults in America* as saying: "Life's losers are likely to find the smiling faces and dogmatic statements of cult leaders almost irresistible. Most people believe that they can, through their own actions, affect the world around them and make their way in it. But there are some who—because their parents really did not care enough for them to teach them how to be effective in life—are desperate to put their lives in the hands of a strong father-figure who promises love coupled with strong guidance and rigid discipline."[16]

Allen Tate Wood, who described his experiences as a member of the Unification Church in the book *Moonstruck,* suggested that the simplification of life for its members is an important reason for joining a cult, regardless of its specific nature. He wrote: "All the questions surrounding growing up—like what profession to choose, coming to terms with one's sexual orientation, where to live, how to find friends who share one's concerns, how to establish emotional independence from one's parents, whom to vote for in the next election—are precluded."[17]

Ronald Enroth also noted that "... cults tend to attract a disproportionate number of young adults who lack self-direction, purpose, and who need an external source of authority to provide a framework for their lives." He added other reasons for joining: "Ultimately, the quest for identity involves the quest for meaning, a spiritual search.... Not only are they involved in a genuine spiritual search, but young people who are highly vulnerable to cultic appeals are also usually very idealistic."[18]

David Hanna also described a common theme that he applied to all cults: "People who are drifting and discontented can find instant comradeship and a sense of self-worth in a cult."[19]

The quotations cited above have emphasized the common aspects of cult joining, implying that individuals who are particularly vulnerable or who happen to find themselves in particularly stressful situations will become members regardless of the nature of the group. However, it is important to view cult joining from another perspective, that there are characteristics of particular groups that attract particular types of people.

Gini Graham Scott, for instance, in her book *Cult and Countercult,* matched the characteristics of individuals with the attributes of groups in the following way: "Typically, lower-income and conservative types were attracted to the neo-Christian and born-again groups; middle- and upper-income liberals to the Eastern religions or quasi-religious self-help groups. There was also a sorting out by age—for example, more communal and total groups like the Unification Church and the Children of God appealed mainly to those under twenty-five, while more intellectual or casual groups like the Theosophists and spiritualists attracted a forty-plus age group. Also, groups that stressed techniques for achievement and monetary success proved especially attractive to middle- and upper-class members, while lower/working-class types were especially drawn to groups that featured emotional expression and magical aids to health, love, and money."[20]

My own research has confirmed the suggestions of Scott. Participants in A.R.E., *est,* Wainwright House, the Institute for Psycho-Integrity, and Scientology are generally older than members of the other organizations. Moreover, I have found that while members of all of the groups have been looking for something, they are generally searching for different kinds of answers. Thus a group that is attractive to one person may not be at all appealing to another individual. The groups do not seem to be interchangeable. The human potential type groups attract individuals who are striving for personal and interpersonal development. Present members of new religions generally report that they joined their group because it provided a logical, comprehensive theological system. In this regard, I spoke to many group members who indicated absolute certainty of their adherence to a particular belief system. Even when they demonstrated tolerance about other new religions (and many did not, to my surprise), they reflected that they had joined a particular group because of its specific theological tenets. Former members of these groups, however, generally suggested social and psychological reasons for joining these organizations.

What accounts for this discrepant perception? First, it may be that the different motivations for remaining in or leaving a group result in different distortions. If the individuals who left the groups were questioned while they were still members, the perception of their rationale for maintaining commitment might be quite similar to the perception of those remaining in the group. This perception only changes once the commitment to the group has been eliminated, i.e., everyone has a need to rationally justify his/her present and past actions, particularly to potential critics and to the social milieu from which he/she comes. However, a second factor may also be at work, namely that those who do join for theological reasons are predisposed to remain committed to the movement, whereas those who join for more personal or social reasons will eventually drop out or be successfully deprogrammed.

Brainwashing or Conversion

One of the most controversial issues facing the new religious movements is whether individuals join after a true conversion process or because they have been successfully programmed or brainwashed by the group. There does not appear to be a clear-cut answer to this difficult and very significant question and certainly no consensus appears in the pertinent literature. Various models have been suggested and several will be elucidated below. Flo Conway and Jim Siegelman argued that cults have definitely brainwashed their members, first by getting the "victims" hooked by deceptively establishing trust, then indoctrinating the recruit through the use of fear, guilt, hate, self-doubt, and rituals. They further argued that the recruits are alienated and isolated from their friends and families until they "snap" or undergo a "sudden, drastic alteration of personality in all its many forms."[21]

Psychiatrist John Clark, with his colleagues Michael Langone, a psychologist; Robert E. Schecter, a historian; and Reverend Roger C.B. Daly, developed a model of conversion which they describe in a monograph published by the Center on Destructive Cultism of the American Family Foundation. They discussed compelling conversion techniques that are used by cult groups to exploit vulnerable potential recruits who are likely "to be found among travelers and others in unfamiliar surroundings, among people in various sorts of distress, and especially among young people who are, whatever their formal attachments, making psychological transitions to maturity." Once a potential member is identified, the following steps are followed, according to this model: enticement, which is similar to the "hooking" phase described by Lofland in his description of the Unification Church; conversion, in which there is continuous activity and personalized attention to the prospect resulting in a narrowing of attention and an increase in suggestibility (during a period as short as a day or two or as long as several months); and acculturation, in which the prospect is led to "a full and unquestioned adoption of the cult's world view" through repeated espousal and practice of the group's beliefs and behaviors.[22]

David Hanna described a similar conversion process in which a new personality develops gradually in the cult member: "It requires various forms of sense deprivation inoculated through loss of sleep, low-protein diets, and exhausting rounds of chanting, praying and indoctrination in the thought of the new father-figure, the cult leader."[23]

Una McManus, a one-time member of the Children of God, described her experiences in *Not for a Million Dollars.* She wrote about common recruiting techniques employed by all cults: "I began to see a pattern of conversion and beliefs that cult members hold in common, no matter what name the cult bears. We were all recruited with a bombardment of 'love' and pressured into giving up thinking for ourselves. We were expected to follow our leaders blindly. We all went through different degrees of alienation from our families and isolation from the world."[24]

Dr. Paul A. Verdier, a clinical psychologist, suggested that frequently mass hypnosis is the major recruiting tool of religious cults. He further pointed to several factors that are facilitative aspects of brainwashing in these groups: threat of death, isolation from friends or family, loss of sleep, ego destruction, and repetition of the message, among others.[25] Earlier, Joost Meerloo had suggested that almost anyone could be brainwashed if the conditions were right. He noted that the process of brainwashing combines classical conditioning (in which associations, which were not previously present, are made), sensory deprivation, and early training in compliance and conformity.[26] Cult critics have argued that Meerloo's model can be applied to many new religions in their attempts to recruit members.

Robert Jay Lifton described eight psychological themes which, when present in a particular environment, serve to foster brainwashing (or thought reform). Lifton further noted: "The more clearly an environment expresses these eight psychological themes, the greater its resemblance to ideological totalism. . . . " The most basic of the eight factors is "milieu control," which means that all forms of input and output including seeing, hearing, reading, writing, experiencing, and thinking, are carefully controlled. The other features of the thought-reform environment are: (1) "mystical manipulation," the creation of a mystical aura around the group, a sense of higher purpose; (2) "the demand for purity," the division of the world into good or pure (that which is consistent with the totalist ideology) and bad or impure (everything else); (3) repeated confessions; (4) maintenance of "an aura of sacredness" around its basic dogma; (5) "loading the language" by reducing the complexity of human problems into "thought-terminating cliches"; (6) the primacy of the doctrine of the group over the individual; and (7) distinguishing between those "whose right to existence can be recognized, and those who possess no such right."[27]

Many critics of religious cults noted that although Lifton had originally applied his model to Communist China in the 1950's, it could be equally applicable to contemporary cults. They suggested that many or all of these conditions are apparent in cults, and thus concluded that members, rather than joining of their own volition, have been brainwashed into joining.

Critics of the brainwashing view of cult commitment argue that, while the conditions that Lifton described may be present in the new religions, they also exist in other situations or organizations, such as the military, particular branches of psychotherapy, and some established religions.

The criticism of brainwashing has not only been leveled against the religious organizations, but has also been leveled against human potential groups. For example, Vanessa Weber, who has been active in the Citizens Freedom Foundation, suggested in a talk at her old school that *est* uses brainwashing techniques and "coercive persuasion."[28] A different, less negative model of cult joining was offered by Gini Graham Scott. She described a five-stage socialization process, whereby newcomers gradually become more firmly entrenched in a group. During the initial contact stage, preliminary information gathering occurs and the individual decides if group members are sufficiently similar to him/herself to continue to the next phase. The "provisional inquiry" period allows the potential member to learn more about the group. The dropout rate, according to Scott, is quite high during this phase as newcomers test their interest in the movement. The first formal commitment to the group occurs in the "preliminary commitment" stage, through some initiation activity. This stage is followed by "confirmation and identification of commitment," during which time members further participate in group activities and apply the group's perspective. The final stage requires a "full commitment," which is manifested as complete identification with the group and acceptance of its beliefs and practices.[29] Scott further noted that "[e]ven though an individual may choose his commitment freely, if we do not like the group, we may charge he has been misled, brainwashed, or deceived."[30] Social psychologists Jonathan L. Freedman and Scott C. Fraser's description of the "foot-in-the-door" technique may be applicable here. They suggested that if individuals are first asked to make a small commitment, it is considerably easier to induce them to comply with a later request for a greater commitment.[31] Thus, the process of joining a group may initially involve a small commitment followed by increasingly greater commitments of time, money, energy, and beliefs.

An alternative model of cult joining was suggested by research conducted by Robert Balch and David Taylor in their study of a UFO cult. They noted that members of the UFO group "were not converts in the true sense of the word." Rather, becoming a follower could be interpreted as "a logical extension of their spiritual quest." These individuals did not relinquish one identity for another. Rather, by joining the UFO cult, they were demonstrating "a *reaffirmation* of their seekership."[32] These are the individuals who are likely to go from one group to another, constantly searching for answers.

Opponents of the use of the concept of brainwashing are as adamant in their claims as are proponents of that viewpoint. Psychiatrist Thomas Szasz, for example, argued: "Like many dramatic terms, brainwashing is a metaphor. A person can no more wash another's brain with coercion or conversation than he can make him bleed with a cutting remark. If there is no such thing as brainwashing, what does the metaphor stand for? It stands for one of the most universal human experiences and events, namely, for one peson influencing another. However, we do not call all types of personal or psychological influence 'brainwashing.' We reserve this term for influence of which we disapprove."[33]

Thomas Robbins and Dick Anthony concurred with Szasz, stating: "The metaphor of brainwashing can probably best be understood as a social weapon which provides a libertarian rationale for persecuting unpopular social movements and ideologies." They noted three aspects of the metaphor. First, there is the subjective nature of the concept, namely, "[b]rainwashing divorced from physical restraint is generally in the eye of the beholder." Second, proponents of the brainwashing concept argue that they are concerned with the way in which beliefs have been inculcated or in which they are presently held, rather than with the content of the beliefs. However, Robbins and Anthony contended that that is not the case; rather cult opponents are indeed concerned with the content of the belief system. Third, Robbins and Anthony argued that proponents of the brainwashing concept deny that unpopular beliefs could be voluntarily chosen.[34]

Social psychologist Leon Festinger's concept of cognitive

dissonance may provide a partial explanation for some of what is occurring in this controversial area. This concept refers to the fact that when our attitudes and/or behaviors conflict, we are motivated to change one to reduce the uncomfortable state of dissonance in which we find ourselves.[35] Thus, the greater our investment of time, money, energy, etc., the more we may need to believe in the group's activities and ideals. Another illustration of this phenomenon may be that former cult members may want (or need) to believe they were brainwashed rather than take responsibility for a behavior (i.e., joining the group) that they now see as foolish. Thus we avoid the discomfort of dissonant cognitions by changing one of them.

In my own investigation, I have found that although there is often obvious peer pressure to join and many instances of deception in recruiting, there is certainly no evidence of physical coercion or clear-cut instances of brainwashing. It appears that people probably join new religious movements because of a combination of personal and situational factors. The kind of manipulation that I observed most often is quite subtle, similar to that which occurs in many other groups and situations (for example, trying to sell a product). If you are not ready or willing to participate in a human potential group experience, you are made to feel that this is an indication of your problems; thus, you really need the experience. This is no more manipulative in itself than the recruiting efforts of a college fraternity or sorority which make potential initiates feel that if they do not join, they will not be part of the social elite of the campus. The manipulation, deceptive practices, and pressures that exist in new religious movements and human potential groups are probably not peculiar to those kinds of organizations.

Family Reactions

Another difficult subject concerns the response of family members to cult membership in a child (or spouse or sibling) and the relationship between family structure and cult conversion. Most parents are somewhat apprehensive when they first find out about their child's new affiliation. In time, some learn to accept their child's membership in the group. Indeed, some parents are actually quite pleased by their child's cult membership for a number of reasons. For instance, the child seems to have found a satisfying and meaningful lifestyle and is happier than previously. In some instances, the cult has saved the child from a worse fate—a life of drugs and drifting. In others, because of the emphasis on family relationships in the group's ideology, children may actually be encouraged to repair previously poor relationships. On the other hand, some parents become increasingly distraught by their child's new life, totally turning against him/her in an attempt to force a reversal of the new commitment. However, the opposite often occurs. Criticism may lead to greater commitment to the new group by reinforcing the child's belief that not only does the parent not understand, but makes no attempt to do so. Moreover, parental criticism strengthens the child's desire for autonomy.

A number of authors have suggested preventive measures that can be employed by parents. For example, Enroth suggested that "one of the best protections against the possibility of cultic involvement is a strong, supportive, loving family in which communication is open and honest and in which children develop early a positive self-image and a healthy sense of autonomy."[36] Robbins and Anthony suggested that parents may need to believe that their children were brainwashed into joining a particular group "to absolve themselves of responsibility for their children's defection."[37]

Advice to parents has also been offered by former cult members. One ex-Moonie, who left the group on her own, told me: "It is important that a parent not say: 'You're wrong.' That strengthens the ties to the group. It's important that a relationship continue to exist, as it did between my mother and myself."

Keeping the lines of communication open seems to be essential regardless of the parents' views of their children's membership. Franklin G. Maleson, a psychiatrist who has treated former cult members, advised clinicians who are working with parents "to take a careful history and to advise parents who have not studied their child's group to do so thoroughly. Organized countercult groups may be quite helpful by providing literature, personal accounts, practical advice, and emotional support. It is advisable, however, to recommend exploration of additional information sources, as in my experience the countercult groups can also be doctrinaire, at times overgeneralizing about cults and being a bit too enthusiastic about deprogramming."[38]

Distressed family members should be aware that most children leave the groups on their own with no encouragement or interference from their parents.

Language

Sharing common terminology or jargon is one of the ways that a group can increase its sense of cohesiveness. Each of the groups studied has developed certain "in" words or concepts that are understandable to members, but incomprehensible to most outsiders. For example, Moonies discuss God's "heart," Scientologists are "high tone" or "low tone," ISKCON members become "Krishna conscious," *est* trainees "get it," and Guru Maharaj Ji's followers are "premies," who strive for "Knowledge." In fact, after several months of investigation, I had become capable of categorizing an individual into a group by their use of specialized words without having to request identification.

The use of jargon allows group members to perceive themselves as similar to each other, which is an important component of interpersonal attraction. The attraction among group participants is a significant basis for a sense of belongingness within an organization. Moreover, exclusive language facilitates a perspective of shared identity and purpose, resulting in enhanced self-esteem which is particularly meaningful to those having poor self-concepts prior to joining. Thus, the development and maintenance of a linguistic system that sets the group apart from others strengthens intragroup bonds.

Deprogramming

Deprogramming is a term introduced by Ted Patrick and its use has been described in his book (with Tom Dulack) *Let Our Children Go*. Many instances of this practice have already been described in previous chapters. Its proponents and opponents are equally vociferous in their arguments. Because of the intensity and significance of the experience, there are probably distortions of reality on both sides.

Three different types of deprogramming are described in the literature. Voluntary deprogramming generally occurs on a visit home, when the child is persuaded to seek counseling concerning his/her cult membership. With involuntary deprogramming or kidnapping, a deprogramming team is hired by the parents to forcibly apprehend and deprogram the cult member. Deprogramming via the conservatorship route would involve the parents receiving custody of their child who is deemed to be incompetent by the courts. State legislative bills which would give parents temporary guardianship over their children have been strongly supported by cult opponents, but seen as a threat to freedom of religion by opponents of such legislation.

Deprogramming in general has been opposed by many religious organizations because of its perceived threat to religious liberty. For example, the National Council of the Churches of Christ in the U.S.A. adopted a resolution on February 28, 1974, stating, in part, that "...religious liberty...is grossly violated by forcible abduction and protracted efforts to change a person's religious commitments by duress. Kidnapping for ransom is heinous indeed, but kidnapping to compel religious deconversion is equally criminal."

It is certainly understandable that parents would resort to the use of involuntary deprogramming when they perceive that they have lost their child to an all-encompassing religious cult with beliefs and practices that are foreign to them, or when they see significant personality changes in their offspring after they have joined such an organization. However, parents should recognize that deprogramming is not a simple straightforward procedure that invariably works.

Numerous instances of failed deprogramming efforts have been documented. An unsuccessful deprogramming is likely to result in loss of trust in one's family and the consequent strengthening of group ties. One Unification Church member whose parents twice tried to have her deprogrammed said: "I didn't expect my life to be like this. I have to live almost like a criminal, always on the run. I always have to be on guard, to be very careful." She remembered that her parents were very upset when she joined the Church and her mother had said to her, "What are we going to tell our relatives? What are we going to tell our neighbors?" Debbie was surprised by her parents' negative reaction: "I couldn't understand it. The doctrine of Divine Principle wasn't so different from what I had grown up with. I thought my parents would be happy that I would be joining." Six weeks after joining the church, the first deprogramming attempt was made, after an invitation to have lunch with her parents. She was taken to a house where several of her relatives and others were present. She described the experience: "One women introduced herself and told me she was there to deprogram me. I applied my newfound faith believing that God would get me out of this. Another deprogrammer was there also. He was trying to break my faith in God. He called me 'a prostitute,' 'a bitch.' He told me that I was worshipping the Satan snake. It started softly, but as hours went on his voice became more and more intense. But he never touched me physically; he was very careful.... I was told that I was taking advantage of other people, that I was brainwashing others." With regard to the relationship with her parents she commented: "I really loved my parents, but the deprogrammers were trying to break down the trust between me and my parents.... My parents had been told that if they didn't do this to me, they were terrible parents." For a month she was moved from place to place and was carefully watched. Then one day she told her parents she was going to the store, took the car, and left, returning to the Unification Church.

The second deprogramming attempt occurred just several months later after her parents had "promised they wouldn't try it again." Debbie recalled that the second experience was even worse than the first, involving "constant degradation and humiliation. The more they carried it on, the more I knew it was wrong." After the initial phase of this deprogramming she was committed to a rehabilitation center where she "escaped with the help of another Unification Church member that I met there." She reflected that it took five years to rebuild the relationship with her parents, but she still never saw them alone; she was usually accompanied by her husband on these visits.

However, in other instances deprogramming was reportedly successful, and the former members expressed profound gratitude to their parents for getting them out of the group, even when some initial force (such as being pushed into a car) was employed. These individuals remembered their deprogramming in a markedly different light from those reported by individuals who remained in the groups. For example, a former Hare Krishna member said: "I didn't even call it a deprograming until two months later. I thought it was going to be much more frightening. All they did basically was to talk to me until I finally understood what was going on. Later I realized that mine was not so unusual."

Many of the deprogrammers are ex-cult members. Their involvement in this activity may be a reflection of some degree of defensiveness, that is, a reinforcement of their own deprogramming experience and the action of leaving the group. Another reason for their involvement was suggested by one deprogrammer, who had lived in a Divine Light Mission ashram for three years: "I have nothing else to do and I do this well." However, others also pointed out that their work was important and necessary "in order to free cult participants from the slavery of mind-control."

Those who argue for the use of deprogramming contend that it is a necessary strategy to restore free will to individuals who have been brainwashed into apparent conversion, in spite of the risks of failure, because the parents have, in essence, lost their children anyway. Critics, on the other hand, argue that the method of involuntary deprogramming bears a close resemblance to brainwashing. Anson D. Shupe, Jr., Roger Spielmann, and Sam Stigall, in their analysis of deprogramming, noted that "it is ironic that while modern anticultists perceive commitment to cults' doctrines as the result of brainwashing, their own attempts to restore their loved ones to 'normality' closely resemble the very phenomena they profess to despise."[39]

Along the same lines, J. Stillson Judah commented: "In other words, to belong to any one of these particular movements meant that you were 'mind-controlled,' and therefore a subject to be deprogrammed. The psychiatrists have, of course, worked with the legal branches of our government continually, you might say, acting the way the inquisitors in the past did to decide what were the 'right' religions to believe in, what were the heresies. And, of course, the new religions have become the heresies of our present day."[40]

Theologian Herbert Richardson suggestd that part of the motivation for the involvement of psychiatrists in the deprogramming movement is a monetary one. "When we ask how the selfish interests of psychiatrists are served by anti-conversion legislation, the answer is obvious. It gives them more dollars and cents. Can anyone, therefore, take seriously the claims of psychiatrists to be scientifically disinterested when they, more than any other group, stand to profit financially from the proposed changes in the law? Moreover, since psychiatrists specialize in adjusting people to the status quo, 'society and its viable values,' rather than changing it, they are the perfect therapists to set in opposition to religious prophets who seek to change the world."[41]

The preceding section certainly underscores the complexity of the subject of deprogramming with its political, religious, social, and emotional overtones. Those who need to make decisions about its use do not have an easy task.

Leaders

The leader's role in a movement is of such great significance that groups often change their very nature and may even be dissolved when the leader dies or leaves the organization. Ellwood described the latter problem: "The crisis of the second generation—of continuing a movement after the passing of the charismatic founder and the original enthusiasts sparked by his or her fire—is especially acute in cases where there is little social reinforcement."[42]

Some observers predicted the demise of the International Society for Krishna Consciousness after the death of its spiritual leader, Bhaktivedanta Prabhupada. However, this did not occur, although the movement has not grown in size in the United States in recent years. Louis Stewart pointed out that while Bhaktivedanta was "influential and revered," he was "not the movement's guru.... The guru is Krishna."[43]

Much of the anticult criticism addresses itself to the issue of the authoritarian nature of leadership. For instance, Enroth wrote: "Rigid, charismatic, authoritarian leadership is the keystone of all cultic movements.... Such a leader exudes certitude, self-confidence, and self-importance. He or she must be able to kindle and fan a sense of hope and trust within the ranks of the faithful."[44] Enroth further described the motivation of cult leaders: "First, they are able to exercise power over people. The ability to manipulate and control other people's lives can be very ego-satisfying. . . . Second, they are in it for the money. . . . Third, cult leaders may sincerely believe what they preach."[45]

Martin Ebon described the relationship between cult members and their leaders as follows: "A cult results from the emotional drive of its founder to be unique, to have a hot line to the Almighty, the Infinite, or powerful extra-terrestrial beings. And then, followers gather around this self-appointed leader, eager to fill a vacuum within their own lives."[46] A somewhat less negative view of this relationship is expressed by Gini Graham Scott, who wrote: "The key to group control seems to be having a strong, demanding leader who requires his followers' total loyalty to himself and to the group, and followers who are willing to give it in return for the belonging, esteem, meaning, and other benefits they derive from the group."[47]

These observations, and my own, point to the importance of a strong leader in maintaining commitment to the group. Each of the movements described in the preceding pages has a strong figurehead or guru at its center, with the exception of Wainwright House, where no one particular person appears to be firmly established as *the* leader. Wainwright House is also the most eclectic organization of the nine, perhaps not a coincidental finding. In some situations, individuals have been elevated to a status that was not intended when the group was originally founded. For instance, Edgar Cayce (and other members of the A.R.E. staff) warned against his being "worshipped." But some members have developed an absolute dedication to him anyway, perhaps reflecting their own motivation in joining the group (i.e., a need to follow a strong leader).

Future Outlook

The continued survival of the groups described in this book may be dependent upon a number of psychosocial factors. Rosabeth Moss Kanter conducted a sociological analysis of social practices, which appeared to "generate and sustain the commitment"[48] of members of 19th-century communes. It is plausible that the presence of these commitment mechanisms in new religions and human potential movements will be correlated with the continued existence of these groups. Kanter cited the following mechanisms: sacrifice, which includes abstinence from certain foods, drugs, and other substances, and celibacy; investment, financial and labor; renunciation, discouraging of both relationships to the outside world and family units within the group; communion, regular group contact, communal sharing of property, similarity of background; mortification, development of a new identity based "on the power and meaningfulness of group membership" through such techniques as confession and sanctions; transcendence, existence of meaning and power in the community through an elaborate philosophical system and special powers, privileges, and forms of address for leaders.[49]

Robert Wuthnow suggested that a particular social movement will have greater impact "if large numbers of people have *heard* of it than if only a few have; if a lot more people are *attracted* to it than are turned off by it; and if at least a significant number of those who hear about it also decide to *take part* in its activities."[50] This consideration may explain the great effort the groups investigated in this book have expended in attempting to enhance their image in their public's eye.

Christopher Evans pointed out another dimension that may offer a clue to the longevity of these movements: ". . . any really successful systems to replace the old religions must either offer more ideas . . . or alternatively offer ideas which are richer, deeper, or more enigmatic. The key here may lie in the word enigma, for the great religions of the past have always thrived on their mysteries and have weakened once they become pressurized, or feel obliged to unravel them."[51]

Another issue which, according to Robert Ellwood, "may be just over the horizon, is the question of multiple church or religious membership." Ellwood noted that "in the Orient it doesn't bother anybody if you belong to several religions at once.... In this country we have the deep-seated notion that if you're a Baptist, you can't be a Roman Catholic at the same time."[52] Thus, multiple church membership may be one means for incorporating new religions into mainstream society. One former cult member expressed the value of the new religions for traditional society in the following way: "Belonging to a cult could be good in a negative way to make religions and educational systems question what they're doing, to get people to use their judgment."

It is already becoming apparent that some of the practices of new religions and human potential groups are being employed by traditional religious and secular groups (e.g., meditation training for Roman Catholic nuns, sensitivity groups for executives in large corporations). One participant in a human potential group, who is also a psychotherapist, reflected on the importance of the diversity of available religious and human potential options: "I think it's wonderful that there are so many things that people are interested in. If there was only one kind of person, it would be very boring. I'm the first to caution people about the kinds of things they get into. Ninety percent of religious groups and human potential groups are very valuable; they're very good. There are, of course, charlatans in any activity. If they are legitimate organizations, attempting to raise consciousness, then we are all going to the same place, via different roads. It's like eating. We can't all want the same food." While there are some signs of growing tolerance for new religions, there is also striking evidence for the rapid growth of anticult groups.

It is becoming increasingly evident that work needs to be done to clarify further some of the issues discussed in this book. To gain a better understanding of the effect of new religions and human potential groups on personality variables, systematic pre-, during, and post-membership comparisons must be made. Other investigations could compare individuals who are currently members with those who have never joined such organizations and those who have left voluntarily. The latter, who are rarely studied because they quietly leave groups and do not usually seek therapy, may be relatively more honest and less defensive in their appraisal of group conditions and practices.

Antecedent family variables related to cult membership in children also need further study. Findings of present investigations may be confounded when the research is conducted after the fact. That is, differences between cult members' families and non-cult members' families may arise *after* the individual joins the group as a function of stress related to that event.

Regardless of what is studied, more information must become available to the public. Much of the debate about new religions and the human potential movement goes on in the absence of sufficient background. Moreover the discussion should concern itself with real issues and avoid the bitterness, name-calling, and defensiveness that is so apparent today. James W. Sire, a strong critic of cult groups, makes that point: "It is true, of course, that those who are misled by error and who propagate error are not to be followed and should, in fact, be made aware of their position before God. But cult believers and evangelists are still human. And all human beings must be treated with respect."[53]

A call for reason and moderation is also made by Gini Graham Scott: "Thus, our concern should be about the nature of the cults that emerge, rather than about cults per se. . . . The difference is in the cult's characteristics and whether these provide safeguards against excesses or whether they are conducive to the group member preserving personal control. . . .

"Thus, because of a few tragic events in the past few years, we must not necessarily reject the cult experience itself. For some individuals, cult involvement can be as valuable as another form of free religious expression, and the cults can do much good for the individual personally by providing self-improvement methods, personal satisfaction, meaning, and esteem, and for society as a whole by offering activities that contribute to society."[54]

People can and should attack groups on real issues—when they engage in illegal actions such as fraud and kidnapping, for instance. In a letter to Congressman Richard L. Ottinger, dated September 3, 1980, Dean M. Kelley, Executive for Religious and Civil Liberty of the National Council of the Churches of Christ in the U.S.A., wrote: ". . . If organizations claiming to be religious are engaged in 'coercion, fraud, violation of immigration laws, and acting covertly as agents of foreign governments and enterprises,' then appropriate steps can and should be taken under the criminal or immigration or other laws, irrespective of the claim of religion." However, to blindly attack these groups poses a significant threat to our liberties and our lifestyles. It is important to look at the issues in as unbiased a way as is possible and to recognize the inherent complexity of these phenomena. Even though it may be easier to search for simple answers, these, unfortunately, do not exist.

Notes

Notes to the Introduction

1. Flinn, "Laws, Language and Religion," *New ERA, a newsletter of the New Ecumenical Research Association,* I, No. 2 (May/June, 1981), 3.
2. *Ibid.,* p. 4.
3. Singer, "Coming Out of the Cults," *Psychology Today,* XII, No. 8 (1979), 72.
4. Sire, *Scripture Twisting: Twenty Ways the Cults Misread the Bible,* p. 20.
5. Ellwood, *Alternative Altars: Unconventional and Eastern Spirituality in America,* p. 13.
6. *Ibid.,* p. 12.
7. Flo Conway and Jim Siegelman, *Snapping: America's Epidemic of Sudden Personality Change.*
8. Enroth, *The Lure of the Cults,* p. 29.
9. Howard, *Please Touch,* pp. 20-21.
10. Ferguson, *op. cit.,* p. 139.
11. Cinnamon and Farson, *Cults and Cons: The Exploitation of the Emotional Growth Consumer,* p. xvi.
12. *Loc. cit.*
13. *Ibid.,* p. 4.
14. *Ibid.,* p. 27.
15. Hunt, *The Cult Explosion,* p. 28.
16. Ferguson, participating in a conference sponsored by the Rockefeller Foundation, *New Religious Movements in America.*

Notes to Chapter 1

1. Stoner and Parke, *All God's Children: The Cult Experience—Salvation or Slavery,* p. 55.
2. Sontag, *Sun Myung Moon and the Unification Church,* pp. 84-85.
3. *Ibid.,* pp. 87-88.
4. *Ibid.,* p. 88.

5. *Ibid.*, pp. 91-92.
6. *Ibid.*, p. 130.
7. *Ibid.*, p. 131.
8. Moon, Commencement Address, in *The Cornerstone* (publication of the Unification Theological Seminary), July, 1981, p. 3.
9. *Ibid.*
10. *Ibid.*
11. *Declaration of Unification Theological Affirmations.*
12. Joe Tully, Principle of Creation Lecture, in M. Darrol Bryant (ed.), *Proceedings of the Virgin Islands' Seminar on Unification Theology*, pp. 9-10.
13. Bryant and Hodges (eds.), *Exploring Unification Theology*, p. 83.
14. Sontag, *op. cit.*, p. 98.
15. Bryant and Hodges, p. 5.
16. *Ibid.*, p. 6.
17. Joe Stenson, cited in Bryant and Hodges, p. 9.
18. Thomas McGowan, "The Unification Church," in *The Ecumenist*, 1979, p. 22.
19. Sontag, p. 108.
20. "Master Speaks" (Sun Myung Moon talk), December 29, 1971, cited in Sontag, p. 119.
21. *Ibid.*, p. 121.
22. *Ibid.*, p. 123.
23. *Ibid.*, p. 124.
24. McGowan, *loc. cit.*
25. Sontag, p. 149.
26. Lofland, *op. cit.* (2d ed.), p. 345.
27. *Ibid.*, p. 68.
28. *Ibid.*, p. 75.
29. *Ibid.*, p. 309.
30. *Ibid.*, pp. 313-314.
31. *Ibid.*, p. 306.
32. McGowan, "Conversion and Human Development," in Herbert Richardson (ed.), *New Religions and Mental Health*, pp. 157-158.
33. *Ibid.*, pp. 160-161.
34. Barker, "Who'd be a Moonie? A Comparative Study of Those Who Join the Unification Church in Britain," in Bryan Wilson (ed.), *The Social Impact of New Religious Movements*, p. 67.
35. *Ibid.*, p. 83.
36. *Ibid.*, p. 84.
37. *Ibid.*, p. 88.
38. *Ibid.*
39. *Ibid.*, p. 94.
40. Mike Butler, "Dynamics of Joining and Leaving the U.C.," in *The Cornerstone*, V (3) (March, 1981), 1.
41. Baughman, *A Look at Unification Discipline*, paper presented at the Conference of Unification Life Style, p. 29.
42. Moon, *The Contrast Between Secular People and Us.*

43. Moon, *Our Position.*
44. Baughman, *loc. cit.*
45. Moon, *The Contrast....*
46. Baughman, *op. cit.*, pp. 26-27.
47. McGowan in Richardson, p. 163.
48. Joseph H. Fichter, "Marriage, Family, and Sun Myung Moon," in M. Darrol Bryant and Herbert W. Richardson (eds.), *A Time for Consideration: A Scholarly Appraisal of the Unification Church*, p. 133.
49. *Parents: Magazine of the Parents' Association of The Unification Church of Great Britain*, No. 5., p. 3.
50. Burnett, in *Parents*, No. 5, p. 17.
51. *Parents*, No. 5, pp. 22-23.
52. *120-Day Training Manual of the Unification Church*, p. 43.
53. *Ibid.*, p. 369.
54. *Ibid.*, p. 64.
55. Wood, p. 131.
56. *Manual*, p. 72.
57. *Ibid.*, p. 95.
58. Stoner and Parke, *op. cit.*, pp. 177-200.
59. National Council of the Churches of Christ in the U.S.A., "A Critique of the Theology of the Unification Church as Set Forth in 'Divine Principle'," p. 4.
60. *Ibid.*, p. 5.
61. Wood, *op. cit.*, pp. 171-172.

Notes to Chapter 2

1. Bry, *est (Erhard Seminars Training): 60 Hours That Transform Your Life*, p. 12.
2. Bartley, *Werner Erhard: The Transformation of a Man, The Founding of* est, p. 38.
3. *Ibid.*, p. 41.
4. *Ibid.*, p. 47.
5. *Ibid.*, p. 58.
6. *Ibid.*, p. 62.
7. *Ibid.*, p. 93.
8. *Ibid.*, p. 109.
9. *Ibid.*, p. 119.
10. *Ibid.*, p. 146.
11. *Ibid.*, p. 147.
12. *Ibid.*, pp. 167-169.
13. *Ibid.*, p. 171.
14. *Ibid.*, p. 172.
15. *Ibid.*, p. 252.
16. *Ibid.*, p. 184.
17. *Ibid.*, p. 185.
18. Bry, *op. cit.*, p. 24.
19. Werner Erhard and Victor Gioscia, "*est:* Communication in a Context of Comparison," in Jules H. Masserman (ed.), *Current Psychiatric Therapies*, p. 124.

20. Bry, p. 46.
21. Erhard and Gioscia, p. 118.
22. *Ibid.*, pp. 118-119.
23. *Ibid.*, p. 119.
24. *Ibid.*, pp. 119-120.
25. *Ibid.*, p. 120.
26. Greene, *est: 4 Days to Make Your Life Work*, p. 73.
27. Erhard and Gioscia, p. 121.
28. Bry, *op. cit.*, p. 63.
29. *Ibid.*, p. 84.
30. *Ibid.*, p. 82.
31. *Ibid.*, p. 85.
32. *Ibid.*, p. 87.
33. Interview of Hal Isen and Phyllis Allen by Ann Overton, "The Training Is the Training, Whenever You Do It," in *The Graduate Review* (*est* magazine), December, 1979/January, 1980, 2.
34. Bry, p. 101.
35. Interview by Overton, *loc. cit.*
36. *Ibid.*, p. 6.
37. Overton, "The Gift," in *The Graduate Review*, December, 1979/January, 1980, pp. 3-29 *passim.*
38. Bry, p. 96.
39. "Graduate Seminars are About Miracles," in *The Graduate Review*, September, 1978, 16.
40. *Loc. cit.*
41. "Celebrating Your Relationships," in *The Graduate Review*, September, 1978, 4.
42. *Ibid.*, p. 6.
43. *The Graduate Review*, March/April, 1981, 24.
44. "Investing in Transformation, Individual and Social," in *The Graduate Review*, July/August, 1981, 11-12.
45. Erhard, "Next Steps," in *The Graduate Review*, July/August, 1981, 10.
46. John Weldon, *The Frightening World of* est, p. 11.
47. Gordon, "Let Them Eat *est*," in *Mother Jones*, December, 1978, p. 43.
48. "Who is the *est* Graduate?," in *The Graduate Review*, September/October, 1980, 4.
49. Garvey, "Anatomy of Erhard's *est*," in *Our Town*, X No. 46 (March 9-15, 1980), 1.
50. Weldon, *op. cit.*, pp. 16-17.
51. Martin, *The New Cults*, pp. 129, 131.
52. Weldon, p. 3.
53. M. Norman (pseudonym), *How I Was Brainwashed by est*, speech given January 27, 1981, p. 2.
54. Martin, p. 123.
55. Baer and Stolz, "A Description of the Erhard Seminars Training *(est)* in the Terms of Behavior Analysis," in *Behaviorism* VI No. 1 (Spring, 1978), 51.
56. Kovel, *A Complete Guide to Therapy from Psychoanalysis to Behavior Modification*, p. 172.

57. "What You Told Us," in *The Graduate Review*, September/October, 1980, 9.
58. *The Graduate Review*, March/April, 1981, 20.
59. Brewer, "Erhard Seminars Training: 'We're Gonna Tear You Down and Put You Back Together'," in *Psychology Today*, IX, No. 3 (August, 1975), 39.
60. Weldon, p. 14.
61. Cited in Bartley, pp. 260-261.
62. Leonard L. Glass, Michael A. Kirsch and Frederick N. Parris, "Psychiatric Disturbances Associated with Erhard Seminars Training: I. A Report of Cases," in *American Journal of Psychiatry*, March, 1977, 245-247.
63. Jane Brody, "Reports of Psychosis after Erhard Course," in *The New York Times*, April 24, 1977, p. 23.
64. Babbie and Stone, *An Evaluation of the est Experience by a National Sample of Graduates*, paper presented at the annual meeting of the American Psychiatric Association, Miami Beach, May 13, 1976.

Notes to Chapter 3

1. L. Ron Hubbard, *Dianetics: The Modern Science of Mental Health*, p. ix.
2. Christopher Evans, *Cults of Unreason*, p. 135.
3. Eugene H. Methvin, "Scientology: Anatomy of a Frightening Cult," in *Reader's Digest*, May, 1980, p. 86.
4. Hubbard, *Dianetics and Scientology Technical Dictionary*, p. 369.
5. Malko, *Scientology: The Now Religion*, p. 64.
6. Hubbard, . . . *Technical Dictionary*, p. 115.
7. Evans, p. 22.
8. *Loc. cit.*
9. L. Ron Hubbard, *Scientology: A New Slant on Life*, pp. 19-20.
10. Cited in Malko, *op. cit.*, p. 32.
11. *L. Ron Hubbard, A Brief Biographical Sketch*, official statement from the Church of Scientology, p. 3.
12. Methvin, *op. cit.*, p. 87.
13. Malko, p. 38.
14. Evans, p. 27.
15. Campbell, "In Times to Come," in *Astounding Science Fiction*, Vol. XLV No. 2 (April, 1950), p. 132.
16. Evans, p. 34.
17. Winter, *A Doctor's Report on Dianetics: Theory and Therapy*, p. 11.
18. Roy Wallis, *The Road to Total Freedom: A Sociological Analysis of Scientology*, p. 43.
19. *Ibid.*, p. 50.
20. *Ibid.*, p. 94.
21. *Ibid.*, p. 103.
22. *Ibid.*, p. 128.
23. *Ibid.*, p. 140.
24. *Ibid.*, p. 142.
25. Ellwood, *op. cit.*, p. 168.
26. Evans, p. 49.
27. Hubbard, *Dianetics . . .*, p. ix.

28. *Ibid.*, p. 69.
29. Wallis, p. 25.
30. Hubbard, *Dianetics:...*, p. 70.
31. *Ibid.*, p. 45.
32. *Ibid.*, p. 72.
33. *Ibid.*, p. 208.
34. *Ibid.*, p. 243.
35. *Ibid.*, p. 241.
36. *Ibid.*, p. 244.
37. *Ibid.*, p. 243.
38. *Ibid.*, pp. 370-371.
39. *Ibid.*, pp. 366-367.
40. *Ibid.*, p. 365.
41. *Ibid.*, p. 38.
42. *Ibid.*, pp. 37-38.
43. Hubbard, *...Technical Dictionary*, p. 128.
44. Hubbard, *Dianetics:...*, p. 38.
45. Hubbard, *...Technical Dictionary*, pp. 128-129.
46. Evans, p. 43.
47. *Ibid.*, p. 40.
48. *Ibid.*, p. 41.
49. Wallis, p. 116.
50. Evans, p. 65.
51. Hubbard, *Scientology:...*, p. 9.
52. *Ibid.*, p. 17.
53. *Ibid.*, p. 37.
54. *Ibid.*, p. 43.
55. *Ibid.*, p. 57.
56. *Ibid.*, p. 68.
57. *Ibid.*, p. 87.
58. *Ibid.*, p. 117.
59. *Ibid.*, p. 157.
60. Evans, p. 105.
61. For example, Hubbard, *Dianetics...*, p. vi.
62. Ellwood, p. 173.
63. Founding Church of Scientology of Washington D.C. *vs.* United States, 409F. 2d 1146 (1969).
64. John Richard Burkholder in Irving I. Zaretsky and Mark P. Leone (eds.), *Religious Movements in Contemporary America*, p. 44.
65. Barr *vs.* Weise, 412F. 2d 338 (1969).
66. Burkholder, *loc. cit.*
67. Snook, *Going Further: Life-and-Death Religion in America*, pp. 93-94.
68. *Ibid.*, p. 97.
69. *Ibid.*, pp. 98-99.
70. *Ibid.*, pp. 102-103.
71. *Ibid.*, p. 100.
72. Malko, *op. cit.*, p. 55.
73. *Ibid.*, p. 58.

74. Wallis, p. 31.
75. *Ibid.* p. 37.
76. Meldal-Johnsen and Lusey, *The Truth About Scientology*, p. 215.
77. *What Is Scientology?*, pp. 239-248 *passim*.
78. Evans, p. 129.
79. Whitehead, "Reasonably Fantastic: Some Perspectives on Scientology, Science Fiction, and Occultism," in Irving I. Zaretsky and Mark P. Leone (eds.), *Religious Movements in Contemporary America*, p. 586.
80. Wallis, pp. 53-55.
81. *Ibid.*, p. 56.
82. *Ibid.*, pp. 62-63.
83. *Op. cit.*, p. 221.
84. Evans, p. 131.
85. *New Viewpoints*, p. 3.
86. *Ibid.*, p. 5.
87. *Ibid.*, p. 10.
88. *Ibid.*, p. 13.
89. *Ibid.*, p. 8.
90. Meldal-Johnsen and Lusey, *op. cit.*, p. 141.
91. Fischer, "Dianetic Therapy: An Experimental Evaluation," School of Education, New York University, 1953, cited in Wallis, p. 72.
92. Colbert, "An Evaluation of Dianetic Theory," School of Education, The City College, New York, 1951, in Wallis, *loc. cit.*
93. *Op. cit.* pp. xvii-xxxi.
94. *What Is Scientology?*, p. 257.
95. *Ibid.*, p. 252.
96. *Ibid.*, p. 253.
97. *Ibid.*, p. 254.
98. *Ibid.*, p. 255.
99. Garrison, *Playing Dirty: The Secret War Against Beliefs*, p. 19.
100. *The Guardian Office of the Church of Scientology*, p. 1.
101. *Ibid.*, p. 8.
102. *Freedom*, XXXI, pp. 3, 8.
103. Methvin, *op. cit.*, pp. 90-91.
104. "Author of a Book on Scientology Tells of Her Eight Years of Torment," in *The New York Times*, January 22, 1980.
105. Statement of Paulette Cooper.
106. *The Guardian Office...*, p. 52.
107. Santa Rosa, Milton, Fla., *Free Press*, October 30, 1975.
108. *The Winner*, June, 1981, p. 2.
109. *Op. cit.*, p. 4.
110. Evans, p. 133.

Notes to Chapter 4

1. Edgar Cayce, *Individual Reference File*, 1957, Question by 1968—P-4 7/25/43, F.33, p. 113.
2. *Ibid.*, Question by 3051-4 F.45, p. 136.

3. *Ibid.*, Question by 365-P-3, 2/27/35, p. 199.
4. *Ibid.*, Question by 276-4, F.17, p. 123.
5. Vaughn, "The Seekers and the Seer," in *The Virginian Pilot/The Ledger Star*, August 31, 1980.
6. Stearn, *Edgar Cayce-The Sleeping Prophet*, p. 26.
7. *Ibid.*, p. 27.
8. Cerminara, *Many Mansions*, pp. 20-21.
9. *Ibid.*, p. 21.
10. Stearn, p. 31.
11. Cerminara, p. 23.
12. Sherrill, *Edgar Cayce: The Man Who Saw Through Time and Space*, (brief biographical statement).
13. Stearn, pp. 25-26.
14. Cerminara, p. 27.
15. Sherrill, p. 5.
16. Cerminara, p. 32.
17. Sherrill, p. 4.
18. Cerminara, p. 40.
19. *Ibid.*, p. 28.
20. Stearn, p. 273.
21. *A.R.E. Fact Sheet*, 1981, p. 3.
22. Cited in Mark Thurston, "The Philosophy of Research," in *A.R.E. Journal*, May, 1973, 119.
23. Reed, "Learning to Remember Dreams," in *Journal of Humanistic Psychology*, XIII No. 3 (1973), 33-48.
24. *A.R.E. Fact Sheet*, 1981, p. 2.
25. Charles Thomas Cayce, "Mail from Members," in *The A.R.E. Journal*, XVI No. 2 (March, 1981), 56.
26. *Ibid.*, p. 57.
27. *A.R.E. Fact Sheet*, 1981, p. 2.
28. Edgar Cayce, Reading 3420-L-1, p. 172.
29. *Ibid.*, Reading 257-P-51, 2/18/43, M.50, p. 101.
30. Richard L. Kohr, "An A.R.E. Survey of Meditation," in *A.R.E. Journal*, XII No. 4 (July, 1977), 174-182.
31. Cited in Vaughn.

Notes to Chapter 5

1. *Summer Programs: The Himalayan International Institute of Yoga Science and Philosophy*, 1981 catalogue, p. 2.
2. Doug Boyd, *Swami*, p. ix.
3. *Summer Programs*, p. 27.
4. Doug Boyd, *Swami*, p. xviii.
5. *Ibid.*, p. 7.
6. *Ibid.*, p. 14.
7. *Ibid.*, pp. 14-16.
8. *Ibid.*, p. 59.
9. *Ibid.*, p. 60.

10. *Ibid.*, pp. 70-74.
11. *Ibid.*, pp. 96-97.
12. *Ibid.*, p. 323.
13. *Summer Programs*, p. 4.
14. *Ibid.*, p. 21.
15. *Ibid.*, p. 22.
16. *Research Bulletin of the Himalayan International Institute / Eleanor N. Dana Laboratory*, III No. 1 (1981).
17. Funk, "Changes in Respiration...," in *Research Bulletin....*, 13-16.
18. Nuernberger, "Meditation in Scientific Research," in *Dawn*, Summer, 1975, 16.
19. Boyd, p. 38.
20. Ballentine, "Ask Rudy: A Column on Medicine and Yoga," in *Dawn*, Summer, 1975, 42.
21. *Loc. cit.*
22. In *Dawn*, Winter, 1975, 40-41.
23. Pandit Usharbudh Arya, "Yoga, Meditation and Christianity," in *Meditation in Christianity*, p. 95.
24. Swami Rama, "Meditation in Christianity," in *Meditation in Christianity*, pp. 17-18.
25. *Ibid.*, p. 21.
26. Nuernberger, pp. 16-19.
27. Anderson, Buegel, and Chernin, *op. cit.*, p. 2.
28. *Ibid.*, p. 3.
29. *Ibid.*, p. 4.
30. *Ibid.*, p. 71.
31. *Ibid.*, p. 75.
32. Swami Rama, *op. cit.*, p. 12.

Notes to Chapter 6

1. Karen Fischer, "Right and Left Brain Radically Different," in *Pocono Record*, March 9, 1981.
2. *The Institute for Psycho-Integrity Presents the Integrity Experience.*
3. *The Institute for Psycho-Integrity Directory of Services.*
4. *Ibid.*
5. *Ibid.*
6. *Ibid.*
7. Lacouture, "Most People Use Only Half a Brain, Randolph Researchers Say," in *The Randolph Reporter*, July 16, 1981.
8. *The Institute for Psycho-Integrity Presents the Integrity Experience.*
9. *Ibid.*
10. *Ibid.*

Notes to Chapter 7

1. Stoner and Parke, *All God's Children: The Cult Experience—Salvation or Slavery*, pp. 40-41.
2. Messer, "Guru Maharaj Ji and the Divine Light Mission," in Charles Y. Glock and Robert N. Bellah (eds.), *The New Religious Consciousness*, p. 63.

3. Stoner and Parke, p. 10.
4. Messer, p. 53.
5. Enroth, *Youth, Brainwashing, and the Extremist Cults,* pp. 137-138.
6. Messer, p. 54.
7. *Ibid.,* p. 58.
8. Stone, "The Human Potential Movement," in Glock and Bellah (eds.), *op. cit.,* p. 102.
9. Messer, pp. 56, 59.
10. Guru Maharaj Ji, in *Love Song* (newsletter distributed by the Divine Light Mission in Los Angeles), May 1976, cited by Enroth, p. 142.
11. Messer, p. 59.
12. *Loc. cit.*
13. Messer, p. 55.
14. Stoner and Parke, pp. 11-12.
15. Enroth, p. 140.
16. *Ibid.,* p. 141.
17. Messer, p. 70.
18. *Ibid.,* pp. 56, 66-67.
19. Stoner and Parke, p. 8.
20. Cox, *op. cit.,* p. 92.
21. Stoner and Parke, pp. 10-11.
22. Robert Jay Lifton, *Thought Reform and the Psychology of Totalism.*
23. *Op. cit.,* pp. 420-429.
24. *Loc. cit.*
25. Messer, p. 72.

Notes to Chapter 8

1. *Wainwright House Summer Programs, 1981* (catalogue).
2. *A History of Wainwright House* (booklet), p. 1.
3. *Ibid.,* p. 2.
4. *Ibid.,* p. 10.
5. *Loc. cit.*
6. *Loc. cit.*
7. *Summer Programs,* p. 3.
8. *Ibid.,* p. 4.
9. John Yungblut, director of the Guild for Spiritual Guidance, cited in *A History of Wainwright House,* p. 12.
10. *Summer Programs,* p. 1.
11. *Ibid.,* p. 8.
12. Ullman, "The Experiential Dream Group," in Wolman, *op. cit.,* pp. 418-420.
13. *Wainwright House Spring Programs, 1981* (catalogue), p. 3.
14. Buzan, interviewed by Eric Frank (ed.), in *Training, Journal of the Institute of Training and Development* VII No. 2 (April 1981).

Notes to Chapter 9

1. Daner, *The American Children or Krsna: A Study of the Hare Krsna Movement,* pp. 34-35.
2. J. Stillson Judah, "The Hare Krishna Movement," in Irving I. Zaretsky and Mark P. Leone (eds.), *Religious Movements in Contemporary America,* p. 465.
3. Daner, p. 23.
4. Judah, p. 468.
5. Daner, p. 26.
6. Judah, p. 468.
7. Daner, pp. 16-17.
8. A.C. Bhaktivedanta, *The Science of Self-Realization,* p. 117.
9. Daner, p. 17.
10. Johnson, "The Hare Krishna in San Francisco," in Charles Y. Glock and Robert N. Bellah (eds.), *The New Religious Consciousness,* p. 33.
11. Daner, pp. 17, 19.
12. Bhaktivedanta, p. 17.
13. Daner, p. 19.
14. Carroll Stoner and Jo Anne Parke, *All God's Children: The Cult Experience—Salvation or Slavery,* p. 64.
15. Johnson, p. 34.
16. Bhaktivedanta, *Life Comes From Life,* p. 17.
17. Bhaktivedanta, *Consciousness, the Missing Link,* p. 15.
18. Bhaktivedanta, *The Science of Self-Realization,* p. 10.
19. Bhaktivedanta, *Life Comes From Life,* p. 68.
20. Daner, p. 33.
21. Swami, Jayadvaita, "Bad Karma," in *Back to Godhead* magazine, XIV No. 9, 7.
22. Daner, p. 33.
23. Bhaktivedanta, *The Science of Self-Realization,* pp. 16-17.
24. Bhaktivedanta, "Hearing from the Right Source," in *Back to Godhead,* XV No. 5, 2.
25. Judah, p. 470.
26. Daner, pp. 60-61.
27. Judah, p. 470.
28. Daner, p. 61.
29. *Ibid.,* pp. 43-44.
30. *Ibid.,* pp. 41-43.
31. *Ibid.,* p. 50.
32. Stoner and Parke, *op. cit.,* p. 144.
33. Faye Levine, *The Strange World of the Hare Krishna,* p. 81.
34. Daner, p. 68.
35. Bhaktivedanta, "Slaughterhouse Civilization," in *Back to Godhead,* XIV No. 9, 3.
36. Krsna-Devi Dasi and Sama-Devi Dasi (eds.), *The Hare Krsna Cookbook,* pp. 8-10.
37. Daner, p. 62.

38. *Ibid.*, p. 74.
39. Stoner and Parke, p. 17.
40. Ruppert, "Looking for Leaders," in *Back to Godhead*, XIV No. 9, 11, 12.
41. Judah, p. 476.
42. Ronald Enroth, *Youth, Brainwashing, and the Extremist Cults*, p. 152.
43. Judah, p. 477.
44. Johnson, p. 38.
45. *Ibid.*, p. 44-45.
46. Stoner and Parke, p. 17.
47. *Ibid.*, pp. 18-19.
48. Levine, p. 49.
49. Judy Steele, "Krishna Story with a Twist," reprinted in *Back to Godhead*, XV No. 5, 7.
50. Levine, pp. 145, 147.
51. Paul Avery, Joe Quintana, and Peter Knutson, "Guns, Profits Cloud Sect's Image," *Sacramento Bee*, June 22, 1980.
52. Avery, Quintana, and Knutson, "Critics Term 'Sankirtan' a Hustle," *Sacramento Bee*, June 24, 1980.
53. Stoner and Parke, p. 44.

Notes to the Conclusions

1. *Open Statement on Jonestown*, The Alliance for the Preservation of Religious Liberty, November 20, 1980.
2. Anthony, participating in a conference sponsored by the Rockefeller Foundation, *New Religious Movements in America*, 1979, p. 12.
3. Schur, *The Awareness Trap*, p. 2.
4. Goffman, *Asylums*.
5. LaBarre, "Materials for History of Studies of Crisis Cults: A Bibliographic Essay," in *Current Anthropology*. XII (1971), 3-44.
6. Eister, "Culture Crises and New Religious Movements: A Paradigmatic Statement of a Theory of Cults," in Irving I. Zaretsky and Mark P. Leone, *Religious Movements in Contemporary America*, pp. 613-614.
7. Colton, Introduction, *New Religious Movements in America* conference.
8. Hanna, *Cults in America*, pp. 11-12.
9. *Ibid.*, p. 227.
10. Marty, in foreword to Robert S. Ellwood, Jr., *Alternative Altars: Unconventional and Eastern Spirituality in America*, p. viii.
11. Ellwood, *op. cit.* in note 10, pp. 171-172.
12. *Ibid.*, p. 34.
13. Meyer and Kitch, cited in Frederick Bird, "Charisma and Ritual in New Religious Movements," in Jacob Needleman and George Baker (eds.), *Understanding the New Religions*, p. 179.
14. Bird, "Charisma and Ritual in New Religious Movements," in Needleman and Baker, *Understanding the New Religions*, pp. 180, 182.
15. Margaret Thaler Singer, "Coming out of the Cults," in *Psychology Today*, XII, No. 8, (1979), 72.
16. Brothers, cited in Hanna, p. 11.

17. Wood, *Moonstruck*, p. 186.
18. Enroth, *The Lure of the Cults*, pp. 48-50.
19. Hanna, p. 256.
20. Scott, *Cult and Countercult: A Study of a Spiritual Growth Group and a Witchcraft Order*, p. 7.
21. Conway and Siegelman, *Snapping: America's Epidemic of Sudden Personality Change*, p. 13.
22. Clark, Langone, Schecter, and Daly, *Destructive Cult Conversion: Theory, Research, and Treatment*, pp. 10-14.
23. Hanna, p. 252.
24. Una McManus and John Charles Cooper, *Not for a Million Dollars*, pp. 135-136.
25. Verdier, *Brainwashing and the Cults: An Expose on Capturing the Human Mind.*
26. Meerloo, *The Rape of the Mind.*
27. Lifton, *Thought Reform and the Psychology of Totalism*, pp. 420-435.
28. Weber, "The Cults, Brainwashing and How They Affect You," in *Oldfields Magazine*, Fall, 1980, 11.
29. Scott, p. 167.
30. *Ibid.*, p. 172.
31. Freedman and Fraser, "Compliance Without Pressure: The Foot-in-the-door Technique," in *Journal of Personality and Social Psychology*, IV (1966), 195-202.
32. Balch and Taylor, "Seekers and Saucers: The Role of the Cultic Milieu in Joining a UFO Cult," *American Behavioral Scientist*, XX No. 6 (July/August 1977), 856-857.
33. Szasz, cited in introduction to Herbert Richardson (ed.), *New Religions and Mental Health: Understanding the Issues*, p. xxiv.
34. Robbins and Anthony, "Available Research Is... Not Consistent with a Model of Psychological Kidnapping," in Joseph Rubinstein and Brent D. Slife (eds.), *Taking Sides: Clashing Views on Controversial Psychological Issues*, pp. 56-59.
35. Festinger, *A Theory of Cognitive Dissonance.*
36. Enroth, p. 99.
37. Robbins and Anthony, p. 61.
38. Maleson, "Dilemmas in the Evaluation and Management of Religious Cultists," in *American Journal of Psychiatry*, CXXXVIII No. 7 (1981), 929.
39. Shupe, Spielmann, and Stigall, "Deprogramming," in *American Behavioral Scientist*, XX No. 6 (1977), 952.
40. Judah, participating in *New Religious Movements in America* conference, p. 21.
41. Richardson, in introduction to Herbert Richardson (ed.), *New Religions and Mental Health: Understanding the Issues*, p. xxv.
42. Ellwood, *op. cit.*, p. 35.
43. Stewart, *Life Forces*, p. 284.
44. Enroth, p. 55.
45. *Ibid.*, p. 61.
46. Ebon, *The World's Weirdest Cults*, p. 1.
47. Scott, p. 178.

48. Kanter, *Commitment and Community: Communes and Utopias in Sociological Perspective,* p. 75.
49. *Ibid.,* p. 103.
50. Wuthnow, "The New Religions in Social Context," in Charles Y. Glock and Robert N. Bellah (eds.), *The New Religious Consciousness,* p. 269.
51. Evans, *Cults of Unreason,* p. 247.
52. Ellwood, participating in a conference sponsored by the Rockefeller Foundation, *New Religious Movements in America,* p. 7.
53. Sire, *Spiritual Twisting: Twenty Ways the Cults Misread the Bible,* p. 19.
54. Scott, p. 180.

Bibliography

Anderson, David, Dale Buegel, and Dennis Chernin. *Homeopathic Remedies for Physicians, Laymen and Therapists*. Honesdale, Pa.: Himalayan International Institute, 1978.

A.R.E., Association for Research and Enlightenment Introductory Brochure.

A.R.E. Fact Sheet, 1981.

A.R.E. Membership Benefits for You and Your Family, flyer.

Arya, Pandit Usharbudh. "Yoga, Meditation and Christianity," in *Meditation in Christianity,* pp. 77-92. Honesdale, Pa.: Himalayan International Institute of Yoga Science and Philosophy, 1979.

"Author of a book on Scientology Tells of her Eight Years of Torment," in *The New York Times,* January 22, 1980.

Avery, Paul, Joe Quintana, and Peter Knutson. "Critics Term 'Sankirtan' a Hustle," in *The Sacramento Bee,* June 24, 1980.

———. "Guns, Profits Cloud Sect's Image," in *The Sacramento Bee,* June 22, 1980.

Babbie, Earl, and Donald Stone. *An Evaluation of the* est *Experience by a National Sample of Graduates,* paper presented at the Annual Meeting of the American Psychiatric Association, Miami Beach, May 13, 1976.

Baer, Donald M., and Stephanie B. Stolz. "A Description of the Erhard Seminars Training *(est)* in the Terms of Behavior Analysis," in *Behaviorism* VI No. 1 (Spring, 1978), 45-70.

Balch, Robert W. and David Taylor. "Seekers and Saucers: The Role of the Cultic Milieu in Joining a UFO Cult," in *American Behavioral Scientist,* XX No. 6 (1977), 839-860.

Ballentine, Rudolph. "Ask Rudy: A Column on Medicine and Yoga," in *Dawn,* Winter, 1975, 38-42; Summer, 1975, 40-44.

Barker, Eileen. "Who'd be a Moonie? A Comparative Study of Those Who

Join the Unification Church in Britain," in Bryan Wilson (ed.), *The Social Impact of New Religious Movements,* pp. 59-96. New York: The Rose of Sharon Press, Inc., 1981.

Bartley, III, William Warren. *Werner Erhard: The Transformation of a Man, The Founding of est.* New York: Clarkson N. Potter, Inc., 1978.

Baughman, James A. *A Look at Unification Discipline,* paper presented at the Conference on Unification Lifestyle, sponsored by the Unification Theological Seminary. San Juan, Puerto Rico, January, 1981.

Baybak, Michael (ed.). *New Viewpoints.* Los Angeles: Information Service of the U.S. Churches of Scientology, 1976.

Bhaktivedanta, A.C. *Consciousness: the Missing Link.* Los Angeles: International Society for Krishna Consciousness, 1979.

______. "Hearing from the Right Source," in *Back to Godhead,* XV no. 5, 2, 4, 30.

______. *Life Comes From Life,* Los Angeles: International Society for Krishna Consciousness, 1979.

______. *The Science of Self-Realization.* Los Angeles: International Society for Krishna Consciousness, 1977.

______. "Slaughterhouse Civilization," in *Back to Godhead,* XIV No. 9, 3-5.

Bird, Frederick. "Charisma and Ritual in New Religious Movements," in Jacob Needleman and George Baker (eds.), *Understanding the New Religions,* pp. 173-189. New York: The Seabury Press, 1978.

Books, Tapes, Records From A.R.E., catalogue, Winter/Spring, 1981.

Boyd, Doug. *Swami.* New York: Random House, 1976.

Breuer, Joseph and Sigmund Freud. *Studies in Hysteria,* Vol. II of the Standard Edition of the Complete Psychological Works of Sigmund Freud. London: Hogarth Press, 1955.

Brewer, Mark. "Erhard Seminars Training: 'We're gonna tear you down and put you back together'," *Psychology Today,* IX No. 3 (August, 1975), 35-36, 39-40, 83, 88-89.

Brody, Jane. "Reports of Psychosis After Erhard Course," in *The New York Times,* April 24, 1977, p. 23.

Bry, Adelaide. *est (Erhard Seminars Training): 60 Hours That Transform Your Life.* New York: Harper & Row, 1976.

Bryant, M. Darrol (ed.), *Proceedings of the Virgin Islands' Seminar on Unification Theology.* New York: The Rose of Sharon Press, Inc., 1980.

Bryant, M. Darrol, and Susan Hodges (eds.), *Exploring Unification Theology,* Second Edition. New York: Rose of Sharon Press, 1978.

Burkholder, John Richard. "The Law Knows No Heresy: Marginal Religious Movements and the Courts," in Irving I. Zaretsky and Mark

P. Leone (eds.), *Religious Movements in Contemporary America.* Princeton: Princeton University Press, 1974, pp. 27-50.
Burnett, Laurie. "If Your Child Joins the 'Moonies'" in *Parents: Magazine of the Unification Church of Great Britain,* No. 5, 17.
Butler, Mike. "Dynamics of Joining and Leaving the U.C.," in *The Cornerstone,* V No. 3 (March 1981), 1.
Campbell, John, Jr. "In Times to Come," in *Astounding Science Fiction.* XLV No. 2 (April, 1950), 132.
Cayce, Charles Thomas. "Mail from Members." *The A.R.E. Journal,* XVI No. 2 (March, 1981), 55-63.
Cayce, Edgar. *Individual Reference File,* Virginia Beach: Association for Research and Enlightenment, Inc., 1957.
"Celebrating your Relationships," in *The Graduate Review.* September, 1978. 2-10.
Cerminara, Gina. *Many Mansions.* New York: The New American Library, Inc., 1967.
Cinnamon, Kenneth, and Dave Farson. *Cults and Cons: The Exploitation of the Emotional Growth Consumer.* Chicago: Nelson-Hall, Inc., 1979.
Clark, John G., Michael D. Langone, Robert E. Schecter, and Roger C.B. Daly. *Destructive Cult Conversion: Theory, Research, and Treatment.* Boston: American Family Foundation, 1981.
Conway, Flo, and Jim Siegelman. *Snapping: America's Epidemic of Sudden Personality Change.* New York: J.P. Lippincott Co., 1978.
Cosgrove, Vincent. "DA to Probe Six Deaths," in *New York Daily News,* May 7, 1977.
A Critique of the Theology of the Unification Church as Set Forth in 'Divine Principle.' Commission on Faith and Order of the National Council of the Churches of Christ in the U.S.A.
Cox, Harvey. *Turning East.* New York: Simon and Schuster, 1977.
Daner, Francine Jeanne. *The American Children of Krsna.* New York: Holt, Rinehart and Winston, 1976.
Declaration of Unification Theological Affirmations at Barrytown, New York, Oct. 14, 1976.
Ebon, Martin (ed.), *The World's Weirdest Cults.* New York: A Signet Book. New American Library, 1979.
Eister, Allan W. "Culture Crises and New Religious Movements: A Paradigmatic Statement of a Theory of Cults," in Irving I. Zaretsky and Mark P. Leone, *Religious Movements in Contemporary America.* Princeton: Princeton University Press, pp. 612-627.
Ellwood, Jr., Robert S. *Alternative Altars: Unconventional and Eastern Spirituality in America.* Chicago: University of Chicago Press, 1979.
______. *Religious and Spiritual Groups in Modern America.* Englewood Cliffs, N.J.: Prentice-Hall, 1973.

Enroth, Ronald M. *The Lure of the Cults.* Chappaqua, N.Y.: Christian Herald Books, 1979.

______. *Youth, Brainwashing, and the Extremist Cults.* Grand Rapids, Mich.: The Zondervan Corporation, 1977.

Erhard, Werner. "Next Steps," in *The Graduate Review.* July/August, 1981, 10.

Erhard, Werner and Victor Gioscia. "*est:* Communication in a Context of Compassion," Jules H. Masserman (ed.), *Current Psychiatric Therapies,* XVIII, 117-125. New York: Grune & Stratton, 1979.

Evans, Christopher. *Cults of Unreason.* New York: Farrar, Straus and Giroux, 1974.

Fall Calendar Sponsored by the Institute for Psycho-Integrity, 1981.

Ferguson, Marilyn. *The Aquarian Conspiracy: Personal and Social Transformation in the 1980's.* Los Angeles: J.P. Tarcher, Inc., 1980.

Festinger, Leon. *A Theory of Cognitive Dissonance.* Stanford, Calif.: Stanford University Press, 1957.

Fichter, Joseph H. "Marriage, Family, and Sun Myung Moon," in M. Darrol Bryant and Herbert W. Richardson (eds.), *A Time for Consideration: A Scholarly Appraisal of the Unification Church,* pp. 131-140. New York: Edwin Mellen Press, 1978.

Fischer, Karen. "Right and Left Brain Radically Different," in *Pocono Record,* March 9, 1981.

Flinn, Frank K. "Laws, Language and Religion," in *New ERA,* a newsletter of the New Ecumenical Research Association, I No. 2 (May/June, 1981), 3-6.

Frank, Eric. "Interview of Tony Buzan," in *Training, Journal of the Institute of Training and Development,* VII (April, 1981).

Freedman, J.L. and S.C. Fraser. "Compliance Without Pressure: The Foot-in-the-door Technique," in *Journal of Personality and Social Psychology,* IV (1966), 195-202.

Freudenberger, Herbert, chair, "Cults and the Impact on Society," symposium presented at the Annual Meeting of the American Psychological Association, Los Angeles, 1981.

Funk, Edwin. "Changes in Respiration With a Mental Task: An Experimental Study," in *The Research Bulletin of the Himalayan International Institute/Eleanor N. Dana Laboratory,* III No. 1 (1981), 13-16.

Garrison, Omar V. *Playing Dirty: The Secret War Against Beliefs.* Los Angeles: Ralston-Pilot, Inc., 1980.

Garvey, Kevin. "Anatomy of Erhard's *est,*" in *Our Town,* X No. 46 (March 9-15, 1980), 1, 4.

Glass, Leonard L., Michael A. Kirsch, and Frederick N. Parris. "Psychiatric Disturbances Associated with Erhard Seminars Training: I. A Report of Cases," in *American Journal of Psychiatry,* March, 1977, 245-247.

Goffman, Erving. *Asylums.* Garden City, N.Y.: Doubleday & Co., 1961.

Gordon, Suzanne. "Let them eat *est,*" in *Mother Jones,* December, 1978.

"Graduate Seminars Are About Miracles," in *The Graduate Review,* September, 1978, 16.

Greene, William. *est: 4 Days to Make Your Life Work.* New York: Simon and Shuster, Pocket Books Edition, 1976.

The Guardian Office of the Church of Scientology. Los Angeles: Church of Scientology of California, 1978.

Hanna, David. *Cults in America.* New York: Belmont Tower Books, 1979.

History of Wainwright House, A, booklet, June 14, 1981.

Howard, Jane. *Please Touch.* New York: McGraw-Hill, 1970.

Hubbard, L. Ron. *Dianetics and Scientology Technical Dictionary.* Los Angeles: The Church of Scientology of California Publications Organization, 1975.

———. *Dianetics: The Modern Science of Mental Health.* Los Angeles: The Church of Scientology of California Publications Organization, 1950.

———. *Science of Survival: Prediction of Human Behavior.* Los Angeles: The American Saint Hill Organization, 1951.

———. *Scientology: A New Slant on Life.* Los Angeles: The Church of Scientology of California Publications Organization, 1972.

Hunt, Dave. *The Cult Explosion.* Irvine, Calif.: Harvest House Publishers, 1980.

Institute for Psycho-Integrity Directory of Services, The.

Institute for Psycho-Integrity Presents the Integrity Experience, The.

Investing in Transformation, Individual and Social," in *The Graduate Review.* July/August, 1981, 11-12.

Johnson, Gregory. "The Hare Krishna in San Francisco," in Charles Y. Glock and Robert N. Bellah (eds.), *The New Religious Consciousness,* pp. 31-51. Berkeley, Calif.: Univ. of Calif. Press, 1976.

Judah, J. Stillson. "The Hare Krishna Movement," in Irving I. Zaretsky and Mark P. Leone (eds.), *Religious Movements in Contemporary America,* pp. 463-478. Princeton: Princeton University Press, 1974.

Kanter, Rosabeth Moss. *Commitment and Community: Communes and Utopias in Sociological Perspective.* Cambridge, Mass.: Harvard University Press, 1972.

Kohr, Richard L. "An A.R.E. Survey of Meditation," in *A.R.E. Journal,* XII No. 4 (July, 1977), 174-182.

Kovel, Joel. *A Complete Guide to Therapy from Psychoanalysis to Behavior Modification.* New York: Pantheon Books, 1976.

Krsna-Devi Dasi and Sama-Devi Dasi (eds.), *The Hare Krsna Cookbook.* Los Angeles: International Society for Krishna Consciousness, 1973.

LaBarre, Weston. "Materials for History of Studies of Crisis Cults: A Bibliographic Essay," in *Current Anthropology,* XII (1971), 3-44.

Lacouture, Sheila. "Most People Use Only Half a Brain, Randolph Researchers Say," in *The Randolph Reporter,* July 16, 1981.

Levine, Faye. *The Strange World of the Hare Krishna.* Greenwich, Conn: Fawcett Publications, 1974.

Lifton, Robert Jay. *Thought Reform and the Psychology of Totalism.* New York: W.W. Norton & Co., 1961.

Lofland, John. *Doomsday Cult* (2d ed.). New York: Irvington Publishers, 1977.

L. Ron Hubbard, A Brief Biographical Sketch. Los Angeles: Church of Scientology of California Publications Organization, 1977.

Maleson, Franklin G. "Dilemmas in the Evaluation and Management of Religious Cultists," in *American Journal of Psychiatry,* CXXXVIII No. 7 (1981), 925-929.

Malko, George. *Scientology: The Now Religion.* New York: Delacorte Press, 1970.

Martin, Walter. *The New Cults,* Santa Ana, Calif.: Vision House, 1980.

Maslow, Abraham. *Toward a Psychology of Being.* New York: Van Nostrand-Reinhold Books, 1968.

McGowan, Thomas. "Conversion and Human Development," in Herbert Richardson (ed.,), *New Religions and Mental Health: Understanding the Issues,* pp. 127-173. New York: Edwin Mellen Press, 1980.

______. "The Unification Church," in *The Ecumenist,* XVII No. 2 (1979), 21-25.

McManus, Una and John Charles Cooper. *Not for a Million Dollars.* Nashville: Impact Books, a division of the Benson Co., 1980.

Meditation in Christianity. Honesdale, Pa.: The Himalayan International Institute of Yoga Science and Philosophy, 1979.

Meerloo, Joost A. *The Rape of the Mind.* New York: Grosset and Dunlap, 1956.

Meldal-Johnsen, Trevor, and Patrick Lusey. *The Truth About Scientology.* New York: Tempo Books, Grosset & Dunlap, 1980.

Messer, Jeanne. "Guru Maharaj Ji and The Divine Light Mission," in Charles Y. Glock and Robert N. Bellah (eds.), *The New Religious Consciousness,* pp. 52-72. Berkeley, Calif,: Univ. of Calif. Press, 1976.

Methvin, Eugene H. "Scientology: Anatomy of a Frightening Cult," in *Reader's Digest,* CXVI No. 697 (May, 1980), 86-91.

Moon, Sun Myung. *The Contrast Between Secular People and Us,* speech, Dec. 23, 1979.

______. Commencement Address, in *The Cornerstone,* publication of the Unification Theological Seminary. V No. 7 (July, 1981), 3-4.
______. *Our Position,* speech, Jan. 2, 1979.
New Religious Movements in America, conference sponsored by The Rockefeller Foundation, September, 1979.
Norman, M. (pseudonym). *How I was Brainwashed by* est, speech given at Women's O.R.T., Jan. 27, 1981.
Nuernberger, E. Phillip. "Meditation in Scientific Research," in *Dawn.* Summer, 1975, 16-19.
Open Statement on Jonestown. The Alliance for the Preservation of Religious Liberty. New York, Nov. 20, 1980.
Overton, Ann. "The Gift," in *The Graduate Review,* December, 1979/ January 1980, 3-29.
______. "The Training Is the Training, Whenever You Do It," in *The Graduate Review.* December, 1979/January, 1980, 2, 6.
Patrick, Ted and Tom Dulack. *Let Our Children Go.* New York: E.P. Dutton, 1976.
Rama, Swami. "Meditation in Christianity," in *Meditation in Christianity.* Honesdale, Pa.: The Himalayan International Institute of Yoga Science and Philosophy, 1979, pp. 1-23.
Rank, Otto. *The Trauma of Birth.* New York: Harcourt Brace & Co., 1929.
Reed, Henry. "Learning to Remember Dreams," in *Journal of Humanistic Psychology,* XIII, No. 3 (1973), 33-48.
Richardson, Herbert (ed.), *New Religions and Mental Health: Understanding the Issues.* New York: The Edwin Mellen Press, 1980.
Robbins, Thomas and Dick Anthony. "Available Research Is... Not Consistent With a Model of Psychological Kidnapping," in Joseph Rubinstein and Brent D. Slife (eds.), *Taking Sides: Clashing Views on Controversial Psychological Issues,* pp. 47, 56-64. Guilford, Conn: The Dushkin Publishing Group, 1980.
Ruppert, Ray. "Looking for Leaders," interview of Srila Hamsaduta Swami, in *Back to Godhead,* XIV No. 9, 11-13.
Schur, Edwin. *The Awareness Trap.* New York: Quadrangle/The New York Times Book Co., 1976.
"Scientologists Achieve Prison Reform in New Zealand," in *The Winner,* No. 2, June, 1981, 4.
Scott, Gini Graham. *Cult and Countercult: A Study of a Spiritual Growth Group and a Witchcraft Order.* Westport, Conn.: Greenwood Press, 1980.
Sherrill, Peter. *Edgar Cayce: The Man Who Saw Through Time and Space,* monograph of The Association for Research and Enlightenment. Virginia Beach, Va., 1973.

Shupe, Jr., Anson D., Roger Spielmann, and Sam Stigall. "Deprogramming: the New Exorcism," in *American Behavioral Scientist,* XX No. 6 (1977), 941-958.

Singer, Margaret Thaler. "Coming Out of the Cults," in *Psychology Today,* XII No. 8 (1979), 72-82.

Sire, James W. *Scripture Twisting: Twenty Ways the Cults Misread the Bible.* Downers Grove, Ill.: Intervarsity Press, 1980.

Snook, John B. *Going Further: Life-and-Death Religion in America.* Englewood Cliffs, N.J.: Prentice-Hall, 1973.

Sontag, Frederick. *Sun Myung Moon and the Unification Church.* Nashville: Abingdon, 1977.

Spring/Summer Calendar Sponsored by the Institute for Psycho-Integrity, 1981.

Stearn, Jess. *Edgar Cayce—The Sleeping Prophet.* Garden City, N.Y.: Doubleday & Co., 1967.

Steele, Judy. "Krishna Story With a Twist," originally in *The Idaho Statesman,* reprinted in *Back to Godhead,* XV No. 5, 7.

Stewart, Louis. *Life Forces: A Contemporary Guide to the Cult and Occult.* Kansas City, Mo.: Andrews and McNeel, Inc., 1980.

Stone, Donald. "The Human Potential Movement," in Charles Y. Glock and Robert N. Bellah (eds.), *The New Religious Consciousness,* pp. 93-115. Berkeley, Calif.: University of California Press, 1976.

Stoner, Carroll and Jo Anne Parke. *All God's Children: The Cult Experience—Salvation or Slavery.* Radnor, Pa.: Chilton Book Co., 1977.

Summer Programs: The Himalayan International Institute of Yoga Science and Philosophy, catalogue, 1981.

"There's Hope for the Mentally Retarded . . . ," in *Santa Rosa Free Press,* I No. 27 (Oct. 30, 1975).

Thurston, Mark. "The Philosophy of Research." in *A.R.E. Journal,* May, 1973, 118-126.

Ullman, Montague. "The Experiential Dream Group," in Benjamin B. Wolman (ed.), *Handbook of Dreams: Research, Theories and Application.* New York: Van Nostrand-Reinhold Co., 1979, pp. 406-423.

UP (Unification Parents) Newsletter, I No. 1.

Vaughn, Melissa. "The Seekers and the Seer," in *The Virginian-Pilot/The Ledger Star,* Aug. 31, 1980.

Verdier, Paul A. *Brainwashing and the Cults: An Expose on Capturing the Human Mind.* Hollywood: Wilshire Book Co., 1977.

Wainwright House Spring Programs, catalogue, 1981.

Wainwright House Summer Programs, catalogue, 1981.

Wallis, Roy. *The Road to Total Freedom: A Sociological Analysis of Scientology.* London: Heinemann, 1976.

Weber, Vanessa. "The Cults, Brainwashing and How They Affect You," in *Oldfields Magazine,* Fall, 1980, 11-14.

Welden, John. *The Frightening World of* est, booklet by Spiritual Counterfeits Project, Berkeley, California.

What Is Scientology. Los Angeles: Church of Scientology of California, 1978.

"What You Told Us," in *The Graduate Review.* September/October, 1980, 5-11.

Whitehead, Harriet. "Reasonably Fantastic: Some Perspectives on Scientology, Science Fiction, and Occultism," in Irving I. Zaretsky and Mark P. Leone (eds.), *Religious Movements in Contemporary America,* pp. 547-587. Princeton: Princeton Univ. Press, 1974.

Whitman, Kenneth J. "A Special Message to All Scientologists," in *The Winner,* The Guardian Office Journal for Scientologists, No. 2, June, 1981, 2.

"Who Is the *est* Graduate?" in *The Graduate Review.* September/October, 1980, 4.

Winter, Joseph A. *A Doctor's Report on Dianetics: Theory and Therapy.* New York: Julian Press, 1951.

Wood, Allen Tate with Jack Vitek. *Moonstruck: A Memoir of My Life in a Cult.* New York: William Morrow and Co., 1979.

Wuthnow, Robert. "The New Religions in Social Context," in Charles Y. Glock and Robert N. Bellah, (eds.) *The New Religious Consciousness,* pp. 267-293. Berkeley, Calif.: University of California Press, 1976.

Glossary

aratrika service—greeting of the Lord involving singing praises to Krishna.
ARC triangle—refers to the relationship among the Scientology concepts of affinity, reality, and communication.
ashram—communal living quarters for celibate followers of Maharaj Ji
auditing—Dianetics treatment using an E-meter.
auditor—an individual skilled in the practice of Dianetics therapy.
Ayurvedic medicine—traditional system of Indian medicine extending back several thousand years; term *ayurvedic* combines *Ayur* meaning "life" and *veda* meaning "science": Science of Life.

Back to Godhead—magazine of the ISKCON movement.
basic-basic—a Scientology concept for the first recorded engram after conception.
Bhagavad-Gita—a Hindu text (translated as the Song of God) used by the members of the International Society for Krishna Consciousness.
Bhakti—constant, absolute loving service to Krishna.
biofeedback—a method of training individuals to perceive and control various physiological activities (such as heart rate or brain waves) through providing continuous information about changes in functioning.
blooper—an individual who has dropped out of the ISKCON movement.
blow—leave the Scientology movement.
brahmacari—celibate student order in ISKCON.
brainwashing—a term first used during the Korean War to refer to the coercive techniques applied by the Communists to extract information and confessions from American prisoners of war.

clear—optimum level of mental and physical functioning to which all Scientologists aspire.
content—lectures or presentation in *est* or about Psycho-Integrity concepts.

darshan—a state of blessedness achieved by followers of Maharaj Ji, resulting from being in the presence of a religious leader.
devotee—member of ISKCON.
dhoti—long draped garment worn by men in the ISKCON movement.

dianetic release—a Scientology state below the level of *clear* purportedly achieved after less than 20 hours of *auditing*.
Dianetics—(according to L. Ron Hubbard) "a system of mental image pictures in relation to psychic (spiritual) trauma."
Dianetics reverie—a Dianetics procedure, induced by an *auditor*, which allows mental return to earlier times in an individual's life.
Divine Principle—scriptures of the Unification Church.
dynamics—eight motives of equal strength described by L. Ron Hubbard.

ekadasi day—fast day for Krishna devotees.
E-meter—(also known as an electropsychometer)—box containing a meter, wire, batteries, and terminals to spot engrams in Dianetics therapy.
engram—a Scientology concept that refers to the complete and permanent mental recording of the perceptions (sounds, smells, sights) involved in a particular experience.
ESP—(extrasensory perception)—mental perception of information obtained through a mechanism other than known human senses.
est—Erhard Seminars Training.
exit-counseling—employed by psychotherapists to refer to their therapeutic intervention with individuals who have left cults either freely or forcibly; also called deprogramming.
faith-breaking—employed by the Unification Church to denote the forcible retrieval of its members and the members of other non-mainstream religions for the purpose of deconversion; generally called deprogramming by the public and cult group opponents.
Four Position Foundation—a basic tenet of Unification Church theology, positing the interrelationships among God, man, woman, and child culminating in a God-centered family.

getting it—experiencing the *est* transformation.
God's heart—a Unification Church term derived from the Korean *shim jung;* refers to God's unconditional loving nature.
grace—coincidental events that occur to followers of Maharaj Ji (premies).
grhastha—married man in ISKCON.

harer-nama ceremony—initiation ceremony in which an ISKCON devotee is provided with a Sanskrit name.
hatha-yoga—a system of postures, breathing, and physical exercises.
holistic (sometimes spelled wholistic) **medicine**—a treatment approach which emphasizes the combined mental, physical, emotional, social, and spiritual aspects of human beings in their total environment.
Home Church—a group of 360 homes or families in a specific area chosen by the Unification Church as a particular community for which a

church member or center has responsibility. These families are not necessarily connected to the Unification Church.

homeopathy—a holistic form of treatment developed in the late 1700's to early 1800's by Samuel Hahnemann, a German physician, in which there is a similarity between the symptoms of an illness and the remedy designed to treat it.

human potential movement—a movement begun in the 1960's by several groups and individuals whose purpose was the development and raised consciousness of the individual and society.

Hunger Project—an organization affiliated with Erhard's Centers Network established to educate the public about the existence of hunger and ways by which it can be eradicated.

indemnity conditions—a wide range of behaviors (such as fundraising and *witnessing*) engaged in by Unification Church members to symbolically remove humankind's "fallen nature" in order to allow the Second Coming of the Messiah.

Individual Reference Files—verbatim excerpts from Edgar Cayce readings.

initiator (or *mahatma*)—a teacher or disciple chosen by Maharaj Ji to guide individuals in meditation techniques and the acquisition of Knowledge.

japa—prayer beads used by followers of Krishna.

karma—from the Sanskrit word meaning "action"; refers to the idea that every action is ultimately followed by an appropriate reaction.

kartals—Indian cymbals used by those chanting Hare Krishna.

Knowledge—the ultimate experience achieved by followers of Maharaj Ji after intense preparation.

Krishna consciousness—the all-encompassing awareness of Lord Krishna that is the goal of all members of ISKCON.

life reading—a psychic discourse that delves into an individual's past lives.

love bombing—the approval, concern, and attention shown by Unification Church members to potential recruits.

Mahamatra—great chanting of Hare Krishna.

mahatma—see *initiator*.

mantra—the repetition of a word or sound employed to enhance a meditative or prayer state.

maya—materialistic, pleasure-seeking aspects of life.

MEST—Matter, Energy, Space, and Time in Scientology.

Mind—described by Werner Erhard as an intrinsically unsatisfying state;

contains a record of personal experiences that are necessary for survival.

mind map—a diagram in which various aspects of a subject are represented by key terms and/or images which extend from a center image; used in the Learning Method Group (LMG) presently offered at Wainwright House.

Mobile Fundraising Teams (MFTs)—groups of Moonies who fundraise together, generally using a van as their means of transportation from one site to another.

Moonie—Unification Church member (follower of Reverend Sun Myung Moon).

Narconon—a Scientology organization established to prevent drug abuse and to rehabilitate drug abusers.

prasadam—food which has first been offered to Krishna.

premie—follower of Maharaj Ji.

process—a guided group experience or exercise in *est.*

psychokinesis—moving of an object without the use of any physical force.

psychosynthesis—a theory and a set of techniques for fostering healthy personality developed by Italian psychiatrist Robert Assagioli; combines concepts from psychology of religion, psychosomatic medicine, anthropology, parapsychology, and other disciplines.

pujari—caretaker of the deities in the ISKCON movement.

reading—a psychic discourse given while in a trance state.

sankirtana—dancing and chanting the praises of Krishna.

sannyasa—renounced, celibate order in ISKCON.

satsang—a practice in which followers of Maharaj Ji meet to discuss their experiences as premies.

Sea Org—a fleet of Scientology vessels reserved for executives of the movement.

Self—described by Werner Erhard as an intrinsically satisfying state, the achievement of which is the prime goal of *est.*

sikha—strands of hair worn loose or braided by men in the ISKCON movement.

spiritual parent (also spiritual mother or spiritual father)—used by Unification Church members to refer to the individual who has been most influential in recruiting them into the Church.

Study Groups—small groups established around the world to test the usefulness of Edgar Cayce readings in their daily lives.

swami—master.

thetan—a Scientology term referring to the nonphysical, immortal part of every human being.
tone scale—Scientology classification of human emotions.

vanaprastha—retired order in ISKCON.
Vedic—pertaining to the entire body of Hindu sacred writings.

wholistic—see *holistic*.
wins—successes or accomplishments in Scientology jargon.
witnessing—proselytizing or providing testimony to one's faith.
wog—a non-Scientologist, an outsider.

Index

Dr. Harriet S. Mosatche, the author of *Searching,* is chairperson of the Department of Psychology, College of Mount St. Vincent, Riverdale, New York.

Searching was printed and bound by BookCrafters, Inc., Chelsea, Michigan.

DATE DUE

APR 11 1988			
NOV 7 1988			
OCT 27 1989			
OCT 15 1990			
NOV 29 1990			
APR 13 1999			
APR 07 2000			
NOV 19 2006			
OCT 20 2009			